DATE DUE

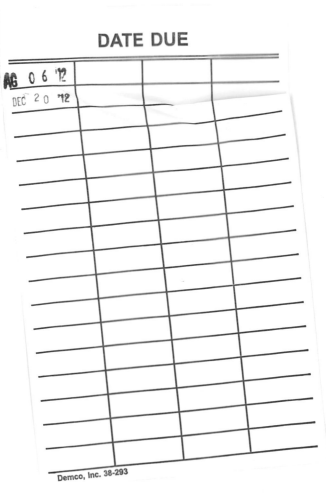

AG 0 6 '12			
DEC 2 0 '12			

Demco, Inc. 38-293

STUDIES

IN

HISTORY AND JURISPRUDENCE

STUDIES IN HISTORY AND JURISPRUDENCE

BY

JAMES BRYCE, D.C.L.

Vol. I.

Essay Index Reprint Series

BOOKS FOR LIBRARIES PRESS
FREEPORT, NEW YORK

First Published 1901
Reprinted 1968

LIBRARY OF CONGRESS CATALOG CARD NUMBER:

68-8444

PRINTED IN THE UNITED STATES OF AMERICA

THIS VOLUME WAS TO HAVE BEEN OFFERED
TO HENRY SIDGWICK (LATE PROFESSOR OF
MORAL PHILOSOPHY IN THE UNIVERSITY OF
CAMBRIDGE) WITH WHOM I HAD OFTEN DISCUSSED
THE TOPICS IT DEALS WITH, AND IN WHOM
I HAD ADMIRED, DURING AN INTIMATE FRIEND-
SHIP OF NEARLY FORTY YEARS, A SUBTLE AND
FERTILE MIND, A CHARACTER OF SINGULAR PURITY
AND BEAUTY, AND AN UNFAILING LOVE OF TRUTH.

IT IS NOW DEDICATED TO HIS MEMORY.

PREFACE

THIS volume contains a collection of Studies composed at different times over a long series of years. It treats of diverse topics: yet through many of them there runs a common thread, that of a comparison between the history and law of Rome and the history and law of England. I have handled this comparison from several points of view, even at the risk of some little repetition, applying it in one essay to the growth of the Roman and British Empires (Essay I), in another to the extension over the world of their respective legal systems (Essay II), in another to their Constitutions (Essay III), in others to their legislation (Essays XIV and XV), in another to an important branch of their private civil law (Essay XVI). The topic is one profitable to a student of the history of either nation; and it has not been largely treated by any writers known to me; as indeed few of our best known historians touch upon the legal aspects of history.

Two Essays (III and IV) embody an effort to examine political constitutions generally from comparatively unfamiliar points of view. Five (IX, X, XI, XII and XIII) are devoted to the discussion, in a non-technical way, of problems in jurisprudence which have both a theoretical and a historical—to some extent also a practical—side. Another sketches in outline the early history of Iceland, and the very peculiar constitution of the primitive Icelandic Republic. Three others relate to modern constitutions. One contains reflections on the history of the constitution of the United States, a second describes the systems of the two Dutch Repub-

lics in South Africa, and a third analyses and comments
on the constitution recently created for the new Commonwealth of Australia.

My aim throughout the book has been to bring out
the importance, sometimes overlooked, of the constitutional and legal element in history, and to present topics
which, because somewhat technical, often repel people
by their apparent dryness, in a way which shall make
them at least intelligible—since they can hardly be made
seductive—to a reader who does not add to a fair general knowledge of history any special knowledge of law.
Technicalities cannot be wholly avoided; but I hope
to have indulged in none that were not absolutely
necessary.

The longer one lives the more is one impressed by
the close connexion between the old Greco-Italian
world and our own. We are still very near the ancients;
and have still much to learn from their writings and
their institutions. The current of study and education
is at present setting so strongly towards the sciences
of nature that it becomes all the more needful for those
who value historical inquiry and the literature of the
past to do what they can to bring that old world into
a definite and tangible relation with the modern time,
a relation which shall be not only stimulative but also
practically helpful.

None of these Studies have previously appeared in
print except two, viz. those relating to the United States
and to the two Dutch Republics; and both of these have
been enlarged and revised. My thanks are due to my
friend Professor Herbert B. Adams of Johns Hopkins
University, Baltimore, and to the proprietors of the
Forum magazine respectively for permission to repub-
lish these two.

Some Studies were (in substance) delivered as Public
Lectures at Oxford, during the years 1870-1893 (when
I held the Regius Professorship of Civil Law there),
pursuant to the custom which exists in that University

for a professor to deliver from time to time discourses dealing with the wider and less technical aspects of his subject. All these have, however, been rewritten for publication; and whoever has had a similar experience will know how much more time and trouble it takes to rewrite a discourse than to compose one *de novo*. Two Lectures, delivered one when I entered on and the other when I resigned the professorship, have been appended, in the belief that they may have some interest for members of the University and for those who watch with sympathy the development of legal teaching in England.

I have endeavoured to bring up to date all references to recent events, so that when such events are mentioned the book may be taken to speak as from 1900 or 1901.

As it is now nine years since I was obliged (when I entered Mr. Gladstone's Ministry in 1892) to intermit any minute study either of Roman or of English law, it is probable that the book may disclose an imperfect knowledge of facts and views given to the world during those nine years. Under these conditions I might have wished to keep the book longer before publishing it. But life is short. Some of the friends to whose comments and criticisms I had most looked forward while composing these Studies have already passed away. So it seemed better to let what I have written, under the constant pressure of other duties, go forth now.

Among the friends whom I have to thank for information or suggestions are Professors A. V. Dicey, Sir F. Pollock, Henry Goudy, and Henry Pelham of Oxford, Sir Courtenay Ilbert (Parliamentary Counsel to the Treasury), Dr. C. L. Shadwell and Mr. Edward Jenks of Oxford, Dr. F. Sigel of Warsaw, and Mr. Jón Stefánsson of Iceland.

The Index has been prepared by Mr. J. S. Cotton, to whom I am indebted for the care he has bestowed upon it.

June 27, 1901.

CONTENTS

ESSAY I

CONTENTS

ESSAY VI

ESSAY VII

ESSAY VIII

ESSAY IX

ESSAY XII

ESSAY XIII

ESSAY XIV

ESSAY XV

I

THE ROMAN EMPIRE AND THE BRITISH EMPIRE IN INDIA

In several of the Essays contained in these volumes comparisons are instituted between Rome and England in points that touch the constitutions and the laws of these two great imperial States. This Essay is intended to compare them as conquering and ruling powers, acquiring and administering dominions outside the original dwelling-place of their peoples, and impressing upon these dominions their own type of civilization.

This comparison derives a special interest from a consideration of the position in which the world finds itself at the beginning of the twentieth century. The great civilized nations have spread themselves out so widely, and that with increasing rapidity during the last fifty years, as to have brought under their dominion or control nearly all the barbarous or semi-civilized races. Europe—that is to say the five or six races which we call the European branch of mankind—has annexed the rest of the earth, extinguishing some races, absorbing others, ruling others as subjects, and spreading over their native customs and beliefs a layer of European ideas which will sink deeper and deeper till the old native life dies out. Thus, while the face of the earth is being changed by the application of European science, so it seems likely that within a measurable time European forms of thought and ways of life will come to prevail everywhere, except possibly in China, whose

vast population may enable her to resist these solvent
influences for several generations, perhaps for several
centuries. In this process whose agencies are migration,
conquest, and commerce, England has led the way and
has achieved the most. Russia however, as well as
France and Germany, have annexed vast areas inhabited
by backward races. Even the United States has, by
occupying the Hawaiian and the Philippine Islands,
entered, somewhat to her own surprise, on the same
path. Thus a new sort of unity is being created among
mankind. This unity is seen in the bringing of every
part of the globe into close relations, both commercial
and political, with every other part. It is seen in the
establishment of a few 'world languages' as vehicles
of communication between many peoples, vehicles which
carry to them the treasures of literature and science
which the four or five leading nations have gathered. It
is seen in the diffusion of a civilization which is everywhere the same in its material aspects, and is tolerably
uniform even on its intellectual side, since it teaches men
to think on similar lines and to apply similar methods
of scientific inquiry. The process has been going on for
some centuries. In our own day it advances so swiftly
that we can almost foresee the time when it will be complete. It is one of the great events in the history of the
world.

Yet it is not altogether a new thing. A similar process
went on in the ancient world from the time of Alexander
the Macedonian to that of Alaric the Visigoth. The Greek
type of civilization, and to some extent the Greek population also, spread out over the regions around the eastern Mediterranean and the Euxine. Presently the conquests of Rome brought all these regions, as well as the
western countries as far as Caledonia, under one government. This produced a uniform type of civilization
which was Greek on the side of thought, of literature,
and of art, Roman on the side of law and institutions.
Then came Christianity which, in giving to all these

countries one religion and one standard of morality, created a still deeper sense of unity among them. Thus the ancient world, omitting the barbarous North and the semi-civilized heathen who dwelt beyond the Euphrates, became unified, the backward races having been raised, at least in the upper strata of their population, to the level of the more advanced. One government, one faith, and two languages, were making out of the mass of races and kingdoms that had existed before the Macedonian conquest, a single people who were at once a Nation and a World Nation.

The process was not quite complete when it was interrupted by the political dissolution of the Roman dominion, first through the immigrations of the Teutonic peoples from the north, then by the terrible strokes dealt at the already weakened empire by the Arab conquerors from the south-east. The results that had been attained were not wholly lost, for Europe clung to the Greco-Romano-Christian civilization, though in a lowered form and with a diminished sense of intellectual as well as of political unity. But that civilization was not able to extend itself further, save by slow degrees over the north and towards the north-east. Several centuries passed. Then, at first faintly from the twelfth century onwards, afterwards more swiftly from the middle of the fifteenth century, when the intellectual impulse given by the Renaissance began to be followed by the rapid march of geographical discovery along the coasts of Africa, in America, and in the further east, the process was resumed. We have watched its later stages with our own eyes. It embraces a far vaster field than did the earlier one, the field of the whole earth. As we watch it, we are naturally led to ask what light the earlier effort of Nature to gather men together under one type of civilization throws on this later one. As Rome was the principal agent in the earlier, so has England been in the later effort. England has sent her language, her commerce, her laws and institutions forth from herself over an even wider and more populous area than that whose races were moulded into new forms by the laws and institutions of Rome. The conditions are, as we shall see, in many respects different. Yet there is in the parallel enough to make it instructive for the present, and possibly significant for the future.

The dominions of England beyond the seas are, however, not merely too locally remote from one another, but also too diverse in their character to be compared as one whole with the dominions of Rome, which were contiguous in space, and were all governed on the same system. The Britannic Empire falls into three territorial groups, the self-governing colonies, the Crown colonies, and the Indian territories ruled by or dependent on the sovereign of Britain. Of these three groups, since they cannot be treated together, being ruled on altogether different principles, it is one group only that can usefully be selected for comparison with the Roman Empire. India contains that one group. She is fitter for our purpose than either of the other two groups, because the self-governing colonies are not subject territories administered from England, but new Englands planted far away beyond the oceans, reproducing, each in its own way, the features of the constitution and government of the old country, while the Crown colonies are so scattered and so widely diverse in the character of their inhabitants that they cannot profitably be dealt with as one body. Jamaica, Cyprus, Basutoland, Singapore, and Gibraltar, have little in common except their dependence on Downing Street. Neither set of colonies is sufficiently like the dominion of Rome to make it possible for us to draw parallels between them and it. India, however, is a single subject territory, and India is compact, governed on the same principles and by the same methods over an area not indeed as wide as that of the Roman Empire but more populous than the Roman Empire was in its palmiest days. British India (including Burma) covers about 965,000 square miles, and the protected States (including Kashmir, but not Nepal and Bhotan), about 600,000 square miles, making a total of (roughly) 1,565,000 square miles, with a population of nearly 290 millions. The area of the territories included in the Roman Empire at its greatest extent (when Dacia and the southern part of what is now Scotland belonged to it) may have been nearly 2,500,000 square miles. The population of that area is now, upon a very rough estimate, about 210 millions. What it was in ancient times we have no data even for guessing, but it must evidently have been much smaller, possibly not 100 millions, for although large regions, such as parts of Asia Minor and Tunisia, now almost deserted, were then filled by a dense industrial population, the increase in the inhabitants of France and England, for instance, has far more than compensated this decline.

The Spanish Empire in America as it stood in the sixteenth and seventeenth centuries was still vaster in area, as is the Russian Empire in Asia to-day. But the population of Spanish America was extremely small in comparison with that of the Roman Empire or that of India, and its organization much looser and less elaborate[1]. Both the Spanish and the Russian Empires, however, furnish illustrations which we shall have occasion presently to note.

Of all the dominions which the ancient world saw, it is only that of Rome that can well be compared with any modern civilized State. The monarchies of the Assyrian and Egyptian conquerors, like those of the Seleucid kings and of the Sassanid dynasty in Persia, stood on a far lower level of culture and administrative efficiency than did the Roman. Neither was there in the Middle Ages any far stretching dominion fit to be matched with that of Rome, for the great Ommiad Khalifate and the Mogul monarchy in India were both of them mere aggregates of territories, not really unified

[1] The total area of the Russian Empire exceeds 8,000,000 square miles, and the population is about 130,000,000.

by any administrative system, while the authority or
suzerainty of the Chinese sovereigns over Turkistan,
Mongolia, and Tibet presents even fewer points of resemblance. So when we wish to examine the methods and
the results of British rule in India by the light of any
other dominion exercised under conditions even remotely similar, it is to the Roman Empire of the centuries between Augustus and Honorius that we must go.

When one speaks of conditions even remotely similar
one must frankly admit the existence of an obvious and
salient point of contrast. Rome stood in the middle of
her dominions, Britain stands, by the Red Sea route,
six thousand miles from the nearest part of hers. She
can reach them only by water, and she conquered them
by troops which had been sent around the Cape over
some thirteen thousand miles of ocean. Here there is
indeed an unlikeness of the utmost significance. Yet,
without minimizing the importance of the contrast, we
must remember that Britain can communicate more
quickly with the most distant part of her territories than
Rome could with hers. It takes only twenty-two days
to reach any part of British India (except Kashmir and
Upper Assam) from London. But it took a nimble, or
as Herodotus says, a 'well girt traveller,' perhaps forty
days from Rome to reach Derr on the Nile, the last for-
tress in Nubia where Roman masonry can be seen, or
Gori, at the foot of the Caucasus, also a Roman stronghold, or Old Kilpatrick (near Dumbarton) where the
rampart of Antoninus touches the Clyde; not to add that
the sea part of these journeys might be much longer if
the winds were adverse. News could be carried not
much faster than an official could travel, whereas Britain
is, by the electric telegraph, in hourly communication
with every part of India: and the difference in speed
between the movement of an army and that of a traveller
was, of course, greater in ancient times than it is now.

Thus, for the purposes both of war and of administration, England is better placed than Rome was as respects

those outlying parts of the Roman Empire which were
most exposed to attack. Dangers are more quickly
known at head quarters; troops can reach the threatened frontier in a shorter time; errors in policy can be
more adequately corrected, because explanations can be
asked, and blundering officials can be more promptly
dismissed. Nevertheless the remoteness of India has
had results of the highest moment in making her relation to England far less close than was that of Rome
to the provinces.

This point will be considered presently. Meantime
our comparison may begin with the points in which the
two Empires resemble and illustrate one another. The
first of these turns upon the circumstances of their respective origins.

Empire is retained, says a famous maxim, by the same
arts whereby it was won. Some Empires have been
won easily. Spain acquired hers through the pertinacity
and daring of a Genoese sailor. She had comparatively
little fighting to do, for the only opponents she encountered, who added to valour some slight tincture of civilization, were the Mexicans.

Russia has met with practically no resistance in occupying her vast territories in Northern Asia; though she
had some sharp tussles with the nomad Turkmans, and
tedious conflicts both with Shamyl and with the Circas-
sians in the Caucasus. But both Rome and England
had to fight long and fight hard for what they won. The
progress of Roman and British expansion illustrates the
remark of Oliver Cromwell that no one goes so far as
he who does not know whither he is going. Neither
power set out with a purpose of conquest, such as
Alexander the Great, and perhaps Cyrus, had planned
and carried out before them. Just as Polybius, writing
just after the destruction of Carthage in B. C. 146, already
perceived that Rome was, by the strength of her government and the character of her people, destined to be
the dominant power of the civilized world, so it was

prophesied immediately after the first victories of
Clive that the English would come to be the masters
of all India. Each nation was drawn on by finding
that one conquest led almost inevitably to another because restless border tribes had to be subdued, because formidable neighbours seemed to endanger
the safety of subjugated but often discontented provinces, because allies inferior in strength passed gradually into the position first of dependants and then of
subjects.

The Romans however, though they did not start out
with the notion of conquering even Italy, much less the
Mediterranean world, came to enjoy fighting for its own
sake, and were content with slight pretexts for it. For
several centuries they were always more or less at war
somewhere. The English went to India as traders,
with no intention of fighting anybody, and were led
into the acquisition of territory partly in order to recoup
themselves for the expensive efforts they had made to
support their first allies, partly that they might get
revenue for the East India Company's shareholders,
partly in order to counterwork the schemes of the
French, who were at once their enemies in Europe and
their rivals in the East. One may find a not too fanciful
analogy to the policy of the English in the days of Clive,
when they were drawn further and further into Indian
conflicts by their efforts to check the enterprises of
Dupleix and Lally, in the policy of the Romans when
they entered Sicily to prevent Carthage from establishing her control over it. In both cases an effort which
seemed self-protective led to a long series of wars and
annexations.

Rome did not march so swiftly from conquest to conquest as did England. Not to speak of the two centuries during which she was making herself supreme in
Italy, she began to conquer outside its limits from the
opening of the First Punic War in B. C. 264, and did
not acquire Egypt till B. C. 30, and South Britain till

A. D. 43-85 [1]. Her Eastern conquests were all the easier because Alexander the Great's victories, and the wars waged by his successors, had broken up and denationalized the East, much as the Mogul conquerors afterwards paved the way for the English in India. England's first territorial gains were won at Plassy in A. D. 1757 [2]: her latest acquisition was the occupation of Mandalay in 1885. Her work was done in a century and a quarter, while that of Rome took fully three centuries. But England had two great advantages. Her antagonists were immeasurably inferior to her in arms as well as in discipline. As early as A. D. 1672 the great Leibnitz had in a letter to Lewis XIV pointed out the weakness of the Mogul Empire; and about the same time Bernier, a French physician resident at the Court of Aurungzeb, declared that 20,000 French troops under Condé or Turenne could conquer all India [3]. A small European force, and even a small native force drilled and led by Europeans, was as capable of routing huge Asiatic armies as the army of Alexander had proved capable of overthrowing the immensely more numerous hosts of Darius Codomannus. Moreover, the moment when the English appeared on the scene was opportune. The splendid Empire of Akbar was crumbling to pieces. The Mahratta confederacy had attained great military power, but at the battle of Paniput, in 1761, it received from the Afghans under Ahmed Shah Durani a terrific blow which for the time arrested its conquests. Furthermore, India, as a whole, was divided into numerous principalities, the feeblest of which lay on the coasts of the Bay of Bengal. These principalities were frequently at war with one another, and glad to obtain European aid in their strife.

---

[1] Dacia was taken by Trajan in A. D. 107, and lost in A. D. 251. Mesopotamia and Arabia Petraea were annexed by Trajan about the same time, but the former was renounced so soon afterwards that ts conquest can hardly be considered a part of the regular process of expansion.

[2] Territorial authority may be said to date from the grant of the Diwani in 1765.

[3] See the admirably clear and thoughtful book of Sir A. C. Lyall, *Rise of British Dominion in India*, pp. 52 and 126.

And England had a third advantage in the fact that she encountered the weakest of her antagonists first. Had she, in those early days when her forces were slender, been opposed by the valour of Marathas or Sikhs, instead of by the feeble Bengalis and Madrassis, her ambitions might have been nipped in the bud. When she found herself confronted by these formidable foes she had already gained experience and had formed a strong native army. But when the Romans strove against the Achaean League and Macedon they had to fight troops all but equal to themselves. When Carthage was their antagonist, they found in Hamilcar a commander equal, in Hannibal a commander superior to any one they could send against him. These earlier struggles so trained Rome to victory that her later conquests were made more easily. The triumphs of the century before and the century after Julius Caesar were won either over Asiatics, who had discipline but seldom valour, or over Gauls, Iberians, Germans, and Caledonians, who had valour but not discipline. Occasional reverses were due to the imprudence of a general, or to an extreme disparity of forces; for, like the English, the Romans did not hesitate to meet greatly superior numbers. The defeat of Crassus by the Parthians and the catastrophe which befel Varus in the forests of Paderborn find a parallel in the disastrous retreat of the English army from Cabul in 1843. Except on such rare occasions the supremacy of Roman arms was never seriously challenged, nor was any great calamity suffered till the barbarian irruption into Italy in the reign of Marcus Aurelius. A still graver omen for the future was the overthrow of Valerian by the Persians in A. D. 260. The Persians were inferior in the arts of civilization and probably in discipline: but the composition of the Roman armies was no longer what it had been three centuries earlier, for the peasantry of Italy, which had formed the kernel of their strength, were no longer available. As the provincial subjects became less and less warlike, men from beyond the frontier

were enrolled, latterly in bodies under their native chiefs
—Germans, or Arabs, or, in still later days, Huns—just
as the native army in British India, which has now become far more peaceful than it was a century ago, is re-
cruited by Pathans and Ghurkas from the hills outside
British territory as well as by the most warlike among
the Indian subjects of the Crown. The danger of the
practice is obvious. Rome was driven to it for want
of Roman fighting-men[1]. England guards against its
risks by having a considerable force of British troops
alongside her native army.

The fact that their dominions were acquired by force
of arms exerted an enduring effect upon the Roman
Empire and continues to exert it upon the British in
imprinting upon their rule in India a permanently military character. The Roman administration began with
this character, and never lost it, at least in the frontier
provinces. The governors were pro-consuls or propraetors, or other officials, entrusted with the exercise
of an authority in its origin military rather than civil.
A governor's first duty was to command the troops
stationed in the province. The camps grew into towns,
and that which had been a group of *canabae* or market
stalls, a sort of bazaar for the service of the camp, sometimes became a municipality. One of the most efficient
means of unifying the Empire was found in the bringing
of soldiers born in one part of it to be quartered for many
years together in another. Military distinction was open
to every subject, and military distinction might lead to
the imperial throne. So the English in India are primarily soldiers. True it is that they went to India three
centuries ago as traders, that it was out of a trading company that their power arose, and that this trading company did not disappear till 1858. The covenanted civil
service, to which Clive for instance belonged, began as a
body of commercial clerks. Nothing sounds more paci-

---

[1] And indeed the employment of these barbarians to resist the outer barbarians
probably prolonged the life of the Empire.

fic. But the men of the sword very soon began to eclipse
the men of the quill and account book. Being in the majority, they do so still, although foɪ forty years there
have been none but petty frontier wars. Society is not in
India, as it is in England, an ordinary civil society occupied with the works and arts of peace, with an extremely
small military element. It is military society, military
first and foremost, though with an infusion of civilian
officials, and in some towns with a small infusion of lawyers and merchants, as well as a still smaller infusion of
missionaries. Military questions occupy every one's
thoughts and talk. A great deal of administrative or
diplomatic work is done, and often extremely well done,
by officers in civil employment. Many of the railways
are primarily strategic lines, as were the Roman roads.
The railway stations are often placed, for military reasons, at a distance from the towns they serve: and the
cantonments where the Europeans, civilians as well as
soldiers, reside, usually built some way off from the native
cities, have themselves, as happened in the Roman Empire, grown into regular towns. The traveller from
peaceful England feels himself, except perhaps in Bombay, surrounded by an atmosphere of gunpowder all the
time he stays in India.

Before we pass from the military aspects of the comparison let it be noted that both Empires have been
favoured in their extension and their maintenance by
the frontiers which Nature had provided. The Romans,
when once they had conquered Numidia, Spain, and
Gaul, had the ocean and nothing but the ocean (save
for the insignificant exception of barbarous Mauretania)
to the west and north-west of them, an awesome and
untravelled ocean, from whose unknown further shore
no enemy could appear. To the south they were defended by the equally impassable barrier of a torrid
and waterless desert, stretching from the Nile to the
Atlantic. It was only on the north and east that there
were frontiers to be defended; and these two sides

remained the quarters of danger, because no natural barrier, arresting the progress of armies or constituting a defensible frontier, could be found without pushing all the way to the Baltic in one direction or to the ranges of Southern Kurdistan, perhaps even to the deserts of Eastern Persia in the other. The north and the east ultimately destroyed Rome. The north sent in those Teutonic tribes which occupied the western provinces and at last Italy herself, and those Slavonic tribes which settled between the Danube, the Aegean, and the Adriatic, and permeated the older population of the Hellenic lands. Perhaps the Emperors would have done better for the Empire (whatever might have been the ultimate loss to mankind) if, instead of allowing themselves to be disheartened by the defeat of Varus, they had pushed their conquests all the way to the Baltic and the Vistula, and turned the peoples of North and Middle Germany into provincial Romans. The undertaking would not have been beyond the resources of the Empire in its vigorous prime, and would have been remunerative, if not in money, at any rate in the way of providing a supply of fighting-men for the army. So too the Emperors might possibly have saved much suffering to their Romanized subjects in South Britain had they followed up the expedition of Agricola and subdued the peoples of Caledonia and Ierne, who afterwards became disagreeable as Picts and Scots. The east was the home of the Parthians, of the Persians, so formidable to the Byzantine Emperors in the days of Kobad and Chosroes Anushirwan, and of the tribes which in the seventh and eighth centuries, fired by the enthusiasm of a new faith and by the prospect of booty, overthrew the Roman armies and turned Egypt, Syria, Africa, Spain, and ultimately the greater part of Asia Minor into Muhamadan kingdoms. Had Rome been menaced on the south and west as she was generally menaced on the east and sometimes on the north, her Empire could hardly have lived so long. Had she possessed a natural barrier on the east like that which the Sahara provided on the south she might have found it easy to resist, and not so very hard even to subjugate, the fighting races of the north.

Far more fortunate has been the position of the English in India. No other of the great countries of the world is protected by such a stupendous line of natural entrenchments as India possesses in the chain of the Himalayas from Attock and Peshawur in the west to the point where, in the far east, the Tsanpo emerges from Tibet to become in Upper Assam the Brahmaputra. Not only is this mountain mass the loftiest and most impassable to be found anywhere on our earth; it is backed by a wide stretch of high and barren country, so thinly peopled as to be incapable of constituting a menace to those who live in the plains south of the Himalayas. And in point of fact the relations, commercial as well as political, of India with Tibet, and with the Chinese who are suzerains of Tibet, have been, at least in historical times, extremely scanty. On the east, India is divided from the Indo-Chinese peoples, Talains, Burmese and Shans, by a belt of almost impenetrable hill and forest country: nor have these peoples ever been formidable neighbours. It is only at its northwestern angle, between Peshawur and Quetta (for south of Quetta as far as the Arabian Sea there are deserts behind the mountains and the Indus) that India is vulnerable. The rest of the country is protected by a wide ocean. Accordingly the masters of India have had only two sets of foes to fear; European maritime powers who may arrive by sea after a voyage which, until our own time, was a voyage of three or four months, and land powers who, coming from the side of Turkistan or Persia, may find their way, as did Alexander the Great and Nadir Shah, through difficult passes into the plains of the Punjab and Sindh. This singular natural isolation of India, as it facilitated the English conquest by preventing the native princes from forming alliances with or obtaining help from powers beyond the mountains or the sea, so has it also enabled the English to maintain their hold with an army extraordinarily small in proportion to the population of the country. The total strength of the Roman military establishment in the days of Trajan, was for an area of some two and a half millions of square miles and population of possibly one hundred millions, between 280,000 and 320,000 men. Probably four-fifths of this force was stationed on the Rhine, the Danube, and the Euphrates. There were so few in most of the inner provinces that, as some one said, the nations wondered where were the troops that kept them in subjection.

The peace or 'established' strength of the British army in India is nearly 230,000 men, of whom about 156,000 are natives and 74,000 Englishmen. To these there may be added the so-called 'active reserve' of natives who have served with the colours, about 17,000 men, and about 30,000 European volunteers. Besides these there are of course the troops of the native princes, estimated at about 350,000 men, many of them, however, far from effective. But as these troops, though a source of strength while their masters are loyal, might under altered circumstances be conceivably a source of danger, they can hardly be reckoned as part of the total force disposable by the British Government. Recently, however, about 20,000 of them have been organized as special contingents of the British army, inspected and advised by British officers, and fit to take their place with regiments of the line.

It would obviously be impossible to defend such widely extended dominions by a force of only 230,000 or 250,000 men, but for the remoteness of all possibly dangerous assailants. The only formidable land neighbour is Russia, the nearest point of whose territories in the Pamirs is a good long way from the present British outposts, with a very difficult country between. The next nearest is France on the Mekong River, some 200 miles from British Burma, though a shorter distance from Native States under British influence. As for sea powers, not only is Europe a long way off, but the navy of Britain holds the sea. It was by her command of the sea that Britain won India. Were she to cease to hold it, her position there would be insecure indeed.

In another respect also the sharp severance of India from all the surrounding countries may be deemed to have proved a benefit to the English. It has relieved them largely if not altogether from the temptation to go on perpetually extending their borders by annexing contiguous territory. When they had reached the natural boundaries of the Himalayas and the ranges of Afghanistan, they stopped. Beyond these lie rugged and unprofitable highlands, and still more unprofitable wildernesses. In two regions only was an advance possible: and in those two regions they have yielded to temptation. They have crossed the southern part of the Soliman mountains into Baluchistan in search for a more ' scientific ' frontier, halting for the present on the Amram range, north-west of Quetta, where from the Khojak heights the eye, ranging over a dark-brown arid plain, descries seventy miles away the rocks that hang over Kandahar. They moved on from Arakhan and Tenasserim into Lower Burma, whence in 1885 they conquered Upper Burma and proclaimed their suzerainty over some of the Shan principalities lying further to the east. But for the presence of France in these regions, which makes them desire to keep Siam in existence as a so-called ' Buffer State,' manifest destiny might probably lead them ultimately eastward across the Menam and Mekong to Annam and Cochin China.

The Romans too sought for a scientific frontier, and hesitated often as to the line they should select, sometimes pushing boldly eastward beyond the Rhine and the Euphrates, sometimes receding to those rivers. Not till the time of Hadrian did they create a regular system of frontier defence, strengthened at many points by fortifications, among which the forts that lie along the Roman Wall from the Tyne to the Solway are perhaps the best preserved. So the English wavered for a time between the line of the Indus and that of the Soliman range; so in the wild mountain region beyond Kashmir they have, within the last few years, alternately occupied and retired from the remote outpost of Chitral. It has been their good fortune to have been obliged to fortify a comparatively small number of points, and all of these are on the north-west frontier.

There have been those who would urge them to occupy Afghanistan and entrench themselves therein to resist a possible Russian invasion. But for the present wiser counsels have prevailed. Afghanistan is a more effective barrier in the hands of its own fierce tribes than it would be as a part of British territory. A parallel may be drawn between the part it has played of late years and that which Armenia played in the ancient world from the days of Augustus to those of Heraclius. Both countries had been the seats of short-lived Empires, Armenia in the days of Tigranes, Afghanistan in those of Ahmed Shah. Both are wild and rugged regions, the dwelling-places of warlike races. Christian Armenia was hostile from religious sentiment to the enemies whom Rome had to fear, the Persian Fire-worshippers. Musulman Afghanistan dreads the power of Christian Russia. But the loyalty or friendship of the Armenian princes was not always proof against the threats of the formidable Sassanids, and the action of the Afghans is an element of uncertainty and anxiety to the British rulers of India.

To make forces so small as those on which Rome relied and those which now defend British India adequate for the work they have to do, good means of communication are indispensable. It was one of the first tasks of the Romans to establish such means. They were the great—indeed one may say, the only—road builders of antiquity. They began this policy before they had completed the conquest of Italy; and it was one of the devices which assured their supremacy throughout the peninsula. They followed it out in Gaul, Spain, Africa, Britain,

2

and the East, doing their work so thoroughly that in Britain some of the roads continued to be the chief avenues of travel down till the eighteenth century. So the English have been in India a great engineering people, constructing lines of communication, first roads and afterwards railways, on a scale of expenditure unknown to earlier ages. The potentates of elder days, Hindu rajahs, and subsequently Pathans and Moguls, with other less famous Musulman dynasties, have left their memorials in temples and mosques, in palaces and tombs. The English are commemorating their sway by railway works, by tunnels and cuttings, by embankments and bridges. If India were to relapse into barbarism the bridges, being mostly of iron, would after a while perish, and the embankments would in time be swept away by torrential rains, but the rock-cuttings and the tunnels would remain, as the indestructible paving-stones of the Roman roads, and majestic bridges, like the Pont du Gard in Languedoc, remain to witness to the skill and thoroughness with which a great race did its work.

The opening up of India by railroads suggests not a few interesting questions which, however, I can do no more than indicate here. Railroad construction has imposed upon the Indian exchequer a strain all the heavier because some lines, especially those on the north-west frontier, having been undertaken from strategic rather than commercial motives, will yield no revenue at all proportionate to their cost. It has been suggested that although railroads were meant to benefit the peasantry, they may possibly have increased the risk of famine, since they induce the producer to export the grain which was formerly locally stored up in good years to meet the scarcity of bad years. The comparative quickness with which food can be carried by rail into a famine area does not— so it is argued—compensate for the loss of these domestic reserves. Railways, bringing the numerous races that inhabit India into a closer touch with one another than was possible before, are breaking down, slowly but

surely, the demarcations of caste, and are tending towards an assimilation of the jarring elements, racial and
linguistic, as well as religious, which have divided India
into a number of distinct, and in many cases hostile,
groups. Centuries may elapse before this assimilation
can become a source of political danger to the rulers of
the country: yet we discern the beginnings of the process now, especially in the more educated class. The
Roman roads, being highways of commerce as well as
of war, contributed powerfully to draw together the
peoples whom Rome ruled into one imperial nationality.
But this was a process which, as we shall presently note,
was for Rome an unmixed gain, since it strengthened
the cohesion of an Empire whose inhabitants had every
motive for loyalty to the imperial Government, if not
always to the particular sovereign. The best efforts
of Britain may not succeed in obtaining a similar attachment from her Indian subjects, and their union into a
body animated by one national sentiment might become
an element of danger against which she has never yet
been required to take precautions.

The excellence of the highways of communication
provided by the wise energy of the Romans and of the
English has contributed not only to the easier defence
of the frontiers of both Empires, but also to the maintenance of a wonderfully high standard of internal
peace and order. Let any one think of the general state
of the ancient world before the conquests of Rome, and
let him then think of the condition not merely of India
after the death of the Emperor Aurungzeb, but of the
chief European countries as they stood in the seventeenth century, if he wishes to appreciate what Rome did
for her subjects, or what England has done in India. In
some parts of Europe private war still went on two hundred and fifty years ago. Almost everywhere robber
bands made travelling dangerous and levied tribute upon
the peasantry. Even in the eighteenth century, and
even within our own islands, Rob Roy raided the farm-

ers of Lennox, and landlords in Connaught fought pitched battles with one another at the head of their retainers. Even a century ago the coasts of the Mediterranean were ravaged by Barbary pirates, and brigandage reigned unchecked through large districts of Italy. But in the best days of the Roman Empire piracy was unknown; the peasantry were exempt from all exactions except those of the tax-gatherer; and the great roads were practically safe for travellers. Southern and western Europe, taken as a whole, would seem to have enjoyed better order under Hadrian and the Antonines than was enjoyed again until nearly our own times. This was the more remarkable because the existence of slavery must have let loose upon society, in the form of runaway slaves, a good many dangerous characters. Moreover, there remained some mountainous regions where the tribes had been left practically to themselves under their own rude customs. These enclaves of barbarism within civilized territory, such as was Albania, in the central mountain knot of which no traces of Roman building have been found, and the Isaurian country in Asia Minor, and possibly the Cantabrian land on the borders of southwestern Gaul and northern Spain, where the Basque tongue still survives, do not appear to have seriously interfered with the peace and well-being of the settled population which dwelt around them, probably because the mountaineers knew that it was only by good behaviour that they could obtain permission to enjoy the measure of independence that had been left to them. The parts of provincial Africa which lay near the desert were less orderly, because it was not easy to get behind the wild tribes who had the Sahara at their back.

The internal peace of the Roman Empire was, however, less perfect than that which has been established within the last sixty years in India. Nothing surprises the visitor from Europe so much as the absolute confidence with which he finds himself travelling unprotected across this vast country, through mountains and jungles,

among half savage tribes whose languages he does not
know, and that without seeing, save at rare intervals, any
sign of European administration. Nor is this confined
to British India. It is almost the same in Native States.
Even along the lofty forest and mountain frontier that
separates the native (protected) principality of Sikkim
from Nepal—the only really independent Indian State—
an Englishman may journey unarmed and alone, except
for a couple of native attendants, for a week or more.
When he asks his friends at Darjiling, before he starts,
whether he ought to take a revolver with him, they smile
at the question. There is not so complete a security
for native travellers, especially in Native States, for here
and there bands of brigands called Dacoits infest the
tracks, and rob, sometimes the wayfarer, sometimes the
peasant, escaping into the recesses of the jungle when
the police are after them. But dacoity, though it occasionally breaks out afresh in a few districts, has become
much less frequent than formerly. The practice of
Thuggi which seventy years ago still caused many murders, has been extirpated by the unceasing energy of
British officers. Crimes of violence show a percentage
to the population which appears small when one considers how many wild tribes remain. The native of
course suffers from violence more frequently than does
the European, whose prestige of race, backed by the
belief that punishment will surely follow on any injury
done to him, keeps him safe in the wildest districts [1].

I have referred to the enclaves within the area of the
Roman Empire where rude peoples were allowed to live
after their own fashion so long as they did not disturb
the peace of their more civilized neighbours. One finds
the Indian parallel to these districts, not so much in the
Native States, for these are often as advanced in the

---

[1] An incident like the murder in 1889 of the British Resident at Manipur, a small
Protected State in the hill country between Assam and Burma, is so rare and excites so much surprise and horror as to be the best proof of the general tranquil-
lity. In that case there had been some provocation, though not on the part of the
Resident himself, an excellent man of conciliatory temper.

arts of life, and, in a very few instances, almost as well administered, as British territory, but rather in the hill tribes, which in parts of central, of north-western, and of southern India, have retained their savage or semi-savage customs, under their own chiefs, within the provinces directly subject to the Crown. These tribes, as did the Albanians and Basques, cleave to their primitive languages, and cleave also to their primitive forms of ghost-worship or nature-worship, though Hinduism is beginning to lay upon them its tenacious grasp. Of one another's lives and property they are not very careful. But they are awed by the European and leave him unmolested.

The success of the British, like that of the Roman administration in securing peace and good order, has been due, not merely to a sense of the interest which a government has in maintaining conditions which, because favourable to industry are favourable also to revenue, but also to the high ideal of the duties of a ruler which both nations have set before themselves. Earlier Empires, like those of the Persian Achaemenids or of the successors of Alexander, had been content to tax their subjects and raise armies from them. No monarch, except perhaps some of the Ptolemies in Egypt, seems to have set himself to establish a system from which his subjects would benefit. Rome, with larger and higher views, gave to those whom she conquered some compensations in better administration for the national independence she extinguished. Her ideals rose as she acquired experience, and as she came to feel the magnificence of her position. Even under the Republic attempts were made to check abuses of power on the part of provincial governors. The proceedings against Verres, which we know so well because Cicero's speeches against that miscreant have been preserved, are an instance of steps taken in the interests of a province whose discontent was so little likely to harm Rome that no urgent political necessity prescribed them. Those proceedings showed how defective was the machinery for controlling or punishing a provincial governor; and it is clear enough that a great deal of extortion and misfeasance went on under proconsuls and propraetors in the later days of the Republic, to the enrichment, not only of those functionaries, but of the hungry swarm who followed them, including men who, like the poet Catullus, were made for better things [1]. With the establishment of a monarchy administration improved. The Emperor had a more definite responsibility for securing the welfare and contentment of the provinces than had been felt by the Senate or the jurors of the Republic, swayed by party interest or passion, not to speak of more sordid motives. He was, moreover, able to give effect to his wishes more promptly and more effectively. He could try an incriminated official in the way he thought best, and mete out appropriate punishment. It may indeed be said that the best proof of the incompetence of the Republican system for the task of governing the world, and of the need for the concentration of powers in a single hand, is to be found in the scandals of provincial administration, scandals which, so far as we can judge, could not have been remedied without a complete change either in the tone and temper of the ruling class at Rome, or in the ancient constitution itself.

On this point the parallel with the English in India is interesting, dissimilar as the circumstances were. The English administration began with extortions and corruptions. Officials were often rapacious, sometimes unjust, in their dealings with the native princes. But the statesmen and the public opinion of England, even in the latter half of the eighteenth century, had higher standards than those of Rome in the days of Sulla and Cicero, while the machinery which the House of Commons provided for dealing with powerful offenders was

---

[1] Poems x and xxviii. It is some comfort to know that Catullus obtained in Bithynia only themes for some of his most charming verses (see poems iv and xlvi). Gains would probably have been ill-gotten.

more effective than the Roman method of judicial proceedings before tribunals which could be, and frequently
were, bribed. The first outbreak of greed and corruption in Bengal was dealt with by the strong hand of
Clive in 1765. It made so great an impression at home
as to give rise to a provision in a statute of 1773, making
offences against the provisions of that Act or against the
natives of India, punishable by the Court of King's Bench
in England. By Pitt's Act of 1784, a Special Court, consisting of three judges, four peers, and six members of
the House of Commons, was created for the trial in England of offences committed in India. This singular tribunal, which has been compared with the *quaestio perpetua*
(*de pecuniis repetundis*) of Senators created by a Roman
statute of B. C. 149 to try offences committed by Roman
officials against provincials, has never acted, or even been
summoned [1]. Soon after it came the famous trial which
is more familiar to Englishmen than any other event in
the earlier relations of England and India. The impeachment of Warren Hastings has often been compared with
the trial of Verres, though Hastings was not only a far
more capable, but a far less culpable man. Hastings,
like Verres, was not punished. But the proceedings
against him so fixed the attention of the nation upon the
administration of India as to secure for wholesome
principles of conduct a recognition which was never
thereafter forgotten. The Act of 1784 in establishing
a Board of Control responsible to Parliament found a
means both for supervising the behaviour of officials and
for taking the large political questions which arose in
India out of the hands of the East India Company. This
Board continued till India was placed under the direct
sway of the British Crown in 1858. At the same time
the appointment of Governors-General who were mostly
men of wealth, and always men of rank and position at
home, provided a safeguard against such misconduct as

[1] See Sir C. P. Ilbert's *Government of India*, p. 68. The provision creating this
Court has never been repealed.

the proconsuls under the Roman Republic had been prone to commit. These latter had little to fear from prosecution when their term of office was over, and the opinion of their class was not shocked by offences which would have fatally discredited an English nobleman. The standard by which English public opinion judges the behaviour of Indian or Colonial officials has, on the whole, risen during the nineteenth century; and the idea that the government of subject-races is to be regarded as a trust to be discharged with a sense of responsibility to God and to humanity at large has become generally accepted. Probably the action of the Emperors, or at least of such men as Trajan and his three successors, raised the standard of opinion in the Roman Empire also. It was, however, not so much to that opinion as to their sovereign master that Roman officials were responsible. The general principles of policy which guided the Emperors were sound, but how far they were applied to check corruption or oppression in each particular case is a matter on which we are imperfectly informed. Under an indolent or vicious Emperor, a governor who had influence at Court, or who remitted the full tribute punctually, may probably have sinned with impunity.

The government of India by the English resembles that of her provinces by Rome in being thoroughly despotic. In both cases, whatever may have been done for the people, nothing was or is done by the people. There was under Rome, and there is in British India, no room for popular initiative, or for popular interference with the acts of the rulers, from the Viceroy down to a district official. For wrongs cognizable by the courts of law, the courts of law were and are open, doubtless more fully open in India than they were in the Roman Empire. But for errors in policy or for defects in the law itself, the people of a province had no remedy available in the Roman Empire except through petition to the sovereign. Neither is there now in India any recourse open to the inhabitants except an appeal to the

Crown or to Parliament, a Parliament in which the Indian subjects of the Crown have not been, and cannot be, represented. This was, and is, by the nature of the case, inevitable.

In comparing the governmental systems of the two Empires, it is hardly necessary to advert to such differences as the fact that India is placed under a Viceroy to whom all the other high functionaries, Governors, Lieutenant-Governors and Chief Commissioners, are subordinated, whereas, in the Roman world every provincial governor stood directly under the Emperor. Neither need one dwell upon the position in the English system of the Secretary of State for India in Council as a member of the British Cabinet. Such details do not affect the main point to which I now come.

The territories conquered by the Romans were of three kinds. Some, such as Egypt, Macedonia, and Pontus, had been, under their own princes, monarchies practically despotic. In these, of course, there could be no question of what we call popular government. Some had been tribal principalities, monarchic or oligarchic, such as those among the Iceni and Brigantes in Britain, the Arverni in Gaul, the Cantabrian mountaineers in Spain. Here, again, free institutions had not existed before, and could hardly have been created by the conqueror. The third kind consisted of small commonwealths, such as the Greek cities. These were fitted for self-government, which indeed they had enjoyed before they were subjected by Rome. Very wisely, municipal self-government was to a large extent left to them by the Emperors down till the time of Justinian. It was more complete in some cities than in others; and it was in nearly all gradually reduced by the equalizing pressure of the central authority. But they were all placed under the governor of the province; most of them paid taxes, and in most both the criminal and the higher civil jurisdiction were in the hands of imperial officials. Of the introduction of any free institutions for the empire at large, or even for any province as a whole, there seems never to have been any question. Among the many constitutional inventions we owe to the ancient world representative government finds no place. A generation before the fall of the Republic, Rome had missed her opportunity when the creation of such a system was most needed and might have been most useful. After her struggle against the league of her Italian allies, she consented to admit them to vote in her own city tribes, instead of taking what seems to us moderns the obvious expedient of allowing them to send delegates to an assembly which should meet in Rome. So it befell that monarchy and a city republic or confederation of such republics remained the only political forms known to antiquity [1].

India is ruled despotically by the English, not merely because they found her so ruled, but because they conceive that no other sort of government would suit a vast population of different races and tongues, divided by the religious animosities of Hindus and Musulmans, and with no sort of experience of self-government on a scale larger than that of the Village Council. No more in India than in the Roman Empire has there been any question of establishing free institutions either for the country as a whole, or for any particular province. But the English, like the Romans, have permitted such self-government as they found to subsist. It subsists only in the very rudimentary but very useful form of the Vil-

[1] The nearest approach to any kind of provincial self-government and also the nearest approach to a representative system was made in the Provincial Councils which seem from the time of Augustus down to the fifth century to have existed in all or nearly all the provinces. They consisted of delegates from the cities of each province, and met annually in some central place, where stood the temple or altar to Rome and Augustus. They were presided over by the priest of these divinities, and their primary functions were to offer sacrifices, provide for the expense of the annual games, and elect the priest for next year. However they seem to have also passed resolutions, such as votes of thanks to the outgoing priest or to a departing governor, and to have transmitted requests or inquiries to the Emperor. Sometimes they arranged for the prosecution of a governor who had misgoverned them ; but on the whole their functions were more ceremonial and ornamental than practically important ; nor would the emperors have suffered them to exert any real power, though they were valued as useful vehicles of provincial opinion (see Marquardt, *Römische Staatsverwaltung*, vol. i, and an article in *Eng. Hist. Review* for April, 1893, by Mr. E. G. Hardy).

lage Council just referred to, called in some parts of India the Panchayet or body of five. Of late years municipal constitutions, resembling at a distance those of English boroughs, have been given to some of the larger cities as a sort of experiment, for the sake of training the people to a sense of public duty, and of relieving the provincial government of local duties. So far the experiment has in most cities been only a moderate success. The truth is that, though a few intelligent men, educated in European ideas, complain of the despotic power of the Anglo-Indian bureaucracy, the people of India generally do not wish to govern themselves. Their traditions, their habits, their ideas, are all the other way, and dispose them to accept submissively any rule which is strong and which neither disturbs their religion and customs nor lays too heavy imposts upon them.

Here let an interesting contrast be noted. The Roman Emperors were despots at home in Italy, almost as much, and ultimately quite as much, as in the provinces. The English govern their own country on democratic, India on absolutist principles. The inconsistency is patent but inevitable. It affords an easy theme for declamation when any arbitrary act of the Indian administration gives rise to complaints, and it may fairly be used as the foundation for an argument that a people which enjoys freedom at home is specially bound to deal justly and considerately with those subjects to whom she refuses a like freedom. But every one admits in his heart that it is impossible to ignore the differences which make one group of races unfit for the institutions which have given energy and contentment to another more favourably placed.

A similar inconsistency presses on the people of the United States in the Philippine Isles. It is a more obtrusive inconsistency because it has come more abruptly, because it has come, not by the operation of a long series of historical causes, but by the sudden and little considered action of the American Republic itself, and because the American Republic has proclaimed, far more loudly and clearly than the English have ever done, the principle contained in the Declaration of Independence that the consent of the governed is the only foundation of all just government. The Americans will doubtless in time either reconcile themselves to their illogical position or alter it. But for the present it gives to thoughtful men among them visions of mocking spirits, which the clergy are summoned to exorcize by dwelling upon the benefits which the diffusion of a pure faith and a commercial civilization will confer upon the lazy and superstitious inhabitants of these tropical isles.

Subject to the general principle that the power of the Emperor was everywhere supreme and absolute, the Romans recognized, at least in the earlier days of the Empire, considerable differences between the methods of administering various provinces. A distinction was drawn between the provinces of the Roman people, to which proconsuls or propraetors were sent, and the provinces of Caesar, placed under the more direct control of the Emperor, and administered in his name by an official called the *praeses* or *legatus Caesaris*, or sometimes (as was the case in Judaea, at the time when it was ruled by Pontius Pilate) by a *procurator*, an officer primarily financial, but often entrusted with the powers of a *praeses*. Egypt received special treatment because the population was turbulent and liable to outbursts of religious passion, and because it was important to keep a great cornfield of the Empire in good humour. These distinctions between one province and another tended to vanish as the administrative system of the whole Empire grew better settled and the old republican forms were forgotten. Still there were always marked differences between Britain, for instance, at the one end of the realm and Syria at the other. So there were all sorts of varieties in the treatment of cities and tribes which had never been conquered, but passed peaceably through alliance into subjection. Some of the Hellenic cities retained their republican institutions till far down in imperial times. Distinctions not indeed similar, yet analogous, have existed between the different parts of British India. There is the old distribution of provinces into Regulation and Non-Regulation. The name ' Province,' one may observe in passing, a name unknown elsewhere in the dominions of Britain [1] (though a recent and vulgar usage sometimes applies it to the parts of England outside of London) except as a relic of French dominion in Canada, bears witness to an authority which began, as in Canada, through conquest. Though the names of Regulation and Non-Regulation provinces are now no longer used, a distinction remains between the districts to the higher posts in which none but members of the covenanted service are appointed, and those in which the Government have a wider range of choice, and also between those districts for which the Governor-General can make ordinances in his executive capacity, and those which are legislated for by him in Council in the ordinary way. There are also many differences in the administrative systems of the different Presidencies and other territories, besides of course all imaginable diversities in the amount of independence left to the different ' Protected States,' some of which are powerful kingdoms, like Hyderabad, while many, as for instance in Gujarat, are petty principalities of two or three dozen square miles.

The mention of these protected States suggests another point of comparison. Rome brought many principalities or kingdoms under her influence, especially in the eastern parts of the Empire ; and dealt with each upon the basis of the treaty by which her supremacy had been acknowledged, allowing to some a wider, to some a narrower measure of autonomy [2]. Ultimately, however, all these, except a few on the frontiers, passed under her direct sway : and this frequently happened in cases where

---

[1] The use of the word to denote the two great ecclesiastical divisions of England (Province of Canterbury and Province of York) is a relic of the Roman imperial system.

[2] For instance, Cappadocia, Pontus, and Commagene were left as subject kingdoms till 17 A. D., 63 A. D., and 72 A. D. respectively.

the native dynasty had died out, so that the title lapsed to the Emperor. The Iceni in Britain seem to have been such a protected State, and it was the failure of male heirs that caused a lapse. So the Indian Government was wont, when the ruling family became extinct or hopelessly incompetent, to annex to the dominions of the British Crown the principality it had ruled. From the days of Lord Canning, however, a new policy has been adopted. It is now deemed better to maintain the native dynasties whenever this can be done, so a childless prince is suffered to adopt, or provide for the adoption of, some person approved by the Government; and the descendants of this person are recognized as rulers [1]. The incoming prince feels that he owes his power to the British Government, while adoption gives him a title in the eyes of his subjects.

The differences I have mentioned between the British provinces are important, not only as respects administration, but as respects the system of landholding. All over India, as in many other Oriental countries, it is from the land that a large part of revenue, whether one calls it rent or land tax, is derived. In some provinces the rent is paid direct to the Government by the cultivator, in others it goes to intermediary landlords, who in their turn are responsible to the State. In some provinces it has been permanently fixed, by what is called a Land-settlement [2], and not always on the same principles. The subject is far too large and intricate to be pursued here. I mention it because in the Roman Empire also land revenue was the mainstay of the im-

[1] 'The extent to which confidence has been restored by Lord Canning's edict is shown by the curious fact that since its promulgation a childless ruler very rarely adopts in his own lifetime. An heir presumptive, who knows that he is to succeed and who may possibly grow restive if his inheritance is delayed, is for various obscure reasons not the kind of person whom an Oriental ruler cares to see idling about his palace, so that a politic chief oftens prefers leaving the duty of nominating a successor to his widows, who know his mind and have every reason for wishing him long life.'—Sir A. C. Lyall in *Law Quarterly Review* for October, 1893.

[2] One finds something similar to this Land-settlement in the Roman plan of determining the land revenue of a province by what was called the *lex provinciae*.

perial treasury. Where territory had been taken in war, the fact of conquest was deemed to have made the Roman people ultimate owners of the land so acquired, and the cultivators became liable to pay what we should call rent for it. In some provinces this rent was farmed out to contractors called *publicani*, who offered to the State the sum equivalent to the rent of the area contracted for, minus the expense of collection and their own profit on the undertaking, and kept for themselves whatever they could extract from the peasantry. This vicious system, resembling that of the tithe farmers in Ireland seventy years ago, was regulated by Nero and abolished by Hadrian, who placed the imperial procurator in charge of the land revenue except as regarded the forests and the mines. It exists to-day in the Ottoman Empire. Convenient for the State as it seems, it is wasteful, and naturally exposes the peasant, as is conspicuously the case in Asiatic Turkey, to oppressions perhaps even harder to check than are those of State officials. When the English came to India they found it in force there; and the present landlord class in Bengal, called Zemindars, are the representatives of the rent or land tax-farmers under the native princes who were, perhaps unwisely, recognized as landowners by the British a century ago. This kind of tax-farming is, however, no longer practised in India, a merit to be credited to the English when we are comparing them with the Romans of the Republic and the earlier Empire.

Where the revenue of the State comes from the land, the State is obliged to keep a watchful eye upon the condition of agriculture, since revenue must needs decline when agriculture is depressed. There was not in the Roman world, and there is not in India now, any question of agricultural depression arising from foreign competition, for no grain came into the Empire from outside, or comes now into India [1]. But a year of drought, or, in a long course of years, the exhaustion

[1] Rice, however, is sent from Lower Burma into India proper.

of the soil, tells heavily on the agriculturist, and may render him unable to pay his rent or land tax. In bad years it was the practice of the more indulgent Emperors to remit a part of the tax for the year: and one of the complaints most frequently made against harsh sovereigns, or extravagant ones like Justinian, was that they refused to concede such remissions. A similar indulgence has to be and is granted in India in like cases.

Finance was the standing difficulty of the Roman as it is of the Anglo-Indian administrator. Indeed, the Roman Empire may be said to have perished from want of revenue. Heavy taxation, and possibly the exhaustion of the soil, led to the abandonment of farms, reducing the rent derivable from the land. The terrible plague of the second century brought down population, and was followed by a famine. The eastern provinces had never furnished good fighting material: and the diminution of the agricultural population of Italy, due partly to this cause, partly to the growth of large estates worked by slave labour, made it necessary to recruit the armies from the barbarians on the frontiers. Even in the later days of the Republic the native auxiliaries were beginning to be an important part of a Roman army. Moreover, with a declining revenue, a military establishment such as was needed to defend the eastern and the northern frontiers could not always be maintained. The Romans had no means of drawing a revenue from frontier customs, because there was very little import trade; but dues were levied at ports and there was a succession tax, which usually stood at five per cent. In most provinces there were few large fortunes on which an income or property tax could have been levied, except those of persons who were already paying up to their capacities as being responsible for the land tax assessed upon their districts. The salt tax was felt so sorely by the poor that Aurelian was hailed as a benefactor when he abolished it.

India has for many years past been, if not in financial

3

straits, yet painfully near the limit of her taxable resources. There too the salt tax presses hard upon the
peasant; and the number of fortunes from which much
can be extracted by an income or property tax is, relatively to the population, very small. Comparing her
total wealth with her population, India is a poor country,
probably poorer than was the Roman Empire in the
time of Constantine [1]. A heavy burden lies upon her in
respect of the salaries of the upper branches of the
Civil Service, which must of course be fixed at figures
sufficient to attract a high order of talent from England,
and a still heavier one in respect of military charges.
On the other hand, she has the advantage of being able,
when the guarantee of the British Government is given
for the loan, to borrow money for railways and other
public works, at a rate of interest very low as compared with what the best Native State would be obliged
to offer, or as compared with that which the Roman
Government paid.

Under the Republic, Rome levied tribute from the
provinces, and spent some of it on herself, though of
course the larger part went to the general expenses of
the military and civil administration. Under the Emperors that which was spent in Rome became gradually
less and less, as the Emperor became more and more
detached from the imperial city, and after Diocletian,
Italy was treated as a province. England, like Spain in
the days of her American Empire and like Holland now,
for a time drew from her Indian conquests a substantial
revenue. An inquiry made in 1773 showed that, since
1765, about two millions a year had been paid by the

[1] The total revenue of British India was, in A. D. 1840, 200,000,000 of rupees, and
in 1898-9, 1,014,427,000 rupees, more than a fourth of which was land revenue and
less than one-fourth from railways. (The exchange value of the rupee, formerly
about two shillings, is now about one shilling and four pence.) £190,000,000 has
been expended upon railways in British India and the Native States. The land
revenue is somewhat increasing with the bringing of additional land under cultivation. It is estimated that forty-two per cent. of the cultivable area is available
for further cultivation. The funded debt of India is now £195,000,000, the un-
funded about £12,000,000.

Company to the British exchequer. By 1773, however, the Company had incurred such heavy debts that the exchequer had to lend them money: and since that time Britain has drawn no tribute from India. She profits by her dominion only in respect of having an enormous market for her goods, industrial or commercial enterprises offering comparatively safe investments for her capital, and a field where her sons can make a career. Apart from any considerations of justice or of sentiment, India could not afford to make any substantial contribution to the expenses of the non-Indian dominions of the Crown. It is all she can do to pay her own way.

Those whom Rome sent out to govern the provinces were, in the days of the Republic and in the days of Augustus, Romans, that is to say Roman citizens and natives of Italy. Very soon, however, citizens born in the provinces began to be admitted to the great offices and to be selected by the Emperor for high employment. As early as the time of Nero, an Aquitanian chief, Julius Vindex, was legate of the great province of Gallia Lugdunensis. When the imperial throne itself was filled by provincials, as was often the case from Trajan onwards, it was plain that the pre-eminence of Italy was gone. If a man, otherwise eligible, was not a full Roman citizen, the Emperor forthwith made him one. By the time of the Antonines (A. D. 138-180) there was practically no distinction between a Roman and a provincial citizen; and we may safely assume that the large majority of important posts, both military and civil, were held by men of provincial extraction. Indeed merit probably won its way faster to military than to civil distinction, for in governments which are militant as well as military, promotion by merit is essential to the success of the national arms, and the soldier identifies himself with the power he serves even faster than does the civilian. So, long before full citizenship was granted to the whole Roman world (about A. D. 217), it is clear that not only the lower posts in which provincials had always been employed, but the highest also were freely open to all subjects. A Gaul might be sent to govern Cilicia, or a Thracian Britain, because both were now Romans rather than Gauls or Thracians. The fact that Latin and Greek were practically familiar to nearly all highly educated civil servants, because Latin was the language of law as well as the tongue commonly spoken in the West, while Greek was the language of philosophy and (to a great extent) of letters, besides being the spoken tongue of most parts of the East, made a well-educated man fit for public employment everywhere, for he was not (except perhaps in Syria and Egypt and a few odd corners of the Empire) obliged to learn any fresh language. And a provincial was just as likely as an Italian to be highly educated. Thus the officials could easily get into touch with the subjects, and felt hardly more strange if they came from a distance than a Scotchman feels if he is appointed to a professorship in Quebec, or an Irishman if he becomes postmaster in a Norfolk village. Nothing contributed more powerfully to the unity and the strength of the Roman dominion than this sense of an imperial nationality.

The English in India have, as did the Romans, always employed the natives in subordinate posts. The enormous majority of persons who carry on the civil administration there at this moment are Asiatics. But the English, unlike the Romans, have continued to reserve the higher posts for men of European stock. The contrast in this respect between the Roman and the English policy is instructive, and goes down to the foundation of the differences between English and Roman rule. As we have seen, the City of Rome became the Empire, and the Empire became Rome. National independence was not regretted, for the East had been denationalized before the Italian conqueror appeared, and the tribes of the West, even those who fought best for freedom, had not reached a genuine

national life when Spain, Gaul, and Britain were brought
under the yoke. In the third century A. D. a Gaul, a
Spaniard, a Pannonian, a Bithynian, a Syrian called
himself a Roman, and for all practical purposes was a
Roman. The interests of the Empire were his interests,
its glory his glory, almost as much as if he had been
born in the shadow of the Capitol. There was, therefore, no reason why his loyalty should not be trusted,
no reason why he should not be chosen to lead in war,
or govern in peace, men of Italian birth. So, too, the
qualities which make a man capable of leading in war
or administering in peace were just as likely to be
found in a Gaul, or a Spaniard, or a German from the
Rhine frontier as in an Italian. In fact, men of Italian
birth play no great part in later imperial history [1].

It is far otherwise in India, though there was among
the races of India no nation. The Englishman does
not become an Indian, nor the Indian an Englishman.
The Indian does not as a rule, though of course there
have been not a few remarkable exceptions to the rule,
possess the qualities which the English deem to be
needed for leadership in war or for the higher posts of
administration in peace [2]. For several reasons, reasons
to be referred to later, he can seldom be expected to feel
like an Englishman, and to have the same devotion to
the interests of England which may be counted on in
an Englishman. Accordingly the English have made
in India arrangements to which there was nothing similar in the Roman Empire. They have two armies, a
native and a European, the latter of which is never suffered to fall below a certain ratio to the former. The
latter is composed entirely of Englishmen. In the former all military posts in line regiments above that of

[1] After the fifth century, Armenians, Isaurians, and Northern Macedonians
figure more largely in the Eastern Empire than do natives of the provinces round
the Aegaean.

[2] Among these exceptions may be mentioned Sir Syed Ahmed of Aligurh, and
the late Mr. Justice Trimbak Telang of Bombay, both men of remarkable force
and elevation of character.

subahdar (equivalent to captain) are reserved to Englishmen [1]. The artillery and engineer services are kept in English hands, *i.e.* there is hardly any native artillery. It is only, therefore, in the native contingents already referred to that natives are found in the higher grades. These contingents may be compared with the auxiliary barbarian troops under non-Roman commanders whom we find in the later ages of Rome, after Constantine. Such commanders proved sometimes, like the Vandal Stilicho, energetic defenders of the imperial throne, sometimes, like the Suevian Ricimer, formidable menaces to it [2]. But apart from these, the Romans had but one army; and it was an army in which all subjects had an equal chance of rising.

In a civil career, the native of India may go higher under the English than he can in a military one. A few natives, mostly Hindus, and indeed largely Bengali Hindus, have won their way into the civil service by passing the competitive Indian Civil Service examination in England, and some of these have risen to the posts of magistrate and district judge. A fair proportion of the seats on the benches of the Supreme Courts in Calcutta, Madras, Bombay, Allahabad, and Lahore have been allotted to native barristers of eminence, several of whom have shown themselves equal in point of knowledge and capacity, as well as in integrity, to the best judges selected from the European bar in India or sent out from the English bar. No native, however, has ever been thought of for the great places, such as those of Lieutenant-Governor or Chief Commissioner, although all British subjects are legally eligible for any post in the service of the Crown in any part of the British Dominions.

[1] The subahdar, however, is rather a non-commissioned than a commissioned officer, and is not a member of the British officers' mess.

[2] Russia places Musulmans from the Caucasian provinces in high military posts. But she has no army corresponding to the native army in India, and as she has a number of Musulman subjects in European Russia it is all the more natural for her to have a Colonel Temirhan Shipsheff at Aralykh and a General Alikhanoff at Merv.

Regarding the policy of this exclusion there has been much difference of opinion. As a rule, Anglo-Indian officials approve the course which I have described as that actually taken. But I know some who think that there are natives of ability and force of character such as to fit them for posts military as well as civil, higher than any to which a native has yet been advanced, and who sees advantages in selecting a few for such posts. They hold, however, that such natives ought to be selected for civil appointments, not by competitive examination in England but in India itself by those who rule there, and in respect of personal merits tested by service. Some opposition to such a method might be expected from members of the regular civil service, who would consider their prospects of promotion to be thereby prejudiced.

Here we touch an extremely interesting point of comparison between the Roman and the English systems. Both nations, when they started on their career of conquest, had already built up at home elaborate constitutional systems in which the rights of citizens, both public and private civil rights, had been carefully settled and determined. What was the working of these rights in the conquered territories ? How far were they extended by the conquerors, Roman and English, and with what results ?

Rome set out from the usual practice of the city republics of the ancient world. No man enjoyed any rights at all, public or private, except a citizen of the Republic. A stranger coming to reside in the city did not, no matter how long he lived there, nor did his son or grandson, obtain those rights unless he was specially admitted to become a citizen. From this principle Rome, as she grew, presently found herself obliged to deviate. She admitted one set of neighbours after another, sometimes as allies, sometimes in later days, as conquered and incorporated communities, to a citizenship which was sometimes incomplete, including only private civil rights, sometimes

complete, including the right of voting in the assembly
and the right of being chosen to a public office. Before
the dictatorship of Julius Caesar practically all Italians,
except the people of Cisalpine Gaul, which remained a
province till B. C. 43, had been admitted to civic rights.
Citizenship, complete or partial (*i.e.* including or not
including public rights) had also begun to be conferred
on a certain number of cities or individuals outside Italy.
Tarsus in Cilicia, of which St. Paul was a native, enjoyed
it, so he was born a Roman citizen. This process of en-
larging citizenship went on with accelerated speed, in
and after the days of the Flavian Emperors. Under
Hadrian, the whole of Spain seems to have enjoyed civic
rights. Long before this date the ancient right of voting
in the Roman popular Assembly had become useless,
but the other advantages attached to the status of citizen
were worth having, for they secured valuable immunities.
Finally, early in the third century A. D., every Roman
subject was by imperial edict made a citizen for all purposes whatsoever. Universal eligibility to office had,
as we have seen, gone ahead of this extension, for all
offices lay in the gift of the Emperor or his ministers;
and when it was desired to appoint any one who might
not be a full citizen, citizenship was conferred along with
the office. Thus Rome at last extended to all her subjects the rights that had originally been confined to her
own small and exclusive community.

In England the principle that all private civil rights
belong to every subject alike was very soon established,
and may be said to have never been doubted since the
final extinction of serfdom in the beginning of the seventeenth century. Public civil rights, however, did not
necessarily go with private. Everybody, it is true, was
(subject to certain religious restrictions now almost
entirely repealed) eligible to any office to which he
might be appointed by the Crown, and was also (subject
to certain property qualifications which lasted till our
own time) capable of being chosen to fill any elective

post or function, such as that of member of the House
of Commons. But the right of voting did not necessarily go along with other rights, whether public or
private, and it is only within the last forty years that it
has been extended by a series of statutes to the bulk
of the adult male population. Now when Englishmen
began to settle abroad, they carried with them all their
private rights as citizens, and also their eligibility to
office; but their other public rights, *i. e.* those of voting
they could not carry, because these were attached to
local areas in England. When territories outside England were conquered, their free inhabitants, in becoming subjects of the Crown, became therewith entitled to
all such rights of British subjects as were not connected
with residence in Britain: that is to say, they had all the
private civil rights of Englishmen, and also complete
eligibility to public office (unless of course some special
disqualification was imposed). The rights of an English
settler in Massachusetts in the seventeenth and eighteenth centuries were those of an Englishman, except
that he could not vote at an English parliamentary election because he was not resident in any English constituency; and the same rule became applicable to a French
Canadian after the cession of Canada to the British
Crown.

So when India was conquered, the same principles
were again applied. Every free Indian subject of the
Crown soon became entitled to the private civil rights
of an Englishman, except so far as his own personal
law, Hindu or Musulman or Parsi or Jain, might modify
those rights; and if there was any such modification,
that was recognized for his benefit rather than to his
prejudice. Thus the process which the Romans took
centuries to complete was effected almost at once in
India by the application of long established doctrines of
English law. Accordingly we have in India the singular
result that although there are in that country no free
institutions (other than those municipal ones previously

referred to) nor any representative government, every Indian subject is eligible to any office in the gift of the Crown anywhere, and to any post or function to which any body of electors may select him. He may be chosen by a British constituency a member of the British House of Commons, or by a Canadian constituency a member of the House of Commons of Canada. Two natives of India (both Parsis) have already been chosen, both by London constituencies, to sit in the British House. So a native Hindu or Musulman might be appointed by the Crown to be Lord Chief Justice of England or Governor-General of Canada or Australia. He might be created a peer. He might become Prime Minister. And as far as legal eligibility goes, he might be named Governor-General of India, though as a matter of practice, no Indian has ever been placed in any high Indian office. Neither birth, nor colour, nor religion constitutes any legal disqualification. This was expressly declared as regards India by the India Act of 1833, and has been more than once formally declared since, but it did not require any statute to establish what flowed from the principles of our law. And it need hardly be added that the same principles apply to the Chinese subjects of the Crown in Hong Kong or Singapore and to the negro subjects of the Crown in Jamaica or Zululand. In this respect at least England has worthily repeated the liberal policy of Rome. She has done it, however, not by way of special grants, but by the automatic and probably uncontemplated operation of the general principles of her law.

As I have referred to the influence of English constitutional ideas, it is worth noting that it is these ideas which have led the English of late years not only to create in India city municipalities, things entirely foreign to the native Indian mind, but also to provide by statute (in 1892) for the admission of a certain number of nominated non-official members to the legislative councils of the Governors in Bengal, Bombay, Madras, the North-West Provinces and Oudh, and the Punjab. These

members are nominated, not elected, because it has been
found difficult to devise a satisfactory scheme of election.
But the provision made for the presence of native non-
officials testifies to the wish of the English Government to secure not only a certain amount of outside
opinion, but also a certain number of native councillors
through whom native sentiment may be represented,
and may obtain its due influence on the conduct of
affairs.

The extension of the civil rights of Englishmen to the
subjects of the Crown in India would have been anything but a boon had it meant the suppression and
extinction of native law and custom. This of course it
has not meant. Neither had the extension of Roman
conquest such an effect in the Roman Empire; and
even the grant of citizenship to all subjects did not
quite efface local law and usage. As the position and
influence of English law in India, viewed in comparison
with the relation of the older Roman law to the Roman
provinces, is the subject of another of these Essays,
I will here pass over the legal side of the matter, and
speak only of the parallel to be noted between the political action of the conquering nations in both cases.

Both have shown a prudent wish to avoid disturbing,
any further than the fixed principles of their policy made
needful, the usages and beliefs of their subjects. The
Romans took over the social and political system which
they found in each of the very dissimilar regions they
conquered, placed their own officials above it, modified
it so far as they found expedient for purposes of revenue
and civil administration generally, but otherwise let it
stand as they found it and left the people alone. In
course of time the law and administration of the conquerors, and the intellectual influences which literature
called into play, did bring about a considerable measure
of assimilation between Romans and provincials, especially in the life and ideas of the upper classes. But
this was the result of natural causes. The Romans did

not consciously and deliberately work for uniformity. Especially in the sphere of religion they abstained from all interference. They had indeed no temptation to interfere either with religious belief or with religious practice, for their own system was not a universal but a strictly national religion, and the educated classes had begun to sit rather loose to that religion before the process of foreign conquest had gone far. According to the theory of the ancient world, every nation had its own deities, and all these deities were equally to be respected in their own country. Whether they were at bottom the same deities under different names, or were quite independent divine powers, did not matter. Each nation and each member of a nation was expected to worship the national gods: but so long as an individual man did not openly reject or insult those gods, he might if he pleased worship a god belonging to some other country, provided that the worship was not conducted with shocking or demoralizing rites, such as led to the prohibition of the Bacchanalian cult at Rome [1]. The Egyptian Serapis was a fashionable deity among Roman women as early as the time of Catullus. We are told that Claudius abolished Druidism on account of its savage cruelty, but this may mean no more than that he forbade the Druidic practice of human sacrifices [2]. There was therefore, speaking broadly, no religious persecution and little religious intolerance in the ancient world, for the Christians, it need hardly be said, were persecuted not because of their religion but because they were a secret society, about which, since it was new, and secret, and Oriental, and rejected all the gods of all the nations alike, the wildest calumnies were readily believed. The first religious persecutors were the Persian Fire-worshipping kings of the Sassanid dynasty, who occasionally worried their Christian subjects.

[1] Constantine prohibited the immoral excesses practised by the Syrians of Heliopolis.

[2] ' Druidarum religionem apud Gallos dirae immanitatis et tantum civibus sub Augusto interdictam penitus abolevit.'—Sueton, *Vita Claud.* c. 25.

Neither, broadly speaking, was religious propagandism known to the ancient world. There were no missions, neither foreign missions nor home missions. If a man did not sacrifice to the gods of his own country, his fellow citizens might think ill of him. If he was accused of teaching that the gods did not exist, he might possibly, like Socrates, be put to death, but nobody preached to him. On the other hand, if he did worship them, he was in the right path, and it would have been deemed not only impertinent, but almost impious, for the native of another country to seek to convert him to another faith, that is to say, to make him disloyal to the gods of his own country, who were its natural and time-honoured protectors. The only occasions on which one hears of people being required to perform acts of worship to any power but the deities of their country are those cases in which travellers were expected to offer a prayer or a sacrifice to some local deity whose territory they were traversing, and whom it was therefore expedient to propitiate, and those other cases in which a sort of worship was required to be rendered to the monarch, or the special protecting deity of the monarch, under whose sway they lived. The edict attributed to Nebuchadnezzar in the book of Daniel may in this connexion be compared with the practice in the Roman Empire of adoring the spirit that watched over the reigning Caesar. To burn incense on the altar of the Genius of the Emperor was the test commonly proposed to the persons accused of being Christians.

All this is the natural result of polytheism. With the coming of faiths each of which claims to be exclusively and universally true, the face of the world was changed. Christianity was necessarily a missionary religion, and unfortunately soon became also, forgetting the precepts of its Founder, a persecuting religion. Islam followed in the same path, and for similar reasons. In India the strife of Buddhism with Hinduism gave rise to ferocious persecutions, which however were perhaps as much political as religious. When the Portuguese and Spaniards began to discover and conquer new countries beyond the oceans, the spread of religion was in the mouths of all the adventurers, and in the minds of many of the baser as well as of the better sort. Spain accordingly forced her faith upon all her subjects, and found no great resistance from the American peoples, though of course their Christianity seldom went deep, as indeed it remains to-day in many parts of Central and South America, a thin veneer over the ancient superstitions of the aborigines. Portugal did the like, so far as she could, in India and in Africa. So too the decrees by which the French colonizing companies were founded in the days of Richelieu provided that the Roman Catholic faith was to be everywhere made compulsory, and that converted pagans were to be admitted to the full civil rights of Frenchmen [1]. But when the English set forth to trade and conquer they were not thinking of religion. The middle of the eighteenth century, when Bengal and Madras were acquired, was for England an age when persecution had died out and missionary propagandism had scarcely begun. The East India Company did not at first interfere in any way with the religious rites it found practised by the people, however cruel or immoral they might be. It gave no advantages to Christian converts, and for a good while it even discouraged the presence of missionaries, lest they should provoke disturbances. Bishops were thought less dangerous, and one was appointed, with three Archdeacons under him, by the Act of 1813. A sort of miniature church establishment, for the benefit of Europeans, still exists and is supported out of Indian revenues. After a time, however, some of the more offensive or harmful features of native worship began to be forbidden. The human sacrifices that occasionally occurred among the hill tribes were treated as murders, and the practice of Sutti—the self-immolation of the Hindu widow on her husband's

[1] I owe this fact to Sir A. C. Lyall (*op. cit.* p. 66).

funeral pyre—was forbidden as far back as 1829. No hindrance is now thrown in the way of Christian missions: and there is perfect equality, as respects civil rights and privileges, not only between the native votaries of all religions, but also between them and Europeans.

So far as religion properly so-called is concerned, the policy of the English is simple and easy to apply. But as respects usages which are more or less associated with religion in the native mind, but which European sentiment disapproves, difficulties sometimes arise. The burning of the widow was one of these usages, and has been dealt with at the risk of offending Hindu prejudice. Infanticide is another; and the British Government try to check it, even in some of the protected States. The marriage of young children is a third: and this it has been thought not yet prudent to forbid, although the best native opinion is beginning to recognize the evils that attach to it. Speaking generally, it may be said that the English have, like the Romans but unlike the Spaniards, shown their desire to respect the customs and ideas of the conquered peoples. Indifferentism has served them in their career of conquest as well as religious eclecticism served the Romans, so that religious sentiment, though it sometimes stimulated the valour of their native enemies, has not really furnished any obstacle to the pacification of a conquered people. The English have, however, gone further than did the Romans in trying to deter their subjects from practices socially or morally deleterious.

As regards the work done by the English for education in the establishment of schools and Universities, no comparison with Rome can usefully be drawn: because it was not deemed in the ancient world to be the function of the State to make a general educational provision for its subjects. The Emperors, however, appointed and paid teachers of the liberal arts in some of the greater cities. That which the English have done, however, small as it may appear in comparison

with the vast population they have to care for[1], witnesses
to the spirit which has animated them in seeking to
extend to the conquered the opportunities of progress
which they value for themselves.

The question how far the triumphs of Rome and of
England are due to the republican polity of the one,
and the practically republican (though not until 1867
or 1885 democratic) polity of the other, is so large
a one that I must be content merely to indicate it as
well deserving a discussion. Several similar empires
have been built up by republican governments of the
oligarchic type, as witness the empire of Carthage in
the ancient, and that of Venice in the later mediaeval
world. One can explain this by the fact that in such
governments there is usually, along with a continuity of
policy hardly to be expected from a democracy, a constant succession of capable generals and administrators
such as a despotic hereditary monarchy seldom provides,
for a monarchy of that kind must from time to time
have feeble or dissolute sovereigns, under whom bad
selections will be made for important posts, policy will
oscillate, and no adequate support will be given to the
armies or fleets which are maintaining the interests of
the nation abroad. A republic is moreover likely to
have a larger stock of capable and experienced men on
which to draw during the process of conquering and
organizing. The two conspicuous instances in which
monarchies have acquired and long held vast external
dominions are the Empires of Spain and Russia. The
former case is hardly an exception to the doctrine just
stated, because the oceanic Empire of Spain was won
quickly and with little fighting against opponents immeasurably inferior, and because it had no conterminous enemies to take advantage of the internal decay
which soon set in. In the case of Russia the process

[1] There are in India five examining and degree-granting Universities, with
about 8,000 matriculated students, nearly all of them taught in the numerous af-
filiated colleges. The total number of persons returned as receiving instruction in
India is 4,357,000, of whom 402,000 are girls.

has been largely one of natural expansion over regions so thinly peopled and with inhabitants so backward that no serious resistance was made to an advance which went on rather by settlement than by conquest. It is only in the Caucasus and in Turkistan that Russia has had to establish her power by fighting. Her conflicts even with the Persians and the Ottoman Turks have been, as Moltke is reported to have said, battles of the one-eyed against the blind. But it must be added that Russia has shown during two centuries a remarkable power of holding a steady course of foreign policy. She sometimes trims her sails, and lays the ship upon the other tack, but the main direction of the vessel's course is not altered. This must be the result of wisdom or good fortune in the choice of ministers, for the Romanoff dynasty has not contained more than its fair average of men of governing capacity.

There is one other point in which the Romans and the English may be compared as conquering powers. Both triumphed by force of character. During the two centuries that elapsed between the destruction of Carthage, when Rome had already come to rule many provinces, and the time of Vespasian, when she had ceased to be a city, and was passing into a nation conterminous with her dominions, the Romans were the ruling race of the world, small in numbers, even if we count the peoples of middle Italy as Romans, but gifted with such talents for war and government, and possessed of such courage and force of will as to be able, not only to dominate the whole civilized world and hold down its peoples, but also to carry on a succession of bloody civil wars among themselves without giving those peoples any chance of recovering their freedom. The Roman armies, though superior in discipline to the enemies they had to encounter, except the Macedonians and Greeks, were not generally superior in arms, and had no resources of superior scientific knowledge at their command. Their adversaries in Africa, in Greece, and in Asia Minor were as far

4

advanced in material civilization as they were themselves. It was their strenuous and indomitable will,
buoyed up by the pride and self-confidence born of a long
succession of victories in the past, that enabled them to
achieve this unparalleled triumph. The triumph was a
triumph of character, as their poet felt when he penned
the famous line, *Moribus antiquis stat res Romana virisque.*
And after the inhabitants of the City had ceased to be
the heart of the Empire, this consciousness of greatness passed to the whole population of the Roman
world when they compared themselves with the barbarians outside their frontiers. One finds it even in
the pages of Procopius, a Syrian writing in Greek,
after the western half of the Empire had been dismem-
bered by barbarian invasions.

The English conquered India with forces much
smaller than those of the Romans; and their success
in subjugating a still vaster population in a shorter
time may thus appear more brilliant. But the English had antagonists immeasurably inferior in valour, in
discipline, in military science, and generally also in the
material of war, to those whom the Romans overcame.
Nor had they ever either a first-rate general or a monarch
of persistent energy opposed to them. No Hannibal,
nor even a Mithradates, appeared to bar their path.
Hyder Ali had no nation behind him; and fortune
spared them an encounter with the Afghan Ahmed
Shah and the Sikh Ranjit Singh. Their most formidable opponents might rather be compared with the
gallant but untrained Celtic Vercingetorix, or the
showy but incompetent Antiochus the Great. It was
only when Europeans like Dupleix came upon the scene
that they had men of their own kind to grapple with;
and Dupleix had not the support from home which
Clive could count on in case of dire necessity. Still the
conquest of India was a splendid achievement, more
striking and more difficult, if less romantic, than the
conquest of Mexico by Hernan Cortez or the conquest of

Peru by Francisco Pizarro, though it must be admitted
that the courage of these two adventurers in venturing
far into unknown regions with a handful of followers has
never been surpassed. Among the English, as among
the Romans, the sense of personal force, the conscious
ascendency of a race so often already victorious, with
centuries of fame behind them, and a contempt for
the feebler folk against whom they were contending,
were the main source of that dash and energy and
readiness to face any odds which bore down all resistance. These qualities have lasted into our own time.
No more brilliant examples were ever given of them
than in the defence of the Fort at Lucknow and in the
siege of Delhi at the time of the Indian Mutiny of
1857-8. And it is worth noting that almost the only
disasters that have ever befallen the British arms have
occurred where the general in command was either
incompetent, as must sometimes happen in every army,
or was wanting in boldness. In the East, more than
anywhere else, confidence makes for victory, and one
victory leads on to another.

It is by these qualities that the English continue to
hold India. In the higher grades of the civil administration which they fill there are only about one thousand
persons: and these one thousand control two hundred
and eighty-seven millions, doing it with so little friction
that they have ceased to be surprised at this extraordinary fact. The English have impressed the imagination of the people by their resistless energy and their
almost uniform success. Their domination seems to
have about it an element of the supernatural, for the
masses of India are still in that mental condition which
looks to the supernatural for an explanation of whatever
astonishes it. The British Raj fills them with a sense of
awe and mystery. That nearly three hundred millions
of men should be ruled by a few palefaced strangers
from beyond the great and wide sea, strangers who all
obey some distant power, and who never, like the

lieutenants of Oriental sovereigns, try to revolt for their own benefit—this seems too wonderful to be anything but the doing of some unseen and irresistible divinity. I heard at Lahore an anecdote which, slight as it is, illustrates the way in which the native thinks of these things. A tiger had escaped from the Zoological Gardens, and its keeper, hoping to lure it back, followed it. When all other inducements had failed, he lifted up his voice and solemnly adjured it in the name of the British Government, to which it belonged, to come back to its cage. The tiger obeyed.

Now that we have rapidly surveyed the more salient points of resemblance or analogy between these two empires, it remains to note the capital differences between them, one or two of which have been already incidentally mentioned. On the most obvious of all I have already dwelt. It is the fact that, whereas the Romans conquered right out from their City in all directions—south, north, west, and east—so that the capital, during the five centuries from B. C. 200 (end of the Second Punic War) to A. D. 325 (foundation of Constantinople), stood not far from the centre of their dominions, England has conquered India across the ocean, and remains many thousands of miles from the nearest point of her Indian territory. Another not less obvious difference is perhaps less important than it seems. Rome was a city, and Britain is a country. Rome, when she stepped outside Italy to establish in Sicily her first province, had a free population of possibly only seventy or eighty thousand souls. Britain, when she began her career of conquest at Plassy, had (if we include Ireland, then still a distinct kingdom, but then less a source of weakness than she has sometimes since been) a population of at least eleven or twelve millions. But, apart from the fact that the distance from Britain to India round the Cape made her larger population less available for action in India than was the smaller population of Rome for action in the Mediterranean, the comparison must not

really be made with Rome as a city, but with Rome as
the centre of a large Italian population, upon which
she drew for her armies, and the bulk of which had,
before the end of the Republic, become her citizens.
On this point of dissimilarity no more need be said,
because its significance is apparent. I turn from it to
another of greater consequence.

The relations of the conquering country to the conquered country, and of the conquering race to the
conquered races, are totally different in the two cases
compared. In the case of Rome there was a similarity
of conditions which pointed to and ultimately effected
a fusion of the peoples. In the case of England there
is a dissimilarity which makes the fusion of her people
with the peoples of India impossible.

Climate offers the first point of contrast. Rome, to
be sure, ruled countries some of which were far hotter
and others far colder than was the valley of the Tiber.
Doubtless the officer who was stationed in Nubia com-
plained of the torrid summer, much as an English
officer complains of Quetta or Multan; nor were the
winters of Ardoch or Hexham agreeable to a soldier
from Apulia. But if the Roman married in Nubia, he
could bring up his family there. An English officer
cannot do this at Quetta or Multan. The English race
becomes so enfeebled in the second generation by living without respite under the Indian sun that it would
probably die out, at least in the plains, in the third
or fourth. Few Englishmen feel disposed to make
India their home, if only because the physical conditions of life there are so different from those under
which their earlier years were passed. But the Italian
could make himself at home, so far as natural conditions went, almost anywhere from the Dnieper to the
Guadalquivir.

The second contrast is in the colour of the races.
All the races of India are dark, though individuals may
be found among high-caste Brahmins and among the

Parsis of Poona or Gujarat who are as light in hue as many Englishmen. Now to the Teutonic peoples, and especially to the English and Anglo-Americans, the difference of colour means a great deal. It creates a feeling of separation, perhaps even of a slight repulsion. Such a feeling may be deemed unreasonable or unchristian, but it seems too deeply rooted to be effaceable in any time we can foresee. It is, to be sure, not nearly so strong towards members of the more civilized races of India, with their faces often full of an intelligence and refinement which witnesses to many generations of mental culture, as it is in North America towards the negroes of the Gulf Coast, or in South Africa towards the Kafirs. Yet it is sufficient to be, as a rule, a bar to social intimacy, and a complete bar to intermarriage.

Among the highest castes of Hindus and among the most ancient princely families, such as those famous Rajput dynasties whose lineage runs back further than does that of any of the royal houses of Europe, there is a corresponding pride of race quite as strong as that felt by the best-born European. So, too, some of the oldest Musulman families, tracing their origin to the relatives of the Prophet himself, are in respect of long descent equal to any European houses. Nevertheless, although the more educated and tactful among the English pay due honour to these families, colour would form an insurmountable barrier to intermarriage, even were the pride of the Rajputs disposed to invite it. The oldest of the Rajput dynasties, that of Udaipur, always refused to give a daughter in marriage even to the Mogul Emperors.

There was no severing line like this in the ancient world. The only dark races (other than the Egyptians) with whom the Romans came in contact were some of the Numidian tribes, few of whom became really Romanized, and the Nubians of the Middle Nile, also scarcely within the pale of civilization. The question, therefore, did not arise in the form it has taken in India. Probably, however, the Romans would have felt and acted not like Teutons, but rather as the Spanish and Portuguese have done. Difference of colour does not repel members of these last-named nations. Among them, unions, that is to say legitimate unions, of whites with dark-skinned people, are not uncommon, nor is the mulatto or quadroon offspring kept apart and looked down upon as he is among the Anglo-Americans. Nothing contributed more to the fusion of the races and nationalities that composed the Roman Empire than the absence of any physical and conspicuous distinctions between those races, just as nothing did more to mitigate the horrors of slavery than the fact that the slave was usually of a tint and type of features not markedly unlike those of his master. Before the end of the Republic there were many freedmen in the Senate, though their presence there was regarded as a sign of declension. The son of a freedman passed naturally and easily—as did the poet Horace—into the best society of Rome when his personal merits or the favour of a great patron gave him entrance, though his detractors found pleasure in reminding one another of his origin. In India it is otherwise. Slavery, which was never harsh there, has fortunately not come into the matter, in the way it did in the Southern States of America and in South Africa. But the population is sharply divided into whites and natives. The so-called Eurasians, a mixed race due to the unions of whites with persons of Indian race, give their sympathies to the whites, but are treated by the latter as an inferior class. They are not numerous enough to be an important factor, nor do they bridge over the chasm which divides the rulers from the ruled. It is not of the want of political liberty that the latter complain, for political liberty has never been enjoyed in the East, and would not have been dreamt of had not English literature and English college teaching im-

planted the idea in the minds of the educated natives.
But the hauteur of the English and the sense of social
incompatibility which both elements feel, are unfortunate features in the situation, and have been so from
the first. Even in 1813 the representatives of the East
India Company stated to a committee of the House of
Commons that 'Englishmen of classes not under the
observation of the supreme authorities were notorious
for the contempt with which, in their ignorance and
arrogance, they contemplated the usages and institutions of the natives, and for their frequent disregard of
justice and humanity in their dealings with the people
of India [1].' And the Act of 1833 requires the Government of India 'to provide for the protection of the
natives from insult and outrage in their persons, religions, and opinions [2].'

It may be thought that, even if colour did not form
an obstacle to intermarriage, religion would. Religion,
however, can be changed, and colour cannot. In North
America blacks and whites belong to the same religious
denominations, but the social demarcation remains complete. Still it is true that the difference of religion does
constitute in India a further barrier not merely to intermarriage but also to intimate social relations. Among
the Musulmans the practice, or at any rate the legal
possibility of polygamy, naturally deters white women
from a union they might otherwise have contemplated.
(There have, however, been a few instances of such
unions.) Hinduism stands much further away from
Christianity than does Islam; and its ceremonial rules
regarding the persons in whose company food may be
partaken of operate against a form of social intercourse
which cements intimacy among Europeans [3].

One must always remember that in the East religion
constitutes both a bond of union and a dividing line

---

[1] See Ilbert's *Government of India*, p. 77.   [2] Ibid. p. 91.

[3] The number of Hindus in all India is estimated at 207 millions, that of Musulmans at fifty-seven millions, aboriginal races nine millions, Christians two millions.

of severance far stronger and deeper than it does in Western Europe. It largely replaces that national feeling which is absent in India and among the Eastern peoples (except the Chinese and Japanese) generally. Among Hindus and Musulmans religious practices are inwoven with a man's whole life. To the Hindu more especially caste is everything. It creates a sort of nationality within a nationality, dividing the man of one caste from the man of another, as well as from the man who stands outside Hinduism altogether. Among Muslims there is indeed no regular caste (though evident traces of it remain among the Muhamadans of India); but the haughty exclusiveness of Islam keeps its votaries quite apart from the professors of other faiths. The European in India, when he converses with either a Hindu or a Musulman, feels strongly how far away from them he stands. There is always a sense of constraint, because both parties know that a whole range of subjects lies outside discussion, and must not be even approached. It is very different when one talks to a native Christian of the upper ranks. There is then no great need for reserve save, of course, that the racial susceptibilities of the native gentleman who does not belong to the ruling class must be respected. Community of religion in carrying the educated native Christian far away from the native Hindu or Muslim, brings him comparatively near to the European. Because he is a Christian he generally feels himself more in sympathy with his European rulers than he does with his fellow subjects of the same race and colour as himself.

Here I touch a matter of the utmost interest when one thinks of the more remote future of India. Political consequences greater than now appear may depend upon the spread of Christianity there, a spread whose progress, though at present scarcely perceptible in the upper classes, may possibly become much more rapid than it has been during the last century. I do not

say that Hinduism or Islam is a cause of hostility to
British rule. Neither do I suggest that a Christian
native population would become fused with the European or Eurasian population. But if the number of
Christians, especially in the middle and upper ranks
of Indian society, were to increase, the difficulty of
ascertaining native opinion, now so much felt by Indian administrators, would be perceptibly lessened, and
the social separation of natives and Europeans might
become less acute, to the great benefit of both sections
of the population.

When we turn back to the Roman Empire how striking is the absence of any lines of religious demarcation! One must not speak of toleration as the note of
its policy, because there was nothing to tolerate. All
religions were equally true, or equally useful, each for
its own country or nation. The satirist of an age which
had already lost belief in the Olympian deities might
scoff at the beast-gods of Egypt and the fanaticism which
their worship evoked. But nobody thought of converting the devotees of crocodiles or cats. A Briton brought
up by the Druids, or a Frisian who had worshipped
Woden in his youth, found, if he was sent to command a
garrison in Syria, no difficulty in attending a sacrifice to
the Syrian Sun-god, or in marrying the daughter of the
Sun-god's priest. Possibly the first injunctions to have
regard to religion in choosing a consort that were ever
issued in the ancient world were such as that given by
St. Paul when he said, ' Be not unequally yoked together
with unbelievers.' Christianity had a reason for this
precept which the other religions had not, because to it
all the other religions were false and pernicious, drawing men away from the only true God. We may accordingly say that, old-established and strong as some
of the religions were which the Romans found when they
began to conquer the Mediterranean countries, religion
did not constitute an obstacle to the fusion of the peoples of those countries into one Roman nationality.

When the Monotheistic religions came upon the scene, things began to change. Almost the only rebellions against Rome which were rather religious than political, were those of the Jews. When in the fourth, fifth, sixth, and seventh centuries, sharp theological controversies began to divide Christians, especially in the East; dangers appeared such as had never arisen from religious causes in the days of heathenism. Schisms, like that of the Donatists, and heresies, began to trouble the field of politics. The Arian Goths and Vandals remained distinct from the orthodox provincials whom they conquered. In Egypt, a country always prone to fanaticism, the Monophysite antagonism to the orthodoxy of the Eastern Emperors was so bitter that the native population showed signs of disaffection as early as the time of Justinian, and they offered, a century later, scarcely any resistance to those Musulman invaders from Arabia whom they disliked no more than they did their own sovereign at Constantinople.

A fourth agency working for fusion which the Roman Empire possessed, and which the English in India want, is to be found in language and literature. The conquests of Rome had been preceded by the spread of the Greek tongue and of Greek culture over the coasts of the Eastern Mediterranean. Even in the interior of Asia Minor and Syria, though the native languages continued to be spoken in the cities as late as the time of Tiberius [1], and probably held their ground in country districts down till the Arab conquest, Greek was understood by the richer people, and was a sort of *lingua franca* for commerce from Sicily to the Euphrates [2]. Greek literature was the basis of education, and formed the minds of the cultivated class. It was indeed familiar to that class even in the western half of the Empire, through which, by the time of the Antonines, Latin had

[1] As in Lycaonia ; cf. Acts xiv.
[2] There is a curious story that when the head of Crassus was brought to the Parthian king a passage from the *Bacchae* of Euripides was recited by a Greek who was at the Court.

begun to be generally spoken, except in remote regions such as the Basque country and the banks of the Vaal and North-Western Gaul. As the process of unification usually works downwards from the wealthier and better educated to the masses, it was of the utmost consequence that the upper class should have, in these two great languages, a factor constantly operative in the assimilation of the ideas of peoples originally distinct, in the diffusion of knowledge, and in the creation of a common type of civilization. Just as the use of Latin and of the Vulgate maintained a sort of unity among Christian nations and races even in the darkest and most turbulent centuries of the Middle Ages, so the use of Latin and Greek throughout the whole Roman Empire powerfully tended to draw its parts together. Nor was it without importance that all the subjects of the Empire had the same models of poetic and prose style in the classical writers of Greece and in the Latin writers of the pre-Augustan and Augustan age. Virgil in particular became the national poet of the Empire, in whom imperial patriotism found its highest expression.

Very different have been the conditions of India. When the British came, they found no national literature, unless we can apply that name to the ancient Sanskrit epics, written in a tongue which had ceased to be spoken many centuries before. Persian and Arabic were cultivated languages, used by educated Musulmans and by a few Hindu servants of the Musulman princes. The *lingua franca* called Hindustani or Urdu, which had sprung up in the camps of the Mogul Emperors, was becoming a means of intercourse over Northern India, but was hardly used throughout the South. Only a handful of the population were sufficiently educated to be accessible to the influences of any literature, or spoke any tongue except that of their own district. At present five great languages [1], branches of the Aryan family, divide between them

[1] Hindi, Bengali, Marathi, Punjabi, and Gujarati.

Northern, North-Western, and Middle India, and four others [1] of the Dravidian type cover Southern India: while many others are spoken by smaller sections of the people. The language of the English conquerors, which was adopted as the official language in 1835, is the parent tongue of only about 250,000 persons out of 287,000,000, less than one in one thousand. An increasing number of natives of the educated class have learnt to speak it, but even if we reckon in these, it affects only the most insignificant fraction of the population. I have already observed that it was an advantage for England in conquering India, and is an advantage for her in ruling it, that the inhabitants are so divided by language as well as by religion and (among the Hindus) by caste that they could not combine to resist her. Rome had enjoyed, in slighter measure, a similar advantage. But whereas in the Roman Empire Greek and Latin spread so swiftly and steadily that the various nationalities soon began to blend, the absence in India of any two such dominant tongues and the lower level of intellectual progress keep the vast bulk of the Indian population without any general vehicle for the interchange of thought or for the formation of any one type of literary and scientific culture. There is therefore no national literature for India, nor any prospect that one will arise. No Cicero forms prose style, no Virgil inspires an imperial patriotism. The English have established places of higher instruction on the model not so much of Oxford and Cambridge as of the Scottish Universities and the new University Colleges which have recently sprung up in England, together with five examining Universities. Through these institutions they are giving to the ambitious youth of India, and especially to those who wish to enter Government employment or the learned professions, an education of a European type, a type so remote from the natural quality and proclivities of the Indian mind that it is not likely to give birth

[1] Telugu, Tamil, Kanarese, Malayalam.

to any literature with a distinctively Indian character. Indeed the chief effect of this instruction has so far been to make those who receive it cease to be Hindus or Musulmans without making them either Christians or Europeans. It acts as a powerful solvent, destroying the old systems of conventional morality, and putting little in their place. The results may not be seen for a generation or two. When they come they may prove far from happy.

If in the course of ages any one language comes to predominate in India and to be the language not only of commerce, law, and administration, but also of literature, English is likely to be that language; and English will by that time have also become the leading language of the world [1]. This will tend both to unify the peoples of India and (in a sense) to bring them nearer to their rulers. By that time, however, if it ever arrives, so many other changes will also have arrived that it is vain to speculate on the type of civilization which will then have been produced.

These considerations have shown us how different have been the results of English from those of Roman conquest. In the latter case a double process began from the first. The provinces became assimilated to one another, and Rome became assimilated to them, or they to her. As her individuality passed to them it was diluted by their influence. Out of the one conquering race and the many conquered races there was growing up a people which, though many local distinctions remained, was by the end of the fourth century A. D. tending to become substantially one in religion, one in patriotism, one in its type of intellectual life and of material civilization. The process was never completed, because the end of the fourth century was just the time when the Empire began, not from any internal dissensions, but from

---

[1] It is estimated that English is at present spoken by about 115 millions of persons, Russian by 80 millions, German by 70, Spanish by 50, French by 45. Of these English is increasing the most swiftly, Russian next, and then German.

financial and military weakness, to yield to invasions and immigrations which forced its parts asunder. But it was so far completed that Claudian could write in the days of Honorius: 'We who drink of the Rhone and the Orontes are all one nation.' In this one huge nation the city and people of Rome had been merged, their original character so obliterated that they could give their name to the world. But in India there has been neither a fusion of the conquerors and the conquered, nor even a fusion of the various conquered races into one people. Differences of race, language, and religion have prevented the latter fusion: yet it may some day come. But a fusion of conquerors and conquered seems to be forbidden by climate and by the disparity of character and of civilization, as well as by antagonisms of colour and religion. The English are too unlike the races of India, or any one of those races, to mingle with them, or to come to form, in the sense of Claudian's words, one people.

The nations and tribes that were overcome and incorporated by Rome were either the possessors of a civilization as old and as advanced as was her own, or else, like the Gauls and the Germans, belonged to stocks full of intellectual force, capable of receiving her lessons, and of rapidly rising to the level of her culture. But the races of India were all of them far behind the English in material civilization. Some of them were and are intellectually backward; others, whose keen intelligence and aptitude for learning equals that of Europeans, are inferior in energy and strength of will. Yet even these differences might not render an ultimate fusion impossible. It is religion and colour that seem to place that result beyond any horizon to which our eyes can reach. The semi-barbarous races of Southern Siberia will become Russians. The Georgians and Armenians of Transcaucasia, unless their attachment to their national churches saves them, may become Russians. Even the Turkmans of the Khanates will be Russians one day, as the Tatars of Kazan and the Crimea are already on the way to become. But the English seem destined to remain quite distinct from the natives of India, neither mingling their blood nor imparting their character and habits.

So too, it may be conjectured, there will not be, for ages to come, any fusion of Americans with the races of the Philippine Isles.

The observation that Rome effaced herself in giving her name and laws to the world suggests an inquiry into what may be called the retroactive influence of India upon England. In the annals of Rome, war, conquest, and territorial expansion pervade and govern the whole story. Her constitutional, her social, her economic history, from the end of the Samnite wars onwards, is substantially determined by her position as a ruling State, first in Italy and then in the Mediterranean world. It was the influence upon the City of the phenomena of her rule in the provinces that did most to destroy not only the old constitution but the old simple and upright character of the Roman people. The provinces avenged themselves upon their conquerors. In the end, Rome ceases to have any history of her own, except an architectural history, so completely is she merged in her Empire. To a great extent this is true of Italy as well as of Rome. Italy, which had subjected so many provinces, ends by becoming herself a province —a province no more important than the others, except in respect of the reverence that surrounded her name. Her history, from the time of Augustus till that of Odovaker and Theodorich the Ostrogoth, is only a part of the history of the Empire. Quite otherwise with England. Though England has founded many colonies, sent out vast bodies of emigrants, and conquered wide dominions, her domestic history has been, since she lost Normandy and Aquitaine, comparatively little affected by these frequent wars and this immense expansion. One might compose a constitutional history of England, or an economic and industrial history, or an ecclesiastical history, or a literary history, or a social history, in which only few and slight references would need to be made to either the colonies or India. England was a great European power before she had any colonies or any Indian territories: and she would be a great European power if all of these transmarine possessions were to drop off. Only at a few moments in the century and a half since the battle of Plassy have Indian affairs gravely affected English politics. Every one remembers Fox's India Bill, in 1783, and the trial of Warren Hastings, and the way in which the Nabobs seemed for a time to be demoralizing society and politics. It was in India that the Duke of Wellington first showed his powers. It was through the Indian opium trade that England first came into collision with China. The notion that Russian ambition might become dangerous to the security of Britain in India had something to do with the Crimean War, and with the subsequent policy towards the Turks followed by England down to 1880. The deplorable Afghan War of 1878-9 led, more perhaps than anything else, to the fall of Lord Beaconsfield's Ministry in 1880. Other instances might be added in which Indian questions have told upon the foreign policy of Great Britain, or have given rise to parliamentary strife; although, by a tacit convention between the two great parties in England, efforts are usually made—and made most wisely— to prevent questions of Indian administration from becoming any further than seems absolutely necessary matters of party controversy. Yet, if these instances be all put together, they are less numerous and momentous than might have been expected when one considers the magnitude of the stake which Britain holds in India. And even when we add to these the effect of Indian markets upon British trade, and the undeniable influence of the possession of India upon the thoughts and aspirations of Englishmen, strengthening in them a sense of pride and what is called an imperial spirit, we shall still be

surprised that the control of this vast territory and of
a population more than seven times as large as that of
the United Kingdom has not told more forcibly upon
Britain, and coloured her history more deeply than
it has in fact done. Suppose that England had not
conquered India. Would her domestic development,
whether constitutional or social, have taken a course
greatly different from that which it has actually followed? So far as we can judge, it would not. It has been
the good fortune of England to stand far off from the
conquered countries, and to have had a population too
large to suffer sensibly from the moral evils which
conquest and the influx of wealth bring in their train [1].

The remark was made at the outset of this discussion
that the contact of the English race with native races
in India, and the process by which the former is giving
the material civilization, and a tincture of the intellectual culture of Europe to a group of Asiatic peoples,
is only part of that contact of European races with
native races and of that Europeanizing of the latter by
the former which is going on all over the world. France
is doing a similar work in North Africa and Madagascar.
Russia is doing it in Turkistan and on the Amur; and
may probably be soon engaged upon it in Manchuria.
Germany is doing it in tropical Africa. England is
doing it in Egypt and Borneo and Matabililand. The
people of the United States are entering upon it in the
Philippine Islands. Every one of these nations professes to be guided by philanthropic motives in its action.
But it is not philanthropy that has carried any of them
into these enterprises, nor is it clear that the result will
be to increase the sum of human happiness.

It is in India, however, that the process has been in
progress for the longest time and on the largest scale.
Even after a century's experience the results cannot
be adequately judged, for the country is in a state

[1] The absence of slavery and the existence of Christianity will of course present
themselves to every one's mind as other factors in differentiating the conditions
of the modern from those of the Roman world.

of transition, with all sorts of new factors, such as railways, and newspapers, and colleges, working as well upon the humbler as upon the wealthier sections of the people. Three things, however, the career of the English in India has proved. One is, that it is possible for a European race to rule a subject native race on principles of strict justice, restraining the natural propensity of the stronger to abuse their power. India has been, and is, ruled upon such principles. When oppression or cruelty is perpetrated, it is not by the European official but by his native subordinates, and especially by the native police, whose delinquencies the European official cannot always discover. Scorn or insolence is sometimes displayed towards the natives by Europeans, and nothing does more to destroy the good effects of just government than such displays of scorn. But again, it is seldom the European civil officials, but either private persons or occasionally junior officers in the army, who are guilty of this abuse of their racial superiority.

The second thing is that a relatively small body of European civilians, supported by a relatively small armed force, can maintain peace and order in an immense population standing on a lower plane of civilization, and itself divided by religious animosities bitter enough to cause the outbreak of intestine wars were the restraining hand withdrawn.

The third fact is that the existence of a system securing these benefits is compatible with an absolute separation between the rulers and the ruled. The chasm between them has in these hundred years of intercourse grown no narrower. Some even deem it wider, and regret the fact that the European official, who now visits England more easily and frequently, does not identify himself so thoroughly with India as did his predecessors some seventy years ago. As one of the greatest problems of this age, and of the age which will follow, is and must be the relation between the European races as a whole on the one hand, and the more backward races of a different colour on the other hand, this incompatibility of temper, this indisposition to be fused, or, one may almost say, this impracticability of fusion, is a momentous result, full of significance for the future. It was quite otherwise with that first effort of humanity to draw itself together, which took shape in the fusion of the races that Rome conquered, and the creation of one Greco-Roman type of civilization for them. But the conditions of that small ancient world were very different from those by which mankind finds itself now confronted.

It is impossible to think of the future and to recall that first impluse towards the unity of mankind which closed fourteen centuries ago, without reverting once more to the Roman Empire, and asking whether the events which caused, and the circumstances which accompanied, its dissolution throw any light on the probable fate of British dominion in the East.

Empires die sometimes by violence and sometimes by disease. Frequently they die from a combination of the two, that is to say, some chronic disease so reduces their vitality that a small amount of external violence suffices to extinguish the waning life. It was so with the dominion of Rome. To outward appearance it was the irruption of the barbarians from the north that tore away the provinces in the west, as it was the assault of the Turks in 1453 that gave the last death blow to the feeble and narrowed Empire which had lingered on in the East. But the dissolution and dismemberment of the western Roman Empire, beginning with the abandonment of Britain in A. D. 411, and ending with the establishment of the Lombards in Italy in A. D. 568, with the conquest of Africa by the Arab chief Sidi Okba in the seventh century, and with the capture of Sicily by Musulman fleets in the ninth, were really due to internal causes which had been for a long time at work. In some provinces at least the administration had become inefficient or corrupt, and the humbler classes were oppressed by the more powerful. The population had in many regions been diminished. In nearly all it had become unwarlike, so that barbarian levies, raised on the frontier, had taken the place of native troops. The revenue was unequal to the task of maintaining an army sufficient for defence. How far the financial straits to which the government was reduced were due to the exhaustion of the soil, how far to maladministration is not altogether easy to determine. They had doubtless been aggravated by the disorders and invasions of A. D. 260-282. Neither can we tell whether the intellectual capacity of the ruling class and the physical vigour of the bulk of the population may not have declined. But it seems pretty clear that the armies and the revenue that were at the disposal of Trajan would have been sufficient to defend the Empire three centuries later, when the first fatal blows were struck; and we may therefore say that it was really from internal maladies, from anaemia or atrophy, from the want of men and the want of money, perhaps also from the want of wisdom, rather than from the appearance of more formidable foes, that the Empire perished in the West.

British power in India shows no similar signs of weakness, for though the establishment of internal peace is beginning to make it less easy to recruit the native army with first-class fighting-men, such as the Punjab used to furnish, it has been hitherto found possible to keep that army up to its old standard of numbers and efficiency. Still the warning Rome has bequeathed is a warning not to be neglected. Her great difficulty was finance and the impoverishment of the cultivator. Finance and the poverty of the cultivator, who is always in danger of famine, and is taxed to the full measure of his capacity—these are the standing difficulties of Indian administration; and they do not grow less, for, as population increases, the struggle for food is more severe, and the expenditure on frontier defence, including strategic railways, has gone on rapidly increasing.

As England seems to be quite as safe from rebellion within India as was Rome within her Empire, so is she stronger against external foes than Rome was, for she has far more defensible frontiers, viz. the sea which she commands, and a tremendous mountain barrier in whose barren gorges a comparatively small force might repel invaders coming from a distance and obliged to carry their food with them. There is really, so far as can be seen at present, only one danger against which the English have to guard, that of provoking discontent among their subjects by laying on them too heavy a burden of taxation. It has been suggested that when the differences of caste and religion which now separate the peoples of India from one another have begun to disappear, when European civilization has drawn them together into one people, and European ideas have created a large class of educated and restless natives ill disposed to brook subjection to an alien race, new dangers may arise to threaten the permanence of British power. Such possibilities, however, belong to a future which is still far distant.

It is, of course, upon England in the last resort that the defence of India rests. The task is well within her strength, though serious enough to make it fitting that a prudent and pacific spirit should guide her whole foreign and colonial policy, that she should neither embark on needless wars nor lay on herself the burden of holding down disaffected subjects.

England must be prepared to command the sea, and to spare 80,000 of her soldiers to garrison the country. Were she ever to find herself unable to do this, what would become of India? Its political unity, which depends entirely on the English Raj, would vanish like a morning mist. Wars would break out, wars of ambition, or plunder, or religion, which might end in the ascendency of a few adventurers, not necessarily belong-

ing to the reigning native dynasties, but probably either
Pathans, or Sikhs, or Musulmans of the north-west.
The Marathas might rise in the West. The Nepalese
might descend upon Bengal. Or perhaps the country
would, after an interval of chaos, pass into the hands
of some other European Power. To India severance
from England would mean confusion, bloodshed, and
pillage. To England however, apart from the particular events which might have caused the snapping
of the tie, and apart from the possible loss of a market,
severance from India need involve no lasting injury.
To be mistress of a vast country whose resources for
defence need to be supplemented by her own, adds
indeed to her fame, but does not add to her strength.
England was great and powerful before she owned
a yard of land there, and might be great and powerful
again with no more foothold in the East than would
be needed for the naval fortresses which protect her
commerce.

Happily, questions such as these are for the moment
purely speculative.

II

THE EXTENSION OF ROMAN AND ENGLISH LAW THROUGHOUT THE WORLD

I. The Regions covered by Roman and English Law.

From a general comparison of Rome and England as powers conquering and administering territories beyond their original limits, it is natural to pass on to consider one particular department of the work which territorial extension has led them to undertake, viz. their action as makers of a law which has spread far out over the world. Both nations have built up legal systems which are now—for the Roman law has survived the Roman Empire, and is full of vitality to-day—in force over immense areas that were unknown to those who laid the foundations of both systems. In this respect Rome and England stand alone among nations, unless we reckon in the law of Islam which, being a part of the religion of Islam, governs Musulmans wherever Musulmans are to be found.

Roman law, more or less modified by national or local family customs or land customs and by modern legislation, prevails to-day in all the European countries which formed part either of the ancient or of the mediaeval Roman Empire, that is to say, in Italy, in Greece and the rest of South-Eastern Europe (so far as the Christian part of the population is concerned), in Spain, Portugal, Switzerland, France, Germany (including the German and Slavonic parts of the Austro-Hungarian monarchy), Belgium, Holland. The only exception is South Britain, which lost its Roman law with the coming of the Angles and Saxons in the fifth century. The leading principles of Roman jurisprudence prevail also in some other outlying countries which have borrowed much of their law from some one or more of the countries already named, viz. Denmark, Norway, Sweden, Russia, and Hungary. Then come the non-European colonies settled by some among the above States, such as Louisiana, the Canadian province of Quebec, Ceylon, British Guiana, South Africa (all the above having been at one time colonies either of France or of Holland), German Africa, and French Africa, together with the regions which formerly obeyed Spain or Portugal, including Mexico, Central America, South America, and the Philippine Islands. Add to these the Dutch and French East Indies, and Siberia. There is also Scotland, which has since the establishment of the Court of Session by King James the Fifth in 1532 built up its law out of Roman Civil and (to some slight extent) Roman Canon Law [1].

English law is in force not only in England, Wales, and Ireland but also in most of the British colonies. Quebec, Ceylon, Mauritius, South Africa, and some few of the West Indian islands follow the Roman law [2]. The rest, including Australia, New Zealand, and all Canada except Quebec, follow English; as does also the United States, except Louisiana, but with the Hawaiian Islands, and India, though in India, as we shall see, native law is also administered.

---

[1] There is scarcely a trace of Celtic custom in modern Scottish law. The law of land, however, is largely of feudal origin ; and commercial law has latterly been influenced by that of England.

[2] In these West Indian islands, however, that which remains of Spanish law, as in Trinidad and Tobago, and of French law, as in St. Vincent, is now comparatively slight ; and before long the West Indies (except Cuba and Puerto Rico, Guadeloupe and Martinique) will be entirely under English law. See as to the British colonies generally, C. P. Ilbert's *Legislative Methods and Forms*, chap. ix.

Thus between them these two systems cover nearly the whole of the civilized, and most of the uncivilized world. Only two considerable masses of population stand outside—the Musulman East, that is, Turkey, North Africa, Persia, Western Turkistan and Afghanistan, which obey the sacred law of Islam, and China, which has customs all her own. It is hard to estimate the total number of human beings who live under the English common law, for one does not know whether to reckon in the semi-savage natives of such regions as Uganda, for instance, or Fiji. But there are probably one hundred and thirty millions of civilized persons (without counting the natives of India) who do: and the number living under some modern form of the Roman law is still larger.

It is of the process by which two systems which had their origin in two small communities, the one an Italian city, the other a group of Teutonic tribes, have become extended over nine-tenths of the globe that I propose to speak in the pages that follow. There are analogies between the forms which the process took in the two cases. There are also contrasts. The main contrast is that whereas we may say that (roughly speaking) Rome extended her law by conquest, that is, by the spreading of her power, England has extended hers by settlement, that is, by the spreading out of her race. In India, however, conquest rather than colonization has been the agency employed by England, and it is therefore between the extension of English law to India and the extension of Roman law to the Roman Empire that the best parallel can be drawn. It need hardly be added that the Roman law has been far more changed in descending to the modern world and becoming adapted to modern conditions of life than the law of England has been in its extension over new areas. That extension is an affair of the last three centuries only, and the whole history of English law is of only some eleven centuries reckoning from Kings Ine and Alfred, let us say, to A. D. 1900, or of eight, if we begin with King Henry the Second, whereas that of Roman law covers twenty-five centuries, of which all but the first three have witnessed the process of extension, so early did Rome begin to impose her law upon her subjects. To the changes, however, which have passed on the substance of the law we shall return presently. Let us begin by examining the causes and circumstances which induced the extension to the whole ancient world of rules and doctrines that had grown up in a small city.

II. The Diffusion of Roman Law by Conquest.

The first conquests of Rome were made in Italy. They did not, however, involve any legal changes, for conquest meant merely the reduction of what had been an independent city or group of cities or tribes to vassalage, with the obligation of sending troops to serve in the Roman armies. Local autonomy was not (as a rule) interfered with; and such autonomy included civil jurisdiction, so the Italic and Greco-Italic cities continued to be governed by their own laws, which in the case at least of Oscan and Umbrian communities usually resembled that of Rome, and which of course tended to become assimilated to it even before Roman citizenship was extended to the Italian allies. With the annexation of part of Sicily in A. D. 230 the first provincial government was set up, and the legal and administrative problems which Rome had to deal with began to show themselves. Other provinces were added in pretty rapid succession, the last being Britain (invaded under Claudius in A. D. 43). Now although in all these provinces the Romans had to maintain order, to collect revenue and to dispense justice, the conditions under which these things, and especially the dispensing of justice, had to be done differed much in different provinces. Some, such as Sicily, Achaia, Macedonia and the provinces of Western Asia Minor, as well as Africa (*i. e.* such parts of that province as Carthage had permeated), were civilized countries, where law-courts already existed in the cities[1]. The laws had doubtless almost everywhere been created by custom, for the so-called Codes we hear of in Greek cities were often rather in the nature of political constitutions and penal enactments than summarized statements of the whole private law; yet in some cities the customs had been so summarized [2]. Other provinces, such as those of Thrace, Transalpine Gaul, Spain, and Britain, were in a lower stage of social organization, and possessed, when they were conquered, not so much regular laws as tribal usages, suited to their rude inhabitants. In the former set of cases not much new law was needed. In the latter set the native customs could not meet the needs of communities which soon began to advance in wealth and culture under Roman rule, so law had to be created.

There were also in all these provinces two classes of inhabitants. One consisted of those who enjoyed Roman citizenship, not merely men of Italian birth settled there but also men to whom citizenship had been granted (as for instance when they retired from military service), or the natives of cities on which (as to Tarsus in Cilicia, St. Paul's birthplace) citizenship had been conferred as a boon[3]. This was a large class, and went on rapidly increasing. To it pure Roman law was applicable, subject of course to any local customs.

The other class consisted of the provincial subjects who were merely subjects, and, in the view of the Roman law, aliens (*peregrini*). They had their own laws

---

[1] Cicero says of Sicily, 'Siculi hoc iure sunt ut quod civis cum cive agat, domi certet suis legibus; quod Siculus cum Siculo non eiusdem civitatis, ut de eo praetor iudices sortiatur'; *In Verrem*, ii. 13, 32.

[2] The laws of Gortyn in Crete, recently published from an inscription discovered there, apparently of about 500 B. C., are a remarkable instance. Though not a complete code, they cover large parts of the field of law.

[3] When I speak of citizenship, it is not necessarily or generally political citizenship that is to be understood, but the citizenship which carried with it private civil rights (those rights which the Romans call *connubium* and *commercium*), including Roman family and inheritance law and Roman contract and property law. Not only the civilized Spaniards but the bulk of the upper class in Greece seem to have become citizens by the time of the Antonines.

or tribal customs, and to them Roman law was primarily inapplicable, not only because it was novel and unfamiliar, so strange to their habits that it would have been unjust as well as practically inconvenient to have applied it to them, but also because the Romans, like the other civilized communities of antiquity, had been so much accustomed to consider private legal rights as necessarily connected with membership of a city community that it would have seemed unnatural to apply the private law of one city community to the citizens of another. It is true that the Romans after a time disabused their minds of this notion, as indeed they had from a comparatively early period extended their own private civil rights to many of the cities which had become their subject allies. Still it continued to influence them at the time (B. C. 230 to 120) when they were laying out the lines of their legal policy for the provinces.

Of that legal policy I must speak quite briefly, partly because our knowledge, though it has been enlarged of late years by the discovery and collection of a great mass of inscriptions, is still imperfect, partly because I could not set forth the details without going into a number of technical points which might perplex readers unacquainted with the Roman law. It is only the main lines on which the conquerors proceeded that can be here indicated.

Every province was administered by a governor with a staff of subordinate officials, the higher ones Roman, and (under the Republic) remaining in office only so long as did the governor. The governor was the head of the judicial as well as the military and civil administration, just as the consuls at Rome originally possessed judicial as well as military and civil powers, and just as the praetor at Rome, though usually occupied with judicial work, had also both military and civil authority. The governor's court was the proper tribunal for those persons who in the provinces enjoyed Roman citizenship, and in it Roman law was applied to such

persons in matters touching their family relations, their
rights of inheritance, their contractual relations with one
another, just as English law is applied to Englishmen
in Cyprus or Hong Kong. No special law was needed
for them. As regards the provincials, they lived under
their own law, whatever it might be, subject to one important modification. Every governor when he entered
his province issued an Edict setting forth certain rules
which he proposed to apply during his term of office.
These rules were to be valid only during his term, for
his successor issued a fresh Edict, but in all probability
each reproduced nearly all of what the preceding Edict
had contained. Thus the same general rules remained
continuously in force, though they might be modified in
detail, improvements which experience had shown to be
necessary being from time to time introduced[1]. This
was the method which the praetors followed at Rome,
so the provincial governors had a precedent for it and
knew how to work it. Now the Edict seems to have
contained, besides its provisions regarding the collection
of revenue and civil administration in general, certain
more specifically legal regulations, intended to indicate
the action which the governor's court would take not
only in disputes arising between Roman citizens, but
also in those between citizens and aliens, and probably
also to some extent in those between aliens themselves. Where the provisions of the Edict did not
apply, aliens would be governed by their own law.
In cities municipally organized, and especially in the
more civilized provinces, the local city courts would
doubtless continue to administer, as they had done
before the Romans came, their local civil law; and in
the so-called free cities, which had come into the Empire
as allies, these local courts had for a long time a wide
scope for their action. Criminal law, however, would
seem to have fallen within the governor's jurisdiction,
at any rate in most places and for the graver offences,

---

[1] As to this see Essay XIV, p. 692 sqq.

because criminal law is the indispensable guarantee
for public order and for the repression of sedition
or conspiracy, matters for which the governor was of
course responsible [1]. Thus the governor's court was
not only that which dispensed justice between Roman
citizens, and which dealt with questions of revenue, but
was also the tribunal for cases between citizens and
aliens, and for the graver criminal proceedings. It was
apparently also a court which entertained some kinds
of suits between aliens, as for instance between aliens
belonging to different cities, or in districts where no
regular municipal courts existed, and (probably) dealt
with appeals from those courts where they did exist.
Moreover where aliens even of the same city chose to
resort to it they could apparently do so. I speak of
courts rather than of law, because it must be remembered that although we are naturally inclined to think
of law as coming first, and courts being afterwards
created to administer law, it is really courts that come
first, and that by their action build up law partly out
of customs observed by the people and partly out of
their own notions of justice. This, which is generally
true of all countries, is of course specially true of countries where law is still imperfectly developed, and of
places where different classes of persons, not governed
by the same legal rules, have to be dealt with.

The Romans brought some experience to the task
of creating a judicial administration in the provinces,
where both citizens and aliens had to be considered, for
Rome herself had become, before she began to acquire
territories outside Italy, a place of residence or resort
for alien traders, so that as early as B. C. 247 she created
a magistrate whose special function it became to handle
suits between aliens, or in which one party was an
alien. This magistrate built up, on the basis of mer-

---

[1] In St. Paul's time, however, the Athenian Areopagus would seem to have retained its jurisdiction ; cf. Acts xvii. 19. The Romans treated Athens with special
consideration.

cantile usage, equity, and common sense, a body of
rules fit to be applied between persons whose native
law was not the same; and the method he followed
would naturally form a precedent for the courts of the
provincial governors.

Doubtless the chief aim, as well as the recognized
duty, of the governors was to disturb provincial usage
as little as they well could. The temptations to which
they were exposed, and to which they often succumbed,
did not lie in the direction of revolutionizing local law
in order to introduce either purely Roman doctrines
or any artificial uniformity [1]. They would have made
trouble for themselves had they attempted this. And
why should they attempt it ? The ambitious governors
desired military fame. The bad ones wanted money.
The better men, such as Cicero, and in later days
Pliny, liked to be fêted by the provincials and have
statues erected to them by grateful cities. No one
of these objects was to be attained by introducing legal
reforms which theory might suggest to a philosophic
statesman, but which nobody asked for. It seems safe
to assume from what we know of official human nature
elsewhere, that the Roman officials took the line of least
resistance compatible with the raising of money and
the maintenance of order. These things being secured,
they would be content to let other things alone.

Things, however, have a way of moving even when
officials may wish to let them rest. When a new and
vigorous influence is brought into a mixture of races
receptive rather than resistent (as happened in Asia
Minor under the Romans), or when a higher culture
acts through government upon a people less advanced
but not less naturally gifted (as happened in Gaul under
the Romans), changes must follow in law as well as in
other departments of human action. Here two forces

---

[1] One of the charges against Verres was that he disregarded all kinds of law
alike. Under him, says Cicero, the Sicilians 'neque suas leges neque nostra senatus consulta neque communia iura tenuerunt'; *In Verr.* i. 4, 13.

were at work. One was the increasing number of persons who were Roman citizens, and therefore lived by the Roman law. The other was the increasing tendency of the government to pervade and direct the whole public life of the province. When monarchy became established as the settled form of the Roman government, provincial administration began to be better organized, and a regular body of bureaucratic officials presently grew up. The jurisdiction of the governor's court extended itself, and was supplemented in course of time by lower courts administering law according to the same rules. The law applied to disputes arising between citizens and noncitizens became more copious and definite. The provincial Edicts expanded and became well settled as respects the larger part of their contents. So by degrees the law of the provinces was imperceptibly Romanized in its general spirit and leading conceptions, probably also in such particular departments as the original local law of the particular province had not fully covered. But the process did not proceed at the same rate in all the provinces, nor did it result in a uniform legal product, for a good deal of local customary law remained, and this customary law of course differed in different provinces. In the Hellenic and Hellenized countries the pre-existing law was naturally fuller and stronger than in the West; and it held its ground more effectively than the ruder usages of Gauls or Spaniards, obtaining moreover a greater respect from the Romans, who felt their intellectual debt to the Greeks.

It may be asked what direct legislation there was during this period for the provinces. Did the Roman Assembly either pass statutes for them, as Parliament has sometimes done for India, or did the Assembly establish in each province some legislative authority ? So far as private law went Rome did neither during the republican period [1]. The necessity was not felt,

---

[1] The *Lex Sempronia* mentioned by Livy, xxxv. 7, seems to be an exception, due to very special circumstances.

6

because any alterations made in Roman law proper altered it for Roman citizens who dwelt in the provinces no less than for those in Italy, while as to provincial aliens, the Edict of the governor and the rules which the practice of his courts established were sufficient to introduce any needed changes. But the Senate issued decrees intended to operate in the provinces, and when the Emperors began to send instructions to their provincial governors or to issue declarations of their will in any other form, these had the force of law, and constituted a body of legislation, part of which was general, while part was special to the province for which it was issued.

Meantime—and I am now speaking particularly of the three decisively formative centuries from B. C. 150 to A. D. 150—another process had been going on even more important. The Roman law itself had been changing its character, had been developing from a rigid and highly technical system, archaic in its forms and harsh in its rules, preferring the letter to the spirit, and insisting on the strict observance of set phrases, into a liberal and elastic system, pervaded by the principles of equity and serving the practical convenience of a cultivated and commercial community. The nature of this process will be found described in other parts of this volume[1]. Its result was to permeate the original law of Rome applicable to citizens only (*ius civile*) with the law which had been constructed for the sake of dealing with aliens (*ius gentium*), so that the product was a body of rules fit to be used by any civilized people, as being grounded in reason and utility, while at the same time both copious in quantity and refined in quality.

This result had been reached about A. D. 150, by which time the laws of the several provinces had also been largely Romanized. Thus each body of law—if we may venture for this purpose to speak of provincial law as a whole—had been drawing nearer to the other.

[1] See Essay XI, and Essay XIV, p. 706.

The old law of the city of Rome had been expanded and improved till it was fit to be applied to the provinces. The various laws of the various provinces had been constantly absorbing the law of the city in the enlarged and improved form latterly given to it. Thus when at last the time for a complete fusion arrived the differences between the two had been so much reduced that the fusion took place easily and naturally, with comparatively little disturbance of the state of things already in existence. One sometimes finds on the southern side of the Alps two streams running in neighbouring valleys. One which has issued from a glacier slowly deposits as it flows over a rocky bed the white mud which it brought from its icy cradle. The other which rose from clear springs gradually gathers colouring matter as in its lower course it cuts through softer strata or through alluvium. When at last they meet, the glacier torrent has become so nearly clear that the tint of its waters is scarcely distinguishable from that of the originally bright but now slightly turbid affluent. Thus Roman and provincial law, starting from different points but pursuing a course in which their diversities were constantly reduced, would seem to have become so similar by the end of the second century A. D. that there were few marked divergences, so far as private civil rights and remedies were concerned, between the position of citizens and that of aliens.

Here, however, let a difference be noted. The power of assimilation was more complete in some branches of law than it was in others; and it was least complete in matters where old standing features of national character and feeling were present. In the Law of Property and Contract it had advanced so far as to have become, with some few exceptions [1], substantially identical. The same may be said of Penal Law and the system of legal procedure. But in the Law of

---

[1] Such as the technical peculiarities of the Roman *stipulatio*, and the Greek *syngraphe*.

Family Relations and in that of Inheritance, a matter closely connected with family relations, the dissimilarities were still significant; and we shall find this phenomenon reappearing in the history of English and Native Law in India.

Two influences which I have not yet dwelt upon had been, during the second century, furthering the assimilation. One was the direct legislation of the Emperor which, scanty during the first age of the monarchy, had now become more copious, and most of which was intended to operate upon citizens and aliens alike. The other was the action of the Emperor as supreme judicial authority, sometimes in matters brought directly before him for decision, more frequently as judge of appeals from inferior tribunals. He had a council called the Consistory which acted on his behalf, because, especially in the troublous times which began after the reign of Marcus Aurelius and presaged the ultimate dissolution of the Empire, the sovereign was seldom able to preside in person. The judgements of the Consistory, being delivered in the Emperor's name as his, and having equal authority with statutes issued by him, must have done much to make law uniform in all the provinces and among all classes of subjects [1].

III. The Establishment of One Law for the Empire.

Finally, in the beginning of the third century A. D., the decisive step was taken. The distinction between citizens and aliens vanished by the grant of full citizenship to all subjects of the Empire, a grant however which may have been, in the first instance, applied only to organized communities, and not also to the backward sections of the rural population, in Corsica,

---

[1] These *decreta* of the Emperor were reckoned among his *Constitutiones* (as to which see Essay XIV, p. 720 sqq.). There does not seem to have been any public record kept and published of them, but many of them would doubtless become diffused through the law schools and otherwise. The first regular collections of imperial constitutions known to us belong to a later time.

for instance, or in some of the Alpine valleys. Our information as to the era to which this famous Edict of Caracalla's belongs is lamentably scanty. Gaius, who is the best authority for the middle period of the law, lived fifty or sixty years earlier. The compilers of Justinian's *Digest*, which is the chief source of our knowledge for the law as a whole, lived three hundred years later, when the old distinctions between the legal rights of citizens and those of aliens had become mere matters of antiquarian curiosity. These compilers therefore modified the passages of the older jurists which they inserted in the *Digest* so as to make them suit their own more recent time. As practical men they were right, but they have lessened the historical value of these fragments of the older jurists, just as the modern restorer of a church spoils it for the purposes of architectural history, when he alters it to suit his own ideas of beauty or convenience. Still it may fairly be assumed that when Caracalla's grant of citizenship was made the bulk of the people, or at least of the town dwellers, had already obtained either a complete or an incomplete citizenship in the more advanced provinces, and that those who had not were at any rate enjoying under the provincial Edicts most of the civil rights that had previously been confined to citizens, such for instance as the use of the so-called Praetorian Will with its seven seals.

How far the pre-existing local law of different provinces or districts was superseded at one stroke by this extension of citizenship, or in other words, what direct and immediate change was effected in the modes of jurisdiction and in the personal relations of private persons, is a question which we have not the means of answering. Apparently many difficulties arose which further legislation, not always consistent, was required to deal with [1]. One would naturally suppose that where

---

[1] See upon this subject the learned and acute treatise (by which I have been much aided) of Dr. L. Mitteis, *Reichsrecht und Volksrecht in den östlichen Provinzen des Römischen Kaiserreichs*, Chap. VI.

Roman rules differed materially from those which a provincial community had followed, the latter could not have been suddenly substituted for the former.

A point, for instance, about which we should like to be better informed is whether the Roman rules which gave to the father his wide power over his children and their children were forthwith extended to provincial families. The Romans themselves looked upon this paternal power as an institution peculiar to themselves. To us moderns, and especially to Englishmen and Americans, it seems so oppressive that we cannot but suppose it was different in practice from what it looks on paper. And although it had lost some of its old severity by the time of the Antonines, one would think that communities which had not grown up under it could hardly receive it with pleasure.

From the time of Caracalla (A. D. 211-217) down till the death of Theodosius the Great (A. D. 395) the Empire had but one law. There was doubtless a certain amount of special legislation for particular provinces, and a good deal of customary law peculiar to certain provinces or parts of them. Although before the time of Justinian it would seem that every Roman subject, except the half-barbarous peoples on the frontiers, such as the Soanes and Abkhasians of the Caucasus or the Ethiopic tribes of Nubia, and except a very small class of freedmen, was in the enjoyment of Roman citizenship, with private rights substantially the same, yet it is clear that in the East some Roman principles and maxims were never fully comprehended by the mass of the inhabitants and their legal advisers of the humbler sort, while other principles did not succeed in displacing altogether the rules to which the people were attached. We have evidence in recently recovered fragments of an apparently widely used law-book, Syriac and Armenian copies of which remain, that this was the case in the Eastern provinces, and no doubt it was so in others also. In Egypt, for instance, it may be gathered from the fragments of papyri which are now being published, that the old native customs, overlaid or re-moulded to some extent by Greek law, held their ground even down to the sixth or seventh century [1]. Still, after making all allowance for these provincial variations, philosophic jurisprudence and a levelling despotism had done their work, and given to the civilized world, for the first and last time in its history, one harmonious body of legal rules.

The causes which enabled the Romans to achieve this result were, broadly speaking, the five following:—

(1) There was no pre-existing body of law deeply rooted and strong enough to offer resistance to the spread of Roman law. Where any highly developed system of written rules or customs existed, it existed only in cities, such as those of the Greek or Graecized provinces on both sides of the Aegean. The large countries, Pontus, for instance, or Macedonia or Gaul, were in a legal sense unorganized or backward. Thus the Romans had, if not a blank sheet to write on, yet no great difficulty in overspreading or dealing freely with what they found.

(2) There were no forms of faith which had so interlaced religious feelings and traditions with the legal notions and customs of the people as to give those notions and customs a tenacious grip on men's affection. Except among the Jews, and to some extent among the Egyptians, Rome had no religious force to overcome such as Islam and Hinduism present in India.

(3) The grant of Roman citizenship to a community or an individual was a privilege highly valued, because it meant a rise in social status and protection against

---

[1] This is carefully worked out both as to Syria and to Egypt by Dr. Mitteis, *op. cit.* He thinks (pp. 30-33) that the law of the Syrian book, where it departs from pure Roman law as we find it in the *Corpus Iuris*, is mainly of Greek origin, though with traces of Eastern custom. He also suggests that the opposition, undoubtedly strong, of the Eastern Monophysites to the Orthodox Emperors at Constantinople may have contributed to make the Easterns cling the closer to their own customary law. The Syrian book belongs to the fifth century A.D., and is therefore earlier than Justinian (Bruns und Sachau, *Syrisch-römisches Rechtsbuch aus dem fünften Jahrhundert*).

arbitrary treatment by officials. Hence even those who might have liked their own law better were glad to part with it for the sake of the immunities of a Roman citizen.

(4) The Roman governor and the Roman officials in general had an administrative discretion wider than officials enjoy under most modern governments, and certainly wider than either a British or an United States legislature would delegate to any person. Hence Roman governors could by their Edicts and their judicial action mould the law and give it a shape suitable to the needs of their province with a freedom of handling which facilitated the passage from local law or custom to the jurisprudence of the Empire generally.

(5) Roman law itself, *i.e.* the law of the city, went on expanding and changing, ridding itself of its purely national and technical peculiarities, till it became fit to be the law of the whole world. This process kept step with, and was the natural expression of, the political and social assimilation of Rome to the provinces and of the provinces to Rome.

At the death of Theodosius the Great the Roman Empire was finally divided into an Eastern and a Western half; so that thenceforward there were two legislative authorities. For the sake of keeping the law as uniform as possible, arrangements were made for the transmission by each Emperor to the other of such ordinances as he might issue, in order that these might be, if approved, issued for the other half of the Empire. These arrangements, however, were not fully carried out: and before long the Western Empire drifted into so rough a sea that legislation practically stopped. The great Codex of Theodosius the Second (a collection of imperial enactments published in A.D. 438) was however promulgated in the Western as well as in the Eastern part of the Empire, whereas the later Codex and Digest of Justinian, published nearly a century later, was enacted only for the East, though presently extended (by re-conquest) to Italy, Sicily, and Africa. Parts of the

Theodosian Codex were embodied in the manuals of law made for the use of their Roman subjects by some of the barbarian kings. It continued to be recognized in the Western provinces after the extinction of the imperial line in the West in A. D. 476: and was indeed, along with the manuals aforesaid, the principal source whence during a long period the Roman population drew their law in the provinces out of which the kingdoms of the Franks, Burgundians, and Visigoths were formed.

Then came the torpor of the Dark Ages.

IV. The Extension of Roman Law after the Fall of the Western Empire.

Upon the later history of the Roman law and its diffusion through the modern world I can but briefly touch, for I should be led far away from the special topic here considered. The process of extension went on in some slight measure by conquest, but mainly by peaceful means, the less advanced peoples, who had no regular legal system of their own, being gradually influenced by and learning from their more civilized neighbours to whom the Roman system had descended. The light of legal knowledge radiated forth from two centres, from Constantinople over the Balkanic and Euxine countries between the tenth and the fifteenth centuries, from Italy over the lands that lay north and west of her from the twelfth to the sixteenth century. Thereafter it is Germany, Holland, and France that have chiefly propagated the imperial law, Germany by her universities and writers, France and Holland both through their jurists and as colonizing powers.

In the history of the mediaeval and modern part of the process of extension five points or stages of especial import may be noted.

The first is the revival of legal study which began in

Italy towards the end of the eleventh century A. D., and
the principal agent in which was the school of Bologna,
famous for many generations thereafter. From that
date onward the books of Justinian, which had before
that time been superseded in the Eastern Empire, were
lectured and commented on in the universities of Italy,
France, Spain, England, Germany, and have continued
to be so till our own day. They formed, except in
England where from the time of Henry the Third
onwards they had a powerful and at last a victorious
rival in the Common Law, the basis of all legal training
and knowledge.

The second is the creation of that vast mass of rules
for the guidance of ecclesiastical matters and courts—
courts whose jurisdiction was in the Middle Ages far
wider than it is now—which we call the Canon Law.
These rules, drawn from the canons of Councils and
decrees of Popes, began to be systematized during
the twelfth century, and were first consolidated into
an ordered body by Pope Gregory the Ninth in the
middle of the thirteenth [1]. They were so largely based
on the Roman law that we may describe them as being
substantially a development of it, partly on a new side,
partly in a new spirit, and though they competed with
the civil law of the temporal courts, they also extended
the intellectual influence of that law.

The third is the acceptance of the Roman law as
being of binding authority in countries which had not
previously owned it, and particularly in Germany and
Scotland. It was received in Germany because the
German king (after the time of Otto the Great) was
deemed to be also Roman Emperor, the legitimate successor of the far-off assemblies and magistrates and
Emperors of old Rome; and its diffusion was aided
by the fact that German lawyers had mostly received
their legal training at Italian universities. It came in
gradually as subsidiary to Germanic customs, but the

[1] Other parts were added later.

judges, trained in Italy in the Roman system, required the customs to be proved, and so by degrees Roman doctrines supplanted them, though less in the Saxon districts, where a native law-book, the *Sachsenspiegel*, had already established its influence. The acceptance nowhere went so far as to supersede the whole customary law of Germany, whose land-rights, for instance, retained their feudal character. The formal declaration of the general validity of the *Corpus Iuris* in Germany is usually assigned to the foundation by the Emperor Maximilian I, in 1495, of the Imperial Court of Justice (Reichskammergericht). As Holland was then still a part of the Germanic Empire, as well as of the Burgundian inheritance, it was the law of Holland also, and so has become the law of Java, of Celebes, and of South Africa. In Scotland it was adopted at the foundation of the Court of Session, on the model of the Parlement of Paris, by King James the Fifth. Political antagonism to England and political attraction to France, together with the influence of the Canonists, naturally determined the King and the Court to follow the system which prevailed on the European continent.

The fourth stage is that of codification. In many parts of Gaul, though less in Provence and Languedoc, the Roman law had gone back into that shape of a body of customs from which it had emerged a thousand years before ; and in Northern and Middle Gaul some customs, especially in matters relating to land, were not Roman. At last, under Lewis the Fourteenth, a codifying process set in. Comprehensive Ordinances, each covering a branch of law, began to be issued from 1667 down to 1747. These operated throughout France, and, being founded on Roman principles, further advanced the work, already prosecuted by the jurists, of Romanizing the customary law of Northern France. That of Southern France (the *pays du droit écrit*) had been more specifically Roman, for the South had been less affected by Frankish conquest and settlement. The five Codes

promulgated by Napoleon followed in 1803 to 1810 [1].
Others reproducing them with more or less divergence
have been enacted in other Romance countries.

In Prussia, Frederick the Second directed the preparation of a Code which became law after his death,
in 1794. From 1848 onwards parts of the law of Germany (which differed in different parts of the country)
began to be codified, being at first enacted by the several
States, each for itself, latterly by the legislature of the
new Empire. Finally, after twenty-two years of labour,
a new Code for the whole German Empire was settled,
was passed by the Chambers, and came into force on the
first of January, 1900. It does not, however, altogether
supersede pre-existing local law. This Code, far from
being pure Roman law, embodies many rules due to
mediaeval custom (especially custom relating to land-
rights) modernized to suit modern conditions, and also
a great deal of post-mediaeval legislation [2]. Some German jurists complain that it is too Teutonic; others that
it is not Teutonic enough. One may perhaps conclude
from these opposite criticisms that the codifiers have
made a judiciously impartial use of both Germanic and
Roman materials.

Speaking broadly, it may be said that the groundwork
of both the French and the German Codes—that is to
say their main lines and their fundamental legal conceptions—is Roman. Just as the character and genius
of a language are determined by its grammar, irrespective of the number of foreign words it may have
picked up, so Roman law remains Roman despite the
accretion of the new elements which the needs of modern
civilization have required it to accept.

The fifth stage is the transplantation of Roman law in

---

[1] Among the States in which the French Code has been taken as a model are
Belgium, Italy, Spain, Portugal, Mexico, and Chili. See an article by Mr. E.
Schuster in the *Law Quarterly Review* for January, 1896.

[2] An interesting sketch of the 'reception' of Roman law in Germany (by Dr.
Erwin Grüber) may be found in the Introduction to Mr. Ledlie's translation of
Sohm's *Institutionen* (1st edition).

its modern forms to new countries. The Spaniards and Portuguese, the French, the Dutch, and the Germans have carried their respective systems of law with them into the territories they have conquered and the colonies they have founded; and the law has often remained unchanged even when the territory or the colony has passed to new rulers. For law is a tenacious plant, even harder to extirpate than is language; and new rulers have generally had the sense to perceive that they had less to gain by substituting their own law for that which they found than they had to lose by irritating their new subjects. Thus, Roman-French law survives in Quebec (except in commercial matters) and in Louisiana, Roman-Dutch law in Guiana and South Africa.

The cases of Poland, Russia and the Scandinavian kingdoms are due to a process different from any of those hitherto described. The law of Russia was originally Slavonic custom, influenced to some extent by the law of the Eastern Roman Empire, whence Russia took her Christianity and her earliest literary impulse. In its present shape, while retaining in many points a genuinely Slavonic character, and of course far less distinctly Roman than is the law of France, it has drawn so much, especially as regards the principles of property rights and contracts, from the Code Napoléon and to a less degree from Germany, that it may be described as being Roman 'at the second remove,' and reckoned as an outlying and half-assimilated province, so to speak, of the legal realm of Rome. Poland, lying nearer Germany, and being, as a Catholic country, influenced by the Canon Law, as well as by German teaching and German books, adopted rather more of Roman doctrine than Russia did [1]. Her students learnt Roman law first at Italian, afterwards at German Univer-

---

[1] In Lithuania the rule was that where no express provision could be found governing a case, recourse should be had to 'the Christian laws.' Speaking generally, one may say that it was by and with Christianity that Roman law made its way in the countries to the east of Germany and to the north of the Eastern Empire.

sities, and when they became judges, naturally applied its principles. The Scandinavian countries set out with a law purely Teutonic, and it is chiefly through the German Universities and the influence of German juridical literature that Roman principles have found their way in and coloured the old customs. Servia, Bulgaria and Rumania, on the other hand, were influenced during the Middle Ages by the law of the Eastern Empire, whence they drew their religion and their culture. Thus their modern law, whose character is due partly to these Byzantine influences—of course largely affected by Slavonic custom—and partly to what they have learnt from France and Austria, may also be referred to the Roman type.

V. The Diffusion of English Law.

England, like Rome, has spread her law over a large part of the globe. But the process has been in her case not only far shorter but far simpler. The work has been (except as respects Ireland) effected within the last three centuries; and it has been effected (except as regards Ireland and India) not by conquest but by peaceful settlement. This is one of the two points in which England stands contrasted with Rome. The other is that her own law has not been affected by the process. It has changed within the seven centuries that lie between King Henry the Second and the present day, almost if not quite as much as the law of Rome changed in the seven centuries between the enactment of the Twelve Tables and the reign of Caracalla. But these changes have not been due, as those I have described in the Roman Empire were largely due, to the extension of the law of England to new subjects. They would apparently have come to pass in the same way and to the same extent had the English race remained confined to its own island.

England has extended her law over two classes of territories.

The first includes those which have been peacefully settled by Englishmen—North America (except Lower Canada), Australia, New Zealand, Fiji, the Falkland Isles. All of these, except the United States, have remained politically connected with the British Crown.

The second includes conquered territories. In some of these, such as Wales, Ireland, Gibraltar, the Canadian provinces of Ontario and Nova Scotia, and several of the West India Islands, English law has been established as the only system, applicable to all subjects [1]. In others, such as Malta, Cyprus, Singapore, and India, English law is applied to Englishmen and native law to natives, the two systems being worked concurrently. Among these cases, that which presents problems of most interest and difficulty is India. But before we consider India, a few words may be given to the territories of the former class. They are now all of them, except the West Indies, Fiji and the Falkland Isles, self-governing, and therefore capable of altering their own law. This they do pretty freely. The United States have now forty-nine legislatures at work, viz. Congress, forty-five States, and three Organized Territories. They have turned out an immense mass of law since their separation from England. But immense as it is, and bold as are some of the experiments which may be found in it, the law of the United States remains (except of course in Louisiana) substantially English law. An English barrister would find himself quite at home in any Federal or State Court, and would have nothing new to master, except a few technicalities of procedure and the provisions of any statutes which might affect the points he had to argue. And the patriarch of American teachers of law (Professor C. C. Langdell of the Law School in Harvard Univer-

---

[1] It has undergone little or no change in the process. The Celtic customs disappeared in Wales; the Brehon law, though it was contained in many written texts and was followed over the larger part of Ireland till the days of the Tudors, has left practically no trace in the existing law of Ireland, which is, except as respects land, some penal matters, and marriage, virtually identical with the law of England.

sity), consistently declining to encumber his expositions with references to Federal or State Statutes, continues to discourse on the Common Law of America, which differs little from the Common Law of England. The old Common Law which the settlers carried with them in the seventeenth century has of course been developed or altered by the decisions of American Courts. These, however, have not affected its thoroughly English character. Indeed, the differences between the doctrines enounced by the Courts of different States are sometimes just as great as the differences between the views of the Courts of Massachusetts or New Jersey and those of Courts in England.

The same is true of the self-governing British colonies. In them also legislation has introduced deviations from the law of the mother country. More than forty years ago New Zealand, for instance, repealed the Statute of Uses, which is the corner-stone of English conveyancing; and the Australian legislatures have altered (among other things) the English marriage law. But even if the changes made by statute had been far greater than they have been, and even if there were not, as there still is, a right of appeal from the highest Courts of these colonies to the Crown in Council, their law should still remain, in all its essential features, a genuine and equally legitimate offspring of the ancient Common Law.

We come now to the territories conquered by England, and to which she has given her law whether in whole or in part. Among these it is only of India that I shall speak, as India presents the phenomena of contact between the law of the conqueror and that of the conquered on the largest scale and in the most instructive form. What the English have done in India is being done or will have to be done, though nowhere else on so vast a scale, by the other great nations which have undertaken the task of ruling and of bestowing what are called the blessings of civilization upon the backward races, Russia, France, Germany, and now the United

States also, all see this task before them. To them therefore, as well as to England, the experience of the British
Government in India may be profitable.

VI. English Law in India.

When the English began to conquer India they found
two great systems of customary law in existence there,
the Musulman and the Hindu. There were other
minor bodies of custom, prevailing among particular
sects, but these may for the present be disregarded.
Musulman law regulated the life and relations of all
Musulmans; and parts of it, especially its penal provisions, were also applied by the Musulman potentates
to their subjects generally, Hindus included. The
Musulman law had been most fully worked out in the
departments of family relations and inheritance, in some
few branches of the law of contract, such as money loans
and mortgages and matters relating to sale, and in
the doctrine of charitable or pious foundations called
Wakuf.

In the Hindu principalities, Hindu law was dominant,
and even where the sovereign was a Musulman, the
Hindu law of family relations and of inheritance was
recognized as that by which Hindus lived. There were
also of course many land customs, varying from district
to district, which both Hindus and Musulmans observed,
as they were not in general directly connected with
religion. In some regions, such as Oudh and what are
now the North-West provinces, these customs had been
much affected by the land revenue system of the Mogul
Emperors. It need hardly be said that where Courts
of law existed, they administered an exceedingly rough
and ready kind of justice, or perhaps injustice, for
bribery and favouritism were everywhere rampant.

There were also mercantile customs, which were
generally understood and observed by traders, and
which, with certain specially Musulman rules recog-

7

nized in Musulman States, made up what there was of a law of contracts.

Thus one may say that the law (other than purely religious law) which the English administrators in the days of Clive and Warren Hastings found consisted of—

First, a large and elaborate system of Inheritance and Family Law, the Musulman pretty uniform throughout India, though in some regions modified by Hindu custom, the Hindu less uniform. Each was utterly unlike English law and incapable of being fused with it. Each was closely bound up with the religion and social habits of the people. Each was contained in treatises of more or less antiquity and authority, some of the Hindu treatises very ancient and credited with almost divine sanction, the Musulman treatises of course posterior to the Koran, and consisting of commentaries upon that Book and upon the traditions that had grown up round it.

Secondly, a large mass of customs relating to the occupation and use of land and of various rights connected with tillage and pasturage, including water-rights, rights of soil-accretion on the banks of rivers, and forest-rights. The agricultural system and the revenue system of the country rested upon these land customs, which were of course mostly unwritten and which varied widely in different districts.

Thirdly, a body of customs, according to our ideas comparatively scanty and undeveloped, but still important, relating to the transfer and pledging of property, and to contracts, especially commercial contracts.

Fourthly, certain penal rules drawn from Musulman law and more or less enforced by Musulman princes.

Thus there were considerable branches of law practically non-existent. There was hardly any law of civil and criminal procedure, because the methods of justice were primitive, and would have been cheap, but for the prevalence of corruption among judges as well as witnesses. There was very little of the law of Torts or Civil

Wrongs, and in the law of property of contracts and of crimes, some departments were wanting or in a rudimentary condition. Of a law relating to public and constitutional rights there could of course be no question, since no such rights existed.

In this state of facts the British officials took the line which practical men, having their hands full of other work, would naturally take, viz. the line of least resistance. They accepted and carried on what they found. Where there was a native law, they applied it, Musulman law to Musulmans, Hindu law to Hindus, and in the few places where they were to be found, Parsi law to Parsis, Jain law to Jains. Thus men of every creed —for it was creed, not race nor allegiance by which men were divided and classified in India—lived each according to his own law, as Burgundians and Franks and Romanized Gauls had done in the sixth century in Europe. The social fabric was not disturbed, for the land customs and the rules of inheritance were respected, and of course the minor officers, with whom chiefly the peasantry came in contact, continued to be natives. Thus the villager scarcely felt that he was passing under the dominion of an alien power, professing an alien faith. His life flowed on in the same equable course beside the little white mosque, or at the edge of the sacred grove. A transfer of power from a Hindu to a Musulman sovereign would have made more difference to him than did the establishment of British rule; and life was more placid than it would have been under either a rajah or a sultan, for the marauding bands which had been the peasants' terror were soon checked by European officers.

So things remained for more than a generation. So indeed things remain still as respects those parts of law which are inwoven with religion, marriage, adoption (among Hindus) and other family relations, and with the succession to property. In all these matters native law continues to be administered by the Courts the English have set up; and when cases are appealed from the highest of those Courts to the Privy Council in England, that respectable body determines the true construction to be put on the Koran and the Islamic Traditions, or on passages from the mythical Manu, in the same business-like way as it would the meaning of an Australian statute [1]. Except in some few points to be presently noted, the Sacred Law of Islam and that of Brahmanism remain unpolluted by European ideas. Yet they have not stood unchanged, for the effect of the more careful and thorough examination which the contents of these two systems have received from advocates, judges, and text-writers, both native and English, imbued with the scientific spirit of Europe, has been to clarify and define them, and to develop out of the half-fluid material more positive and rigid doctrines than had been known before. Something like this may probably have been done by the Romans for the local or tribal law of their provinces.

In those departments in which the pre-existing customs were not sufficient to constitute a body of law large enough and precise enough for a civilized Court to work upon, the English found themselves obliged to supply the void. This was done in two ways. Sometimes the Courts boldly applied English law. Sometimes they supplemented native custom by common sense, *i.e.* by their own ideas of what was just and fair. The phrase 'equity and good conscience' was used to embody the principles by which judges were to be guided when positive rules, statutory or customary, were not forthcoming. To a magistrate who knew no law at all, these words would mean that he might follow his own notions of 'natural justice,' and he would probably give more satisfaction to suitors than would his more learned

---

[1] It is related that a hill tribe of Kols, in Central India, had a dispute with the Government of India over some question of forest-rights. The case having gone in their favour, the Government appealed to the Judicial Committee. Shortly afterwards a passing traveller found the elders of the tribe assembled at the sacrifice of a kid. He inquired what deity was being propitiated, and was told that it was a deity powerful but remote, whose name was Privy Council.

brother, trying to apply confused recollections of Black-stone or Chitty. In commercial matters common sense would be aided by the usage of traders. In cases of Tort native custom was not often available, but as the magistrate who dealt out substantial justice would give what the people had rarely obtained from the native courts, they had no reason to complain of the change. As to rules of evidence, the young Anglo-Indian civilian would, if he were wise, forget all the English technicalities he might have learnt, and make the best use he could of his mother-wit [1].

For the first sixty years or more of British rule there was accordingly little or no attempt to Anglify the law of India, or indeed to give it any regular and systematic form. Such alterations as it underwent were the natural result of its being dispensed by Europeans. But to this general rule there were two exceptions, the law of Procedure and the law of Crimes. Courts had been established in the Presidency towns even before the era of conquest began. As their business increased and subordinate Courts were placed in the chief towns of the annexed provinces, the need for some regular procedure was felt. An Act of the British Parliament of A.D. 1781 empowered the Indian Government to make regulations for the conduct of the provincial Courts, as the Court at Fort William (Calcutta) had already been authorized to do for itself by an Act of 1773. Thus a regular system of procedure, modelled after that of England, was established; and the Act of 1781 provided that the rules and forms for the execution of process were to be accommodated to the religion and manners of the natives.

As respects penal law, the English began by adopting that which the Musulman potentates had been accustomed to apply. But they soon found that many

---

[1] For the facts given in the following pages I am much indebted to the singularly lucid and useful treatise of Sir C. P. Ilbert (formerly Legal Member of the Viceroy's Council) entitled *The Government of India*.

of its provisions were such as a civilized and nominally Christian government could not enforce. Mutilation as a punishment for theft, for instance, and stoning for sexual offences, were penalties not suited to European notions; and still less could the principle be admitted that the evidence of a non-Musulman is not receivable against one of the Faithful. Accordingly a great variety of regulations were passed amending the Musulman law of crimes from an English point of view. In Calcutta the Supreme Court did not hesitate to apply English penal law to natives; and applied it to some purpose at a famous crisis in the fortunes of Warren Hastings when (in 1775) it hanged Nuncomar for forgery under an English statute of 1728, which in the opinion of many high authorities of a later time had never come into force at all in India. It was inevitable that the English should take criminal jurisdiction into their own hands—the Romans had done the same in their provinces—and inevitable also that they should alter the penal law in conformity with their own ideas. But they did so in a very haphazard fashion. The criminal law became a patchwork of enactments so confused that it was the first subject which invited codification in that second epoch of English rule which we are now approaching.

Before entering on this remarkable epoch, one must remember that the English in India, still a very small though important class, were governed entirely by English law. So far as common law and equity went, this law was exactly the same as the contemporaneous law of England. But it was complicated by the fact that a number of Regulations, as they were called, had been enacted for India by the local government, that many British statutes were not intended to apply and probably did not apply to India (though whether they did or not was sometimes doubtful), and that a certain number of statutes had been enacted by Parliament expressly for India. Thus though the law under which the

English lived had not been perceptibly affected by Indian customs, it was very confused and troublesome to work. That the learning of the judges sent from home to sit in the Indian Courts was seldom equal to that of the judges in England was not necessarily a disadvantage, for in traversing the jungle of Indian law the burden of English case lore would have too much impeded the march of justice.

The first period of English rule, the period of rapid territorial extension and of improvised government, may be said to have ended with the third Maratha war of 1817-8. The rule of Lord Amherst and Lord William Bentinck (1823-35) was a comparatively tranquil period, when internal reforms had their chance, as they had in the Roman Empire under Hadrian and Antoninus Pius. This was also the period when a spirit of legal reform was on foot in England. It was the time when the ideas of Bentham had begun to bear fruit, and when the work begun by Romilly was being carried on by Brougham and others. Both the law applied to Englishmen, and such parts of native law as had been cut across, filled up, and half re-shaped by English legal notions and rules, called loudly for simplification and reconstruction.

The era of reconstruction opened with the enactment, in the India Charter Act of 1833, of a clause declaring that a general judicial system and a general body of law ought to be established in India applicable to all classes, Europeans as well as natives, and that all laws and customs having legal force ought to be ascertained, consolidated, and amended. The Act then went on to provide for the appointment of a body of experts to be called the Indian Law Commission, which was to inquire into and report upon the Courts, the procedure and the law then existing in India. Of this commission Macaulay, appointed in 1833 legal member of the Governor-General's Council, was the moving spirit: and with it the work of codification began. It prepared a Penal Code, which however was not passed into law until 1860, for its activity declined after Macaulay's return to England and strong opposition was offered to his draft by many of the Indian judges. A second Commission was appointed under an Act of 1853, and sat in England. It secured the enactment of the Penal Code, and of Codes of Civil and of Criminal Procedure. A third Commission was created in 1861, and drafted other measures. The Government of India demurred to some of the proposed changes and evidently thought that legislation was being pressed on rather too fast. The Commission, displeased at this resistance, resigned in 1870; and since then the work of preparing as well as of carrying through codifying Acts has mostly been done in India. The net result of the sixty-six years that have passed since Macaulay set to work in 1834 is that Acts codifying and amending the law, and declaring it applicable to both Europeans and natives, have been passed on the topics following :—

Crimes (1860).

Criminal Procedure (1861, 1882, and 1898).

Civil Procedure (1859 and 1882).

Evidence (1872).

Limitation of Actions (1877).

Specific Relief (1877).

Probate and Administration (1881).

Contracts (1872) (but only the general rules of contract with a few rules on particular parts of the subject).

Negotiable Instruments (1881) (but subject to native customs).

Besides these, codifying statutes have been passed which do not apply (at present) to all India, but only to parts of it, or to specified classes of the population, on the topics following :—

Trusts (1882).

Transfer of Property (1882).

Succession (1865).

Easements (1882).

Guardians and Wards (1890).

These statutes cover a large part of the whole field of law, so that the only important departments not yet dealt with are those of Torts or Civil Wrongs (on which a measure not yet enacted was prepared some years ago); certain branches of contract law, which it is not urgent to systematize because they give rise to lawsuits only in the large cities, where the Courts are quite able to dispose of them in a satisfactory way; Family Law, which it would be unsafe to meddle with, because the domestic customs of Hindus, Musulmans, and Europeans are entirely different; and Inheritance, the greater part of which is, for the same reason, better left to native custom. Some points have, however, been covered by the Succession Act already mentioned. Thus the Government of India appear to think that they have for the present gone as far as they prudently can in the way of enacting uniform general laws for all classes of persons. Further action might displease either the Hindus or the Musulmans, possibly both: and though there would be advantages in bringing the law of both these sections of the population into a more clear and harmonious shape, it would in any case be impossible to frame rules which would suit both of them, and would also suit the Europeans. Here Religion steps in, a force more formidable in rousing opposition or disaffection than any which the Romans had to fear.

In such parts of the law as are not covered by these enumerated Acts, Englishmen, Hindus and Musulmans continue to live under their respective laws. So do Parsis, Sikhs, Buddhists (most numerous in Burma), and Jains, save that where there is really no native law or custom that can be shown to exist, the judge will naturally apply the principles of English law, handling them, if he knows how, in an untechnical way. Thus beside the new stream of united law which has its source in the codifying Acts, the various older streams of law, each representing a religion, flow peacefully on.

The question which follows—What has been the action on the other of each of these elements? resolves itself into three questions :—

How far has English Law affected the Native Law which remains in force ?

How far has Native Law affected the English Law which is in force ?

How have the codifying Acts been framed—*i.e.* are they a compromise between the English and the native element, or has either predominated and given its colour to the whole mass ?

The answer to the first question is that English influence has told but slightly upon those branches of native law which had been tolerably complete before the British conquest, and which are so interwoven with religion that one may almost call them parts of religion. The Hindu and Musulman customs which regulate the family relations and rights of succession have been precisely defined, especially those of the Hindus, which were more fluid than the Muslim customs, and were much less uniform over the whole country. Trusts have been formally legalized, and their obligation rendered stronger. Adoption has been regularized and stiffened, for its effects had been uncertain in their legal operation. Where several doctrines contended, one doctrine has been affirmed by the English Courts, especially by the Privy Council as ultimate Court of Appeal, and the others set aside. Moreover the Hindu law of Wills has been in some points supplemented by English legislation, and certain customs repugnant to European ideas, such as the self-immolation of the widow on the husband's funeral pyre, have been abolished. And in those parts of law which, though regulated by local custom, were not religious, some improvements have been effected. The rights of the agricultural tenant have been placed on a more secure basis. Forest-rights have been ascertained and defined, partly no doubt for the sake of the pecuniary interests which the Government claims in them, and which the peasantry do not always admit. But no attempt has been made to Anglify these branches of law as a whole.

On the other hand, the law applicable to Europeans only has been scarcely (if at all) affected by native law. It remains exactly what it is in England, except in so far as the circumstances of India have called for special statutes.

The third question is as to the contents of those parts of the law which are common to Europeans and Natives, that is to say, the parts dealt by the codifying Acts already enumerated. Here English law has decisively prevailed. It has prevailed not only because it would be impossible to subject Europeans to rules emanating from a different and a lower civilization, but also because native custom did not supply the requisite materials. Englishmen had nothing to learn from natives as respects procedure or evidence. The native mercantile customs did not constitute a system even of the general principles of contract, much less had those principles been worked out in their details. Accordingly the Contract Code is substantially English, and where it differs from the result of English cases, the differences are due, not to the influence of native ideas or native usage, but to the views of those who prepared the Code, and who, thinking the English case-law susceptible of improvement, diverged from it here and there just as they might have diverged had they been preparing a Code to be enacted for England. There are, however, some points in which the Penal Code shows itself to be a system intended for India. The right of self-defence is expressed in wider terms than would be used in England, for Macaulay conceived that the slackness of the native in protecting himself by force made it desirable to depart a little in this respect from the English rules. Offences such as dacoity (brigandage by robber bands), attempts to bribe judges or witnesses, the use of torture by policemen, kidnapping, the offering

of insult or injury to sacred places, have been dealt with
more fully and specifically than would be necessary in
a Criminal Code for England. Adultery has, conformably to the ideas of the East, been made a subject for
criminal proceedings. Nevertheless these, and other
similar, deviations from English rules which may be
found in the Codes enacted for Europeans and natives
alike, do not affect the general proposition that the codes
are substantially English. The conquerors have given
their law to the conquered. When the conquered had
a law of their own which this legislation has effaced, the
law of the conquerors was better. Where they had one
too imperfect to suffice for a growing civilization, the
law of the conquerors was inevitable.

VII. THE WORKING OF THE INDIAN CODES.

Another question needs to be answered. It has a
twofold interest, because the answer not only affects
the judgement to be passed on the course which the
English Government in India has followed, but also
conveys either warning or encouragement to England
herself. This question is—How have these Indian
Codes worked in practice ? Have they improved the
administration of justice ? Have they given satisfaction
to the people ? Have they made it easier to know the
law, to apply the law, to amend the law where it proves
faulty ?

When I travelled in India in 1888-9 I obtained
opinions on these points from many persons competent
to speak. There was a good deal of difference of view,
but the general result seemed to be as follows. I take
the four most important codifying Acts, as to which
it was most easy to obtain profitable criticisms.

The two Procedure Codes, Civil and Criminal, were
very generally approved. They were not originally
creative work, but were produced by consolidating and
simplifying a mass of existing statutes and regulations,

which had become unwieldy and confused. Order was evoked out of chaos, a result which, though beneficial everywhere, was especially useful in the minor Courts, whose judges had less learning and experience than those of the five High Courts at Calcutta, Madras, Bombay, Allahabad and Lahore.

The Penal Code was universally approved; and it deserves the praise bestowed on it, for it is one of the noblest monuments of Macaulay's genius. To appreciate its merits, one must remember how much, when prepared in 1834, it was above the level of the English criminal law of that time. The subject is eminently fit to be stated in a series of positive propositions, and so far as India was concerned, it had rested mainly upon statutes and not upon common law. It has been dealt with in a scientific, but also a practical common-sense way: and the result is a body of rules which are comprehensible and concise. To have these on their desks has been an immense advantage for magistrates in the country districts, many of whom have had but a scanty legal training. It has also been claimed for this Code that under it crime has enormously diminished: but how much of the diminution is due to the application of a clear and just system of rules, how much to the more efficient police administration, is a question on which I cannot venture to pronounce[1].

No similar commendation was bestowed on the Evidence Code. Much of it was condemned as being too metaphysical, yet deficient in subtlety. Much was deemed superfluous, and because superfluous, possibly perplexing. Yet even those who criticized its drafting admitted that it might possibly be serviceable to untrained magistrates and practitioners, and I have myself heard some of these untrained men declare that they

---

[1] The merits of this Code are discussed in an interesting and suggestive manner by Mr. H. Speyer in an article entitled *Le Droit Pénal Anglo-indien*, which appeared in the *Revue de l'Université de Bruxelles* in April, 1900.

did find it helpful. They are a class relatively larger in India than in England.

It was with regard to the merits of the Contract Code that the widest difference of opinion existed. Any one who reads it can see that its workmanship is defective. It is neither exact nor subtle, and its language is often far from lucid. Every one agreed that Sir J. F. Stephen (afterwards Mr. Justice Stephen), who put it into the shape in which it was passed during his term of office as Legal Member of Council, and was also the author of the Evidence Act, was a man of great industry, much intellectual force, and warm zeal for codification. But his capacity for the work of drafting was deemed not equal to his fondness for it. He did not shine either in fineness of discrimination or in delicacy of expression. Indian critics, besides noting these facts, went on to observe that in country places four-fifths of the provisions of the Contract Act were superfluous, while those which were operative sometimes unduly fettered the discretion of the magistrate or judge, entangling him in technicalities, and preventing him from meting out that substantial justice which is what the rural suitor needs. The judge cannot disregard the Act, because if the case is appealed, the Court above, which has only the notes of the evidence before it, and does not hear the witnesses, is bound to enforce the provisions of the law. In a country like India, law ought not to be too rigid: nor ought rights to be stiffened up so strictly as they are by this Contract Act. Creditors had already, through the iron regularity with which the British Courts enforce judgements by execution, obtained far more power over debtors than they possessed in the old days, and more than the benevolence of the English administrator approves. The Contract Act increases this power still further. This particular criticism does not reflect upon the technical merits of the Act in itself. But it does suggest reasons which would not occur to a European mind, why it may be inexpedient by making the law too precise to narrow the path in which the judge has to walk. A stringent administration of the letter of the law is in semi-civilized communities no unmixed blessing.

So much for the rural districts. In the Presidency cities, on the other hand, the Contract Code is by most experts pronounced to be unnecessary. The judges and the bar are already familiar with the points which it covers, and find themselves—so at least many of them say—rather embarrassed than aided by it. They think it cramps their freedom of handling a point in argument. They prefer the elasticity of the common law. And in point of fact, they seem to make no great use of the Act, but to go on just as their predecessors did before it was passed.

These criticisms may need to be discounted a little, in view of the profound conservatism of the legal profession, and of the dislike of men trained at the Temple or Lincoln's Inn to have anything laid down or applied on the Hooghly which is not being done at the same moment on the Thames. And a counterpoise to them may be found in the educational value which is attributed to the Code by magistrates and lawyers who have not acquired a mastery of contract law through systematic instruction or through experience at home. To them the Contract Act is a manual comparatively short and simple, and also authoritative; and they find it useful in enabling them to learn their business. On the whole, therefore, though the Code does not deserve the credit which has sometimes been claimed for it, one may hesitate to pronounce its enactment a misfortune. It at any rate provides a basis on which a really good Code of contractual law may some day be erected.

Taking the work of Indian codification as a whole, it has certainly benefited the country. The Penal Code and the two Codes of Procedure represent an unmixed gain. The same may be said of the consolidation of the statute law, for which so much was done by the energy

and skill of Mr. Whitley Stokes. And the other codifying acts have on the whole tended both to improve the
substance of the law and to make it more accessible.
Their operation has, however, been less complete than
most people in Europe realize, for while many of them
are confined to certain districts, others are largely
modified by the local customs which they have (as expressed in their saving clauses) very properly respected.
If we knew more about the provinces of the Roman
Empire we might find that much more of local custom
subsisted side by side with the apparently universal and
uniform imperial law than we should gather from reading
the compilations of Justinian.

It has already been observed that Indian influences
have scarcely at all affected English law as it continues
to be administered to Englishmen in India. Still less
have they affected the law of England at home. It seems
to have been fancied thirty or forty years ago, when law
reform in general and codification in particular occupied
the public mind more than they do now, that the enactment of codes of law for India, and the success which
was sure to attend them there, must react upon England
and strengthen the demand for the reduction of her law
into a concise and systematic form. No such result has
followed. The desire for codification in England has
not been perceptibly strengthened by the experience of
India. Nor can it indeed be said that the experience
of India has taught jurists or statesmen much which
they did not know before. That a good code is a very
good thing, and that a bad code is, in a country which
possesses competent judges, worse than no code at
all—these are propositions which needed no Indian experience to verify them. The imperfect success of the
Evidence and Contract Acts has done little more than
add another illustration to those furnished by the Civil
Code of California and the Code of Procedure in New
York of the difficulty which attends these undertakings.
Long before Indian codification was talked of, Savigny

had shown how hard it is to express the law in a set of definite propositions without reducing its elasticity and impeding its further development. His arguments scarcely touch penal law, still less the law of procedure, for these are not topics in which much development need be looked for. But the future career of the Contract Act and of the projected Code of Torts, when enacted, may supply some useful data for testing the soundness of his doctrine.

One reason why these Indian experiments have so little affected English opinion may be found in the fact that few Englishmen have either known or cared anything about them. The British public has not realized how small is the number of persons by whom questions of legal policy in India have during the last seventy years been determined. Two or three officials in Downing Street and as many in Calcutta have practically controlled the course of events, with little interposition from outside. Even when Commissions have been sitting, the total number of those whose hand is felt has never exceeded a dozen. It was doubtless much the same in the Roman Empire. Indeed the world seldom realizes by how few persons it is governed. There is a sense in which power may be said to rest with the whole community, and there is also a sense in which it may be said, in some governments, to rest with a single autocrat. But in reality it almost always rests with an extremely small number of persons, whose knowledge and will prevail over or among the titular possessors of authority.

Before we attempt to forecast the future of English law in India, let us cast a glance back at the general course of its history as compared with that of the law of Rome in the ancient world.

8

VIII. Comparison of the Roman Law with English Law in India.

Rome grew till her law became first that of Italy, then that of civilized mankind. The City became the World, *Urbs* became *Orbis*, to adopt the word-play which was once so familiar. Her law was extended over her Empire by three methods:—

Citizenship was gradually extended over the provinces till at last all subjects had become citizens.

Many of the principles and rules of the law of the City were established and diffused in the provinces by the action of Roman Magistrates and Courts, and especially by the Provincial Edict.

The ancient law of the City was itself all the while amended, purged of its technicalities, and simplified in form, till it became fit to be the law of the World.

Thus, when the law of the City was formally extended to the whole Empire by the grant of citizenship to all subjects, there was not so much an imposition of the conqueror's law upon the conquered as the completion of a process of fusion which had been going on for fully four centuries. The fusion was therefore natural; and because it was natural it was complete and final. The separation of the one great current of Roman law into various channels, which began in the fifth century A.D. and has continued ever since, has been due to purely historical causes, and of late years (as we shall see presently) the streams that flow in these channels have tended to come nearer to one another.

During the period of more than four centuries (B.C. 241 to A.D. 211-7), when these three methods of development and assimilation were in progress, the original law of the City was being remoulded and amended in the midst of and under the influence of a non-Roman population of aliens (*peregrini*) at Rome and in the provinces, and that semi-Roman law which was ad-

ministered in the provinces was being created by
magistrates and judges who lived in the provinces and
who were, after the time of Tiberius, mostly themselves of provincial origin. Thus the intelligence, reflection, and experience of the whole community played
upon and contributed to the development of the law.
Judges, advocates, juridical writers and teachers as well
as legislators, joined in the work. The completed law
was the outcome of a truly national effort. Indeed it was
largely through making a law which should be fit for both
Italians and provincials that the Romans of the Empire
became almost a nation.

In India the march of events has been different,
because the conditions were different. India is ten
thousand miles from England. The English residents
are a mere handful.

The Indian races are in a different stage of civilization from the English. They are separated by religion;
they are separated by colour.

There has therefore been no fusion of English and
native law. Neither has there been any movement of
the law of England to adapt itself to become the law of
her Indian subjects. English law has not, like Roman,
come halfway to meet the provinces. It is true that
no such approximation was needed, because English
law had already reached, a century ago, a point of
development more advanced than Roman law had
reached when the conquest of the provinces began,
and the process of divesting English law of its archaic
technicalities went on so rapidly during the nineteenth
century under purely home influences, that neither the
needs of India nor the influences of India came into
the matter at all.

The Romans had less resistance to meet with from
religious diversities than the English have had, for the
laws of their subjects had not so wrapped their roots
round religious belief or usage as has been the case in
India. But they had more varieties of provincial custom

to consider, and they had, especially in the laws of the Hellenized provinces, systems more civilized and advanced first to recognize and ultimately to supersede than any body of law which the English found.

There is no class in India fully corresponding to the Roman citizens domiciled in the provinces during the first two centuries of the Roman Empire. The European British subjects, including the Eurasians, are comparatively few, and they are to a considerable extent a transitory element, whose true home is England. Only to a very small extent do they enjoy personal immunities and privileges such as those that made Roman citizenship so highly prized, for the English, more liberal than the Romans, began by extending to all natives of India, as and when they became subjects of the British Crown, the ordinary rights of British subjects enjoyed under such statutes as Magna Charta and the Bill of Rights. The natives of India have entered into the labours of the barons at Runnymede and of the Whigs of 1688.

What has happened has been that the English have given to India such parts of their own law (somewhat simplified in form) as India seemed fitted to receive. These parts have been applied to Europeans as well as to natives, but they were virtually applicable to Europeans before codification began. The English rulers have filled up those departments in which there was no native law worthy of the name, sometimes, however, respecting local native customs. Here one finds an interesting parallel to the experience of the Romans. They, like the English, found criminal law and the law of procedure to be the departments which could be most easily and promptly dealt with. They, like the English, were obliged to acquiesce in the retention by a part of the population of some ancient customs regarding the Family and the Succession to Property. But this acquiescence was after all partial and local; whereas the English have neither applied to India the more technical parts of their own law, such as that relating to land, nor attempted to supersede those parts of native law which are influenced by religion, such as the parts which include family relations and inheritance. Thus there has been no general fusion comparable to that which the beginning of the third century A. D. saw in the Roman Empire.

As respects codification, the English have in one sense done more than the Romans, in another sense less. They have reduced such topics as penal law and procedure, evidence and trusts, to a compact and well-ordered shape, which is more than Justinian did for any part of the Roman law. But they have not brought the whole law together into one *Corpus Iuris*, and they have left large parts of it in triplicate, so to speak, that is to say, consisting of rules which are entirely different for Hindus, for Musulmans, and for Europeans.

Moreover, as it is the law of the conquerors which has in India been given to the conquered practically unaffected by native law, so also the law of England has not been altered by the process. It has not been substantially altered in India. The uncodified English law there is the same (local statutes excepted) as the law of England at home. Still less has it been altered in England itself. Had Rome not acquired her Empire, her law would never have grown to be what it was in Justinian's time. Had Englishmen never set foot in India, their law would have been, so far as we can tell, exactly what it is to-day.

Neither have those natives of India who correspond to the provincial subjects of Rome borne any recognizable share in the work of Indian legal development. Some of them have, as text-writers or as judges, rendered good service in elucidating the ancient Hindu customs. But the work of throwing English law into the codified form in which it is now applied in India to Europeans and natives alike has been done entirely by Englishmen. In this respect also the more advanced civilization has shown its dominant creative force.

IX. The Future of English Law in India.

Here, however, it is fit to remember that we are not, as in the case of the Romans, studying a process which has been completed. For them it was completed before the fifth century saw the dissolution of the western half of the Empire. For India it is still in progress. Little more than a century has elapsed since English rule was firmly established; only half a century since the Punjab and (shortly afterwards) Oudh were annexed. Although the Indian Government has prosecuted the work of codification much less actively during the last twenty years than in the twenty years preceding, and seems to conceive that as much has now been done as can safely be done at present, still in the long future that seems to lie before British rule in India the equalization and development of law may go much further than we can foresee to-day. The power of Britain is at this moment stable, and may remain so if she continues to hold the sea and does not provoke discontent by excessive taxation.

Two courses which legal development may follow are conceivable. One is that all those departments of law whose contents are not determined by conditions peculiar to India will be covered by further codifying acts, applicable to Europeans and natives alike, and that therewith the process of equalization and assimilation will stop because its natural limits will have been reached. The other is that the process will continue until the law of the stronger and more advanced race has absorbed that of the natives and become applicable to the whole Empire.

Which of these two things will happen depends upon the future of the native religions, and especially of Hinduism and of Islam, for it is in religion that the legal customs of the natives have their roots. Upon this vast and dark problem it may seem idle to speculate; nor can it be wholly dissevered from a consideration of the possible future of the religious beliefs which now hold sway among Europeans. Both Islam and Hinduism are professed by masses of human beings so huge, so tenacious of their traditions, so apparently inaccessible to European influences, that no considerable declension of either faith can be expected within a long period of years. Yet experience, so far as it is available, goes to show that no form of heathenism, not even an ancient and in some directions highly cultivated form like Hinduism, does ultimately withstand the solvent power of European science and thought. Even now, though Hinduism is growing every day, at the expense of the ruder superstitions among the hill-folk, it is losing its hold on the educated class, and it sees every day members of its lower castes pass over to Islam. So Islam also, deeply rooted as it may seem to be, wanes in the presence of Christianity, and though it advances in Central Africa, declines in the Mediterranean countries. It has hitherto declined not by the conversion of its members to other faiths, but by the diminution of the Muslim population; yet one must not assume that when the Turkish Sultanate or Khalifate has vanished, it may not lose much of its present hold upon the East. Possibly both Hinduism and Islam may, so potent are the new forces of change now at work in India, begin within a century or two to show signs of approaching dissolution. Polygamy may by that time have disappeared. Other peculiar features of the law of family and inheritance will tend to follow, though some may survive through the attachment to habit even when their original religious basis has been forgotten.

In the Arctic seas, a ship sometimes lies for weeks together firmly bound in a vast ice-field. The sailor who day after day surveys from the masthead the dazzling expanse sees on every side nothing but a solid surface, motionless and apparently immoveable. Yet all the while this ice-field is slowly drifting to the south, carrying with it the embedded ship. At last, when a warmer region has been reached and the south wind has begun to blow, that which overnight was a rigid and glittering plain is in the light of dawn a tossing mass of ice-blocks, each swiftly melting into the sea, through which the ship finds her homeward path. So may it be with these ancient religions. When their dissolution comes, it may come with unexpected suddenness, for the causes which will produce it will have been acting simultaneously and silently over a wide area. If the English are then still the lords of India, there will be nothing to prevent their law from becoming (with some local variations) the law of all India. Once established and familiar to the people, it will be likely to remain, whatever political changes may befall, for nothing clings to the soil more closely than a body of civilized law once well planted. So the law of England may become the permanent heritage, not only of the hundreds of millions who will before the time we are imagining be living beyond the Atlantic, but of those hundreds of millions who fill the fertile land between the Straits of Manaar and the long rampart of Himalayan snows.

We embarked on this inquiry for the sake of ascertaining what light the experience of the English in India throws upon the general question of the relation of the European nations to those less advanced races over whom they are assuming dominion, and all of whom will before long own some European master [1].

These races fall into two classes, those which do and those which do not possess a tolerably complete system of law. Turks, Persians, Egyptians, Moors, and Siamese belong to the former class; all other non-European races to the latter.

As to the latter there is no difficulty. So soon as Kafirs or Mongols or Hausas have advanced sufficiently to need a regular set of legal rules, they will (if their

[1] Among the 'less advanced races' one must not now include the Japanese, but one may include the Turks and the Persians. The fate of China still hangs in the balance. It is not to be assumed that she will be ruled, though she must come to be influenced, and probably more and more influenced, by Europeans.

European masters think it worth while) become subject
to the law of those masters, of course more or less
differentiated according to local customs or local needs.
It may be assumed that French law will prevail in
Madagascar, and English law in Uganda, and Russian
law in the valley of the Amur.

Where, however, as is the case in the Musulman and
perhaps also in the Buddhist countries belonging to the
former class, a legal system which, though imperfect,
especially on the commercial side, has been carefully
worked out in some directions, holds the field and rests
upon religion, the question is less simple. The experience of the English in India suggests that European
law will occupy the non-religious parts of the native
systems, and will tend by degrees to encroach upon
and permeate even the religious parts, though so long
as Islam (or Brahmanism) maintains its sway the legal
customs and rules embedded in religion will survive.
No wise ruler would seek to efface them so far as they
are neither cruel nor immoral. It is only these ancient
religions—Hinduism, Buddhism, and especially Islam—
that can or will resist, though perhaps only for a time,
and certainly only partially, the rising tide of European
law.

X. Present Position of Roman and English Law in the World.

European law means, as we have seen, either Roman
law or English law, so the last question is: Will either,
and if so which, of these great rival systems prevail
over the other?

They are not unequally matched. The Roman jurists,
if we include Russian as a sort of modified Roman law,
influence at present a larger part of the world's population, but Bracton and Coke and Mansfield might rejoice
to perceive that the doctrines which they expounded
are being diffused even more swiftly, with the swift

diffusion of the English tongue, over the globe. It is an interesting question, this competitive advance of legal systems, and one which would have engaged the attention of historians and geographers, were not law a subject which lies so much outside the thoughts of the lay world that few care to study its historical bearings. It furnishes a remarkable instance of the tendency of strong types to supplant and extinguish weak ones in the domain of social development. The world is, or will shortly be, practically divided between two sets of legal conceptions of rules, and two only. The elder had its birth in a small Italian city, and though it has undergone endless changes and now appears in a variety of forms, it retains its distinctive character, and all these forms still show an underlying unity. The younger has sprung from the union of the rude customs of a group of Low German tribes with rules worked out by the subtle, acute and eminently disputatious intellect of the Gallicized Norsemen who came to England in the eleventh century. It has been much affected by the elder system, yet it has retained its distinctive features and spirit, a spirit specially contrasted with that of the imperial law in everything that pertains to the rights of the individual and the means of asserting them. And it has communicated something of this spirit to the more advanced forms of the Roman law in constitutional countries.

At this moment the law whose foundations were laid in the Roman Forum commands a wider area of the earth's surface, and determines the relations of a larger mass of mankind. But that which looks back to Westminster Hall sees its subjects increase more rapidly, through the growth of the United States and the British Colonies, and has a prospect of ultimately overspreading India also. Neither is likely to overpower or absorb the other. But it is possible that they may draw nearer, and that out of them there may be developed, in the course of ages, a system of rules of private law which

shall be practically identical as regards contracts and
property and civil wrongs, possibly as regards offences
also. Already the commercial law of all civilized countries is in substance the same everywhere, that is to say,
it guarantees rights and provides remedies which afford
equivalent securities to men in their dealings with one
another and bring them to the same goal by slightly
different paths.

The more any department of law lies within the
domain of economic interest, the more do the rules that
belong to it tend to become the same in all countries,
for in the domain of economic interest Reason and
Science have full play. But the more the element of
human emotion enters any department of law, as for
instance that which deals with the relations of husband
and wife, or of parent and child, or that which defines
the freedom of the individual as against the State, the
greater becomes the probability that existing divergences
between the laws of different countries may in that department continue, or even that new divergences may
appear.

Still, on the whole, the progress of the world is
towards uniformity in law, and towards a more evident
uniformity than is discoverable either in the sphere of
religious beliefs or in that of political institutions.

III

FLEXIBLE AND RIGID CONSTI-TUTIONS[1]

I. The Constitutions of Rome and England.

ROME and England are the two States whose con-stitutions have had the greatest interest for the world, and have exerted the greatest influence upon it. Out of the republic on the Tiber, a city with a rural terri-tory round it no bigger than Surrey or Rhode Island, grew a World Empire, and the framework of that Empire retained till its fall traces of the institutions under which the little republic, circled and threatened by a crowd of hostile States, had risen to show her-self the strongest of them all. In England a monarchy, first tribal and then feudal, developed from very small beginnings into a second World Empire of a wholly different type, while at the same time the ancient form of government, through a series of struggles and efforts, guided by an only half-conscious purpose, slowly de-veloped itself into a system monarchical only in name. That system became in the eighteenth century the start-ing-point for all modern political philosophy[2], and in the nineteenth the model for nearly all the schemes of free

[1] This Essay was delivered, in the form of two lectures, in 1884, and the names Flexible and Rigid were then suggested for the two types of Constitution here described. It has been enlarged and revised and brought up to date, but the sub-stance remains the same.

[2] The interest which the English Constitution excited in Montesquieu may be compared with that which the Roman excited in Polybius.

representative polity that have arisen in the Old World as well as for many in the newer countries.

It is, however, not merely the range of their influence, nor merely the fact that, as the Roman Constitution worked upon the whole of the ancient, so the English Constitution has worked upon the whole of the modern world, that makes these two systems deserve constant study. Constitutions are the expression of national character, as they in their turn mould the character of those who use them; and the same causes which made both peoples great have made their political institutions also strong and rich, specially full of instruction for all nations in all times. There were in the fifth century B. C. hundreds of commonwealths in the Mediterranean countries with republican frames of government, many of which bore a general resemblance to that of Rome. There were in the fourteenth century A. D. several monarchies in Europe similar in their constitutional outlines to that of England, and with what seemed an equal promise of rich and free development. Of the former, Rome alone survived, destroying or absorbing all the rest. Of the latter, that of England is the only one which had at the end of the eighteenth century grown into a system at once broad-based and strong, a system which secured both public order and the freedom of the individual citizen, and in which the people were able to make their voice heard and to influence the march of national policy. All the others had either degenerated into despotisms or remained comparatively crude and undeveloped. Thus when, after the flood of Napoleonic conquest had subsided, the peoples of the European continent began to essay the establishment of free constitutions, they found in that of England the model fittest to be followed, and sought to adapt its principles to their own several conditions.

England, moreover, has been the parent of free governments in a further sense. Though she has not, like Rome, stretched her system of government till it embraced the world, she has reproduced it in those parts of her transoceanic dominions where her children have been able to form self-governing communities. Reduced copies of the British Constitution have been created in seventeen self-governing colonies. Seven of these have in North America been united in a Federation whose frame of government is built on British lines. Six others, in Australia, have been similarly grouped in another Federal Government of a not less distinctively British type. And an independent Republic, far vaster in population than all these colonies put together, has, less closely, but yet in the main and essential points, reproduced the principles, although not the form, of the institutions of the motherland. It is, therefore, to Rome and to England that the eye of the student of political constitutions will most often turn. They represent the most remarkable developments of ordered political life for the ancient and for the modern world respectively. And whoever attempts to classify Constitutions and to note the distinctive features of the principal types they present, will find that it is from Rome and from England that illustrations can most frequently and most profitably be drawn [1].

II. THE TRADITIONAL CLASSIFICATION OF CONSTITUTIONS.

The old-fashioned classification of Constitutions which has come down to our own times is based on the distinction of Written and Unwritten Law, itself an ill-expressed and rather confusing distinction, because *ius non scriptum* is intended to denote customs: and when customs have been recorded in writing, they can hardly continue to be called unwritten. This classification places in the category of Written Constitutions those which are expressly set forth in a specially important

[1] As to the countries or peoples in which Constitutions in the proper sense can be said to exist, see Note at the end of this Essay.

document or documents, and in the category of Unwritten those which began, not in formal agreements, but in usage, a usage which lives in men's recollections, and which, even when it has been to a large extent defined, and secured against error, by being committed to writing, is recorded as embodying that which men have observed, and are deemed likely to continue to observe, not as that to which they have bound themselves formally by a law.

These terms are, however, not happy terms, although the distinction they aim at expressing is a real distinction. The line which they attempt to draw between the two classes of Constitutions is not a clear or sharp line, because in all Written Constitutions there is and must be, as we shall presently see, an element of unwritten usage, while in the so-called Unwritten ones the tendency to treat the written record of custom or precedent as practically binding is strong, and makes that record almost equivalent to a formally enacted law, not to add that Unwritten Constitutions, though they began in custom, always include some statutes. Moreover, these names, while they dwell on a superficial distinction, ignore a more essential one to be presently mentioned. Let us therefore try to find a better classification.

If we survey Constitutions generally, in the past as well as in the present, we find them conforming to one or other of two leading types. Some are natural growths, unsymmetrical both in their form and in their contents. They consist of a variety of specific enactments or agreements of different dates, possibly proceeding from different sources, intermixed with customary rules which rest only on tradition or precedent, but are deemed of practically equal authority. Other Constitutions are works of conscious art, that is to say, they are the result of a deliberate effort on the part of the State to lay down once for all a body of coherent provisions under which its government shall be established and conducted. Such Constitutions are usually comprised in one instrument—

possibly, however, in more than one—an instrument solemnly enacted whose form and title distinguish it from ordinary laws. We may provisionally call these two types the Old and the New, because all ancient and mediaeval as well as some few recent Constitutions are of the former kind, while most modern ones belong to the latter. The distinction corresponds roughly to that drawn, in England and America, between common law and statute law, or to the Roman distinction between *ius* and *lex*, so that we might describe the types as Common Law Constitutions and Statutory Constitutions respectively. Yet the line of demarcation is not always a plain one. In countries with constitutions of the Common Law type, statutes are frequently passed, declaring or modifying or abolishing antecedent usage, which supersede and replace parts, possibly large parts, of the common law maxims, so that at last most of the leading rules can be found in a few great statutes. On the other hand, the Statutory Constitutions become developed by interpretation and fringed with decisions and enlarged or warped by custom, so that after a time the letter of their text no longer conveys their full effect. It is, therefore, desirable to have some more definite and characteristic test or criterion whereby to mark off the two types which have been just described in general terms.

III. A Proposed New Classification of Constitutions.

Such a criterion may be found in the relation which each Constitution bears to the ordinary laws of the State, and to the ordinary authority which enacts those laws. Some constitutions, including all that belong to the older or Common Law type, are on the level of the other laws of the country, whether those laws exist in the form of statutes only, or also in the form of recorded decisions defining and confirming a custom. Such con-

stitutions proceed from the same authorities which make
the ordinary laws; and they are promulgated or repealed
in the same way as ordinary laws.   In such cases the term
'Constitution' denotes nothing more than such and so
many of the statutes and customs of the country as determine the form and arrangements of its political system.
And (as will presently appear) it is often difficult to say
of any particular law whether it is or is not a part of the
political Constitution.

Other constitutions, most of them belonging to the
newer or Statutory class, stand above the other laws of
the country which they regulate.   The instrument (or
instruments) in which such a constitution is embodied
proceeds from a source different from that whence spring
the other laws, is repealable in a different way, exerts a
superior force.   It is enacted, not by the ordinary legislative authority, but by some higher or specially empowered person or body.   If it is susceptible of change,
it can be changed only by that authority or by that special
person or body.   When any of its provisions conflict with
a provision of the ordinary law, it prevails, and the ordinary law must give way.   These are features, partly
political, partly legal, which mark off the two types of
Constitution from one another; and although it will
appear that in some few cases the question to which
type the Constitution of a particular State belongs may
be a nice one, still the general legal criteria to be applied
are clear and definite.   In a State possessing a constitution of the former—the older—type, all laws (excluding
of course by-laws, municipal regulations, and so forth)
are of the same rank and exert the same force.   There
is, moreover, only one legislative authority competent
to pass laws in all cases and for all purposes.   But in a
State whose Constitution belongs to the latter—the
newer—type, there are two kinds of laws, one kind higher
than the other, and more universally potent; and there
are likewise two legislative authorities, one superior and
capable of legislating for all purposes whatsoever, the

9

other inferior and capable of legislating only so far as the superior authority has given it the right and function to do so.

The difference of these two types is best explained by illustrative instances. At Rome in the second century B. C. there was but one kind of enactment. All *leges* passed by the general assembly (whether *comitia centuriata* or *comitia tributa*) were of the same generality and the same force. There was but one legislative authority, the people voting in the *comitia*. So in England, during the last few centuries, there has been but one direct legislative authority, viz. Parliament, which is supreme, and all whose acts bind every citizen everywhere. Accordingly in England the laws called constitutional differ only in respect of their subject-matter from other laws, but are of no higher order. Each of such laws, though we call them in their totality ' the British Constitution,' is alterable by the ordinary legislative authority at any moment, just like other laws. Between an Act for making a railway from Manchester to Liverpool and an Act extending the electoral suffrage to all householders or disestablishing the Protestant Episcopal Church in Ireland there is no difference whatever in point of form or in degree of authority. In Switzerland, however, and in France the case is different. The Constitution of the Swiss Confederation is a document which was enacted by the people, and any amendment of which needs to be similarly enacted by them, whereas ordinary laws are passed by the Federal legislature of two Houses [1]. The present Constitution of the French Republic was enacted by the two Chambers sitting together as a Constituent Assembly, and can be amended only by the Chambers sitting together in that capacity, after each Chamber has separately resolved that revision is needed, whereas ordinary laws are passed by

---

[1] It is unnecessary for the present purpose to call attention to the complication introduced in Switzerland by the application of the Referendum plan to ordinary laws.

the two Chambers sitting separately. Thus both in Switzerland and in France there is a distinction in the enacting authority, and therewith also a distinction in the quality and force of the laws enacted, the law which is called the Constitution being entirely superior to the other laws which are passed by the legislature in the ordinary every-day course of its action.

What in the case of each State of the latter or newer type may be the higher (and indeed supreme) authority which is alone competent to enact a Constitution depends upon the provisions of each particular system. It may be the whole people, voting by what is sometimes, though not very happily, called a plebiscite. It may be a body specially elected for the purpose, which dissolves when its work has been completed. It may be certain local bodies, each voting separately on the same instrument submitted to them. It may be, as in the case just mentioned of France, the ordinary legislature sitting in a peculiar way, or acting by a prescribed majority, or rendering several successive votes to the same effect at prescribed intervals of time. These are matters of detail. The essential point is that in States possessing Constitutions of the newer type that paramount or fundamental law which is called the Constitution takes rank above the ordinary laws, and cannot be changed by the ordinary legislative authority.

I have sought in many quarters for names, necessarily metaphorical names, suitable to describe these two types of Constitution. They might be called Moving and Stationary, because those of the older kind are virtually never at rest, but are always undergoing some sort of change, however slight, in the course of ordinary legislation, while those of the newer type abide fixed and stable in their place. Or they might be described, the former as Fluid, and the latter as Solid or Crystallized. When a man desires to change[1] the composition of a liquid, he pours in some other liquid or dissolves a solid

---

[1] *I. e.* to change mechanically, not necessarily chemically.

in the liquid, and shakes the mixture. But he who wishes
to alter the composition of a solid must first dissolve
it or fuse it, and then, having got it into a liquid or gase-
ous state, must mix in or extract (as the case may be) the
other substance. The analogy between these two processes and those whereby a Constitution of the older and
one of the newer type are respectively changed might
justify these names. But there is another and simpler
metaphor, which, though not quite perfect, seems on
the whole preferable. Constitutions of the older type
may be called Flexible, because they have elasticity,
because they can be bent and altered in form while retaining their main features. Constitutions of the newer
kind cannot, because their lines are hard and fixed.
They may therefore receive the name of Rigid Constitutions: and by these two names I propose that we
shall call them for the purposes of this inquiry. If
the characteristics of the two types have not been made
sufficiently clear by what has been already said, they
will probably become clear in the more detailed examination of them, to which we may now proceed.

I begin with Flexible Constitutions, not only because
they are more familiar to students of Roman history
and to Englishmen, but also because they are anterior
in date. They are indeed the only constitutions which
the ancient world possessed, for although, in the absence
of Aristotle's famous treatise *On Polities*, we know comparatively little about most of the constitutions even of
the more famous Greek cities (except Athens), and practically nothing about any others, save those of Rome
and Carthage, there are reasons, to be given presently,
why we may safely assume that all of them belonged
to the Flexible type. But in the modern world they
have become rare. Excluding despotically governed
countries, such as Russia, Turkey, and Montenegro,
there are now only three in Europe, those of the United
Kingdom, of Hungary—an ancient and very interesting
Constitution, presenting remarkable analogies to that

of England—and of Italy, whose constitution, though originally set forth in one document, has been so changed by legislation as to seem now properly referable to the Flexible type. Elsewhere than in Europe, all Constitutions would appear to be Rigid [1].

But a preliminary objection deserves to be first considered. Can we properly talk of a Constitution at all in States which, like Rome and England, draw no formal and technical distinction between laws of different kinds? Since there was at Rome and is in England but one legislative authority, and all its statutes are of equal force, how distinguish those which relate to the general frame of government from those which embody the minor details of administration? The great Reform Act of A. D. 1832, for instance—and the same remark applies to the parliamentary reform Acts of 1867 and 1884—was clearly a constitutional statute. But it contained minor provisions which no one could call fundamental, and some of which were soon changed by other statutes which would scarcely be described as constitutional. There are many statutes of which, as of the Municipal Reform Act of 1834 (and I may add as of the Local Government Acts of 1888 and 1894), it would be hard to say whether they are or are not constitutional statutes, and there are statutes which would not be termed constitutional (such as the Scottish Universities Act of 1852), which have in fact modified such a momentous constitutional document as the Act of Union with Scotland (5 Anne, c. 6, art. xxv).

Technically, therefore, we cannot draw a distinction between constitutional and other laws. There was in strictness no Roman Constitution. There is no British Constitution. That is to say, there are no laws which can be definitely marked off as Fundamental Laws, defining and distributing the powers of government, the mode of creating public authorities, the rights and immu-

---

[1] Except that of the South African Republic (Transvaal). The cases of the British self-governing colonies will be presently referred to.

nities of the citizen. That which we call the Constitution of the Roman State, that which we now call the
Constitution of the United Kingdom, is a mass of precedents, carried in men's memories or recorded in writing,
of dicta of lawyers or statesmen, of customs, usages, un-
derstandings and beliefs bearing upon the methods of
government, together with a certain number of statutes,
some of them containing matters of petty detail, others
relating to private just as much as to public law, nearly
all of them presupposing and mixed up with precedents
and customs, and all of them covered with a parasitic
growth of legal decisions and political habits, apart from
which the statutes would be almost unworkable, or at
any rate quite different in their working from what they
really are. The most skilful classifier could not draw
up a list that would bear criticism of Roman or of British
statutes embodying the Constitution of either State:
and even if such a list were prepared, the statutes so
classified would fail to contain some cardinal doctrines
and rules. Such a list, for instance, of British statutes
would contain nothing about the Cabinet, and very little
about the relations of the House of Commons to the
House of Lords. On such subjects as the control of the
House of Commons over foreign affairs, the obligation of
the Crown to take, or the possible right of the Crown in
certain cases to overrule, the advice of its ministers, no
light would be thrown. Yet the statutes form the clearest
and most manageable part of the materials which make
up the British Constitution. Those other materials which
have been referred to are by their very nature vague
and indeterminate, unsusceptible of classification, and in
many instances incapable of being set forth in definite
rules [1]. A certain part of them is already, or is on the
way to become, obsolete. Another part is matter of
controversy between different schools of jurists or historians. The same thing was true of Rome, for at Rome

[1] This point has been brought out with admirable force in Mr. Dicey's *Law of
the Constitution.*

it would seem that no statute defined the power of the
consuls, nor their relation to the Senate, nor set limits
to the quasi-legislative authority of that great magistrate
the Praetor. So far from being clearly ascertained were
the powers of the Senate, that in Cicero's time it was
matter of constitutional debate whether its decrees had
or had not the full force of law [1] ; and men took one view
or the other according to their political proclivities, just
as in England men at one time differed regarding the
right of the House of Lords to deal with money bills.

These facts are of course obvious enough to-day to
every English lawyer, and indeed to those laymen who
have some tincture of historical or legal knowledge.
It is otherwise with the general public. To them the
word Constitution seems to represent something definite and positive. Much of the current talk about the
danger of altering the British Constitution [2] seems to
spring from the notion that the name represents a concrete thing, an ascertainable and positive definite body
of rules laid down in black and white. The Romans had
no single word to convey what we mean by ' Constitution.' Even in the last days of the Republic Cicero
had to use such phrases as *forma,* or *ratio,* or *genus rei
publicae,* or *leges et instituta;* and what we call ' constitutional law' appears in the jurists of the Empire as
ius quod ad statum rei Romanae spectat [3].

The objection, however, which we have been considering, goes only to misconceptions that may arise
from the word ' Constitution,' not to the use of the word
itself, for some such word is indispensable. The thing
exists, and there must be a name to describe it. A thing
is not the less real because its limits cannot be sharply
defined. A hill is a hill and a plain a plain, though you
cannot fix the point where the hill subsides into the plain.

---

[1] See as to this, Essay XIV, p. 716.

[2] I have allowed these lines to remain, though they were more applicable in
1884 than they are in 1900, when so many changes have been effected that arguments about the danger of changing the Constitution are less frequently heard.

[3] Ulpian in *Digest,* i. 1, 2.

The aggregate of the laws and customs through and
under which the public life of a State goes on may fitly be
called its Constitution; and even the still vaguer phrases,
' Spirit of the Constitution,' ' Principles of the Constitution,' may properly be used, since they too describe a
general quality or tendency pervading the whole mass
of laws and customs that rule a State which gives to this
mass a character differing from that of the Constitution
of any other State; just as each great nation has what we
call a National Character, though this character can be
more easily recognized than defined.

IV. THE ORIGIN OF FLEXIBLE CONSTITUTIONS.

Now let us return to consider the history and the
attributes of Flexible Constitutions. We have seen
that they are older than those of the Rigid type. It
may be thought that this is so because they are more
compatible with a rude condition of society, and because springing out of custom, always the first source
of law, they are the simplest and most obvious form
which regular political society can take. This is true,
but does not fully explain the phenomena.

A Constitution properly so called is a frame of political
society organized through and by law, that is to say, one
in which law has established permanent institutions with
recognized functions and definite rights. Now such
forms of organized political society appear first in small
communities, whether Urban, like the City States of
Greece, or Rural, like those of early England or mediaeval Switzerland. Wherever in the earlier stages of civilization we find large communities, like Egypt, Assyria,
Peru, Russia in the sixteenth century, we find that a
tribal organization has passed into a despotism [1], appa-

---

[1] I use the term ' despotism' for convenience, but of course no monarchy is absolutely despotic, and least of all perhaps in the ruder ages; for monarchs are
always amenable to public opinion, and most so when they are the leaders of a
tribe or people in arms. The real distinction is between a government checked

rently without passing through the intermediate stage
of a more or less restricted monarchy. Now in a small
area men usually organize themselves in a regular community by vesting legal authority in a mass meeting of
the citizens. The Folk Mot of our Teutonic ancestors, like the still surviving Landesgemeinde of Uri or
Appenzell, represents in a rural community what the
ἀγορά represents in Homeric Greece, what the ἐκκλησία
represents in the later Greek cities, and what the *comitia*
represent at Rome; I might add, what (in a more rudimentary form) the popular meeting represents to-day in
Albania and what the similar meeting called a *Pitso* represents among the Basuto and Bechuana Kafirs. Such
meetings, like the New England Town Meeting, are
Primary, not Representative. They consist of all the
freemen within the community, though, in their earlier
stage, it is in practice the leading men who determine
the action of the whole assembly. They make such laws
as there are. Being not only the supreme, but the only
legislative authority, they can at any moment change the
laws they deem fundamental, if there are any such laws,
for the more backward races remain in the stage of mere
custom, and do not reach the conception of a fundamental law. Whether the system of their government is
formally embodied in one group of specially important
laws, or, as more often happens, is left to be collected
from a number of enactments connected and supplemented by usages, that system remains on a level with
all the other laws and usages, because it emanates
from the same source, viz. the governing primary
assembly. It is not till the growth of some scheme of
representation has made familiar the distinction between
the authority of the people themselves and that of their

by religious sentiment consecrating ancient usage and by the fear of insurrection,
and a government checked by well-established institutions and legal rules. As to
Russia, it may be noted that though she has no Constitution in the proper sense,
there are said to exist three Fundamental Laws of the Empire—that declaring
the sovereign's autocratic power, that requiring him (or her) to be a member of
the Orthodox Church of the East, and that fixing the rule of succession to the
throne.

representatives that truly Rigid Constitutions appear, for it is not till then that a method suggests itself of enacting a kind of law which shall be superior to that which the ordinary legislative body creates. Accordingly the Primary Assembly, whether in ancient Greece and Italy or in mediaeval Europe, works for some time, and may create by its constant action what is practically a Constitution (*i.e.* a set of established rules embodying and directing the practice of government), before the idea of a regular political Constitution emerges. That idea comes into being when in the progress of political thought and of jurisprudence men begin to distinguish between laws and customs which relate to the structure of the State and the management of its affairs and those which relate to other matters, such as the civil rights of individuals; and when they also distinguish between rules and usages which are fixed and settled, because generally observed and regularly applied to recurrent facts, and the particular decisions taken in particular cases. In this sense the Romans may have begun to feel they had a Constitution before they had gone far in the conquest of Italy. Our English ancestors reached the same consciousness in the fourteenth century, when much stress began to be laid upon political precedents, and Parliament, by this time a Representative body, and thereby entitled to speak for the nation, had definitely established its rights as against the Crown[1]. The Confirmation of the Charters together with the statute De Tallagio Non Concedendo of A. D. 1297 is often taken as marking the first form of the plainly settled English Constitution, but perhaps the successful resistance of Parliament to King Edward the Third sixty years later is a better point to choose. Anyhow the language of Chief

[1] The history of England illustrates what is here said regarding small and large communities. The Folk Mot of the West Saxons when it passed into the Magnum Concilium of all England, though it remained in theory a Primary Assembly, was practically no longer a meeting of all freemen. It could not have continued to embody and safeguard the constitutional rights of the people but for the later invention of Representation, which made it again a virtually Popular though no longer a Primary Assembly.

Justice Fortescue (under Henry the Sixth) shows how clearly drawn the main lines of the Constitution had become in his time. When this stage has been reached, efforts are sometimes made to give to these constitutional rules, or to certain among them, an exceptional degree of force and permanence. Such rules may be embodied in a document of special sanctity; or they may be protected by oaths. But the creation of a truly Rigid Constitution comes later, when some system of representation has appeared. I shall presently return to examine the causes which produce it.

V. The Strength and Weakness of Flexible Constitutions.

The names 'Flexible' or 'Fluid,' which I have suggested for Constitutions of this type, seem to suggest that they are unstable, with no guarantee of solidity and permanence. They are in a state of perpetual flux, like the river of Heraclitus, into which a man cannot step twice. Not only are new laws constantly passed which more or less affect them, but their mere working tends to alter them daily. Just as every man's character is being every day insensibly modified by the acts he does, by the thoughts he cherishes, by the emotions which each new experience of life brings with it, so every decade saw the Constitution of Rome, and sees the Constitution of England, slightly different at the end of even so short a period from what it was at the beginning. Even a deliberately conservative policy cannot arrest this process of variation. If the change does not for a time appear in the laws, it is in progress in the minds of men, and may have all the more violent a working when it begins to tell upon legislation. A reaction, such as that carried through by Lucius Cornelius Sulla at Rome, or that which followed the fall of the Cromwellian Protectorate in England, is almost as fertile in change as a time of revolution. The past can never be effaced, since the recollection of it is an element in shaping the future, and the measures taken to restore a *status quo ante* always contain much which was not in that *status quo ante*, much which is in itself new, and the source of further novelties. The only cases in which constitutional development can be said to stop are those where, as at Venice and in some of the cities of post-mediaeval Switzerland, an oligarchy gets control of the government, and, in extinguishing the spirit and the habits of freedom, arrests the natural processes of movement and development until some powerful neighbour overthrows the State, or internal economic changes induce a revolution. Even under a despotism, the system of government changes insensibly from century to century, as it did in the old French monarchy, and as it has recently done among a people so stagnant as the Turks. But despotic systems, being scarcely classifiable as Constitutions, do not come within our present inquiry.

These things being so, it seems natural to assume that Flexible (the so-called 'unwritten') Constitutions, having been enacted and being alterable by the ordinary legislative authority, and not being contained in any specially sacred instrument, will in fact be subject to frequent and large changes, and will moreover be so readily transgressed in practice, that they will furnish an insufficient guarantee for public order and for the protection of private rights.

The facts, however, do not support this assumption. Let us take our two typical instances, Rome and England. The Roman Constitution is an extreme case of a Frame of Government capable of being changed in the quickest and simplest way. Nothing was needed but a vote of the *comitia*, on the proposition of a competent magistrate, accompanied by the silence of the tribunes. No doubt any single tribune could paralyse the action of the *comitia*, but in such a community as Rome became in the later days of the Republic it must often have been easy for those who desired a change to 'get at,' or to remove, an obnoxious tribune. Yet the Constitution of Rome, regarded on its legal side, changed comparatively little in the three centuries that lie between the Licinian laws and the age of Sulla, for most of those deviations from ancient usage which, as we can now see, were working towards its fall, were in form quite legal, being merely occasional resorts to expedients which the Constitution recognized, though they had been more rarely and more cautiously used in older and better days. So in England, the exercise of the sovereign power is lodged in an assembly which can, on occasion, act with extraordinary promptitude, as when some while ago (April 9, 1883) the Explosives Act was passed through the House of Commons in a few hours (the standing orders having been suspended), and having been forthwith passed by the House of Lords also, received the royal assent next day. So the most sacred rules and principles of the Constitution might with perfect legality of form be abolished—Magna Charta and the Bill of Rights and the Act of Settlement included—just as quickly as the Explosives Act was passed. Yet the main lines of the English frame of government have since 1689 and 1701 remained legally the same; and the most important changes made since the latter year have been effected after long and strenuous controversies [1]. We all know how hard it is to secure even small constitutional improvements, such as the abolition of the provision, confessedly useless and certainly troublesome, which obliges a member of the House of Commons to vacate his seat and seek re-election on his being appointed a Minister of the Crown.

One explanation of this apparent paradox is (though sometimes neglected) obvious enough. The stability of any constitution depends not so much on its form as on the social and economic forces that stand behind and support it; and if the form of the constitution corre-

---

[1] The two most important changes, the Union with Scotland and the Union with Ireland, were, however, among those most quickly carried through.

sponds to the balance of those forces, their support maintains it unchanged. Two other reasons deserve to be more fully stated.

A Flexible or Common Law Constitution sometimes owes its stability to the very conditions which have enabled it to grow out of isolated laws and mere usages into a firmly settled Frame of Government. There have no doubt been many cases, such as those of most of the Greek cities of antiquity, where the eager restless spirit of the people and the violence of faction never allowed any system of government to last long enough to strike deep root. Such constitutions were often enacted all in one piece, and would have been made Rigid, had the citizens who enacted them known how to make them so. They were seldom the growth of long-continued usage. But the best instances of Flexible Constitutions have been those which grew up and lived on in nations of a conservative temper, nations which respected antiquity, which valued precedents, which liked to go on doing a thing in the way their fathers had done it before them. This type of national character is what enables the Flexible Constitution to develop; this supports and cherishes it. The very fact that the legal right to make extensive changes has long existed, and has not been abused, disposes an assembly to be cautious and moderate in the use of that right. Those who have always enjoyed power are least likely to abuse it [1]. This truth might be illustrated both from Rome and from England; and, indeed, from Switzerland also, though the argument which tries to prove the stupid conservatism of democracy from the habits of rural communities in the last-named country has been pressed too far by Sir H. Maine and others, since in rural communities, where nearly every one is a citizen, and well off, and most men about equally well off, the usual motives for making political changes do not exist.

A further reason may be found in the fact that a con-

---

[1] Ἀρχαιοπλούτων δεσποτῶν πολλὴ χάρις, Aesch. *Agam.* 1002.

stitution which has come down in the form of a mass of laws, precedents and customs is not only more mysterious, and therefore more august, to the minds of the ordinary citizens than one they can read in a document, but is not felt by them to lie at their mercy and to live only by their pleasure. A constitution embodied in a document which they have seen drafted, and have enacted by their votes, has no element of antiquity or mystery. It issues from the sovereignty of the people, it reminds them of their sovereignty, it suggests to them nothing more exalted. Perhaps it has been the work of one party in the State ; and if that party becomes discredited, it may share the discredit. The dignity which a remote and half mythic origin gives to constitutions, as it does to royal families, was in the ancient world and the Middle Ages enhanced by religious associations. In Greece and Italy the tutelary deities of the city watched over the oldest laws. In mediaeval countries the order of the State seemed an expression of the Will of God. Although these sentiments have vanished from the modern world, the fact that an old constitution represents a long course of progressive development, or, to use a somewhat vulgarized term, of evolution, gives it some claim on the respect of imaginative or philosophical minds. These sources of moral strength have been found sufficient in many countries to secure an enduring life for political institutions which the people, or a legislative body, had it in their power to change, and which, in some instances, ought to have been replaced by other institutions more suited to their altered environment.

It would, therefore, be an error to pronounce Flexible Constitutions unstable. Their true note, their distinctive merit, is to be elastic. They can be stretched or bent so as to meet emergencies, without breaking their framework ; and when the emergency has passed, they slip back into their old form, like a tree whose outer branches have been pulled on one side to let a vehicle pass. Just because their form is not rigidly fixed, a temporary change is not felt to be a serious change. The sentiment of respect for the established order is not shaken. The old habits are maintained, and the machine, modified perhaps in some detail which the mass of the people scarcely notice, seems to go on working as before.

Whether the working is really the same is another matter. During two centuries and a half, from Edward the Third till James the First, the Constitution of England remained in its legal aspect scarcely altered. Though at some moments within that period Parliament seemed to have mightily gained on the Crown, and at others the Crown seemed to be dominating Parliament, yet it was, until the Civil War, doubtful whether any permanent change had been effected. From the days of Queen Anne to those of William the Fourth the Constitution preserved a legal character practically the same. But it had been altered essentially in substance. So we may say that while the Flexible character of a constitution sometimes enables it to recover from shocks without injury, that character sometimes conceals the effects of a shock, since these effects may take the form of changes of usage and changes of opinion among the citizens which have not been expressed, perhaps hardly can be expressed, in a definite legal form. The relations to one another of the two Houses of the British Parliament, and the relations of Parliament to the now self-governing British Colonies, are instances in point.

No constitution illustrates these phenomena better than did that of Rome. It was a complicated piece of work, made of many pieces, firmly attached, yet each piece playing freely. It had to be bent, twisted, stretched in many ways, under the pressure of divers exigencies. But it stood the strain of being bent or stretched, and when the force that had bent it was withdrawn, could return so nearly to its original shape as to seem to have never been disturbed. The change from consuls to military tribunes, the frequent appointment of a dictator, the memorable episode of the Decemvirate, the creation of new magistracies, even the admission of new and sometimes large masses of persons to citizenship and voting power, and the adaptation of its old machinery to the new task of governing conquered provinces, did not, during several centuries, permanently disturb its balance or seriously shake its main principles. Suspensions of the ordinary rights of the private citizen, extensions of the ordinary powers of the magistrate, which would have ruined most States by setting dangerous precedents, were at Rome found harmless because law and custom recognized them as expedients available in case of need, and, in legalizing them, took away their revolutionary character. Thus, being parts of the Constitution, though parts to be used only in emergencies, they did not shock conservative sentiment nor encourage attempts pernicious to freedom—did not, that is to say, until at last the character of the city population had so completely changed and the dominions of the Republic had so prodigiously grown that the old Constitution was obviously out of date, unfit for work immensely heavier than that for which it had been constructed.

A Greek city, or an Italian city of the Middle Ages, which delivered itself into the hands of a dictator when pressed by its neighbours, almost invariably found that it had given itself a master who refused to resign his power when the danger was past, but continued to rule as a Tyrant or Signore. This happened not merely because the people were passionate and the leading men ambitious, for there was plenty both of passion and of ambition among the Romans, but largely because in those cities no provision was made for such emergencies; so that when it became necessary to place extraordinary powers in one or few hands, the Constitution received a violent wrench, from which it might not recover. At Rome the contingency had been foreseen, and the mode of meeting it was legal. A spirit had been formed among the body of the people as well as among the leading men which held ambition in check. The dictator was not intoxicated by his elevation. The citizens did not lose their faith in the soundness of their system; and it justified their confidence.

The elasticity of the British Constitution appears in somewhat different features, less striking perhaps than those which mark Rome, but not less useful. We English appoint no dictators, seeing that we have always fortunately had a permanent head of the Executive, though latterly one rather nominal than real, and have seldom been exposed to the dangers which the city-states of the ancient world had to fear. But we have kept in reserve a wide and vague prerogative, which, though it cannot in practice be put in force against the will of the representative House of Parliament, may be employed to effect things far more important than many other things for which express legislative authority is required. The control of the army and navy and the control of foreign policy are instances. There are, moreover, ways in which the normal powers of the Executive may be immensely increased. When a statute, such as the Habeas Corpus Act, is suspended, or when a Vote of Credit for a very large sum of money is passed, the control of the ordinary law and courts in the one case, and the control of the House of Commons in the other case, over the Ministers of the Crown, is for the time being (especially if Parliament is not sitting) and for some purposes practically suspended; and the Sovereign (or rather the Cabinet) of to-day is almost replaced in the position of the last Tudor or the first Stuart. Stringent measures to repress disorder may be taken at home, military operations may be threatened or begun abroad which would be beyond the legal competence of the Crown in the former case and its ordinary discretionary powers and functions, as fixed by custom, in the latter. So too when it became necessary in view, not of an emergency, but of the general convenience of administration, to delegate to inferior authorities the supreme legislative power of Parliament, advantage was taken of the old royal prerogative and of that ancient body the Privy Council. Parliament gave power to the Crown to issue Orders in Council dealing with large classes of matters which must otherwise have been dealt with by statute; and these Orders take effect sometimes at once, sometimes when a certain period has elapsed during which they have lain before Parliament and received from it no disapproval. In this way a vast mass of secondary legislation is annually enacted which, though it does not directly issue from Parliament, carries parliamentary authority, and does not infringe the principle that Parliament is the only true source of law. And, similarly, out of the ancient judicial functions of the Crown and of the Council which advised the Crown, functions which a century ago seemed to be lapsing into desuetude, there has been evolved a new system of judicature. A body called the Judicial Committee of the Privy Council, somewhat resembling the Consistory of the Roman Emperors, has been created, and now acts as a Supreme Court of Appeal for all the transmarine possessions of Britain, whether Indian or Colonial.

The merit of this elastic quality in such Constitutions as the Roman and the British is that it affords a means of preventing or minimizing revolutions by meeting them halfway. Let us note how each kind of Constitution, the Rigid and the Flexible, behaves when a serious crisis arrives, in which one section of the nation is bent on changing the Constitution, and the other on maintaining it. A Rigid Constitution, if the legal means provided for altering it cannot be used for the want of the prescribed legal majority, resists the pressure. It may of course resist successfully, but if so, probably after a conflict which has shaken the State and excited hostility to it in the minds of a large part of the people. It may, however, if the assailing forces are very strong, be broken, and if so, broken past mending. A Flexible Constitution, however, being more easily and promptly alterable, and being usually a less firmly welded and cohesive structure, can bend without breaking, can be modified in such a way as to satisfy popular demands, can escape revolution by the practical submission of one of the contending forces in the particular dispute, that submission being recognized as a precedent which will be followed, even though it has not been embodied in any law or other formal document. The extinction of the right once claimed by the House of Lords to alter money bills is one instance. Or it may be made to evolve some organ which, though really new, conceals its novelty by keeping some of the old colour, and thus it may continue to work with no palpable breach of continuity. The knowledge that a constitution can be changed without any tremendous effort helps to make a party of revolution less violent and a party of resistance less stubborn, disposing both to some compromise. At Rome the resort to the appointment of military tribunes with consular power when the plebs demanded, and the patricians would not yet consent to the election of a plebeian Consul, delayed revolution till opinion had so changed that the danger of revolution had passed away. So, later, the compromise by which a Praetor was created with the functions of a Consul but with a special range of duties appeased conservative feeling and smoothed the passage from the old order to the new. The history of the English Constitution is a history of continual small changes, no single one of which, hardly even the Bill of Rights at the time of the so-called Revolution, or the Reform Act of 1832, made the system look substantially different. Something no doubt was cut away, and something was added, but the structure as a whole seemed the same, because far more of the old was left than there was added of the new.

The two main processes which have turned the government of England from the monarchy of the Tudors into what may be called the plutocratic democracy of to-day have been the limitation of the royal prerogative and the

transference of the right of suffrage from a few to the
multitude. Both processes have gone on slowly, by a
succession of steps, each comparatively small, but all
in the same direction. Accordingly the strife of parties
has been mitigated by the existence at all, or nearly all,
moments, of a large body of persons who desired reform,
but only a moderate reform. They are the persons who
impose compromise on the extremists to the right and
to the left of them, and they can do so because the Constitution permits small reforms to be easily effected.
The party of change, which would be a party of revolution if it was obliged to have large changes or none, is
apt to be divided, and its more moderate section is, or
soon passes into, a party only of reform. The English
Chartists of 1840-50 caused some alarm. But between
them and the old Constitutional Whigs there were several
sections of opinion passing by imperceptible gradations
into one another; and when it was seen that the current
was setting towards changes approximating to those
which the Chartists demanded, their less violent men
were by degrees reabsorbed into the general body of
the Whig or Liberal party, the latter at the same time
moving with the times; and some of those changes, in
particular vote by ballot, were ultimately obtained with
no great friction.

It must nevertheless be remembered that in the history
of most States a crisis is apt to arrive when elasticity
becomes a danger, in that it tempts people to abuse the
facility for change. There is no better sign of strength
in a man's physical constitution than his being able to
make some short, sudden, and violent effort without
suffering afterwards from doing so; and there is nothing
of which the happy possessor of such strength is more
proud. But those men who have reached middle life are
aware that the temptation to strain one's strength in this
exultant spirit is perilous. Repeated impunity is apt to
encourage a man to go on trying experiments when the
conditions are perhaps less favourable, or when the re-

serve of force is less abundant than it was in youth. The story goes that the famous Milo of Croton, passing alone through a forest, saw an oak into which woodmen who were preparing to fell it had driven wedges. Pulling out the wedges, he tried to rive it asunder. But he had no longer the fullness of his youthful strength. The returning tree caught him by the hands and held him fast till he died. In our own days Captain Webb, stimulated by his feat in swimming across the English Channel, sought still bolder exploits, and perished in the Whirlpool Rapid below Niagara Falls. So the Romans, having many a time given exceptional powers for special occasions to their magistrates, found at last that they had created precedents which enabled the old free Constitution to be in substance overthrown. Sulla became a dictator of a new kind. After a while he resigned his power, but the example showed that monarchy was not far off. Julius Caesar also received exceptional authority, and used it to form an army which extinguished the Republic. The dictatorship he had held passed under other forms into permanent absolutism, and what was practically a revolution was ultimately carried through with a certain deference to the old constitutional forms. In England, Parliament, during the sixteenth century, once or twice gave powers to the Crown which brought the Constitution into danger. In the seventeenth century the monarchy was abolished, and a Protectorate set up by revolutionary methods. This was the result of a war which had destroyed a vital part of the old machine, much to the regret of most of those who had in the first instance taken up arms. We have never since that date (except under King James the Second) seen the Constitution in any real danger.

It is, however, often suggested that the enormous power possessed by Parliament might be used to upset fundamental institutions with reckless haste, and that it might therefore be prudent to impose restrictions on parliamentary action. And those who note the way in which Parliament bends and staggers under the increasing burden of work laid on it, coupled with the inadequacy of its rules to secure the prompt dispatch of business [1], have frequently predicted that the House of Commons may one day deliver itself into the hands of the Cabinet, the power of party organization having grown so strong that the head of each Cabinet will be deemed a sort of dictator, drawing his authority, nominally of course, from the House of Commons, but really from a so-called direct 'mandate' of the electors [2]. Others draw a yet more horrible picture of a party machine, which they call the Caucus, dictating a policy to the electors on the one hand, and to the Cabinet on the other, itself reigning in the spirit of a tyrant, but under the forms of the Constitution. If the British Constitution, as we have hitherto known it, should perish, there is little reason to fear it will do so in this eminently ignoble fashion [3].

When Flexible Constitutions come to an end, they do so in one of two ways. Sometimes they pass into an autocracy, either dying a violent death by revolution, or expiring in a more natural manner through the extension and development, under legal forms, of one of their organs, to a point at which it practically supersedes and replaces the other organs. Sometimes, on the other hand, they pass into Rigid Constitutions. The causes which induce this latter change belong,

[1] This was written in 1884. Since that year sweeping changes have been made in the procedure of the House of Commons which have greatly curtailed the rights and opportunities of private members while increasing the powers of the Ministry of the day. They have not, however, made that House able to discharge all or nearly all the work that falls on it ; and it is becoming (under the new rules) less and less careful in the exercise of its powers of voting money.

[2] This apprehension was often expressed between 1880 and 1885. Nothing has occurred since to justify it so far as the dictatorship of any single person is concerned ; and it may have in great part arisen from the fact that from 1867 to 1885 the headships of both the two great parties had been vested in exceptionally vigorous and influential leaders. There can however be no doubt that the power of the Cabinet as against the House of Commons has grown steadily and rapidly : and it appears (1901) to be still growing.

[3] Of this supposed danger also much less is heard now than in 1884. The thing that was then called the 'Birmingham Caucus' has ceased to be used to terrify the timid.

however, to the examination of that second type of Constitution; and will be considered when we have surveyed some further features characteristic of the Flexible type.

VI. Aristocracies and Flexible Constitutions.

Flexible Constitutions have a natural affinity for an aristocratic structure of government. I do not mean merely that they spring up at times when power is in the hands of the well-born or rich, for the stage of society in which constitutions, properly so called, begin to exist, is nearly always oligarchic, even if there be a monarch at the head of it. But there is a sort of natural attraction between an aristocracy and an undefined and elastic form of government, as there has begun to be, in most modern countries, a natural repulsion between such a form and a pure democracy. It needs a good deal of knowledge, skill and experience to work a Flexible Constitution safely, and it is only in the educated classes that these qualities can be looked for. The masses of a modern nation seldom appreciate the worth of ancient usages and forms, or the methods of applying precedents. In small democratic communities, such as are the Forest Cantons of Switzerland, this attachment to custom may be found, because there traditions have passed into the life of the people, and the maintenance of ancient forms has become a matter of local pride. But in a large nation it is only educated men who can comprehend the arrangements of a complicated system with a long history, who can follow its working, and themselves apply its principles to practice. The uninstructed like something plain, simple and direct. The *arcana imperii* inspire suspicion, a suspicion seldom groundless, because the initiated are apt to turn a knowledge of secrets to selfish purposes. Now a Common Law Constitution with its long series of precedents, some half obsolete, some of doubtful interpretation, is full of *arcana*. Even to-day, though the process of clarification and simplification has gone on fast since 1832, dark places are still left in the British Constitution.

There is, however, a further reason why Common Law Constitutions accord better with aristocratic than with democratic sentiment. They allow a comparatively wide discretion to the chief officials of State, such as the higher magistrates at Rome and the Ministers of the Crown in England. The functions of these officials are not very strictly defined, because legal enactments, though they limit power in certain directions (far more rigidly now in England than was the case at Rome), do not draw a completely closed circle round it, but leave certain gaps, through which tradition and precedent permit it, so to speak, to shoot out and play freely. Aristocracies prize this latitude. They prize it because it is mainly to prominent members of their class that offices fall, and these persons are then able to act with freedom, to assert their individual wills, to carry out their views unchecked by the dread of transgressing a statute. On the other hand, the less conspicuous members of the upper class have at any rate little reason to fear harm from the wide authority of the officials, because their social position, and the influence of their family connexions, protect them from arbitrary treatment. The masses of the people have neither advantage. Very few of them can hope to enjoy power. Any one of them may suffer from an exercise of it, which, because not positively illegal, gives him no claim for redress. They have, therefore, everything to gain and nothing to lose if they can restrict it by those definite and fixed limitations which are congenial to Rigid rather than to Flexible Constitutions. And in the history of most peoples a time arrives when, the love of equality being reinforced by the distrust of authority, there is a movement to cut down the powers of the rulers to the lowest point compatible with the safety of the State. The extent to which this process has gone is in any nation a fair test of the gains made by the democratic principle upon the aristocratic. But in this respect the course things have taken in England has been very unlike that which they took at Rome. One of the first events which the authentic history of Rome records is the effort of the plebeians to secure a limitation of the power of the Consuls by having statutes passed to define it. The effort failed. It is characteristic of the Romans that it should have failed. Statutes, known afterwards as the Laws of the Twelve Tables, were enacted, statutes which doubtless on the whole improved the position of the plebeians. But the powers of the Consuls remained wide and legally indefinite down till the time when life went out of them under the shadow of an autocrat who ruled for life. Limited of course these powers had to be as time went on and the popular element in the constitution was developed, but the limitations were imposed, not by narrowing the powers themselves, but by the introduction of new factors. The two Consuls, being chosen from a circle less narrow than in the old days, were more frequently at variance with one another. Other officials were set up over against the Consuls, who could (if they pleased) interfere to restrain the Consuls. And thirdly, the permanent non-representative Council of Elders (the Senate), composed mainly of ex-officials, increased its influence, and could generally hold the magistrates in check. Things went very differently in England. There the prerogative of the Crown was the force of which the nobles as well as the commons stood in dread, and they united in the effort to restrict it down till a time when the commons were strong enough to dispense with the help of more than a section of the landowning magnates. In steadily reducing the prerogative of the Crown, in lopping off some parts of it and strictly defining others, they restricted the powers of the Crown and its Ministers, until at last they had so firmly established the right of the representative assembly to prescribe to the Crown what persons it should employ as Ministers that the old motive for limiting the prerogative vanished. Those who had been feared as masters were now trusted as servants. The people no longer disliked what was left of the royal prerogative, because their representatives could control the persons who wielded it, and the members of the ruling assembly began to feel that it was in the public interest, and not against their own personal interest, to maintain the powers of Ministers, because many things could be done more easily and more promptly through these powers than by the passing of statutes for dealing with each matter in detail. There n ay even be a danger, in this new condition of things, that the royal prerogative will be used too freely, because that prerogative now means the will of the leaders of the parliamentary majority, whose action might at a moment of excitement be applauded and sustained by their followers even should it transcend the limits fixed by constitutional usage.

It has been already remarked that the system of checks in the Roman Constitution differed essentially from that employed in the English. Every constitution must of course have a system of checks, else it will quickly perish, or, to vary the metaphor, it must so dispose the ballast as to enable the vessel to recover her equilibrium after a violent oscillation. At Rome the checks consisted in the coexistence of various magistrates who could arrest one another's action, and in a permanent Senate with a large though somewhat ill-defined control, while the popular assembly, in theory omnipotent, was in fact restrained by a number of curious features in its procedure which made it much less effective than was the primary popular assembly in most of the Greek republics. It could act only when convoked by a magistrate, could have its action stopped by another magistrate, and was frequently overreached or circumvented by the Senate. In England, on the other hand, the Crown, which before the conflicts of the seventeenth century had been the predominant power which needed to be checked, and which frequently was checked, by Parliament, becomes after that time capable only of occasionally baffling (and that less and less as time went on) the now predominant Parliament, while the restraint on hasty or violent action by Parliament was found, partly in the division of Parliament into two Houses, and partly, especially after the Upper House had begun to lose moral weight, and had passed more and more under the control of one party in the State, in the fact that an assembly of representatives, nearly all of whom belonged to the wealthier and so-called upper classes, was pervaded by a conservative temper. A representative body, the members of which are mostly satisfied with the world as it is, and who are sufficiently instructed to respect the traditions of administration, is, except where a question arises which stirs class passions, less prone to ill-considered action than is an assembly of all the citizens, such as was the Ecclesia of Athens or Syracuse, where the large majority were humble folk, and where the sympathy of numbers made the ascendency of emotion over reason doubly dangerous. Thus, as compared with the democracies of the city-states of antiquity, the representative character of the assemblies of modern Europe has been a moderating factor. But these assemblies are now changing their character, as the countries in which they exist have changed. The progress of science has, through the agency of railways and telegraphs, of generally diffused education, and of cheap newspapers, so brought the inhabitants of large countries into close and constant relations with one another and with their representatives, that the conditions of a small city-state are being reproduced. A man living at Kirkwall knows what happened last night in London, eight hundred miles away, sooner and more fully than a man living in Marathon (distant eight hours' walking) knew what had happened the day before in Athens. The same news reaches all the citizens at the same time, the same emotion affects all simultaneously, and is intensified by reverberation through the press. The nation is, so to speak, compressed into a much smaller space than it filled three centuries ago, and has become much more like a primary assembly than it was then. If concurrently with this change there should come, as some presage, a closer and more constant control of the members of the representative assembly by their constituents, the representatives becoming rather delegates acting under instructions than men chosen to speak and vote because they are deemed trusty and intelligent, much of the moderative value which the representative system has possessed will disappear.

It need not be thought that in England at least there is any immediate risk of evils to be expected from the change which has been noted. Representatives have not yet become delegates, and if they do, it will be rather their own fault than that of the electors, for the electors respect courage and value independence. In England the power of party organizations over constituencies and members, if it grows, grows slowly. It is, in fact, not so much these organizations as small sections of opinion or organized 'interests,' seeking some advantage for themselves, that try to terrorize candidates. There is still a valuable check on possible recklessness on the part of Parliament in the fact that it is (unlike some popular assemblies) guided by responsible Ministers, who have hitherto seldom been mere demagogues, and who have experience behind them, prospects of future dignity before them, and the opinion of their own class around them. All that I wish to point out is that a change has passed on the conditions under which representative assemblies act, which in making them more swiftly responsive to public sentiment, increases some of the risks always incident to popular government. History has not spoken her last word about Flexible Constitutions. Rather may she be opening a new stage in their development.

VII. The Influence of Constitutions on the Mind of a Nation.

We have been considering what are the conditions present in a nation which make it prefer a particular kind of constitution. Now let us approach the converse question, and inquire what will be the influence on the political ideas and habits of a nation of these Constitutions of the Common Law, or Flexible type, and what are the features of national character which will enable such constitutions to live on and prosper.

Forms of government are causes as well as effects, and give an intellectual and moral training to the peoples that live under them, as the character of a parent affects the children of the household. Now the Common Law Constitution, with its complexity, its delicately adjusted and balanced machinery, its inconsistencies, its *nuances*—one is driven to French because there is no English word to express the tendency of a tendency—its abundance of unsettled points, in which a refined sense can perceive what the decision ought in each case to be without being able to lay down a plain and positive rule—such a constitution must undoubtedly polish and mature in the governing class a sort of tact and judgement, a subtlety of discrimination and a skill in applying old principles to new combinations of facts, which make it safe for a people to leave wide powers to their magistrates or their governing assembly. A sense grows up among those who have to work the constitution as to what is and is not permissible under it, and that which cannot be expressed in the stiff phrases of a code is preserved in the records of precedents and shines through the traditions which form the minds of the rulers. This kind of constitution lives by what is called its Spirit. ' The letter killeth, but the spirit giveth life.'

Evidently, however, it is only among certain nations with certain gifts that such a constitution will come to maturity and become a subject for science as well as a work of art. Three things seem needful. One is legal-mindedness, a liking and a talent for law. Another is a conservative temper, by which I mean the caution which declines to make changes save when a proved need for change arises, so that changes are made not suddenly, but slowly and bit by bit. The third is that intellectual freshness and activity which refuses to be petrified by respect for law or by aversion to change. It is only where these three qualities are fitly mixed or evenly balanced that either a great system of law or a finely tempered and durable constitution can grow up. Many otherwise gifted peoples have, like the Athenians in ancient and, *longo intervallo*, the Spaniards in modern times, wanted one or other of these qualities, and have therefore failed to enrich the world by law or by constitutions. Perhaps it was partly owing to their possessing other gifts, scarcely compatible with these, that the Athenians did fail.

But although, when a nation has reached the point at which its law begins to be scientific, the law and the constitution become teachers, it must be remembered that the training they give is mainly given to the classes which practise law and administer the State. For though a nation as a whole may come to understand and appreciate in outline its constitution, and may attain to a fairly correct notion of the functions of each organ of government, only a comparatively small section comprehends the system well enough to work it or to criticize its working. For such comprehension there is needed not only some knowledge of history but also close and continuous observation of the machinery in motion, and either participation in the business of governing or association with those who are carrying on that business. The mass of the nation cannot be expected to possess this familiarity. They are like the passengers on board an ocean steamer, who hear the clank of the engine and watch the stroke of the piston and admire the revolution of the larger wheels, and know that steam acts by expansion, but do not know how the less conspicuous but not less essential parts of the machinery play into the other parts, and have little notion of the use of fly-wheels and connecting-rods and regulators. They can see in what direction the vessel is moving, and can conjecture the rate of speed, but they must depend on the engineers for the management of boilers and engines, as they do on the captain for the direction of the ship's course. In the earlier stages of national life, the masses are usually as well content to leave governing to a small upper class as passengers are to trust the captain and the engineers. But when the masses obtain, and feel that they have obtained, the sovereignty of the country, this acquiescence can no longer be counted on. Men without the requisite knowledge or training, men who, to revert to our illustration, know no more than that steam acts by expansion and that a motion in straight lines has to be turned into a rotary one, men who are not even aware of the need for knowledge and training, men with little respect for precedents, and little capacity for understanding their bearing, may take command of engines and ship: and the representative assembly may be filled by those who have no sense of the dangers to which an abuse of the vast powers of the assembly may lead. If such a change arrives, it imposes a severe strain on the constitution; and that elasticity which has been its merit may prove its danger.

It may accordingly be said that one of three conditions is generally necessary for the salvation of a Flexible Constitution. Either (1) the supremacy must remain in the hands of a politically educated and politically upright minority, or (2) the bulk of the people must be continuously and not fitfully interested in and familiar with politics, or (3) the bulk of the people, though legally supreme, must remain content, while prescribing certain general principles, to let the trained minority manage the details of the business of governing. Of these conditions the first has disappeared from nearly all civilized countries. The second has always been rare, and in large industrial countries is at present unattainable. The best chance of success is therefore to be found in the presence of the third; but it needs to be accompanied by a tone and taste and sense of public honour among the people which will recoil from the mere demagogue.

Both the influence of its constitution upon a nation and the need of certain qualities in order to work a Flexible Constitution are well illustrated in the history of the Roman commonwealth. Of all famous constitutions it was the most flexible. It lived long and overcame many perils because it grew up among a people who possessed in an eminent degree the three qualities of legalmindedness, of conservatism, and of keen practical intelligence. It trained the national mind to a respect for order and legality, and had doubtless much to do with the forming of that constructive genius which created the whole system of Roman private law. It fell at last because the mass of the citizens became unfit to discharge their function in the scheme. They did not, it is true, press into the inner circle of the governing class. The success first of the well-born and then of the rich in keeping the offices in their own hands all through is one of the most remarkable features of Roman history. But they were corrupt and reckless in the bestowal of power, and had really ceased to care for the freedom and welfare of the State. The ruling classes, on the other hand, were tempted by the demoralization of the masses to be their corrupters, and lost their old respect for legality. Even a conscientious philosopher like Cicero did not scruple to put prisoners to death without trial, and to justify himself by citing an act of lawless violence done four centuries before. The leading Romans of that day were as fit as ever to work the system, so far as skill and knowledge went, but they had not the old regard for its principles, nor the old sense of public duty; and the prizes which office offered now that Rome was mistress of the world were too huge for average virtue to resist. The moral forces which had enabled the Roman Constitution to work in spite of its extraordinary complexity, and to live, in spite of the risks to which its own nature exposed it, were now fatally enfeebled. These abuses of power on the one hand, and on the other hand the deadlocks which the system of checks caused, grew more frequent and serious. Each successive wrench which the machine received became more violent, because neither faction had patriotism enough to try to ease them off, and so break the force of the shock. From the beginning of the Republic the chief danger had lain in the immense powers vested in the magistrates. These powers had been necessary, because the State was constantly exposed to attacks from without; and nothing but the sense of devotion to the interests of the State had controlled the party spirit which rages more fiercely within the walls of a city than it does in a large and scattered community. Now that Rome had vast dominions to rule, and now that her frontiers extended to the very verge of civilization, involving her in long wars with great monarchies or groups of tribes on those frontiers, large powers had to be entrusted to military chiefs, and entrusted for long periods. Thus the Republican constitution fell through the very faults which had always lain deep in its bosom, though an over-mastering patriotism had in earlier days kept them harmless.

It is never easy, in studying the history of an institution, to determine how much of its success or its failure is due to its own character, how much to the conditions, external and domestic, in the midst of which it has to work. The fortunes of the Roman Constitution would doubtless have been different had Rome been less pressed by foreign enemies in her earlier days, or had she been less of a conquering power in her later. So too it is hard to compare States so different as Rome— whose Constitution was always that of a City, and failed to widen itself so as to become a Constitution for Italy—

and England, whose Constitution has always since the
days of Ecghbert and Alfred been that of a large and
originally a rural and scattered community. If, however,
the comparison is attempted, we may observe that England never, after the fourteenth century, recognized
such vast powers in the Crown (whether in the Crown
personally or as exercised by its Ministers) as Rome
granted to her magistrates. In the sphere of public
law England has applied more successfully than Rome
did the conception of the inviolability of the rights of
the citizen as against the organs of the State, although
that conception is itself Roman. With all their legal
genius the Romans were too much penetrated by the
idea of the necessary amplitude of State power to fix
just limits to the action of the Executive. When it was
necessary to provide for checking a magistrate, they set
up another magistrate to do it, instead of limiting magis-
terial powers by statute. Nor did they ever succeed as
the English have done in disengaging the judicial from
the executive department of government. In both these
respects part of the merits of the English Constitution
may be ascribed to Norman feudalism, whose precise
definition of the respective rights of lord and vassal—all
the lords but one being also vassals, and the greater
vassals being also lords—helped to form and imprint deep
the idea that powers, however strong within a definite
sphere, may be strictly confined to that sphere, and that
the limits of the sphere are fit matter for judicial determination. Perhaps the existence in the clergy of a large
class of men enjoying specific immunities the exact
range of which had to be settled, and, where possible,
judicially settled, may have also contributed to train this
habit of mind. The extent to which England, favoured
no doubt by her insular position, was able to secure
domestic freedom while leaving a large discretionary
authority to the Crown, is usually credited to the rise
of the House of Commons and the vigilance of its control. But much is also to be ascribed to that precise

definition of the rights of the individual which has made life and property secure from injury on the part of the State, to the habit of holding officials liable for acts done in excess of their functions, and to that ultimate detachment of the judiciary from the influence of the Crown which has enabled the individual to secure by legal process the enforcement of his rights. These principles have sunk deep into the mind of the nation, and have been of the utmost service in forming the habits of thought and action by which free constitutions have to be worked. They are just as strong as if they were embodied in a Rigid Constitution, instead of being legally at the mercy of Parliament. But that is because they have centuries of tradition behind them, and because the English are a people who respect tradition and have been trained to appreciate the value of the principles which their ancestors established.

VIII. Capacity of Constitutions for Territorial Expansion.

One point more remains to be mentioned before we quit constitutions of the Flexible type, viz. their suitability to a State which is expanding its territory and taking in other communities whether by conquest or by treaty.

Such constitutions seem especially well suited to countries which are passing through periods of change, whether internal or external. When new classes of the population have to be admitted to share in political power, or when the inhabitants of newly-acquired territories have to be taken in as citizens, this is most quickly and easily effected by the action of the ordinary legislature. Both Rome and England availed themselves of this flexibility in the earlier stages of their growth. England, itself created as a State by the expansion of the West Saxons, enlarged herself to include Wales with no disturbance of her former Constitution, and similarly fused herself with Scotland in 1707 and with Ireland in 1800, in both cases altering the Constitution of the enlarged State no further than by the admission of additional members to the two Houses of Parliament, and by the suppression of certain offices in the smaller kingdoms. The ease with which the earlier expansions were effected may be attributed to the fact that in mediaeval times the prominence of the king made the submission of any tribe or territory to him carry with it the incorporation of that tribe or territory into his former dominions. The popular assembly of a community, such as were the South Saxons, for instance, sank into a secondary place as soon as the king was head of the South Saxons as well as of the West Saxons, for the council of the united people which he summoned and over which he presided became the national assembly for all his subjects. In later times, though Scotland and Ireland had their separate Parliaments, these could be readily united with that of England, because in all three countries the popular House was representative. Here, however, England has stopped. The vast dominions which she possesses beyond the oceans, while legally subject to her Crown and Parliament, have not been brought into the constitutional scheme of the motherland. Indeed they could hardly be brought in without a reconstruction of the present frame of government, which would probably have to be effected by the establishment of a Rigid Constitution.

Similarly the Roman State had its first beginnings in the union of neighbouring tribes, whose popular assemblies coalesced into one assembly. As time went on, the flexibility of the constitution permitted the extension of political rights to a number of communities which had lain outside the old Roman territory. But the process presently stopped (so far as effective political expansion was concerned), because the representative system had not yet been invented. When after the great revolt of the Allies in B. C. 90 Rome was compelled to grant full citizenship to a large number of Italian communities, she did not take what moderns might think the obvious course of creating a representative assembly to which these allied communities might send elected delegates, but merely distributed the new citizens among her old tribes, an expedient which so far improved the position of the Allies that they became legally equal to Roman citizens, and acquired thereby various privileges and exemptions, but which extended to them practically no share in the government, since few could not come to Rome to give their votes in the assembly of the people. It may well have been that neither the oligarchs nor the leaders of the so-called popular party at Rome were willing to resign a substantial part of the power of the inhabitants of the City, with the opportunities of bribing and being bribed, in exchange for the primacy of a Federal or quasi-Federal Italian republic. But that the notion of a representative assembly had not crossed men's minds appears from the circumstance that the Italian Allies themselves, when in the course of their struggle they set up a rival government, merely reproduced the general lines of the Roman constitution, and did not create any representative council, excellently as it might have served their purpose. So strong was the influence of the idea of the city community in the ancient world, and (it may be added) so little power of invention do mankind display in the sphere of political institutions.

When an expanding State absorbs by way of treaty other communities already enjoying a government more or less constitutional, the process now usually takes the form of creating a Federation, and a Federation almost necessarily implies a Rigid Constitution. Cases where the Flexible Constitution of one State is stretched to take in another (as the Constitution of England was stretched to take in Scotland) are rare. The ancient Romano-Germanic Empire had a Flexible Constitution, which, already in an advanced stage of decay, was extinguished by Napoleon. When it was desired to reestablish a German Empire out of a number of practically independent States, this had to be done by the creation of a federal system under a Rigid Constitution. No similar device was required in the case of Italy, because the communities which united themselves to the kingdom of Sardinia between 1859 and 1871 had not theretofore enjoyed constitutional government, had just dismissed their whilome sovereigns, were all eager for union, and in their eagerness for union cared but little for the maintenance of any local rights.

IX. THE ORIGIN OF RIGID CONSTITUTIONS.

We may now pass on to examine the other type of constitution, that for which I have suggested the name Rigid, the specific character whereof resides in the fact that every constitution belonging to it enjoys an authority superior to the authority of the other laws of the State, and can be changed only by a method different from that whereby those other laws are enacted or repealed. This type is younger than the Flexible type. The latter goes back to the very beginning of organized political societies, being the first form which the organization of such societies took. Rigid Constitutions, on the other hand, mark a comparatively advanced stage in political development, when the idea of separating fundamental laws from other laws has grown familiar, and when considerable experience in the business of government and in political affairs generally has been accumulated. Thus they have during the last hundred years been far more in favour than constitutions of the Flexible type.

In Europe they exist in every constitutional country except the United Kingdom, Hungary, and Italy. There are none in the Asiatic continent, but Asia, the cradle of civilization, possesses no constitutional self-governing State whatever, except Japan, the Constitution of which, established in 1889, bears some resemblance to that of the German Empire. America, as a new continent, is appropriately full of them. The Republic of the United States has not only presented the most remarkable instance of this type in the modern world, but has by its success become a pattern which other republics have imitated, just as most modern States in the Old World took England for their model when they established, during the nineteenth century, governments more or less free. The Constitutions of all the forty-five States of the Union are Rigid, being not alterable by the legislatures of those States respectively. This is also true of the Constitution of the Dominion of Canada, which is alterable only by the Imperial Parliament. The Constitutions of the seven Canadian Provinces might, so far as their legislatures are concerned, be deemed Flexible, being (except as respects the office of Lieutenant-Governor) alterable by ordinary provincial statutes, but as all Provincial statutes are subject to a Dominion veto, they are not within the sole power of the legislatures. Mexico and the five republics of Central America, together with the nine republics of South America, have all adopted Constitutions which their legislatures have not received power to change. Africa is the most backward of the continents, but she has in the Orange Free State a tiny republic living under a Rigid Constitution. It has been contended that the Constitution of the South African Republic (Transvaal) is referable to the same category, but it is really *de iure,* and it has always been treated *de facto,* as being a Flexible Constitution [1]. The Constitutions of the Australasian colonies present legal questions of some difficulty, owing to the way in which the imperial Acts creating or confirming them have been drawn. So far as the method of changing these Constitutions has been prescribed by statutes of the colonies in which they exist, it would appear that each can also be changed by the legislature of the colony. Where those methods, however, are prescribed by the British Parliament, or by

[1] See Essay VII, p. 378.

instruments issuing from the Crown, the point is more
doubtful, and would need a fuller discussion than it can
receive here. Questions, however, touching the relations of a legally subordinate to a legally supreme legislature lie in a different plane, so to speak, from that with
which we are here concerned: and we may say that if
these colonial constitutions are regarded solely as respects the legislatures of the colonies themselves, they
are referable to the Flexible type. As to the new Federal
Constitution of Australia there is no doubt at all. It is
Rigid [1], for any alteration in it requires a majority of the
States and a majority of the direct popular vote. All the
acts of every British colony are subject to a power of
disallowance by the Governor or the Crown, but (although it is sometimes provided that constitutional acts
shall be 'reserved' for the pleasure of the Crown) this
power is not confined to acts changing the constitution,
conformably to the English habit of drawing little distinction between constitutional and other enactments.

All the above-mentioned constitutions are products of
the last century and a quarter, and it is doubtful whether
there existed in A. D. 1776 any independent State the
constitution of which the ruling authority of that State
could not have changed in the same way in which it
changed its ordinary laws. The Swiss Confederation
does not come into question, for that Confederation was,
until the French laid hands on it in the last years of the
eighteenth century, a League of States rather than a
State, and could not be said to have any constitution in
the proper sense, not to add that the republics of which
the league consisted could alter the terms of their league
in the same way in which they had formed it. The same
remark applies to the confederation of the seven United
Provinces of the Netherlands.

The beginnings of Rigid Constitutions may, however,

[1] See as to this Constitution Essay VIII, p. 391. As to the Constitutions of the
several Australian and other British colonies, reference may be made to the book
of the late Sir Henry Jenkyns, entitled *British Rule and Jurisdiction beyond the
Seas*, the publication of which is announced for a very early date.

be traced back to the seventeenth century. The first settlers in the British colonies in North America lived under governments created by royal charters which the colonial legislatures could not alter, and thus the idea of an instrument superior to the legislature and to the laws it passed became familiar [1]. In one colony (Connecticut) the settlers drew up for themselves in 1638 a set of rules for their government, called the Fundamental Orders. These Orders, developed subsequently into a royal charter, were really a rudimentary constitution. And almost contemporaneously the conception appeared in England during the Civil War. The Agreement of the People, presented to the Long Parliament in 1647, contains in outline a Frame of Government for England which was meant to stand above Parliament and be not changeable by it. So Oliver Cromwell sought by his Instrument of Government, promulgated in 1653, to create a Rigid Constitution, some at least of whose provisions were to be placed beyond the reach of Parliament, and indeed apparently to be altogether unchangeable. But his own Parliament refused to recognize any part of it as outside their right of interference [2].

From this rapid geographical survey we may now return to examine the circumstances under which constitutions of this type arise. Their establishment is usually due to one or more of the four following motives :—

(1) The desire of the citizens, that is to say, of the part of the population which enjoys political rights, to secure their own rights when threatened, and to restrain the action of their ruler or rulers.

(2) The desire of the citizens, or of a ruler who wishes to please the citizens, to set out the form of the pre-existing system of government in definite and positive terms precluding further controversy regarding it.

---

[1] Observations on this topic may be found in the author's *American Commonwealth*, chap. xxxvii.

[2] These documents are printed in Dr. S. R. Gardiner's *Constitutional Documents of the Puritan Revolution*. A concise account of the Instrument may be found in Mr. Goldwin Smith's *United Kingdom*, vol. i. pp. 605-8.

(3) The desire of those who are erecting a new political community to embody the scheme of polity under which they propose to be governed, in an instrument which shall secure its permanence and make it comprehensible by the people.

(4) The desire of separate communities, or of distinct groups or sections within a large (and probably loosely united) community, to settle and set forth the terms under which their respective rights and interests are to be safe-guarded, and effective joint action in common matters secured, through one government.

Of these four cases, the two former arise where an existing State changes its constitution. The two latter arise where a new State is created by the gathering of individuals into a community, or by the union of communities previously more or less separate into one larger community, as for instance by the forming of a Federation.

Note further that Rigid Constitutions arise in some one of four possible ways.

1. They may be given by a monarch to his subjects in order to pledge himself and his successors to govern in a regular and constitutional manner, avoiding former abuses. Several modern European constitutions have thus come into being, of which that of the Kingdom of Prussia, granted by King Frederick William the Fourth in 1850, is a familiar example. The *Statuto* or Fundamental Law of the Kingdom of Sardinia, now expanded into the Kingdom of Italy, was at one time deemed another instance. It is now, however, held to be a Flexible Constitution. Magna Charta would have been a fragment of such a constitution had it been legally placed out of the possibility of any change being made in it by the Great Council, then the supreme legislature of England, but it was enacted by the king in his Great Council, and has always been alterable by the same authority. The *Charte Constitutionnelle* for France issued by Louis the Eighteenth in 1814, and renewed in an

altered form on the choice of Louis Philippe as king in
1830, and the Constitutions granted by their respective
kings to Spain and to Portugal, are similar instances.

2. They may be created by a nation for itself when
it has thrown off (or been released from) its old form of
government, and desires to create another entirely *de
novo*. The various Constitutions of the various French
Republics from 1790 downwards are instances, as is the
Constitution of the Orange Free State [1] and the present
(A. D. 1901) Constitution of Brazil. To this category also
belong the Constitutions of the original thirteen States
of the American Union. Two of these States, however,
were content to retain the substance of the charter-con-
stitutions under which they had lived as British Colonies,
merely turning them into State constitutions, with nothing but the Confederation above them, that Confederation being then a mere League and not a National
Government. The Constitution of the Austrian part of
the Austro-Hungarian monarchy may also be referred to
this category. It consists of five Fundamental Laws,
enacted in 1867, and alterable by the legislature only
in a specially prescribed manner.

3. They may be created by a new community, not
theretofore a nation, when it deliberately and formally
enters upon organized political life as a self-governing
State, whether or no as also a member of any larger
political body. Such are the Constitutions of the States
of the American Union formed since 1790. Such was
the original Constitution of Belgium, a country which
had been previously a part of the Kingdom of Holland.
Such is the Constitution of the Dominion of Canada,
though it is a peculiar feature of this instrument—and
the same is true of the Constitutions of all the self-
governing British Colonies—that it has been created
not by the community which it regulates but by an
external authority, that of the Parliament of the United
Kingdom, in a statute of A. D. 1867. Being unchange-

[1] See Essay VII, p. 361.

able by the Dominion Legislature, it is a Rigid Constitution within the terms of our definition, although changeable, like any other statute, by the British Parliament. The new Federal Constitution of Australia belongs to the same class and had a like origin [1].

4. They may arise by the tightening of a looser tie which has theretofore existed between various self-governing communities. When external dangers or economic interests have led such communities to desire a closer union than treaties or federative agreements have previously created, such communities may unite themselves into one nation, and give that new nation a government by means of an instrument which is thereafter not only to hold them together but to provide for their action as a single body. This process of turning a League of States (*Staatenbund*) into a Federal State (*Bundesstaat*) is practically certain to create a Rigid Constitution, for the component communities which are so uniting will of course desire that the rights of each shall be safeguarded by interposing obstacles and delays to any action tending to change the terms of their union, and they will therefore place the constitution out of the reach of amendment by the ordinary legislature. Cases may, however, be imagined in which the component communities might be willing to forego this safeguard. The Achaean League did so; and its constitution was therefore a flexible one, but then the Achaean League can hardly be said to have been a single State in the strict sense of the word. It was rather a league, though a close league, of States, like the Swiss Confederation in the eighteenth century.

The most familiar instances of this fourth kind of origin are the United States of North America, the Federation of Mexico (unless it be referred to the second class), and the present Swiss Confederation. To this

[1] As to this Constitution see Essay VIII. Unlike the Constitution of Canada, it can be amended by the people of Australia without the aid of the Imperial Parliament.

class may also be referred the very peculiar case of the new German Empire, which by two steps, in 1866 and in 1871, has created itself out of the pre-existing Germanic Confederation of 1815, that Confederation having been formed by the decay into fragments of the ancient East Frankish or German kingdom, which had, throughout the Middle Ages, a Flexible Constitution resembling that of the England or France or Castile of the thirteenth century.

X. The Enactment and Amendment of Rigid Constitutions.

Before proceeding to consider the methods by which these constitutions may be enacted and changed, it is worth while to suggest an explanation of their compara-tive recent appearance in history. Documentary consti-tutions, *i.e.* those contained in one or several instruments prepared for the purpose, are old. There were many of them in the Greek cities; and efforts were some-times made when they were enacted to secure their permanence by declaring them to be unchangeable. But in the old days when City States (and sometimes also small Rural States) were ruled by Primary Assemblies, consisting of all free citizens, there was no authority higher than the legislature that could be found to enact a constitution, seeing that the legislature consisted of the whole body of the citizens. In those days, accordingly, when it was decided to give peculiar permanence to some political arrangement, so that no subsequent assembly of the people should upset it, two expedients were re-sorted to. One was to make all the leading men, perhaps the whole people, swear solemnly to maintain it, and thereby to bring in the deities of the States as co-enact-ing or at least protecting and guaranteeing parties. Tradition attributed this expedient to Lycurgus at Sparta. The other was to provide in the law intended to be Fundamental that no proposal to repeal it should ever be entertained, or to declare a heavy penalty on the audacious man who should make the proposal. The objection to both these expedients was that they debarred any amendment, however desirable, and however generally desired. Hence they were in practice little regarded, though the exceptionally pious or superstitious Spartans were deemed to be largely deterred from governmental changes by the fear of divine disapproval. Moreover, the second of the above-named devices or barriers could be easily turned by proposing to repeal, not the Fundamental law itself, but the prohibition and the penalty. These having been repealed—and of course the proposal would not be made unless its success were pretty well assured—the Fundamental Law would then itself be forthwith repealed. It must, however, be added that even if the Greek cities had adopted what seems to us the obvious plan of requiring a certain majority of votes (say two-thirds) for a change in the Fundamental Law, or had required it to be passed by four Assemblies in succession at intervals of three months, one may doubt whether such provisions would have restrained a majority in communities which were small, excitable, and seldom legally-minded.

Those who have suggested that the United Kingdom ought to embody certain parts of what we call the British Constitution in a Fundamental Statute (or Statutes) and to declare such a statute unchangeable by Parliament, or by Parliament acting under its ordinary forms, seem to forget that the Act declaring the Fundamental Statute to be Fundamental and unchangeable by Parliament would itself be an Act like any other Act, and could be repealed by another ordinary statute in the ordinary way. All that this contrivance would obtain would be to interpose an additional stage in the process of abolition or amendment, and to call the attention both of the people and the legislature in an emphatic way to the fact that a very solemn decision was being reversed. Some may think that such a security, if imperfect, would be worth having. The restraint imposed would, however, be a moral not a legal one [1].

A constitution placed out of the power of the legislature may or may not be susceptible of alteration in a legal manner. Sometimes no provision has been made, when it was first established, for any change whatever. There are instances of this among constitutions granted by a monarch to his subjects—such seems to be to-day the case in Spain—but in cases of this kind it might possibly be held that the grantor implicitly reserved the power to vary his grant, as there may not have been expressed in the document, and need not be, any bilateral obligation. As already observed, the Constitution of the present Kingdom of Italy was originally granted to the Kingdom of Sardinia by King Charles Albert in 1848; and it was for a long time held that the power to change it resided in the Crown only. It was extended by a succession of popular votes (1859 to 1871) to the rest of Italy, and some conceive that this sanction makes at least its fundamental parts unchangeable. But the view that it is alterable by legislation has prevailed, and it has in fact been so altered in some points. The *Charte Constitutionnelle* granted by Louis XVIII, under which the government of France was carried on for many years,

---

[1] Soon after the above lines were written, the point they deal with came up in Parliament in a practical form. In the debate on the Irish Home Rule Bill of 1886 the question emerged whether Parliament could in constituting a legislature for Ireland and assigning to that legislature a certain sphere of action legally debar itself from recalling its grant or from legislating, upon matters falling within that sphere, over the head of the Irish legislature. It was generally agreed by lawyers that Parliament could not so limit its own powers, and that no statute it might pass could be made unchangeable, or indeed could in any way restrict the powers of future Parliaments.

Upon the general question whether Parliament could so enact any new Constitution for the United Kingdom as to debar itself from subsequently repealing that Constitution, it may be suggested, for the consideration of those who relish technicalities, that Parliament could, if so disposed, divest itself of its present authority by a sort of suicide, *i.e.* by repealing all the statutes under which it is now summoned, and abolishing the common-law right of the Crown to summon it, and thereupon causing itself to be forthwith dissolved, having of course first provided means for summoning such an assembly, or assemblies, as the new Constitution created. There would then be no legal means of summoning another Parliament of the old kind, and the new Constitution, whatever it was, would therefore not be liable to be altered save in such manner as its own terms provided.

was intended to create a sort of parliamentary government, in the first instance by way of gift from the sovereign, but afterwards, under Louis Philippe, by way of a compact, or kind of covenant between monarch and people. The fact that it contained no provisions for alteration, having apparently been designed to last for ever, worked against it; and the discontents of France may have ripened the faster because no constitutional method had been provided for appeasing them by changes in the machinery of government. Nothing human is immortal; and constitution-makers do well to remember that the less they presume on the long life of their work the longer it is likely to live.

The Constitutions of Norway (created in 1814, but subsequently altered) and of Greece (created in 1864) declare that amendments are to be confined to matters not fundamental, but omit to specify the matters falling under that description.

The existing Constitution of France is so far legally unalterable that no proposition for abolishing the republican form of government can be entertained. If it be asked, What is a republican form? one may answer that if ever the question has to be answered, it will be not so much by the *via iuris* as by the *via facti*. So also the Constitution of the United States is in one respect virtually, if not technically, unchangeable. No State can without its own consent be deprived of its equal representation in the Senate. As no State is ever likely to consent to such a change, the change may be deemed legally unattainable; and that any State against which it was attempted to enforce a reduction of its representation effected by constitutional amendments to which it had refused assent would be legally justified in considering itself out of the Union. In accordance with this American precedent, the new Constitution of Australia declares that no State can have its proportionate representation in the Parliament, or the minimum number of its representatives in the House of

12

Representatives, reduced without the approval of a majority·of its electors voting on a constitutional amendment [1].

Among the methods by which constitutions of the Rigid type make, as they now almost invariably do, provision for their own amendment, four deserve to be enumerated.

The first is to give the function to the Legislature, but under conditions which oblige it to act in a special way, different from that by which ordinary statutes are passed. There may, for instance, be required a fixed quorum of members for the consideration of amendments. Belgium fixes this quorum at two-thirds of each House, while also requiring a two-thirds majority of each House for a change. Bavaria requires a quorum of three-fourths of the members of each House; Rumania one of two-thirds. Or again—and this is a very frequent provision, found even when that last-mentioned is wanting—a specified minimum majority of votes may be required to carry an amendment. Sometimes this majority is three-fourths (as in Greece and Saxony, and in the German Empire for a vote of the Federal Council): more frequently it is two-thirds, as in the United States Congress, in the Mexican Chambers, in Norway, Belgium, Rumania, Servia, Bulgaria. Another plan is to require a dissolution of the Legislature, so that the amendments carried in one session may come under the judgement of the electors at a general election, and be thereafter passed, or rejected, by the newly chosen Legislature. This arrangement, often combined with the two-thirds majority rule, prevails in Holland, Norway, Rumania, Portugal, Iceland, Sweden (where the amendment must have been passed in two ordinary successive sessions), and several other States, including some of the republics of Spanish America. It is in substance an appeal to the people as well as to their representatives, and therefore adds a further guarantee against hasty change. Finally,

[1] See Essay VIII.

the two Houses of the Legislature may sit together as a Constituent Assembly. Thus in France (Constitution of 1875) when each Chamber has resolved that the Constitution shall be revised, the two are for the moment fused, and proceed to debate and pass amendments. Haiti (Constitution of 1899) has a similar plan, which, oddly enough, was not borrowed from France, but is as old as 1843. Few will suspect France of borrowing from Haiti.

A second plan is to create a special body for the work of revision. In the United States, where a vast deal of constitution making and revising goes on in the several States, such a body is called a Convention, and is usually elected when it is desired to re-draft the whole constitution, the ultimate approval of the draft being, however, almost always reserved for the people [1]. In Servia and Bulgaria, after amendments have been twice passed by the ordinary Legislature, a sort of Special Assembly, similarly elected, but twice as large, called the Great Skuptschina (in Servia) or Great Sobranje (in Bulgaria), receives and finally decides on the proposed amendments.

The republics of Paraguay, Guatemala, Honduras, Nicaragua, and Salvador also prescribe Conventions, preceded in each case by votes of the Legislature, such votes usually requiring a two-thirds majority [2].

A third plan is to refer the new constitution, or the amendments proposed (if the revision is partial), to a number of minor or local authorities for approval. This course is an obviously suitable one in a federation, and has accordingly been adopted by the United States, by Mexico, by Colombia, by Switzerland, and by the new

---

[1] But the Constitution of Mississippi of 1890 was enacted by a Convention only and never submitted to the people. See as to the United States the author's *American Commonwealth*, ch. xxxvii.

[2] On the whole subject of the modes of amending constitutions reference may be made to the valuable book of my friend M. Charles Borgeaud, Professor at Geneva, *Établissement et Revision des Constitutions*. See also Dareste, *Les Constitutions Modernes*. I owe to these books, and especially to the former, most of the facts here given regarding the minor States.

Australian Commonwealth, in all of which the component States are consulted, the United States requiring a three-fourths majority of States, Switzerland, Australia, and Mexico a bare majority. (Switzerland and Australia also require a majority of the citizens generally.) It is not, however, invariable in federal countries, for the Argentine Confederation entrusts amendment to a Convention, following on a three-fourths majority vote of the Legislature, and Brazil (now a federal country) leaves it to the Legislature alone, acting by a two-thirds majority in three successive debates. Neither is such a plan necessarily confined to a federation, for the existing Constitution of Massachusetts was (in 1780) submitted to the Towns (*i.e.* townships) of the State, acting as communities, and enacted by the majority of them.

The fourth plan is to refer amendments to the direct vote of the people. Originating in the New England States of America, where democracy earliest prevailed, this method has spread to Switzerland and to Australia, both of which require for alterations in the Fundamental Instrument a majority of the electors voting as well as a majority of the States. It prevails now not only in these two federations, but also in the several States of the United States (with very rare exceptions). A bare majority of votes is sufficient, except in Rhode Island, where three-fifths are required, and in Indiana and Oregon, which require a majority of all the qualified voters. The popular vote is also in use in the several Cantons of Switzerland. It was repeatedly employed in France during the first Revolution, and again (under the name of *plébiscite*) by Louis Napoleon under the Second Empire.

These variations in the mode of amending are interesting enough to deserve a few comments.

Broadly speaking, two methods of amendment are most in use: that which gives the function to the Legislature, usually requiring something more than a bare majority, and that which gives it to the People, *i.e.* the qualified voters. The former of these methods often directs a dissolution of the Legislature to precede the final vote on amendments, and in this way secures for the people a means of delivering their judgement on the questions at issue. The latter method is, however, a more distinct and emphatic, because a more direct, recognition of Popular Sovereignty; and it has the advantage of making the constitution appear to be the work of the Nation as a whole, apart from faction, whereas in the Legislature it may have been by a party vote that the amendments have been carried. Thus it supplies the broadest and firmest basis on which a Frame of Government can rest. The Convention system is intermediate between the two others, and has struck no deep roots in the Old World, while in the United States it has been virtually superseded (as respects enactment) by that of the direct Popular Vote.

Geographically regarded, the method of revision by Legislature prevails over Europe and over most of Spanish America (being in the latter region sometimes combined with the Convention method). The Constitution which has most influenced others in Europe and become a type for them in this respect is that of Holland (1814), because it was the earliest one established after the revolutionary period. On the other hand, the United States (except the Federal Government) and the democratic governments of the Swiss and Australian Federations are ruled by the Popular method. The Constitution which has set the type of this method is that of Massachusetts of 1780.

As respects facility of change, it is interesting to note that the Constitutions which are most quickly and easily altered are those of Prussia, which prescribes no safeguard save that of two successive votes separated by an interval of at least twenty-one days, and that of France, which requires an absolute majority of each House for a proposal to revise, and an absolute majority of the two Houses sitting together for the carrying of any amendment. The omission of the French Chambers in 1875 to submit to the people the constitution then framed, or to provide for their sanction to any future amendments, was due to the doubt which each party felt of the result of an appeal to the nation. The Republicans, though able to prevent the establishment of a monarchical constitution by the Legislature, were not quite sure that a republican one would be carried if submitted to a popular vote. Thus it has come about that France, which went further towards popular sovereignty in 1793 than any great country has ever done, has lived since 1875 under an instrument never ratified by the people, and which was originally regarded as purely provisional.

The Constitution which it is most difficult to change is that of the United States. It has in fact never been amended since 1809, except thrice between 1865 and 1870, immediately after and in consequence of the Civil War, and then under conditions entirely abnormal, because some States were under military duress.

The tendency of recent years has been towards easier and swifter methods than those which were in favour during the first half of the nineteenth century: and in Germany lawyers and publicists are now disposed to minimize the difference between constitutional changes and ordinary statutes, partly perhaps because doctrines of popular sovereignty obtain little sympathy from the school dominant in the new Empire. That Empire itself presents quite peculiar phenomena. So far as the Reichstag or Federal Assembly is concerned, the constitution can be altered by ordinary legislation. But in the Federal Council a majority is required large enough to enable either Prussia on the one hand or a combination of the smaller States on the other to prevent any change. This is because the component members of the Federation are not republics, as in America, Switzerland, and Australia, but are (except the three Hanse cities) monarchies, so that the Upper Federal House represents not the people but the governments of the several German States.

It is evident that the greater or less stability of any given constitution will (other things being equal) be determined by the comparative difficulty or ease of carrying changes in one or other of the above methods. As one at least of them, that of committing the function of revision to a Constitutional Convention not followed by a popular vote, seems to interpose no more, and possibly even less, difficulty or delay than does the ordinary process of law-making by a two-chambered legislature, it may be asked why a constitution changeable in such a way should be called Rigid at all. Because inasmuch as the method of changing it is different from that of passing ordinary statutes, the people are led to realize the importance of the occasion, and may be deterred, by the trouble and formalities involved in creating the special body, from too lightly or frequently tampering with their fundamental laws. It seems a more momentous step to create this convention *ad hoc* than to carry a measure through a legislature which already exists, and is daily employed on legislative work. Experience has, moreover, shown in the United States, the country in which this method has been largely used for redrafting, or preparing amendments to, the Constitutions of the several States [1], that a set of men can be found for the work of a Convention better than those who form the ordinary legislature of the State, and that their proceedings when assembled excite more attention and evoke more discussion than do those of a State Legislature, a body which now receives little respect, though perhaps as much as it deserves. Nowadays, however, a draft constitution prepared by a Convention is in an American State almost always submitted to the people for their approval.

---

[1] No Constitutional Convention has ever been held for revising the Federal Constitution of 1787-9, which was drafted by a Convention and adopted by the thirteen States in succession.

The French plan of using the two Houses sitting
together as a Constituent Convention has a certain interest for Englishmen, because the suggestion has been
made that disputes between their House of Lords and
House of Commons might be settled by a vote of both
sitting together, *i.e.* of the whole of the Great Council
of the Nation [1] as it sat in the thirteenth century before
it had formed the habit of debating and voting in two
Houses. It still meets (but does not debate or vote)
as one body when the Sovereign, or a Commission representing the Sovereign, is present, as happens at the
beginning and at the end of each session.

To examine the distinctive qualities of Rigid Constitutions, as I must now do, is virtually to traverse again
the same path which was followed in investigating those
of the Flexible type, for the points in which the latter
were found deficient are those in which Rigid Constitutions excel, while the merits of the Flexible indicate the
faults of the Rigid. The inquiry may, therefore, be brief.
    The two distinctive merits claimed for these Consti-
tutions are their Definiteness and their Stability.

XI. The Definiteness of Rigid Constitutions.

We have seen that the distinctive mark of these Rigid
Constitutions is their superiority to ordinary statutes.
They are not the work of the ordinary legislature, and
therefore cannot be changed by it. They are embodied
in one written document, or possibly in a few documents,
so that their provisions are ascertainable without doubt
by a reference to the documentary terms. This feature
is a legitimate consequence of the importance which belongs to a law placed above all other laws. That which

---

[1] This plan would have more chance of being favourably entertained were the
Upper House now, as it was in 1760, less than two hundred strong. As it is now
nearly as large as the House of Commons, with a majority of about fourteen to
one belonging to one political party, the party which is in a permanent minority
might feel that the chances are not equal.

is to be the sheet-anchor of the State, giving permanent shape to its political scheme, cannot be left unwritten, and cannot be left to be gathered from a comparison of a considerable number of documents which may be confused or inconsistent. Whether it spring from the agreement of the citizens or from the·free gift of a monarch, it must be embodied if possible in one, if not, at any rate in only a few solemn instruments. That which is to be a fundamental law, limiting the power of the legislature, must be set forth in specific and unmistakable terms—else how shall it be known when the legislature is infringing upon or violating it? A Flexible Constitution, which the legislature can modify or destroy at its pleasure, though it might conceivably be embodied in one document only, is in fact almost always to be collected from at least several documents, and is often, like the Flexible Constitution of England, scattered through a multitude of statutes and collections of precedents. But the benefits expected from a Rigid Constitution would be lost were its provisions left in similar confusion.

It is not, however, to be supposed that the citizen of a country controlled by a Rigid Constitution who desires to understand the full scope and nature of his government will find all that he needs in the document itself. No law ever was so written as to anticipate and cover all the cases that can possibly arise under it[1]. There will always be omissions, some left intentionally, because the points not specifically covered were deemed fitter for the legislature to deal with subsequently, some, again, because the framers of the constitution could not agree, or knew that the enacting authority would not agree, regarding them. Other omissions, unnoticed at the time, will be disclosed by the course of events, for questions are sure to arise which the imagination or foresight of those who prepared the constitution never contemplated. There will also be expressions whose meaning is ob-

---

[1] 'Neque leges neque senatus consulta ita scribi possunt, ut omnes casus qui quandoque inciderint comprehendantur.'—Iulianus in *Digest* i. 3, 10.

scure, and whose application to unforeseen cases will be found doubtful when those cases have to be dealt with. Here let us distinguish three classes of omissions or obscurities:—

The first class includes matters, passed over in silence by the written constitution, which cannot be deemed to have been left to be settled either by the legislature or by any other organ of government, because they are too large or grave, as for instance matters by dealing with which the legislature would disturb the balance of the constitution and encroach on the province of the Executive, or the Judiciary, or (in a Federal Government) of the component States. Matters belonging to this class can only be dealt with by an amendment of the constitution itself.

The second class includes gaps or omissions relating to matters not palpably outside the competence of the legislature as defined by the constitution. Here the proper course will be for the legislature to regulate such matters by statute, or else to leave them to be settled by the action of the several organs of government each acting within its own sphere. These organs may by such action create a body of usage which, when well settled, will practically supplement the defects of the constitution, as statutes will do in like manner, so far as they are passed to cover the omitted cases.

The third class consists not of omissions but of matters which are referred to by the constitution, but in terms whose meaning is doubtful. Here the question is what interpretation is to be given to its words by the authority entitled to interpret, that authority being in some countries the legislature, in others the judicial tribunals. To the subject of Interpretation I shall presently return. Meantime, it must be noted that both Legislation and Usage in filling up the vacant spaces in the constitution, and Interpretation in explaining its application to a series of new cases as they arise upon points not expressly covered by its words, expand and develop a constitution, and may make it after a long interval of time different from what it seemed to be to those who watched its infancy. The statutes, usages, and explanations aforesaid will in fact come to form a sort of fringe to the constitution, cohering with it, and possessing practically the same legal authority as its express words have. And it thus may happen that (as in the United States) a large mass of parasitic law grows up round the document or documents which contain the Constitution. Nevertheless there will still remain a distinction between this parasitic law and usage and the provisions of the constitution itself. The latter stand unchangeable, save by constitutional amendment. Statutes, on the other hand, can be changed by the legislature; usage may take a new direction; the decisions given interpreting the constitution may be recalled or varied by the authority that pronounced them. All these are in fact Flexible parasites growing upon a Rigid stem. Thus it will be seen that the apparent definiteness and simplicity of Documentary Constitutions may in any given case be largely qualified by the growth of a mass of quasi-constitutional matter which has to be known before the practical working of the constitution can be understood.

XII. The Stability of Rigid Constitutions.

The stability of a constitution is an object to be much desired both because it inspires a sense of security in the minds of the citizens, encouraging order, industry and thrift, and because it enables experience to be accumulated whereby the practical working of the constitution may be improved. Political institutions are under all circumstances difficult to work, and when they are frequently changed, the nation does not learn how to work them properly. Experiment is the soul of progress, but experiments must be allowed a certain measure of time. The plant will not grow if men frequently uncover the roots to see how they are striking. Constitutions embodied in one legal document and unchangeable by the legislature, are intended to be, and would seem likely to be, peculiarly durable. Being definite, they do not give that opening to small deviations and perversions likely to arise from the vagueness of a Flexible or 'unwritten' Constitution, or from the probable discrepancies between the different laws and traditions of which it consists. They may be battered down, but they cannot easily (save by a method to be presently examined) be undermined. When an attack is made upon them, whether by executive acts violating their provisions, or by the passing of statutes inconsistent with those provisions, such an attack can hardly escape observation. It is a plain notice to the defenders of the constitution to rally and to stir up the people by showing the mischief of an insidious change. The principles on which the government rests, being set forth in a broad and simple form, obtain a hold upon the mind of the community, which, if it has been accustomed to give those principles a general approval, will be unwilling to see them tampered with. Moreover the process prescribed for amendment interposes various delays and formalities before a change can be carried through, pending which the people can reconsider the issues involved, and recede, if they think fit, from projects that may have at first attracted them. Both in Switzerland and in the States of the American Union it has repeatedly happened that constitutional amendments prepared and approved by the legislature have been rejected by the people, not merely because the mass of the people are often more conservative than their representatives, or are less amenable to the pressure of particular 'interests' or sections of opinion, but because fuller discussion revealed objections whose weight had not been appreciated when the proposal first appeared. In these respects the Rigid Constitution has real elements of stability.

Nevertheless it may be really less stable than it appears, for there is in its rigidity an element of danger.

It has already been noted that a constitution of the Flexible type finds safety in the elasticity which enables it to be stretched to meet some passing emergency, and then to resume its prior shape, and that it may disarm revolution by meeting revolution half-way. This is just what the Rigid Constitution cannot do. It is constructed, if I may borrow a metaphor from mechanics, like an iron railway-bridge, built solidly to resist the greatest amount of pressure by wind or water that is likely to impinge upon it. If the materials are sound and the workmanship good, the bridge resists with apparent ease, and perhaps without showing signs of strain or displacement, up to the highest degree of pressure provided for. But when that degree has been passed, it may break suddenly and utterly to pieces, as the old Tay Bridge did under the storm of December, 1879. The fact that it is very strong and all knit tightly into one fabric, while enabling it to stand firm under small oscillations or disturbances, may aggravate great ones. For just as the whole bridge collapses together, so the Rigid Constitution, which has arrested various proposed changes, may be overthrown by a popular tempest which has gathered strength from the very fact that such changes were not and under the actual conditions of politics could not be made by way of amendment. When a party grows up clamouring for some reforms which can be effected only by changing the constitution, or when a question arises for dealing with which the constitution provides no means, then, if the constitution cannot be amended in the legal way, because the legally prescribed majority cannot be obtained, the discontent that was debarred from any legal outlet may find vent in a revolution or a civil war. The history of the Slavery question in the United States illustrates this danger on so grand a scale that no other illustration is needed. The Constitution of 1787, while recognizing the existence of slavery, left sundry questions, and in particular that of the extension of slavery into new territories and States, unsettled. Thirty years later these matters became a cause of strife, and after another thirty years this strife became so acute as to threaten the peace of the country. Both parties claimed that the Constitution was on their side. Had there been no Constitution embodied in an instrument difficult of change, or had it been practicable to amend the Constitution, so that the majority in Congress could have had, at an earlier stage, a free hand in dealing with the question, it is possible—though no one can say that it is certain—that the War of Secession might have been averted. So much may at any rate be noted that the Constitution, which was intended to hold the whole nation together, failed to do. There might no doubt in any case have been armed strife, as there was in England under its Flexible Constitution in 1641. But it is at least equally probable that the slave-holding party, which saw its hold on the government slipping away, hardened its heart because it held that it was the true exponent of the Constitution, and because the Constitution made compromise more difficult than it need have been in a country possessing a fully sovereign legislature.

Two opposing tendencies are always at work in countries ruled by these Constitutions, the one of which tends to strengthen, the other to weaken them. The first is the growth of the respect for the Constitution which increasing age brings. The remark is often made that if husband and wife do not positively dislike one another, and if their respective characters do not change under ill-health or misfortune, every year makes them like one another better. They may not have been warmly attached at first, but the memories of past efforts and hardships, as well as of past enjoyments, endear them more and more to one another, and even if jars and bickerings should unhappily recur from time to time, the strength of habit renders each necessary to the other, and makes that final severance which, at moments of exasperation, they may possibly have contemplated with equanimity, a severe blow when it arrives. So a nation, though not contented with its Constitution, and vexed by quarrels over parts of it, may grow fond of it simply because it has lived with it, has obtained a measure of prosperity under it, has perhaps been wont to flaunt its merits before other nations, and to toast it at public festivities. The magic of self-love and self-complacency turns even its meaner parts to gold, while imaginative reverence for the past lends it a higher sanction. This is one way in which Time may work. But Time also works against it, for Time, in changing the social and material condition of a people, makes the old political arrangements as they descend from one generation to another a less adequate expression of their political needs. Nobody now discusses the old problem of the Best Form of Government, because everybody now admits that the chief merit of any form is to be found in its suitability to the conditions and ideas of those among whom it prevails. Now if the conditions of a country change, if the balance of power among classes, the dominant ideas of reflective men, the distribution of wealth, the sources whence wealth flows, the duties expected from the administrative departments of government, all become different, while the form and constitutionally-prescribed methods of government remain unmodified, it is clear that flaws in the Constitution will be revealed which were previously unseen, and problems will arise with which its arrangements cannot cope. The remedy is of course to amend the Constitution. But that is just what may be impossible, because the requisite majority may be unattainable; and the opponents of amendment, entrenched behind the ramparts of an elaborate procedure, may succeed in averting changes which the safety of the community demands. The provisions that were meant to give security may now be dangerous, because they stand in the way of natural development.

Even where no strong party interest is involved it may be hard to pass the amendments needed. The history of the United States again supplies a case in point. Two defects in its Constitution are admitted by most political thinkers. One is the absence of power to establish a uniform law of marriage and divorce over the whole Union. The other is the method of conducting the election of a President, a method which in 1876 brought the country to the verge of civil war, and may every four years involve the gravest risks. Yet it has been found impossible to procure any amendment on either point, because an enormous force of united public opinion is needed to ensure the concurrence of two-thirds of both Houses of Congress and three-fourths of the States. The first of these two changes excites no sufficient interest among politicians to make them care to deal with it. The second is neglected, because no one has a clear view of what should be substituted, and neither party feels that it has more to gain than has the other by grappling with the problem.

A historical comparison of the two types as regards the smoothness of their working, and the consequent tendency of one or other to secure a quiet life to the State, yields few profitable results, because the circumstances of different nations are too dissimilar to enable close parallels to be drawn, and because much depends upon the skill with which the provisions of each particular instrument have been drawn and upon the greater or less particularity of those provisions. The present Constitution of France, for instance, is contained in two very short and simple documents, which determine only the general structure of the government, and are in size not one-twentieth of the Federal Constitution of Switzerland. Hence it follows that a far freer play is left to the legislature and executive in France than in Switzerland; and that these two authorities have in the former State more power of meeting any change in the conditions of the country, and also more power of doing harm by hasty and unwise action, than is permitted in the latter. As Adaptability is the characteristic merit and insecurity the characteristic defect of a Flexible Constitution, so the drawback which corresponds to the Durability of the Rigid is its smaller capacity for meeting the changes and chances of economic, social and political conditions. A provision strictly defining the structure of the government may prevent the evolution of a needed organ. A prohibition debarring the legislature from passing certain kinds of measures may prove unfortunate when a measure of that kind would be the proper remedy. Every security has its corresponding disadvantage.

XIII. The Interpretation of Rigid Constitutions.

A well-drawn Rigid Constitution will confine itself to essentials, and leave many details to be filled in subsequently by ordinary legislation and by usage. But (as already observed) even the best-drawn instrument is sure to have omitted some things which ought to have been expressly provided for, to have imposed restrictions which will prove inconvenient in practice, to contain provisions which turn out to be susceptible of different interpretations when cases occur raising a point to which the words of those provisions do not seem to be directly addressed. When any of these things happen, the authorities, legislative and executive, who have to work the Constitution find themselves in a difficulty. Steps seem called for which the Constitution either does not give power to do, or forbids to be done, or leaves in such doubt as to raise scruples and controversies. The authorities, or the nation itself, have then three alternative courses open to them. The first is to submit to the restrictions which the Constitution imposes, and abandon a contemplated course of action, though the public interest demands it. This is disagreeable, but if the case is not urgent, may be the best course, though it tends to the disparagement of the Constitution itself. The second course is to amend the Constitution: and it is obviously the proper one, if it be possible. But it may be practically

13

impossible, because the procedure for passing an amendment may be too slow, the need for action being urgent, or because the majority that can be secured for amendment, even if large, may be smaller than the Constitution prescribes. The only remaining expedient is that which is euphemistically called Extensive Interpretation, but may really amount to Evasion. Evasion, pernicious as it is, may give a slighter shock to public confidence than open violation, as some have argued that equivocation leaves a man's conscience less impaired for future use than does the telling of a downright falsehood. Cases occur in which the Executive or the Legislature profess to be acting under the Constitution, when in reality they are stretching it, or twisting it, *i.e.* are putting a forced construction upon its terms, and affecting to treat that as being lawful under its terms which the natural sense of the terms does not justify. The question follows whether such an evasion will be held legal, *i.e.* whether acts done in virtue of such a forced construction as aforesaid will be deemed constitutional, and will bind the citizens as being legally done. This will evidently depend on a matter we have not yet considered, but one of profound importance, viz. the authority in whom is lodged the right of interpreting a Rigid Constitution.

On this point there is a remarkable diversity of theory and practice between countries which follow the English and countries which follow the Roman law. The English attribute the right to the Judiciary. As a constitutional instrument is a law, distinguished from other laws only by its higher rank, principle suggests that it should, like other laws, be interpreted by the legal tribunals, the last word resting, as in other matters, with the final Court of Appeal. This principle of referring to the Courts all questions of legal interpretation may be said to be inherent in the English Common Law, and holds the field in all countries whose systems are built upon the foundation of that Common Law. In particular, it holds good in the United Kingdom and in the United States. As the British Parliament can alter any part of the British Constitution at pleasure, the principle is of secondary political importance in England, for when any really grave question arises on the construction of a constitutional law it is dealt with by legislation. However, the action of the Courts in construing the existing law is watched with the keenest interest when questions arise which the Legislature refuses to deal with, such, for instance, as those that affect the doctrine and discipline of the Established Church. So in the seventeenth century, when constitutional questions were at issue between the King and the House of Commons, which it was impossible to settle by statute, because the king would have refused consent to bills passed by the Commons, the power of the Judges to declare the rules of the ancient Constitution was of great significance. In the United States, where Congress cannot alter the Constitution, the function of the Judiciary to interpret the will of the people as set forth in the Constitution has attained its highest development. The framers of that Constitution perhaps scarcely realized what the effect of their arrangements would be. More than ten years passed before any case raised the point; and when the Supreme Court declared that an Act of Congress might be invalid because in excess of the power granted by the Constitution, some surprise and more anger were expressed. The reasoning on which the Court proceeded was, however, plainly sound, and the right was therefore soon admitted. Canada and Australia have followed the English doctrine, so the Bench has a weighty function under the constitutions of both those Federations.

On the European Continent a different view prevails, and the Legislature is held to be the judge of its own powers under the Constitution, so that no Court of law may question the authority of a statute passed in due form. Such is the rule in Switzerland. There, as in most parts of the European Continent, the separation of the Judiciary from the other two powers has been less complete than in England, and the deference to what Englishmen and Americans call the Rule of Law less profound. The control over governmental action which the right of interpretation implies seems to the Swiss too great, and too political in its nature, to be fit for a legal tribunal. It is therefore vested in the National Assembly, which when a question is raised as to the constitutionality of a Federal Statute or Executive Act, or as to the transgression of the Federal Constitution by a Cantonal Statute, is recognized as the authority competent to decide. The same doctrine seems to prevail in the German Empire, though the point is there not quite free from doubt, and also in the Austrian Monarchy, in France, and in Belgium. In the Orange Free State, living under Roman-Dutch law, the Bench, basing itself on American precedents, claimed the right of authoritative interpretation, but the Legislature hesitated to admit it.

American lawyers conceive that the strength and value of a Rigid Constitution are greatly reduced when the Legislature becomes the judge of its own powers, entitled after passing a statute which really transgresses the Constitution to declare that the Constitution has in fact not been transgressed. The Swiss, however, deem the disadvantages of the American method still more serious, for they hold that it gives the last word to the judges, persons not chosen for or fitted for such a function, and they declare that in point of fact public opinion and the traditions of their government prevent the power vested in their National Assembly from being abused. And it must be added that the Americans have so far felt the difficulty which the Swiss dwell on, that the Supreme Court has refused to pronounce upon the action of Congress in 'purely political cases,' *i. e.* cases where the arguments used to prove or disprove the conformity to the Constitution of the action taken by Congress are of a political nature.

Returning to the question of legislative action alleged

to transgress the Constitution, it is plain that if the Legislature be, as in Switzerland, the arbiter of its own powers, so that the validity of its acts cannot be questioned in a court of law, there is no further difficulty. But where that validity can be challenged, as in the United States, it might be supposed that every unconstitutional statute will be held null, and that thus any such stretching or twisting of the Constitution as has been referred to will be arrested. But experience has shown that where public opinion sets strongly in favour of the line of conduct which the Legislature has followed in stretching the Constitution, the Courts are themselves affected by that opinion, and go as far as their legal conscience and the general sense of the legal profession permit—possibly sometimes even a little farther—in holding valid what the Legislature has done. This occurs most frequently where new problems of an administrative kind present themselves. The Courts recognize, in fact, that ' principle of development ' which is potent in politics as well as in theology. Human affairs being what they are, there must be a loophole for expansion or extension in some part of every scheme of government; and if the Constitution is Rigid, Flexibility must be supplied from the minds of the Judges. Instances of this kind have occurred in the United States, as when some twenty years ago the Supreme Court recognized a power in a State Legislature to deal with railway companies not consistent with the opinions formerly enounced by the Court, though they disclaimed the intention of overruling those opinions [1].

[1] A still more remarkable instance has been furnished, while these pages are passing through the press (June, 1901), by the decisions of the Supreme Court of the United States in the group of cases which arose out of questions relating to the applicability of the Federal Constitution to the island of Puerto Rico, recently ceded by Spain to the United States. The Court had to deal with a constitutional question raising large issues of national policy regarding the application of the Federal Constitution to territories acquired by conquest and treaty: and its judgements in these cases (given in every case by majorities only) have expanded the Constitution, *i.e.* have declared it to have a meaning which may well be its true meaning, but which was not previously ascertained, and certainly by many lawyers not admitted, to be its true meaning.

Does not a danger lurk in this? May not a majority in the Legislature, if and when they have secured the concurrence, honest or dishonest, of the Judiciary, practically disregard the Constitution? May not the Executive conspire with them to manipulate places on the highest Court of Appeal, so as to procure from it such declarations of the meaning of the Constitution as the conspiring parties desire? May not the Constitution thus be slowly nibbled away? Certainly. Such things may happen. It is only public opinion and established tradition that will avail to prevent them. But it is upon public opinion, moulded by tradition, that all free governments must in the last resort rely.

XIV. DEMOCRACIES AND RIGID CONSTITUTIONS.

The mention of traditions, that is to say of the mental and moral habits of judgement which a nation has formed, and which guide its political life, as the habits of each one of us guide his individual life, suggests an inquiry as to the effect of Documentary Constitutions on the ideas and habits of those who live under them. I will not venture on broad generalizations, because it is hard to know how much should be assigned to the racial tendencies of a nation, how much to the circumstances of its history, how much to its institutions. But the cases of Switzerland and the United States seem to show that the tendency of these instruments is to foster a conservative temper. The nation feels a sense of repose in the settled and permanent form which it has given to its government. It is not alarmed by the struggles of party in the legislature, because aware that that body cannot disturb the fundamental institutions. Accordingly it will often, contracting a dislike to change, negative the amendments which the legislature submits to it. This happens in Switzerland, as already observed; and the people of the United States, though liable to sudden and violent waves of political opinion, show so little disposition to innovate that Congress has not proposed any amendments to the State Legislatures since 1870 [1]. I may be reminded that the Constitutions of the several States of the Union are frequently recast or amended in detail. This is true, but the cause lies not so much in a restless changefulness as in the low opinion entertained of the State Legislatures. The distrust felt for these bodies induces the people to take a large part of what is really ordinary legislation out of their hands, and to enact themselves, in a form of a Constitution, the laws they wish. State Constitutions now contain many regulations on matters of detail, and have thus, in most States, ceased to be considered fundamental instruments of government. To revise or amend them has become merely a convenient method of direct popular legislation, similar to the Swiss Popular Initiative and Referendum. But the fundamental parts of these instruments are but slightly changed.

In estimating the influence of Flexible Constitutions in forming the political character of a nation, in stimulating its intelligence and training its judgement, it was remarked that only the governing class, a very small part of the nation even in democratic countries, are directly affected. This is less true of a Rigid Constitution. While a Flexible Constitution like the Roman or English requires much knowledge, tact and courage to work it, and develops these qualities in those who bear a part in the working of it, as legislators or officials or magistrates, a Rigid Constitution tends rather to elicit ingenuity, subtlety and logical acumen among the corresponding class of persons. It is apt to give a legal cast to most questions, and sets a high, perhaps too high, premium on legal knowledge and legal capacity. But it goes further. It affects a much larger part of the community than the Flexible Constitution does. Few even of the governing class can be expected to understand the latter. The average Roman voter in the *comitia* in the

---

[1] Something must, however, be allowed for the provisions which require large majorities for any amendment of the Constitution.

days of Cicero, like the average English voter at the polls to-day, probably knew but little about the legal structure of the government he lived under. But the average Swiss voter, like the average native American voter (for the recent immigrant is a different sort of creature), understands his government, can explain it, and has received a great deal of education from it. Talk to a Swiss peasant in Solothurn or Glarus, and you will be astonished at his mastery of principles as well as his knowledge of details. Very likely he has a copy of the Federal Constitution at home. He has almost certainly learnt it at school. It disciplines his mind much as the Shorter Catechism trained the Presbyterian peasantry of Scotland. As there is no mystery about a scheme of government so set forth, it may be thought that he will have little reverence for that which he comprehends. It is, however, his own. He feels himself a part of the Government, and seems to be usually imbued with a respect even for the letter of the instrument, a wholesome feeling, which helps to form that law-abiding spirit which a democracy needs.

A documentary Constitution appears to the people as the immediate outcome of their power, the visible image of their sovereignty. It is commended by a simplicity which contrasts favourably with the obscure technicalities of an old common law Constitution. The taste of the multitude, and especially of that class which outnumbers all other classes, the thinly-educated persons whose book-knowledge is drawn from dry manuals in mechanically-taught elementary schools, and who in after life read nothing but newspapers, or penny weeklies, or cheap novels—the taste of this class, and that not merely in Europe but perhaps even more in the new countries, such as Western America and the British Colonies, is a taste for ideas level with their comprehension, sentiments which need no subtlety to be appreciated, propositions which can be expressed in unmistakable positives and negatives. Thus the democratic man (as Plato would call him) is pleased to read and know his Constitution for himself. The more plain and straightforward it is the better, for so he will not need to ask explanations from any one more skilled. And a good reason for this love of plainness and directness may be found in the fact that the twilight of the older Constitutions permitted abuses of executive power against which the express enactments of a Rigid Constitution protect the people. Magna Charta, the Bill of Rights, the Twelve Tables, were all fragments, or rather instalments, of such a Constitution, rightly dear to the commons, for they represented an advance towards liberty and order [1].

The theory of democracy assumes that the multitude are both competent and interested; competent to understand the structure of their government and their own functions and duties as ultimately sovereign in it, interested as valuing those functions, and alive to the responsibility of those duties. A Constitution set out in black and white, contained in a concise document which can be expounded and remembered more easily than a Constitution growing out of a long series of controversies and compromises, seems specially fitted for a country where the multitude is called to rule. Only memory and common sense are needed to master it. It can lay down general principles in a series of broad, plain, authoritative propositions, while in the case of the 'historical Constitution' they have to be gathered from various sources, and expressed, if they are to be expressed correctly, in a guarded and qualified form. Now the average man, if intelligent enough to comprehend politics at all, likes general principles. Even if, as some think, he overvalues them, yet his capacity for absorbing them gives him a sort of comprehension of his govern-

---

[1] The 'People's Charter' of 1848 was called for as another such onward step. Its Six Points were to be the basis of a democratic reconstruction of the government.

ment and attachment to it which are solid advantages in a large democracy.

Constitutions of this type have usually arisen when the mass of the people were anxious to secure their rights against the invasions of power, and to construct a frame of government in which their voices should be sure to prevail. They furnish a valuable protection for minorities which, if not liable to be overborne by the tyranny of the mass, are at any rate liable to be disheartened into silence by superior numbers, and so need all the protection which legal safeguards can give them. Thus they have generally been accounted as institutions characteristic of democracy, though the cases of Germany and Japan show that this is not necessarily true.

A change of view has, however, become noticeable within the last few years. In the new democracies of the United States and the British self-governing Colonies—and the same thing is true of popularly governed countries in Europe—the multitude no longer fears abuses of power by its rulers. It is itself the ruler, accustomed to be coaxed and flattered. It feels no need for the protection which Rigid Constitutions give. And in the United States it chafes under those restrictions on legislative power, embodied in the Federal Constitution or State Constitution (as the case may be), which have surrounded the rights of property and the obligation of subsisting contracts with safeguards obnoxious, not only to the party called Socialist, but to reformers of other types. As these safeguards are sometimes thought to prevent the application of needed remedies and to secure impunity for abuses which have become entrenched behind them, the aforesaid constitutional provisions have incurred criticism and censure from various sections, and many attempts have been made by State legislatures, acting at the bidding of those who profess to control the votes of working men, to disregard or evade the restrictions. These attempts are usually defeated by the action of the Courts, whence it happens that both the Federal Constitution and the functions of the Judiciary are often attacked in the country which was so extravagantly proud of both institutions half a century ago. This strife between the Bench as the defender of old-fashioned doctrines (embodied in the provisions of a Rigid Constitution (Federal or State)) and a State Legislature acting at the bidding of a large section of the voters is a remarkable feature of contemporary America.

The significance of this change in the tendency of opinion is enhanced when we find that a similar change has been operative in the opposite camp. The very considerations which have made odious to some American reformers those restrictions on popular power, behind which the great corporations and the so-called ' Trusts ' (and capitalistic interests generally) have entrenched themselves, have led not a few in England to applaud the same restrictions as invaluable safeguards to property. Realizing, a little late in the day, that political power has in England passed from the Few to the Many, fearing the use which the Many may make of it, and alarmed by the precedents which land legislation in Ireland has set, they are anxious to tie down the British legislature, while yet there is time, by provisions which shall prevent interference with a man's control over what he calls his own, shall restrict the taking of private property for public uses, shall secure complete liberty of contracting, and forbid interference with contracts already made. Others in England, in their desire to save political institutions which they think in danger, propose to arrest any sudden popular action by placing those institutions in a class by themselves, out of the reach of the regular action of Parliament. In other words, the establishment in Britain of a species of Rigid Constitution has begun to be advocated, and advocated by the persons least inclined to trust democracy. ' Imagine a country '—so they argue—' with immense accumulated wealth, and a great inequality of fortunes, a country which rules a vast and distant Empire, a country which depends for her prosperity upon manufactures liable to be injured by bad legislation, and upon a commerce liable to be imperilled by unskilful diplomacy, and suppose that such a country should admit to power a great mass of new and untrained voters, to whose cupidity demagogues will appeal, and upon whose ignorance charlatans will practise. Will not such a country need something better for her security than a complicated and delicately-poised Constitution resting largely on mere tradition, a Constitution which can at any moment be fundamentally altered by a majority, acting in a revolutionary transient spirit, yet in a perfectly legal way? Ought not such a country to place at least the foundations of her system and the vital principles of her government out of the reach of an irresponsible parliamentary majority, making the procedure for altering them so slow and so difficult that there will be time for the conservative forces to rally to their defence before any fatal changes can be carried through?'

I refer to these arguments, which were frequently heard in England during some years after the extension of the suffrage in 1884[1], with no intention of discussing their soundness, for that belongs to politics, but solely for the sake of illustrating how different are the aspects which the same institution may come to wear. A century ago revolutionists were the apostles, conservatives the enemies, of Rigid Constitutions. Even forty years ago it was the Flexibility of the historical British Constitution that was its glory in the eyes of admirers of the British system, its Rigidity that was the glory of the American Constitution in the eyes of fervent democrats.

---

[1] They are much less heard now (1900), partly because the public mind is occupied with matters of a different order, partly because the political party which professes to be opposed to innovation has latterly commanded a large majority in the British Legislature.

XV. THE FUTURE OF THE FLEXIBLE AND RIGID TYPES.

A few concluding reflections may be devoted to the probable future of the two types that have been occupying our minds. Are both likely to survive? or if not, which of the two will prevail and outlast the other?

Two reasons suggest themselves for predicting the prevalence of the Rigid type. One is that no new Flexible Constitutions have been born into the world for many years past, unless we refer to this class those of some of the British self-governing colonies [1]. The other is that no country now possessing a Rigid Constitution seems likely to change it for a Flexible one. The footsteps are all the other way. Flexible Constitutions have been turned into Rigid ones. No Rigid one has become Flexible [2]. Even those who complain of the undue conservatism of the American Constitution do not propose to abolish that Constitution altogether, nor to place it at the mercy of Congress, but merely to expunge parts of it, though no doubt parts which (such as the powers of the Judiciary) have been vital to its working.

Against these two arguments may be set the fact that popular power has in most countries made great advances, and does not need the protection of an instrument controlling the legislature and the executive, which are already only too eager to bend to every breeze of popular opinion. If we lived in a time of small States, as the ancients did, the people would themselves legislate in primary assemblies. Why then, it may be asked, should they care to limit the powers of legislatures which are completely at their bidding? The old reasons for holding legislatures and executives in check have disappeared. Why should the people, safe and self-confident, impose a check on themselves? In this there may be

---

[1] The British self-governing Colonies (except the two great federations, see ante, pp. 168-9) have constitutions which may be changed in all or nearly all points by their respective legislatures, but they are not independent States, and the power of the legislatures to alter the constitutions is therefore not complete.

[2] The Constitution of Italy, already referred to, is scarcely an exception.

some truth. But it must be remembered that since modern States are larger than those of former times, and tend to grow larger by the absorption of the small ones, legislatures are necessary, for business could not be carried on by primary popular assemblies, even with the aid of ' plébiscites.' Now legislatures are nowhere rising in the respect and confidence of the people, and it is therefore improbable that any nation which has a documentary Constitution, holding its legislature in sub-jection, will abolish it for the benefit of the legislature, although it may wish to do more and more of its legisla-tion by the direct action of the people, as it does in Switzerland and in some of the States of the American Union. On the whole, therefore, it seems probable that Rigid Constitutions will survive in countries where they already exist.

Two other questions remain. Will existing Flexible Constitutions remain? Are such new States as may arise likely to adopt Constitutions of the Rigid or of the Flexible type?

An inquiry whether countries which, like Hungary and Britain, now live under ancient Flexible Constitu-tions will exchange them for new documentary ones would resolve itself into a general study of the political prospects of those countries. All that can be said, apart from such a study, is that our age shows no such general tendency to change in this respect as did the revolu-tionary and post-revolutionary era of the first sixty years of the nineteenth century. Still, a few lines may be given to considering whether any such alteration of form is likely to pass on the Constitution which has long had the unquestioned pre-eminence in age and honour, that, namely, of the United Kingdom, which is really the ancient Constitution of England so expanded as to include Scotland and Ireland.

So far as internal causes and forces are concerned, this seems improbable. The people are not likely, de-spite the alarms felt and the advice tendered by the uneasy persons to whom reference has already been made, to part with the free play and elastic power of their historical Cabinet and Parliamentary system. England has never yet made any constitutional change either on grounds of theory or from a fear of evils that might arise in the future. All the modifications of the frame of government have been gradual, and induced by actually urgent needs.

But there is another set of causes and forces at work which may, as some think, affect the question. It has already been noted that Rigid Constitutions have arisen where States originally independent or semi-independent have formed Confederations. These States, finding the kind of connexion which treaties had created insufficient for their needs, have united themselves into one Federal State, and expressed their new and closer relation in the form of a documentary Constitution. Such a Constitution has invariably been raised above the legislature it was creating, because the States which were uniting wished to guard jealously such autonomy as they respectively retained, and would not leave those rights at the mercy of the legislature. This happened in the United States in 1787-9, in Switzerland after the fall of Napoleon, in Germany when the North German Confederation and German Empire were created in 1866 and 1870-71. It has happened also in Canada and in Australia.

Two proposals of a federalizing nature have recently been made regarding the United Kingdom, one to split it up into a Federation of four States, the other to make it a member of a large Federation. Neither seems likely to be carried out at present, but both are worth mentioning, because they illustrate the occasions on which, and methods by which, constitutions may be transformed. The United Kingdom stands to its self-governing Colonies in what is practically a permanent alliance as regards all foreign relations, these relations being managed by the mother country, with complete local legislative and administrative autonomy both for each Colony and for the mother country [1]. Many think that this alliance is not a satisfactory, and cannot well be a permanent, form of connexion, because at present almost the whole burden—and it is a heavy one—of naval and military defence falls upon Britain, while the Colonies have no share in the control of foreign relations, and may find themselves engaged in a war, or bound by a treaty, regarding which they have not been consulted. Thus the idea has grown up that some sort of confederation ought to be established, in which there would be a Federal Assembly, containing representatives of the (at present seven) component States [2], and controlling those matters, such as foreign relations and a system of military and naval armaments, which would be common to the whole body. If this idea were ever to take practical shape, it would probably be carried out by a statute establishing a new Constitution for the desired Confederation, and creating the Federal Assembly. Such a statute would be passed by the Parliament of the United Kingdom, and (being expressed to be operative over the whole Empire) would have full legal effect for the Colonies as well as for the mother country. Now if such a statute assigned to the Federal Assembly certain specified matters, as for instance the control of imperial defence and expenditure or (let us say) legislation regarding merchant shipping and copyright, taking them away from the present and future British Parliament as well as from the parliaments of the several Colonies, and therewith debarring the British Parliament from recalling or varying the grant except by the

---

[1] This autonomy is, however, not legally complete as regards the Colonies, for the mother country may, though she rarely does, disallow colonial legislation. In Canada the Dominion Legislature cannot affect the rights of the several Provinces, the power to do so remaining with the Imperial Parliament which passed the Confederation Act of 1867. So too under the Constitution of the Australian Commonwealth the rights of each colony are protected by the instrument of federation.

[2] Viz. the United Kingdom, the two great Colonial Federations (Canada and Australia), and four comparatively small self-governing Colonies, viz. New Zealand, Cape Colony, Natal, and Newfoundland.

consent of the several Colonies (or perhaps of the Federal Assembly itself), it is clear that the now unlimited powers of the British Parliament would have been reduced. A part of the future British Constitution would have been placed beyond its control: and to that extent the British Constitution would have ceased to be a Flexible one within the terms of the definition already given [1]. Parliament would not be fully sovereign; and if either the British or a Colonial Parliament passed laws inconsistent with statutes passed by the Federal Assembly in matters assigned to the latter, the Courts would have to hold the transgressing laws invalid.

Doubtless, if such a Federal Constitution were established, a Supreme Court of Appeal on which some colonial judges should sit would be thought essential to it, and questions arising under the Federation Act (as to the extent of the powers of the Federal Assembly and otherwise) would go before it, sometimes in the first instance, sometimes by way of appeal from inferior Courts.

The other proposal is to turn the United Kingdom itself into a Federation by erecting England, Scotland, Ireland, and Wales into four States, each with a local legislature and ministry controlling local affairs, while retaining the Imperial Parliament as a Central or Federal Legislature for such common affairs as belong in the United States to Congress, and in Canada to the Dominion Parliament, and in Australia to the Commonwealth Parliament. If such a scheme provided, as it probably would provide, for an exclusive assignment to the local legislatures of local affairs, so as to debar the Imperial Parliament from interfering therewith, it would destroy the present Flexible British Constitution and substitute

---

[1] It may of course be observed (see p. 175, ante) that the British Parliament, while it continues to be elected as now, may be unable to divest itself of its general power of legislating for the whole Empire, and might therefore repeal the Act by which it had resigned certain matters to the Federal Assembly and resume them for itself. This is one of those *apices iuris* of which the Romans say *non sunt iura:* and in point of fact no Parliament can be supposed capable of the breach of faith which such a repeal would involve. The supposed legal difficulty might. however, be avoided by some such expedient as that previously suggested.

14

a Rigid one for it. Care would have to be taken to use proper legal means of extinguishing the general sovereign authority of the present Parliament, as for instance by directing the elections for the new Federal Legislature to be held in such a way as to effect a breach of continuity between it and the old Imperial Parliament, so that the latter should absolutely cease and determine when the new Constitution came into force. Upon this scheme also it would be for the Courts of Law to determine whether in any given case either the Federal or one of the Local Legislatures had exceeded its powers.

Some persons have proposed to combine both these proposals so as to make the four parts of the United Kingdom each return members, along with the Colonies, to a Pan-Britannic Federal Legislature, and to place the local legislatures of Scotland, for instance, or Wales, in a line with those of the Australian Commonwealth or New Zealand. On this plan also the British Constitution would become a Rigid one.

The difficulties, both legal and practical, with which these proposals, taken either separately or in conjunction, are surrounded, are greater than those who advocate them have as yet generally perceived.

XVI. Are New Constitutions Likely to Arise?

The remaining question, also somewhat speculative, relates to the prospects the future holds out to us of seeing new States with new Constitutions arise.

New States may arise in one of two ways, either by their establishment in new countries where settled and civilized government has been hitherto unknown, or by the breaking up of existing States into smaller ones, fragments of the old.

The opportunities for the former process have now been sadly curtailed through the recent appropriation by a few great civilized States of some two-thirds of the surface of the globe outside Europe. North America is

in the hands of three such States. Central and South
America, though the States are all weak and most of
them small in population, are so far occupied that no
space is left. The last chance disappeared when the
Argentine Republic asserted a claim to Patagonia, where
it would have been better that some North European
race should have developed a new colony, as the Welsh
settlers were doing on a small scale. Australia is occupied. Asia, excluding China and Japan in the East, and
the two dying Musulman powers in the West, is virtually partitioned between Britain and Russia, with France
holding a bit of the south-east corner. So Africa has
now been (with trifling exceptions) divided between five
European Powers (Portugal, England, France, Germany, Italy). Thus there is hardly a spot of earth left
on which a new independent community can establish
itself, as the Greeks founded a multitude of new commonwealths in the eighth and seventh centuries B. C., and
as the Teutonic invaders founded kingdoms during the
dissolution of the Roman Empire.

If we turn to the possibilities of new States arising
from the ruins of existing ones, whether by revolt or by
peaceful separation, the prospect is not much more encouraging. There is indeed Turkey. Five out of the
six new States that have arisen in Europe during
this century have been carved out of the territories
she claimed—viz. Greece, Rumania, Servia, Bulgaria,
Montenegro: and there is material for one or two more
in Europe and possibly for one or two in Asia, though it
is more probable that both the Asiatic and European
dominions of the Sultan will be partitioned among existing States than that new ones will spring out of them.
The ill-compacted fabric of the Austro-Hungarian monarchy may fall to pieces. Parts of the Asiatic dominions
of Russia may possibly (though in a comparatively distant future) become independent of the old Muscovite
motherland, and the less civilized among the republics
of Central and South America may be broken into parts

or combined into new States, though the saying ' plus
cela change, plus c'est la même chose ' is even more true
of those countries than of that to which it was originally
applied, and gives little hope of interesting novelties.
But on the whole the tendency of modern times is rather
towards the aggregation of small States than towards
the division of large ones.   Commerce and improved
facilities of communication are factors of constantly increasing importance which work in this direction, and
this general tendency for the larger States to absorb the
smaller forbids us to expect the rise, within the next
few generations, of more than a few new Constitutions
which will provide matter for study to the historian or
lawyer of the future.

What type of Constitution will these new States, whatever they be and whenever they come, be disposed to
prefer?   Upon this point it is relevant to observe that
all the new States that have appeared since 1850 have
adopted Rigid Constitutions, with the solitary exception
of Montenegro, which has no Constitution at all, but
lives under the paternal autocracy of the temporal ruler
who has succeeded the ancient ecclesiastical Vladika [1].
Each of them, on beginning its independent life, has felt
the need of setting out the lines of its government in a
formal instrument which it has consecrated as fundamental by placing it above ordinary legislation.   Similar
conditions are likely to surround the birth of any new
States, similar motives to influence those who tend their
infancy.   The only cases in which a Flexible Constitution
is likely to arise would be the division of a country having such a Constitution into two or more fragments,
each of which should cleave to the accustomed system ;
or the revolt of a people or community among whom, as
they grow into a State, usages of government that had
naturally sprung up might, when independence had been
established, continue to be observed and so ripen into a
Constitution.   The chance that either of these cases will

[1] As to Italy, however, see above, pp. 171 and 176.

present itself is not very great. New States will more probably adopt documentary Constitutions, as did the insurgent colonies of England after 1776 and of Spain after 1811, and as the Christians of South-Eastern Europe did when they had rid themselves of the Turk. Upon the whole, therefore, it would seem that the future is rather with Rigid Constitutions than with those of the Flexible type.

It is hardly necessary to close these speculations by adding the warning that all prophecies in politics must be highly conjectural. Circumstances change, opinion changes; knowledge increases, though the power of using it wisely may not increase [1].

The subtlety of nature, and especially the intricacy of the relations she develops between things that originally seemed to lie wide apart, far surpasses the calculating or predicting wit of man. Accordingly many things, both in the political arrangements of the world and in the beliefs of mankind, which now seem permanent may prove transitory. Democracy itself, though most people treat it as a thing likely to grow stronger and advance further, may suffer an eclipse. Human nature no doubt remains. But human nature has clothed itself in the vesture of every sort of institution, and may change its fashions as freely in the future as it has done in the past.

[1] Ἅπανθ' ὁ μακρὸς κἀναρίθμητος χρόνος
φύει τ' ἄδηλα καὶ φανέντα κρύπτεται.
Soph. *Ajax*, 646.

NOTE TO ESSAY III

CONSTITUTIONAL AND OTHER GOVERN-MENTS

THE races and nations of the world may, as respects the forms of Government under which they live, be distributed into four classes :—

I. Nations which have created and maintain permanent political institutions, allotting special functions to each organ of Government, and assigning to the citizens some measure of participation in the business of Government.

In these nations we discover Constitutions in the proper sense of the term. To this class belong all the States of Europe except Russia and Montenegro, and, outside Europe, the British self-governing Colonies, the United States and Mexico, the two republics of South Africa, Japan and Chili, possibly also the Argentine Republic.

II. Nations in which the institutions aforesaid exist in theory, but are seldom in normal action, because they are in a state of chronic political disturbance and mostly ruled, with little regard to law, by military adventurers. This class includes the republics of Central and South America, with the exception of Chili, and possibly of Argentina, whose condition has latterly been tolerably stable.

III. Nations in which, although the upper class is educated, the bulk of the population, being backward, has not begun to desire such institutions as aforesaid, and which therefore remain under autocratic monarchies.

To this class belong Russia and Montenegro. Japan has lately emerged from it: and two or three of the newest European States might, but for the interposition of other nations, have remained in it.

IV. Nations which are, for one reason or another, below the level of intellectual life and outside the sphere of ideas which the permanent political institutions aforesaid presuppose and need for their proper working. This class includes all the remaining peoples of the world, from intelligent races like the Chinese, Siamese, and Persians, down to the barbarous tribes of Africa.

Constitutions, in the sense in which the term is used in the preceding Essay, belong only to the first class, and in a qualified sense to the second. In the modern world they are confined to Europe and her Colonies, adding Japan, which has imitated Europe. In the ancient world they were confined to three races, Greeks, Italians, and Phoenicians, to whom one may perhaps add such races as the Lycians, who had learnt from the Greeks. Their range is somewhat narrower than that of law, that is to say, there are peoples which, like the Musulmans of Turkey, Egypt, and Persia, have law, but have no Constitutions.

No race that has ever lived under a lost Constitutional Government has permanently lost it, except those parts of the Roman Empire which now form part of the Turkish Empire; and the Roman Empire, though its Government never ceased to be in a certain sense constitutional, ultimately extinguished the habit of self-government among its subjects.

IV

THE ACTION OF CENTRIPETAL AND CENTRIFUGAL FORCES ON POLITICAL CONSTITUTIONS [1]

As every government and every constitution is the result of certain forces and tendencies which bring men together in an organized community, so every government and every constitution tends when formed to hold men together thenceforth, training them to direct their efforts to a common end and to sacrifice for that purpose a certain measure of the exercise of their individual wills. So strong is the aggregative tendency, that each community naturally goes on by a sort of law of nature to expand and draw in others, whether persons or groups, who have not previously belonged to it: nor is physical force the prime agent, for the great majority of mankind prefer some kind of political society, even one in whose management they have little or no share, to mere isolation. As this process of expansion and aggregation continues, the different political groups which it has called into being come necessarily in contact with one another. The weaker ones are overcome or peacefully absorbed by the stronger ones, and thus the number of groups is continually lessened. Where two communities of nearly equal strength encounter each other, each may for a time succeed in resisting the attraction of the

[1] This Essay was composed in the early part of 1885. It has been revised throughout, but the substance remains the same.

other. But in this changeful world it almost always happens that sooner or later one becomes so much stronger that the other yields to it : and thus in course of time the number of detached communities, *i.e.* of groups each with its own centre of attraction, becomes very small, because the weak have been swallowed up by the strong. This is the general, though, as we shall see, not the universal course of events. There is also another force at work, which has at some moments in history developed great strength.

I. How the Tendencies to Aggregation and to Disjunction respectively affect Constitutions.

Of the many analogies that have been remarked between Law in the Physical and Law in the Moral World, none is more familiar than that derived from the Newtonian astronomy, which shows us two forces always operative in our solar system. One force draws the planets towards the sun as the centre of the system, the other disposes them to fly off from it into space. So in politics, we may call the tendency which draws men or groups of men together into one organized community and keeps them there a Centripetal force, and that which makes men, or groups, break away and disperse, a Centrifugal. A political Constitution or frame of government, as the complex totality of laws embodying the principles and rules whereby the community is organized, governed, and held together, is exposed to the action of both these forces. The centripetal force strengthens it, by inducing men (or groups of men) to maintain, and even to tighten, the bonds by which the members of the community are gathered into one organized body. The centrifugal assails it, by dragging men (or groups) apart, so that the bonds of connexion are strained, and possibly at last loosened or broken. That no community can be exempt from the former force is obvious. But neither can any wholly escape the latter. For every community has been built out of smaller groups, and the members of such groups have seldom quite lost the attraction which each had to its own particular centre, such attraction being of course dissociative as regards the other groups and their members [1]. Moreover in no large community can there ever be a complete identity of views and wishes, of interests and feelings, between all the members. Many must have something to complain of, something which sets them against the rest and makes them desire to be, for some purposes, differently treated, or (in extreme cases) to be entirely separated. The existence of such a grievance constitutes a centre round which a group is formed, and this group is in so far an element of disjunction. Accordingly the history of every community and every constitution may be regarded as a struggle between the action of these two forces, that which draws together and that which pushes apart, that which unites and that which dissevers.

This subject, it may be thought, belongs either to History, in so far as history attempts to draw general conclusions from the facts she records, or to that branch of political science which may be called Political Dynamics, and is one with which the constitutional lawyer is not directly concerned. The constitutional lawyer, however, must always, if he is to comprehend his subject and treat it fruitfully, be a historian as well as a lawyer. His legal institutions and formulae do not belong to a sphere of abstract theory but to a concrete world of fact. Their soundness is not merely a logical but also a practical soundness, that is to say, institutions and rules must represent and be suited to the particular phenomena they have to deal with in a particular country. It is through history that these phenomena are known. History explains how they have come to be what they are. History shows whether they are the result of tendencies still in-

---

[1] In the pages that follow the word Group is used to denote the section of persons within a larger community who may be held together by some tie, whether of interest or sentiment or race or local habitation, which makes them a sort of minor community inside the larger one.

creasing or of tendencies already beginning to decline. History explains them by parallel phenomena in other times and places. Thus the lawyer who has to consider and advise on any constitutional problem, and still more the lawyer who has to contrive a constitutional scheme for grappling with a political difficulty, must study the matter as a historian, otherwise he will himself err and mislead those whom he advises. Great lawyers often have so erred, and with lamentable results. A lawyer who shall deal with a constitutional problem as he would deal with a technical point in the law of real property will be as much astray as an advocate who should prosecute or defend a political prisoner with a sole regard to the law of treason or sedition which he may find in his books, heedless of the temper and opinion of those from among whom the jury will be drawn.

An obvious illustration may be found in the fact that when any particular community is studied from the constitutional point of view, and the inquiry is raised whether it ought to have a Flexible or a Rigid Constitution, the question of the comparative actual strength of these two forces becomes a vital one. Where the centripetal force is palpably the stronger, either sort of constitution will do to hold the community together : and the choice between the two sorts may be made on other grounds. But where the centrifugal force is potent, and especially where there are reasons to apprehend its further development, the establishment of a Rigid Constitution may become desirable, and yet may be a matter of much delicacy and difficulty. If the constitution be framed in the interests of a centralizing policy, there is a danger that it may assume and require for its maintenance a greater strength in the centripetal forces than really exists, and that for the want of such strength the constitution may be exposed to a strain it cannot resist. Amid the constant change of phenomena, a Rigid Constitution necessarily represents the past, not the present ; and if the tendencies actually operative are towards the dissociation of the component groups of the community, a frame of government which fails to provide scope for these tendencies will soon become out of date and unfit for its work. Where, on the other hand, the existence of distinct groups, each desiring some control of its own affairs, is fully perceived and duly admitted as a factor in the condition of the community, and where it is desired to give legal recognition to the fact, and to protect the other local groups or sub-communities from being over-ridden by the largest among the groups, or by the community as a whole, the creation of a Rigid Constitution offers a valuable means of securing these objects. For such a constitution may be so drawn as to place the local groups under the protection of a fixed body of law, making their privileges an integral part of the frame of government, so that the whole Constitution must stand or fall with the maintenance of the rights enjoyed by the groups [1]. The familiar instance of such a form of Rigid Constitution is a Federal Constitution. It is specially adapted to the case of a country where the centrifugal forces are so strong that it is clear that the groups will not consent to be wholly merged and lost in one community, as under a Flexible Constitution might befall them, yet where they are sufficiently sensible of the advantages of combination to be willing to enter into a qualified and restricted union. And in these cases it has sometimes proved to be an efficient engine for further centralization. That is to say, the best way of strengthening in the long run the centripetal tendencies has been to give so much recognition and play to the centrifugal as may disarm them, and may allow the causes which make for unity to operate quietly without exciting antagonism.

It appears accordingly that the historian who studies constitutions, and still more the draftsman who frames them, must have his eye constantly fixed on these two

---

[1] Subject of course to any provisions for amending the Constitution which may have been inserted. See Essay III, p. 176 sqq.

forces. They are the matter to which the legislator has to give form. They create the state of things which a Constitution has to deal with, so laying down principles and framing rules as on the one hand to recognize the forces, and on the other hand to provide safeguards against their too violent action. Their action will preserve or destroy the Constitution,—preserve it, if it has given them due recognition and scope, destroy it, if its provisions turn out to be opposed to the sweep of irresistible currents. The forces that move society are to the constructive jurist or legislator what the forces of nature are (in the famous Baconian phrase) to man. He is their servant and interpreter. They can be overcome only by obeying them. If he defies or misunderstands them, they overthrow his work. If he knows how to use them, they preserve it. But his difficulty is greater than that of the physicist, because these social forces are more complex than those of inanimate nature, and vary in their working from generation to generation.

II. TENDENCIES WHICH MAY OPERATE EITHER AS CENTRIPETAL OR AS CENTRIFUGAL FORCES.

Now let us see what are the chief among the tendencies which in political society are capable of playing the part either of centripetal or of centrifugal forces.

So far as individual men are concerned, all the tendencies that work on them may be said to be associative tendencies, that is to say, every thing tends to knit individual men together into a band or group, and to make them act together. The repulsion of man from man is so rare that we may ignore it. Even the keenest individualist desires to convert other men to his individualism, and forms a league for the purpose with others who are likeminded.

As regards political societies, the subject wherewith we are here concerned, the tendencies I am going to enumerate may be either associative or dissociative.

Whether in the case of any given State they act as agglutinative and consolidating forces or as splitting and rending forces depends upon whether they are at the moment giving their support to, or are enlisted in the service of, the State as a whole, or are strengthening the group or groups inside the State which are seeking to assert either their rights within the State or their independence of it. Even obedience, the readiness to submit and follow, which might seem primarily a centripetal force, may be centrifugal as against the State if it leads the partisans of a particular recalcitrant group to surrender their wills to the leaders of that group. Even the love of independence, the desire to let each man's individuality have full scope, may act as a centripetal force if it disposes men to revolt against the tyranny of a faction and maintain the rights and interests of the whole people against the attempts of that faction to have its own way. There are always two centres of attraction and two groupings to be considered, the larger, which we call the State, and the smaller, which may be either a subordinate community, such as a province, district or dependency, or only a party or faction. And the centripetal force which draws men to the smaller centre is a centrifugal force as regards the larger.

These two tendencies, which I have referred to as Obedience and Individualism, are so familiar, and the former is a disposition of human nature so generally pervasive, as to need no further discussion. The other tendencies which may operate either centrifugally or centripetally may be classed under the two heads of Interest and Sympathy. Under the head of Interest there fall all those influences which belong to the sphere of Property, including of course Industry and Commerce as means of acquiring property. These influences usually make for consolidation and assimilation. It is a gain to the trader or the producer that the area of consumers which he supplies without the hindrance of an interposed customs tariff should be as wide as possible. It is a gain that communications by sea and land should be safe, easy, swift, and cheap, and these objects are better secured in a large country under a strong government. It is a gain that coinage, weights, and measures should be uniform over the largest possible area and that the standard of the currency should be upheld. It is a gain that the same laws and the same system of courts should prevail in every part of a State—and the larger the State the better, so far as these matters are concerned—and that the law should be steadily enforced and complete public order secured. All these things make not only for the growth of industry and the spread of trade, but also for the value of all kinds of property. And all these influences, derived from the consideration of such gains, which play upon the citizen's mind, are usually aggregative influences, disposing him to desire the extension of the State and the strength of its central authority. Considerations of Interest, therefore, usually operate as a centripetal force. It was through commercial interests that the States of Germany were, after the fall of the old Romano-Germanic Empire, drawn into that Zollverein which became a stage towards, and ultimately the basis of, the present German Empire. It was the increase of trade, after the union of Scotland and England, that by degrees reconciled the Scotch to a measure which was at first most unpopular among them as threatening to extinguish their national existence. It is the absence of any strong commercial motives for political union that has hampered the efforts of those who have striven, so far successfully, to keep Norway and Sweden united.

In exceptional cases, however, the influences of Interest may be centrifugal. A particular group of traders or landowners, for instance, living in a particular district, may think they will gain more by having the power to enact special laws for the conduct of their own affairs or for the exclusion of competing persons than they will by entering or by remaining under the uniform system of a

large State [1]. Trade considerations counted for something in making the planters of the Slave States of
America desire to sever themselves from a government
in which the protectionist party was generally dominant.
It is partly on economic grounds that the various
provinces of the Cis-Leithanian part of the Austro-
Hungarian Monarchy have been allowed, and desire
to maintain, each its autonomy.   It was largely a divergence of economic views and interests that so long
deterred the free trade colony of New South Wales
from linking its fortunes in a federation with the protectionist colonies; nor were there wanting industrial
grounds which made the adhesion of Queensland long
doubtful.

To the head of Sympathy we must refer all the influences which flow not from calculation and the desire of
gain, but from emotion or sentiment.   The sense of
community, whether of belief, or of intellectual conviction, or of taste, or of feeling (be it affection or aversion
towards given persons or things), engenders sympathy,
and draws men together.   To the same class belong the
recognition of a common ancestry, the use of a common
speech, the enjoyment of a common literature.   The importance of these factors has often been exaggerated.
Some of the keenest Irish revolutionaries have been
English by blood and Protestants by faith.   The Borderers of Northumberland and those of Berwickshire did
not hate one another less because they were of the same
stock and spoke the same tongue.   The Celts of Inverness-shire and the Teutons of Lothian are now equally
enthusiastic Scotchmen, though they disliked and despised one another almost down to the days of Walter

---

[1] The case of Ireland shows the same forces of industrial or commercial interest, real or supposed, operating partly as centripetal, partly as centrifugal.
The Nationalist party conceive that economic benefits would result from a local
legislature, which could aid local industries.   The mercantile class, especially in
the north-eastern part of the island, fear commercial loss from anything which
could hamper their trade intercourse with Scotland and England, or which might
be deemed prejudicial to commercial credit.   With the soundness of either view I
am not concerned; it is sufficient to note the facts.

Scott [1]. Mere identity of origin does not count for much,
as witness the ardent Hungarian patriotism of most of
the Germans and Jews settled in Hungary, with perhaps
no drop of Magyar blood in their veins. Community of
language does not any more than a common ancestry
necessarily make for love, and indeed may increase
hatred, because in an age of newspapers each of two dis-
putant parties can read the injurious things said of it by
the other. Civil wars are, like family quarrels, prover-
bially embittered. Tocqueville wrote, in 1833, that he
could imagine no more venomous hatred than the Americans then felt for England. So it may be said that
though the want of these elements of community is usually an obstacle to unity, their presence is no guarantee
for its existence. Somewhat greater value belongs to
identity of traditions and historical recollections, and to
the possession of the materials for a common pride in
past achievements. Most men find a personal satisfaction and take a personal pride in recalling the feats and
struggles of the nation, or the tribe, or the party, or the
sect, to which they belong, so the recollection of exploits
or sufferings becomes an effective rallying point for a
group. We all know how powerful a force such memories have been at various times in stimulating national
feeling in Italy, in Germany, in Hungary, in Scotland,
in Portugal, in Ireland.

Still less necessary is it to dwell upon the influence of
Religion, which, as it touches the deepest chords of
man's nature, is capable of educing the maximum of
harmony or discord. No force has been more efficient
in knitting factions and States together, or in breaking
them up and setting the parts of a State in fierce antagonism to one another. Religion held together the
Eastern Empire, originally a congeries of diverse races,
in the midst of dangers threatening it from every side for

[1] A curious survival of the dislike of the Lowlander to the Highlander may be
found in Carlyle's comments upon the Highland wife of his friend Thomas Campbell the poet.

eight hundred years. Religion now holds together the
Turkish Empire in spite of the hopeless incompetence
of its government. Religion split up the Romano-Germanic Empire after the time of Charles the Fifth. The
instances of the Jews and the Armenians are even more
familiar.

There remains a large and rather miscellaneous category of sources of sympathy which we may call by the
general name of Elements of Compatibility. Traits of
character, ideas, social customs, similarity of intellectual
culture, of tastes, and even of the trivial usages of daily
life, all contribute to link men together, and to assimilate
them further to one another, as the absence of these
things tends to differentiation and dissimilation, because
it supplies points in which the members of one group,
racial or local or social, feel themselves out of touch with
the members of another, and possibly inclined to show
contempt, or to think themselves contemned, on the
ground of the divergence. The natural repulsion which
the Germans usually feel for the Slavs, and the Slavs
for the Germans, seems to have its root in a difference of
character and temperament which makes it hard for
either race to do full justice to the other. That repulsion
is powerfully operative to-day in the Austrian Empire.
In the ancient world the obstinate and passionate Egyptians seem to have displayed, and provoked, a similar
antagonism in their contact with other races, and particularly with the arrogant Persians.

These influences of Sympathy, like those of Interest,
may figure either as centripetal or centrifugal forces,
according as the centre round which they group and
towards which they draw men is the main centre of that
larger circle represented by the State or the centre of
the smaller circle represented by the tribe, the district,
the province, the faith, the sect, the faction. The same
feeling may play the one part or the other according to
the accident of individual view, or taste, or environment.
Thus in a University consisting of a number of autono-

mous colleges, one man may be a centralizer, and seek to bring the colleges into subordination, pecuniary and administrative, to the University, while another man may desire to maintain their independence, and yet both may set a high value on corporate spirit, and be filled with it themselves. In one man this spirit clings to the college, in another it glorifies the University. The patriotism which makes a Magyar desire that Hungary should absorb Croatia, and that which makes a Croat desire to sever his country from Hungary, are essentially the same sentiment, though, as regards the monarchy of the Hungarian Crown, the sentiment operates with the Magyar as an attractive, with the Croat as a repulsive force. This statement is generally true of that complex feeling, based upon affinities of race, of speech, of literature, of historic memories, of ideas, which we call the Sentiment of Nationality, a sentiment comparatively weak in the ancient world and in the Middle Ages, and which did not really become a factor of the first moment in politics till the religious passions of the sixteenth and seventeenth centuries had almost wholly subsided, and the gospel of political freedom preached in the American and French Revolutions had begun to fire men's minds. As regards the historical States of Europe, it is a sentiment which is both aggregative and segregative. It has contributed to create the German Empire: yet it is also a sentiment which makes Bavaria unwilling to merge in that Empire her individual existence. In Bavaria, and still more in the case of Scotland, which had a long and brilliant national history, the sentiment of local has been found compatible with a sentiment of imperial patriotism.

It is a remarkable feature of recent times that the tendency of a common interest to draw groups together and make them prize the unity of the State is often accompanied by the parallel development of an opposite tendency, based on sentiment, to intensify the life of the smaller group and in so far to draw it apart, and thereby

weaken the unity of the State. This arises from the
fact that the march of civilization is material on the one
hand, intellectual and moral on the other. So far as it is
material, it generally makes for unity. On its intellectual and social or moral side it works in two ways. It
tends to break down local prejudices and to create a
uniform type of habits and character over a wide area.
But it also heightens the influence of historical memories. It is apt to rekindle resentment at old injuries.
Filling men's minds with the notion of social and political equality, it disposes them to feel more keenly any
social or political inferiority to which they may be subjected. Raising the estimate they set upon themselves
as individuals and as a race, it makes them more bold in
organizing themselves and claiming what they deem
their rights. And so one notes the singular phenomenon
that men are stirred to disaffection, or impelled towards
separation, by grievances less acute than those which
their ancestors, sunk in ignorance and despondency,
bore almost without a murmur. The Roman Catholic
Irish since 1782 and the Transylvanian Rumans since
1848 are instances in point.

All these tendencies, pulling this way and that, are
among the facts which a given Constitution has to deal
with, are forces which it must use in order to secure its
own strength and permanence. Where, in a free country,
the system of government has grown up naturally, and
can be readily modified by the normal action of the
normal sovereign authority, *i.e.* where the Constitution
is a Flexible one, the presumption is that the rules and
usages of the Constitution conform to and represent the
actual forces, and draw strength therefrom. Yet even
in countries governed on this system there is a risk that
the Constitution which the will of a majority has established may leave a minority discontented and unrestful,
and that such discontent and unrest may impede the
working of the machinery and create an element of instability. In such countries, it may be the part of wis-

dom for the majority to yield something to the minority, modifying the Constitution, so far as it can safely be modified, in order to remove the obstacles to harmony. A centrifugal force which is not strong enough to disrupt the State, because the centripetal forces are on the whole more powerful, may nevertheless be able to cause a harmful friction, and may even, if the State be exposed to external attacks, become a source of peril. Everybody can now see that Rome ought to have admitted the Italian allies to the franchise long before the Social War, that Catholic Emancipation ought to have been enacted by the Irish Parliament in 1796 or by the British Parliament immediately after the Union of 1800, that Denmark ought not to have waited till 1874 before she conceded a qualified autonomy to Iceland, that the same country might probably have retained Schleswig-Holstein if she had yielded long before the war of 1864 some of the demands made by the German inhabitants of those duchies. And, if we may apply the same principle to despotically governed countries, most people will agree that Austria ought to have retired from Lombardy before 1859, and that the Turks gained nothing by clinging to Bulgaria, and may be gaining nothing now by clinging to Macedonia.

III. How Constitutions may use the Centripetal Forces to promote National Unity.

As we are here dealing with constitutions considered in their relation to the forces and tendencies that rule in politics (*i.e.* as a part of political dynamics), we may now inquire what it is that Constitutions can accomplish in the way of regulating or controlling these forces.

Every political Constitution has three main objects.

One is to establish and maintain a frame of government under which the work of the State can be efficiently carried on, the aims of such a frame of government being on the one hand to associate the people with the government, and, on the other hand, to preserve public order, to avoid hasty decisions and to maintain a tolerable continuity of policy.

Another is to provide due security for the rights of the individual citizen as respects person, property, and opinion, so that he shall have nothing to fear from the executive or from the tyranny of an excited majority. This object has fallen into the background since these rights came to be fully recognized. But in earlier times it was the chief purpose of constitutional provisions from Magna Charta down to the Bill of Rights and the Declaration of Independence. The safeguard for these rights which the Constitution of England provided, was the thing which, more perhaps than anything else, moved the admiration of foreign observers who studied that constitution during the eighteenth century.

The third object is to hold the State together, not only to prevent its disruption by the revolt or secession of a part of the nation, but to strengthen the cohesiveness of the country by creating good machinery for connecting the outlying parts with the centre, and by appealing to every motive of interest and sentiment that can lead all sections of the inhabitants to desire to remain united under one government.

In pursuing these objects, a constitution seeks to achieve by means of legal provisions that which in ruder times it was often necessary to accomplish by physical force. No doubt at all times the natural disposition to obey (the sources of which I have analysed elsewhere [1]) was an agent more constant and effective than physical force. Nevertheless, the latter was needed, sometimes from the side of the government to maintain order and compel subjects to bear their share of the public burdens, sometimes from the side of the subjects to abate the abuses into which the possession of power tempts rulers. Troops to keep order and quell revolts, and men handy with their weapons and ready to rise in insur-

[1] See Essay IX, p. 46; sqq.

rection to dethrone bad monarchs or expel bad ministers, were a necessary part of the equipment of political societies in the ruder ages.

A good constitution relieves the government from the necessity of frequently resorting to military force by securing that those who govern shall be persons approved by the bulk of the citizens, as well as by providing for the purposes of coercion machinery so promptly and effectively applicable, that the elements of disturbance either do not break forth or are quickly suppressed. Similarly it relieves the subjects from the need of rising in rebellion by providing machinery whereby the complaints of those who think themselves aggrieved shall be fully made known, and shall, if well founded, have due effect on the rulers by warning them to remove the grievances, or by displacing them if they fail to do so.

How constitutional machinery should be framed and worked for the attainment of the two former objects enumerated above, viz. the establishment of a proper frame of government and the safeguarding of private rights, is a matter which does not fall within the scope of our present inquiry. The third object does, so we have to ask how a constitution should be framed in order to enable it to maintain and strengthen the unity of a State.

It may do this in two ways. One is by setting various centripetal forces to work. The other is by preventing all or some of the centrifugal forces from working.

I have already enumerated the tendencies or influences which operate to draw men together and bind them into a community, be it greater or smaller, and have pointed out that these tendencies may in any given case operate in favour either of the State as a whole, in which case they preserve it, or in favour of some group or section within it, in which case they sap its unity. Let us now consider how the constitutional arrangements of a State may be so devised as to draw together all its members and all the minor groups within it.

The most generally available of these centripetal tendencies is trade, that interchange of commodities which benefits all the producers, by giving them a market, all the consumers by giving them the means of getting what they want, all the middlemen by supplying them with occupation. A Constitution can render no greater service to the unity as well as to the material progress of a nation than by enabling the freest interchange of products to go on within its limits. Nothing did more to keep the districts of each of the great European countries divided during the Middle Ages than the levying of tolls along the rivers and highways by petty potentates, or than the insecurity of those rivers and highways, as well as the want of good roads, for thus the market for the producers of the cheaper articles was narrowed to the small area immediately around them, and men were prevented from realizing, or benefiting by, the greatness of the country they belonged to. England, with an exceptionally strong and centralized government, suffered less from these tolls and this insecurity than did the large States of the Continent, and England arrived at unity sooner than they did. And so, conversely, nothing has done more to unify the vast territories of the United States than the provisions of the Federal Constitution which secure perfect freedom of trade within its limits, and empower the National Government to regulate the means of communication between the several States of the Union. So the Customs Union of the Germanic States, formed under the auspices of Prussia in A.D. 1829, did a great work in stimulating industry, while it showed the people the benefits of united action, and prepared the way for the formation of the new German Empire.

Another influence of moment is the establishment of a common law and a common system of courts. It is not an influence which can be reckoned on so invariably or confidently as can the influence of commerce, for any hasty attempt to change the law (whether customary or statutory) to which men are accustomed may provoke resistance and retard the growth of unity. Great Britain has wisely forborne to impose her own law on the dominions she has acquired by conquest or purchase. Roman-Dutch law remains in South Africa, in Ceylon, and in Guiana; Roman-French law in Lower Canada. So the French Code was left in force not only in Alsace-Lorraine which Germany took in 1871 but also in the German country all along the left bank of the Lower Rhine, when that region was reunited to Germany in 1814. So Roman law has remained in Louisiana, which was once French. But where one legal system can, without exciting resentment, be extended over the whole of a country, it becomes a valuable unifying force. As respects the substance of law, this happens by the formation of certain habits of thought and action, certain ideas of justice and utility. As respects the administration of law, it happens by giving to the central executive an engine for making its power felt, and usually felt for good. In the Middle Ages, the jurisdiction of the king's courts was found the most effective means both in England, from Henry II onward, and (somewhat later) in France, of extending the power of the central government and accustoming the people to rally round the Crown as the representative of national unity as well as of justice. A somewhat similar process has been in progress during the last thirty years among those petty principalities which we call the Laos States, and which lie to the north of the kingdom of Siam. The princes of these States were practically independent, living in a country of forests and hills, and recognizing only a vague titular suzerainty as vested in the Siamese king at Bangkok. But when foresters from British Burma had come among them, desiring to cut down and export the teak trees in those forests which make their only wealth, and when disputes had arisen between the Laos chiefs and these timber traders, the Government of India found it needful to make treaties with the king of Siam, under which a Court presided over by Siamese officials was set up in Chiengmai, the principal State. By means of this Court the Siamese Government has been able gradually to obtain complete control of the forest administration and the revenues thence arising, and incidentally to strengthen its general authority over these Laos States.

Similarly, the jurisdiction of the British Privy Council as a Supreme Court of Appeal from the Colonies and India, and the action of the Supreme Court of the United States as the final Court of Appeal for the whole Union (in certain classes of cases), have done something to make the members of these vast political aggregates realize the bond that links them together. In the case of the United States, respect for the Federal Courts and the keen interest with which their development of the law by judicial interpretation is followed by a large and powerful profession has been an important factor in strengthening the sense of national unity.

After law, religion, not as less potent, for it is more potent, but as more uncertain, because it has been as often a dissevering as a unifying influence. There is, however, a marked distinction between the earlier and the later forms of religion as regards the energy of the force they exert. In the earlier stages of civilization, when tradition and ritual counted for much, and abstract theology had not yet come into being, the worship of the gods of the nation or city was a part, a necessary and sometimes the most deep-rooted part, of the political constitution and the national life. In Egypt the rise or fall of a great deity is often the sign of the rise or fall of a dynasty. Moab, Edom, and Ammon, are each the people of a peculiar God. After the Captivity, when the minor Semitic peoples decline or vanish, Israel continues to be held together by the name of Jehovah, and by the Law He has given. Every Greek and every Italian city has its own distinctive public State worship. A race sometimes pays special honour to one out of its various deities, and the devotion of the Dorians to

Apollo, of the Athenians to the Virgin Goddess, finds a mediaeval parallel in that of the Swedes to Odin, of the Norwegians to Thor. As the Roman Empire included so many races and cities that no one deity or group of deities could be worshipped by all, altars were erected to the Goddess Rome, and the Guardian Spirit or Genius of the reigning Emperor became a common object of devotion for the whole mass of his subjects. In modern times the strong religions are (except Hinduism) World Religions, and therefore not national or local as were those of antiquity. But they exert an even greater political power. For monotheistic religions, however they may develop into elaborate rites and forms of ceremonial observance, are primarily philosophical religions, in which abstract ideas and beliefs take not only a firm but an exclusive grasp of the mind and heart of whosoever holds them. Hence they form a closer tie than did the worships of the ancient Italo-Hellenic world. Christianity created a new cohesion when the provinces of the Roman Empire were beginning to fall asunder. Islam formed a prodigious dominion out of many diverse peoples. The mutually hostile forms of a World Religion, such as the Sunnite and Shiite sects in Islam, act as consolidating or dissevering influences just as the religion itself did before schisms had arisen. When a faith grounded in peculiar dogmas or observances is held by one section of a people and hated by another section, it becomes a formidably centrifugal force. When the great mass of a people have embraced such a faith, their political cohesion is strengthened, and they may attract from other communities persons or groups who share their beliefs. The same principle applies to beliefs which cannot be called religious, but which exert a similar power over men's emotions. Even where no question of the supernatural is involved, the holding in common of certain ideas deemed supremely valuable whether for the individual or for society, may operate as a centrifugal or centripetal force.

A nation with a national religion which all or nearly all citizens cherish possesses a bond of unity which grows the more powerful the more its traditions become entwined with the national life. It is chiefly the influence of the Orthodox Church that has made a people so low in the scale of civilization as Russia was three centuries ago, to-day so united, so strong through its union, and so submissive to its sovereign, for it is not less as Head of the Church than as a secular prince that the Czar commands the reverence of his subjects [1]. Accordingly, whenever a State Church can be set up which embraces practically the whole of the people, and when it can be associated with the government and the movements of public life, the cohesion of the nation and the power of the government which controls the church will be increased. Of the possibly pernicious influence of such arrangements on such a church and on religion I do not speak; that is quite another matter. I am only pointing out that a Constitution will gain strength, and a nation unity, if the ecclesiastical arrangements can be linked to those of the secular government, assuming the people to be all attached to the same form of faith and worship.

Similarly, in so far as those who frame a Constitution can make it provide a system of education which will give the people common ideas and common aspirations, in so far as they can persuade the inhabitants to use a common language, if the country is one where more than one tongue has been spoken, or even to enjoy and meet for the enjoyment of common festivities and games, they will be availing themselves of influences not to be despised. The Prussian Government founded the University of Bonn immediately after the recovery of the left bank of the Rhine from France in 1814, and the University of Strassburg immediately after the recovery of Alsace in 1871, in both cases with the view of bene-

---

[1] There are of course dissenting sects in Russia, some of them counting many adherents, but they have seldom, and in no large measure, affected the political unity of the nation.

fiting these territories and of drawing them closer to
the rest of the country by the afflux of students from
other parts of it, an aim which was realized. Indeed the
non-local character of the German Universities, each
serving the whole of the lands wherein the German
tongue was spoken, powerfully contributed to intensify
the sentiment of a common German nationality throughout the two centuries (1648 to 1870) during which Germany had virtually ceased to be a State. The Olympian,
Pythian, Isthmian, and Nemean games had no contemptible effect in fostering the sentiment of a common
national unity, as against the barbarians, among the
Greeks, who had never enjoyed and did not desire political union. The admission of the Macedonian king to
strive at the Olympian games was a political event of
high significance, for it enabled his descendants Philip
and Alexander the Great to claim to belong to the Hellenic race.

Some of these various engines for promoting the cohesion of a nation may seem to lie rather in the sphere
of governmental action than in that of a Constitution.
Commercial freedom, however, as well as religious com-
pulsion on the one hand, or religious freedom on the
other hand, have been provided for by some Rigid Constitutions. So too has been the use of certain languages.
Where the Constitution is a Flexible one, the question
whether the laws regulating such matters are to be
deemed a part of the Constitution depends entirely on
the practical importance ascribed to them, since in such
a Constitution there is no distinction of form between
fundamental and other provisions.

IV. How Constitutions may Reduce or Regulate the Centrifugal Forces.

Now let us see what Constitutions may effect in the
other of the two above specified ways, viz. what they
may do to meet and grapple with, and if possible disarm,

the tendencies which make for disruption, *i.e.* the forces which, while drawing men together in minor groups within the State, are as regards the State itself centrifugal forces.

What are these tendencies? History tells us that the chief among them are race feeling, resentment for past injuries, grievances in respect of real or supposed ill-treatment in matters of industry, or of trade, or of education, or of language, or of religion, where these grievances or any of them press on a part only of the population. If they press on the whole population, or on the humbler classes as a whole, they are perturbing, but not necessarily nor even probably disruptive, *i.e.* they threaten disaffection or a general revolt against the government, rather than the severance of a particular province or the secession of a particular section of the people. It is only with grievances which affect one section or district, and make it desire an independence to be obtained by separation, that we have here to deal. There must be in every such case either a sentiment of dislike on the part of the disaffected section towards the rest of the nation, or else a belief that great material advantages will be obtained by separation; and the latter of these causes is almost sure to produce the former. When two or more of these tendencies combine in any given case, so much the stronger does the desire for separation become.

A few illustrations will explain better than a long abstract statement what I desire to convey. In the ancient world the thing which we call National Sentiment was seldom a powerful factor, perhaps because the more advanced peoples were divided into small city communities, while the backward peoples, living under large empires like the Persian or that of the Seleucid kings, were allowed to retain their own customs and religion, and often their native princes, feeling the weight of subjection only in having to pay tribute and send a contingent in war. The only nations that gave much trouble to the

Achaemenid kings of Persia were the Egyptians, a race very peculiar and very conceited, and the Greeks of Asia Minor. Under the Roman Empire there were wonderfully few national revolts, probably because the imperial government pressed equally upon all, conceded rights of citizenship pretty freely, and gave the subjects in exchange for their own national sentiment the higher pride of belonging to the majestic World State which had engulfed them. The chief source of disruptive attempts lay in the monotheistic religions. The Jews made more than one obviously hopeless rebellion. When Christianity became the religion of the Empire, schisms and heresies gave trouble. Africa was convulsed by the Donatist movement. Egypt was disaffected owing to Monophysitism, and no doubt gave herself the more readily to the Arab conquerors in respect of this disaffection. The persecuted Montanist sectaries of Phrygia revolted in the sixth century. It was the religious persecution of the Fire-worshipping Sassanid kings that provoked their Armenian vassals to rebellion[1]. So in the fifteenth and sixteenth centuries, the sentiment of nationality having not yet reached its full strength, it was chiefly by religious divisions that the unity of States was threatened. This was what lost the Dutch Netherlands to Spain. This was what split up the Romano-Germanic Empire, and made it, after the Thirty Years' War, the mere shadow of a State. It contributed to keep the Highlanders distinct from the Lowland population of Scotland after the Reformation (though other causes also were at work), and it was of course a still more potent force in Ireland. In our own time it nearly rent Switzerland in two in the war of the Sonderbund. Conversely, any one who notices how little the unity of the nation has been threatened in Spain, a country where the populations and dialects of the different provinces still present striking contrasts, and are accom-

---

[1] The dualistic Zoroastrianism of Persia seems to have taken many of the characteristics of a monotheistic religion.

panied by diversities of character, will be disposed to attribute this fact not merely to the absence of natural boundaries between the provinces, but also to the remarkable religious unity which the nation has always preserved.

In our own time, while religion is a less energetic factor, what is called national sentiment has begun to threaten loosely compacted States. It compelled the transformation in 1868 of the so-called Austrian Empire into the present Dual Monarchy. It shakes the Austrian half of that monarchy now, so sharp is the antagonism between the Czechs of Bohemia and the other Slavic populations of Cis-Leithania and the Germans of the Western and South-Western Crown Lands. Iceland differs from Denmark, with which she has been politically united since 1380 (or 1397), in language, in character, and in habits, and she has therefore struggled for autonomy, a large measure of which she obtained in 1874. She has had some economic grievances, but sentiment has been an even stronger element in her discontent, which, however, stopped short of a wish to separate, as she feels herself too small to stand alone. A strong party in Norway has desired to be divorced from Sweden, to which she was unnaturally yoked in 1814 by the Congress of Vienna, not merely in respect of specific complaints regarding the Foreign Office and the consular service, but also because her people, though Lutherans like the Swedes, are far more democratic in ideas and temper than the latter, and because their high national pride makes them unwilling to appear to be in any way subordinate to the sister kingdom. The case of Poland is a simple one, because she has the memory of an independent kingdom destroyed by force and fraud, and is different in religion, as well as in speech, from the Russians who have annexed her. Had the peasant population of the country shared the patriotism of the upper and middle classes, Poland might possibly have succeeded in shaking off the yoke. Even now her disaffection is a source of weakness to Russia. In Ireland several currents of discontent have joined to produce the passion and prolong the struggle for autonomy, or, in a very few of the more ardent minds, for independence. There is the diversity of faith, which remains, though that of language has almost vanished, a diversity embittered by recollections of persecution. There are economic grievances, the memory of the destruction of an industry in the last century, the more urgent resentment at the exactions of landlords, and the peasants' desire to have a grip of the soil. There is an incompatibility of character and temperament, due partly to historical conditions, partly to the old antagonism of Celt and Teuton. All these have gone to create a passion among the people to be recognized as a nation controlling its own affairs, a passion which is the same in essence among those who would be content with the possession of a subordinate legislature, and those, now fewer than formerly, who would like to go further.

If the sources of the centrifugal force in Ireland are easily explicable, and indeed so strong that had this force acted upon the whole nation instead of only upon a majority which consists mainly of the poorer and weaker part of the population, it would have before now prevailed, those which induced the secession of the Southern States of America are much less evident. Here there was no religious factor, nor any revengeful feeling, nor any sense of an unjust or oppressive control. The South had obtained more than its fair share of power and influence in the councils of the Union. But the planters had persuaded themselves that property in slaves and the whole slave-holding system were threatened by the growing strength in the Northern and Western States of an aversion to slavery, with a determination to check its extension; and the irritation of feeling which a long struggle had engendered, coupled with a growing dissimilarity of habits and ideas, enabled the hot-headed oligarchy which controlled the Southern

16

population to drive it into separation. Possibly these causes would not have been strong enough to provoke an armed conflict in a unified country. It was the existence of State Governments, and the conviction that the rights of the States, supposed to be guaranteed by the Constitution, furnished a legal basis for secession, that spurred the South into its desperate venture.

What then can the framing, or the manipulation in working, of a Constitution do to reduce the power of such disruptive tendencies as we have been considering?

They may of course be resisted by the employment of physical force. If a government is sufficiently strong and resolute, and is supported by the great majority of the nation, it may crush down the discontent of a province or a section. It is however an axiom in free governments, and ought to be an axiom in all governments, that physical force should never be used when peaceful means will suffice. Coercion usually seems easier, and naturally commends itself to the dull, the impatient, and the violent, to imperious princes, arrogant ministers, and excited majorities. But coercion, besides being a fatal expedient if it fails, is often a bad expedient when it appears to succeed, for it leaves smouldering discontent behind among the vanquished, and it is apt to inflict a moral injury upon the victors, perhaps to warp for the future their frame of government and to lower their political traditions. Accordingly whenever a Constitution can be so drawn and worked as to give the disjunctive tendencies just so much recognition as may disarm their violence, and bring all sections of the nation and all parts of the country to acquiesce in unity under one government, this course is to be preferred. It may sometimes fail. Every expedient may fail. But it has generally more promise of ultimate success than force has, for in a free country force is not a remedy, but a confession of past failures and a postponement of dangers likely to recur.

Among the methods which a Constitution may employ for the purpose indicated, the following find a place.

It may enact certain securities against oppression, whether by the executive or by the legislature, giving to such securities a specially solemn sanction, and thus reassuring the minds of the citizens. This was done by Magna Charta, by the Petition of Right, and again by the American Federal and State Constitutions, and by the French Declaration of the Rights of Man of 1789. It is usually done for the protection of all subjects or citizens alike, but of course the benefit of such a protection enures with special value for any section of the population, or any province or group of provinces, likely to be specially exposed at any given time to the abuses of power, because they are a minority whom the Government, or the majority, may view with disfavour.

A Constitution may provide means for varying the general institutions or laws of the State in such a way as to exempt particular parts of the State from any legislation that might be opposed to their special interests or feelings. The retention of Scotland as a distinct kingdom after the union of the crowns in 1603, and as a distinct part of the United Kingdom after the Treaty and Act of Union in 1707, has had most beneficial effects in enabling Scotland to be treated separately where it is fitting she should be. Her faith, her laws and judicature, her system of local government, have remained almost intact, to the satisfaction of her people, and with no injury to the cohesion of the united monarchy [1]. Similarly the maintenance of Finland as a separate Grand Duchy, with her own tongue, religion, laws and privileges, guaranteed by the coronation oath of the Czar, has made the Finns loyal and contented subjects, and has in no wise detracted from the strength of Russia [2]. The cases

---

[1] Though it must be admitted that the passing of legislation disapproved by the majority of Scotch representatives, or the omission to pass legislation which they demand, often elicits murmurs.

[2] This wise policy seems unfortunately to be now (1900) on the point of being abandoned, with results which every lover of freedom and progress must regret.

of Hungary as towards the Austrian Monarchy, and of Croatia as towards Hungary, are also in point.

It may provide for relegating certain classes of affairs to local legislatures, such as those of Croatia or Finland, areas which are not only, like Scotland, political divisions retaining their old laws, but also, unlike Scotland, since the Union, communities enjoying local autonomy. All Federations are managed on this system; and one can see in the case of Canada the advantages it secures, for the Roman Catholics of Quebec are able to have legislation diverse from that which the Protestant majority desires in the other provinces of the Dominion.

It may assign certain administrative and, within limits, certain legislative functions also to the inhabitants of minor local areas, such as counties, empowering them to regulate their local affairs in their own way. Provisions of this nature are not usually embodied in European constitutional instruments. They are, however, to be found in the State Constitutions of the American States. And they are really, in substance, parts of any well-framed Constitution, for nothing contributes more to the smooth working of a central government and to the satisfaction of the people under it, than the habit of leaving to comparatively small local communities the settlement of as many questions as possible. The practice of local self-government and the love for it are not a centrifugal force, but rather tend to ease off any friction that may exist by giving harmless scope for independent action, and thus producing local contentment. It is only where there exist grievances fostering disruptive sentiments that the existence of local bodies with a pretty large sphere of activity need excite disquiet.

It may exclude certain matters altogether from the competence of the central government, and thereby keep them out of the range of controversy. This principle has been wisely followed in the American and Canadian and Swiss Federal Constitutions as regards religion in its relations to the State. In some federations it has been similarly found desirable to disable the several legislatures from dealing with topics likely to produce dissensions among the members of the federation, or otherwise to affect the cohesion of the nation. Thus in the United States no State legislature can impose any duties on goods brought from one State to another, nor in any wise interfere with commerce between the States.

By these means a Constitution may prevent the disruptive forces in a country from threatening the stability of the central government or the unity of the State. To remove part of the material on which they might work is to weaken their working, and to divert into safe channels the political activity they would evoke. Although a Flexible Constitution may accomplish this, if those who work it respect certain fundamental principles and treat their querulous minorities in a conciliatory spirit, the work is best done, and usually has been done, by a Rigid Constitution, because this latter provides a guarantee to minorities, or to subdivisions of the country, stronger than they can have under an omnipotent legislature. In fact the existence of the grounds of contention and possibilities of disruption we have been considering is among the chief causes which have called Federal Governments and Rigid Constitutions into being.

One further observation should be made before quitting this part of the subject. Racial differences and animosities, which have played a large part in threatening the unity of States, are usually dangerous only when the unfriendly races occupy different parts of the country. If they live intermixed, in tolerably equal numbers, and if in addition they are not of different religions, and speak the same tongue, the antagonism will disappear in a generation or two by social intercourse and especially by intermarriage. When the right of full legal intermarriage had been established, the fusion of the patricians and the plebs at Rome began. So the Northmen in the tenth and eleventh centuries, so the Norman-French in the eleventh and twelfth centuries, became blent with the English. The Magyars and Saxons, though generally occupying different parts of the country, and to some extent retaining each their own speech, have in Transylvania now begun to melt into one. It is the fact that they not only speak a different tongue but also profess a different faith that keeps the Rumans of that province apart from both Saxons and Magyars ; and even these differences might in time cease to operate did not these Rumans look across the mountains to a large Ruman State into which they would gladly be absorbed. But in one set of cases no fusion is possible ; and this set of cases forms the despair of the statesman. It presents a problem which no Constitution has solved. It is the juxtaposition on the same soil of races of different colour.

This is a recent phenomenon in history. In the ancient world, almost all the barbarous tribes whom Rome subdued and brought into her Empire were sufficiently near the Italians and Hellenized Asiatics in physical characteristics for intermarriage to go on freely. The Carthaginians, who to be sure were not numerous, seem to have soon lost their distinctive nationality : and that the Jews remained distinct was their own doing, not that of the conquerors [1]. Even as towards Egyptians and Numidians, who were certainly dark, one hears of little repulsion. Besides, both races were intelligent, and the former in their way highly civilized. With the African slave trade a new and a dolorous chapter in history opens. In our own time it is the settlement of Europeans in countries where the native holds his ground against the settler, as the Kafir does in South Africa, and the aboriginal Peruvians and Araucanians do in Western South America, or it is the influx of coloured immigrants, like that of the Chinese in Western America and the Hawaiian Isles, that raises, or threatens to raise in

---

[1] In two respects the Jews under the early Empire would seem to have been above the average level of the civilized subjects of Rome. There was apparently very little slavery among them ; and there must have been an exceptionally large proportion of persons able to read.

the future, this problem in an acute form. A community in which there exist two or more race-elements physically contrasted and socially unsusceptible of amalgamation cannot grow into a really united State. If the coloured people are excluded from political rights, there is created a source of weakness, possibly of danger. If they are admitted, there is admitted a class who cannot fully share the political life of the more civilized and probably smaller element, who will not be consoled by political equality for social disparagement, and who may lower the standard of politics by their incompetence or by their liability to corruption. If the people of colour are dispersed over the country among the Europeans, instead of dwelling in masses by themselves, they may not act as a centrifugal force, threatening secession, but they are a serious hindrance to the working of any form of popular government that has been hitherto devised, for they divide the population, they complicate political issues, they prevent the growth of a genuinely national opinion.

The most noteworthy attempts that Constitutions have made to deal with these cases have been made in the United States, where the latest amendments to the Federal Constitution provide protection for the negroes and forbid the States to exclude any person from the electoral suffrage in respect of race or colour, and where several recent State Constitutions have devised ingenious schemes for disfranchising the vast mass of those whom these very amendments have sought to protect. So far as political rights are concerned, the problem is very far from having been solved in the United States. But as regards private civil rights, it has certainly been an advantage to the negroes that the Federal Constitution guarantees such rights to all citizens : and probably in any country where marked differences, with possible antagonisms, of race exist, it will be prudent to place the private civil rights of every class of persons under the equal protection of the laws, and to make the rights themselves practically identical. It would lead me too far from the main subject to describe the ways in which similar problems have been dealt with in Algeria, in South Africa, and in some of the other colonies of European nations. Nowhere has any quite satisfactory solution been found [1]. But the case of New Zealand deserves to be mentioned as one in which the experiment has been tried of giving parliamentary representation to the natives, who mostly live apart on their own reserved lands. So far, the results have been good. The conditions are favourable, for the Maoris are a brave and intelligent race, and they are now too few in number to excite disquiet.

It was the good fortune of the Roman Empire that the vast majority of the races whom it conquered and absorbed had no conspicuous physical differences from the Italians which prevented intermarriage and fusion. Race and birthplace were no great obstacle to a man of force. Two or three of the Emperors were of African or Arab extraction. Moreover, the peoples of Southern Europe seem to have less repulsion of sentiment towards the dark-skinned races than the Teutons have. The Spanish and Portuguese intermarry not only with the native Indians of Central and Southern America, but also with the negroes. The French of Canada intermarried more freely with the Indians of North America than the English have done.

Summing up, we may say that the aim of a well-framed Constitution will presumably be to give the maximum of scope to the centripetal and the minimum to the centrifugal forces. But this presumption is subject to two countervailing considerations. One is that the energy of civic life may be better secured by giving ample range and sphere of play to local self-government, which will stimulate and train the political interest of the members of the State, and relieve the central au-

[1] In Algeria the electoral suffrage is limited ; but in some of the French tropical colonies it seems to have been granted irrespective of colour.

thority of some onerous duties. The other is that the centrifugal forces may, if too closely pent up, like heated water in the heart of the earth, produce at untoward moments explosions like those of a volcano. Hence it is well to provide, in the Constitution, such means of escape for the steam as can be made compatible with the general safety of the State. Where a Constitution, and especially a Rigid Constitution, has been framed with due regard to these considerations, and turns to account the methods already discussed, it may itself become a new centripetal force, a factor making for the unity and coherence of the community which lives under it. The Rigid Constitution has in this respect one advantage over the Flexible one, that it is more easily understood by the mass of the people, and more capable of coming to form a part of their political consciousness. When such a Constitution is so contrived and worked as to satisfy the bulk of the nation—and it will do so all the more if no single section dislikes it—it attracts the affection and pride of the people, their pride because it is their work, their affection because they enjoy good government under it. Time, if it does not weaken these feelings, strengthens them, because reverence comes with age. By providing a convenient channel or medium through or in which the centripetal forces may act, the Constitution increases the effective strength of those forces. It is a reservoir of energy, an accumulator, if the comparison be permissible, which has been charged by a dynamo, and will go on for some time discharging the energy stored up in it. But, like an accumulator, its energy becomes exhausted if there is not behind it an engine generating fresh power, that is to say, if the real social and political forces which called it into being have become feebler, and those which oppose it have become stronger.

V. Illustrations from Modern History of the Action of Constitutions.

The best instance of the capacity of a Constitution to reinforce and confirm existing centripetal tendencies is supplied by the history of the Rigid Constitution of the United States. That instrument was at first received with so little favour by the people that its ratification was, in many States, obtained with the greatest possible difficulty, and the original document secured acceptance only on the understanding, which was loyally carried out, that it should forthwith receive a number of amendments. Within fifteen years the party which had advocated it was overthrown in the country, and ultimately broke up and vanished. A generation passed away before it began to be generally popular. But after a time it secured so widespread a respect that even during the fierce and protracted struggle which ushered in the Civil War few attacked the Constitution itself, nearly all the combatants on one side or the other claiming that its provisions were really in their favour. It was not round the merits, but round the true construction, of the instrument that controversy raged. Since the Civil War, and the amendments which embodied the results of the Civil War, it has been glorified and extolled in all quarters[1], and has unquestionably been a most potent influence in consolidating the nation, as well as in extending the range and the activity of the central government.

To what is this success due? Regarded as a Frame of Government, *i.e.* as a piece of mechanism for distributing powers between the Executive, the Legislature and the Judiciary, the American system has probably been praised beyond its deserts. Both the mode of electing the President and the working of Congress leave much to be desired. But the Constitution has had two conspicuous merits. It so judiciously estimated the

---

[1] Only since 1890 have complaints begun to be made: see Essay III, p. 202, ante.

centripetal and centrifugal forces as they actually stood at the time when it was framed, frankly recognizing the latter and leaving free play for them, and while throwing its own weight into the scale of the centripetal, doing this only so far as not to provoke a disjunctive reaction, that it succeeded in winning respect from the advocates both of States' Rights and of National Unity [1]. Thus it was able to add more strength to the centripetal tendency than it could have done had it been originally drawn on more distinctly centripetal lines. For—and here comes in the second merit—its provisions defining the functions of the central Government were expressed in such wide and elastic terms as to be susceptible of interpretation either in a more restricted or in a more liberal way, *i.e.* so as to allow either a less wide or a more wide scope of action for the Central Government. During the earlier years, when State sentiment was still stronger than National sentiment, the scope remained limited, because both the executive and the legislature wished to keep it so, and such extensions as there were came from judicial construction. But latterly, and especially since the prodigious development of internal communications has stimulated commerce, and since the death blow given to States' Rights doctrines by the Civil War, the scope has been widened, and has widened quite naturally and gradually, with no violence to the words of the Constitution, but according to that expansive interpretation of them which changing conditions and a corresponding change in national sentiment prescribed [2].

Nowadays one hears in the United States less about the Constitution than about the Flag [3]. But that is

[1] It has been accused of having caused a civil war by omitting to deal with the questions out of which the Civil War arose, and by failing to negative the right of secession. But to this it may be answered that an attempt to deal with those questions or to negative that right might possibly have prevented it from having ever been accepted.

[2] This interpretation has sometimes been at variance with the views of the older interpreters, but no instance occurs to me in which an impartial jurist could have pronounced it inadmissible.

[3] This is still more so to-day (1900) than it was when this Essay was first composed.

partly because the Constitution has done its work, and made the Flag the popular badge of an Unity which it took nearly a century to endear to the nation.

One might go on to illustrate the efficiency of a Constitution in consolidating a people composed of disparate elements from the parallel case of Switzerland, where communities speaking three (it might almost be said four) different languages have been brought much closer together by the Constitutions of 1848 and 1874 than they were before, or could have been without some such arrangement. Switzerland, however, is a more complicated case, because much has turned on the external pressure towards unity exerted by the fear felt for several great bordering Powers. The formidable neighbours of the Confederation have, so to speak, squeezed together into a Swiss people the originally dissimilar Alemannic, Celto-Burgundian, Italian, and Romansch communities.

The two instances of the United States and Switzerland [1], compared with those of unitary countries living under Rigid Constitutions, such as France, Belgium, Holland and Denmark, suggest the observation that the service which Rigid Constitutions may render in strengthening the centripetal tendency can best be rendered where a Federation is to be constructed. For in these cases what is needed is an arrangement by which the several rights of the component communities which are to form the State may be so protected that they need not fear to give their allegiance to the State and cordially support its Central Government. The exist-

[1] One would like to refer to the cases of the numerous so-called republics, most of them federal, of Spanish America. But apart from the difficulty of ascertaining their constitutional history, little of which has been written, some of these republics seem to pay so little regard to their constitutions, living generally in a state of revolution, whether subsiding, or actually raging, or apprehended, like the Atlantic during a series of cyclones following one another along the same track from the Bermudas to the Fastnet, that it is hard to draw any conclusions of value from them. They are in fact republics only in name: and it is surprising that Sir H. Maine in his *Popular Government* condescended to go to them for arguments to discredit democracy. They are military tyrannies, the product of peculiar historical, territorial and racial conditions.

ence of such communities is an expression of forces actually operative which are centrifugal as towards the State as a whole, and therefore need to be studied. By giving a carefully limited scope to these forces, and thereby diminishing their possibilities of danger, the Constitution subserves the cohesion of the States. In a truly unitary country this service is not needed. But there are cases in which States endeavouring to become unitary would have done better had they sought to apply the federal principle, placing it under the protection of a Rigid Constitution. I have already referred to Denmark. Holland might probably have saved Belgium by a concession of some such kind. Whether a similar contrivance might not have been profitably employed within the British Isles in A.D. 1782, or in A.D. 1800, or again later, is a question which will already have presented itself to one who has followed the argument thus far.

In dwelling upon the services which Constitutions may render, by fostering the centripetal forces, or by restraining the violence and softening the action of the centrifugal forces, we must not forget that no scheme of government can hope permanently to resist the action of either tendency if either develops much greater strength than it possessed when the Constitution was framed. If the centripetal forces grow, the Constitution whose provisions have recognized and given scope to the centrifugal will be practically, in some of those provisions, superseded. If the centrifugal grow, it may be overthrown. It is where the forces are nearly balanced, that the weight of the Constitution may turn the scale, and avert conflicts which would have rent the community, or caused a violent subjection of one part of it to the other. And in any case the Constitution ought, where dissimilative and disruptive forces are feared, to be so drawn as to enlist all available motives of interest, to shelter the law behind popular sentiment where possible, to oppose it to sentiment as little as possible, and

to avoid challenging at the same time the hostility of
several kinds of sentiment.

VI. The Probable Action of the Aggregative and the Disjunctive Tendencies in the Future.

Whether in the long run it is the centripetal or the
centrifugal force that will prevail in politics, or, in other
words, whether large States or small States are more
likely to commend themselves to mankind, is a question
which belongs rather to history than to the doctrines of
constitutions, and which could be adequately discussed
only after a long investigation. History shows us first
one force dominant, then the other, though no doubt
the centrifugal is usually more powerful in rude times
and in hilly or mountainous countries, the centripetal
in countries comparatively advanced in civilization, and
in level and fertile regions where wealth is more easily
acquired and stored, and where military operations are
easier. When the mists of antiquity begin to rise sufficiently to show us the Mediterranean and south-west
Asiatic world, we discover both a few great States and a
multitude of small ones. The former have a low, the
latter a high and intense political vitality. From the
time of Menes down to that of Attila the tendency is
generally towards aggregation: and the history of the
ancient nations shows us, not only an enormous number
of petty monarchies and republics swallowed up in the
Empire of Rome, but that empire itself far more highly
centralized than any preceding one had been. When the
Roman dominion began to break up the process was
reversed, and for seven hundred years or more the centrifugal forces had it their own way. Europe and Western Asia were divided up among innumerable petty potentates, and even the large monarchies, such as the two
Khalifates, the Romano-Germanic Empire, the kingdoms of France and Hungary, possessed so feeble a
royal authority that the real organs of government and

centres of attraction were to be sought rather in the vassals than in the nominal sovereign. From the thirteenth century onwards the tide begins to set the other way. One great State indeed—the Empire—first decays and then disappears under the action of centrifugal forces, but all the other chief States expand, absorbing their smaller neighbours, and giving themselves a compact and well-knit organization which makes the central power effective through the whole sphere of its action. This process culminates in the despotic monarchies of the eighteenth century, when the strength of feudal localism has been completely broken, though the picturesque relics of it still cumber the ground, and when at the same time the foundations are laid in the West of a gigantic State which proceeds to cover the temperate area of North America between the two oceans, and, in the East, of the dominion of a European nation which has absorbed the numerous and populous principalities of India. Immediately afterwards the doctrine of popular self-government and the doctrine of nationalities come upon the scene, threatening a disruption of some existing political aggregates. In point of fact, however, these new principles have done as much to unite as to sever, for though five States—Greece, Rumania, Servia, Montenegro and Bulgaria—have been cut off from an effete monarchy, and sixteen republics have been carved out of the American dominions of Spain and Portugal, the doctrine of nationality has substituted two new great States, more important than all the last-mentioned twenty-one put together, for the multitude of kingdoms and principalities which so late as 1859 filled Italy and Germany.

Thus neither Democracy nor the principle of Nationalities has, on the balance of cases, operated to check the general movement towards aggregation which marks the last six centuries.

It may, however, be said—and this question should be faced before we proceed to inquire whether the aggregative movement is likely to continue—that in all this inquiry we have been ignoring two potent factors. One is Conquest—that is to say, military power. We have been examining the forces of Interest and Sympathy, which cover a number of influences social or economic, racial or sentimental. But after all it is Conquest, *i.e.* the might of the strongest, which has created most States as we find them. Is Conquest one of the centripetal forces? and if so, is it not the greatest of them?

The other factor is Family Succession, which both during the Middle Ages and since has done a great deal to consolidate principalities and kingdoms. The United Kingdom owes much to this agency, Austria and France even more.

Conquest and Dynastic Succession are hardly fit to be classed among the centripetal forces, because they are not susceptible of scientific treatment like the other influences. The disposition of the stronger to subdue and annex the weaker neighbour is of course a permanent fact in human nature, and therefore in history. But in each particular instance the success of one or other combatant depends on what may be called historical accidents—on the numbers or the discipline of troops, on the possession of a commander of military genius, on alliances with other states, on the internal dissensions of one state as compared with the unity of another. Physical force belongs to a different sphere from that in which political constitutions work. Constitutions may result from a conquest or may be maintained for a time by arms ; but if they are obliged to rely on and have constant recourse to physical force in order to prevent their overthrow, they are, considered as Constitutions, failures; because the very nature and object of a constitutional Frame of Government is so to express and so to adjust to existing conditions the wishes and aims of the citizens as to make the majority, and if possible the vast majority, of the people desire to support it. According to the proverb, you can do anything with bayonets except sit down on them. Physical force is of course needed to punish occasional infractions of the Constitution or to quell revolts against it. But the system of government which *ex hypothesi* corresponds to the permanently strongest among the moral forces, else it has no right to prevail in a free country, ought not to be surrounded by cannon.

Similarly, the devolution of princedoms or kingdoms by marriage and inheritance, much as it has done to bring States originally independent under one government, lies outside political science in the proper sense of the term. Like conquest, it brings about a new state of things by an event with which the ordinary political and constitutional phenomena of national life have nothing to do, coming into these phenomena as an incommensurable and (so to speak) irrational factor [1].

So soon as either conquest or a union due to hereditary succession has taken place, the normal centripetal and centrifugal tendencies resume their action. Where the territory of one people has been forcibly acquired by another, as Lombardy was acquired by Austria in 1815, or has been occupied in virtue of a title based on succession, as Portugal was claimed by Spain in 1580, such centripetal forces as may exist have the advantage of physical force behind them. But this advantage may be unavailing against the stronger forces which sentiment sends forth to dissever the connexion. Austria lost Lombardy after forty-four years; Spain lost Portugal after sixty. In both cases there was fighting, but it was not so much the balance of military strength as the settled hostility of the subjected people which in both caused the severance. So the acquisition by the English kings of Aquitaine and the subsequent conquest

---

[1] The fact that the custom of a country permits or forbids succession through females makes a great difference in the importance of succession. The union of Castile with Aragon, like the union of England with Scotland, would not have occurred under a different rule of succession. So it may make a difference whether the throne of the larger country passes to the dynasty of the smaller, or vice versa. Had a king of England inherited the throne of Scotland, Scotland might have been more hostile to England. Had a king of Portugal inherited the throne of Spain, the two countries might have remained united.

17

of large part of France, the conquest by the Turks of Transylvania, the union of Holstein with Denmark, the union of Belgium with Holland, the union of Alsace with France, all effected without regard to the will of the people, were all in time brought to an end. The last-mentioned case is a peculiar one. It was not because the Alsatians wished to be reunited to Germany, but because the Germans wished to be reunited to Alsace that a connexion which had lasted nearly two centuries was dissolved in 1871. Military motives, decisive as regards the annexed part of Lorraine, had something to do with the taking of Alsace also; but if Alsace had not been German in language and habits, though not in sentiment, the popular voice of Germany would not have insisted on recovering it against the will of its inhabitants.

Speaking broadly, one may say that Conquest and Inheritance give an opportunity, better in the latter than in the former case, for centripetal forces to work. If the peoples on which they operate are backward, with no pronounced national feeling, that chance may be a good one, and the influences of free commerce, joint government (especially if it is good government), together with the kind of pride which common service in war often produces, may operate to weld two peoples together into a united State. Much depends on language, much on geographical position, much on external pressure from powerful neighbours. But if one of the peoples (or both) has already developed a strong sentiment of nationality, the prospect of fusion is but slender.

The Roman Empire is the capital instance of a vast dominion established by conquest. But there it was the weakness of the centrifugal forces that secured the cohesion of the Empire. The conquered countries were either, like Gaul, Spain and Britain, occupied by tribes between whom there existed so weak a bond that no general national feeling or combined national action was possible, or had been, as in the Eastern Mediterranean

World, ruled by dynasties, most of them sprung from military adventurers [1], so that the sentiment of national life had not centred in the monarchy. The centrifugal forces of interest—the desire for peace, good government, facilities for commerce, and so forth—obtained free play under the imperial administration, and to these was added after a time the sense of pride in Roman citizenship, and in the greatness of a State which included all the highest civilization of the world. So too during the Middle Ages not a few conquests ended in an assimilation of the vanquished, which enlarged without weakening the conquering nation. But during the last three centuries the experience of military powers has been that the acquisition of masses of subjects who, being already civilized, are likely to resist absorption and to remain disaffected, is a doubtful gain and may become a danger to the conquering State. The last conspicuous instance is Poland, partitioned between three Powers, to all of whom her provinces have brought trouble. Conquests continue to be made, but they are now mostly of barbarous or semi-civilized races, so inferior to the conquerors in force and in national spirit that the centrifugal forces are, or at least seem to be, practically negligible.

Is it possible, then, to arrive at any conclusion regarding the respective strength which these two sets of forces are likely to display in the coming centuries? Will the tendency to aggregation continue, and does the future belong to great States? Or may new forces appear which will reverse the process, as it was reversed, though through causes most unlikely to reappear, at the fall of the Roman Empire?

At first sight the probabilities seem to point to further aggregation. Although none of the five great na-

---

[1] There were of course also a certain number of city republics, or leagues of republics, but these were too small to have developed national feeling in the modern sense ; and the Roman system left most of them a certain measure of self-government which modified their regret for an independence the delight in which had been (in many cases) reduced by domestic disorders.

tional States—Russia, Germany, France, Italy, Britain
—is in the least likely to be absorbed by any of the
others, there is reason to think that within the next century some of the smaller states will have disappeared
from the map of Europe. In one or two other parts of
the world—as for instance in South and in Central America—the process by which the great States are expanding is not yet complete. The influences of swifter and
cheaper communications by land and sea, of increasing
commerce, and of the closer intercourse which commerce brings, of the power exerted by the printing press
in extinguishing the languages which prevail over a
small area and diffusing those spoken by vast masses of
men—all these things make for unity within each of the
great States and add to the attractive power which the
greater have for the smaller. These influences, moreover, all promise to be permanent.

Against them we must set the fact that Conquest, so
far as civilized peoples are concerned, seems likely to
play a smaller rôle in the future than in the past, because
it begins to be perceived how tenacious is the sentiment
of nationality in a vanquished people, and how much the
maintenance of that sentiment may endanger the victor
State. As was observed in an earlier page, the progress
of a community in civilization often tends to intensify
both its capacity for political discontent and its peculiar
national sentiment, thus counterworking the influences
of trade and wealth. A people, or a nationality included
in a large State, while feeling the centripetal forces of
material interest, may nevertheless feel the repellent
instinct of an unquenched attachment to its national traditions and cling to the hope of reviving its old national
life.

The problem is, however, a far more complex one than
any comparison of the influences of material interest on
the one side and national sentiment on the other would
suggest. Many phenomena may be imagined which
would affect it as the world moves on. One is a change

in the conditions under which war is waged. Another is a removal of some of the causes which induce war, or a means, better than now exists, of averting its outbreak. Another is the growth of what is called Collectivism and a disposition to apply its principles in small rather than in large areas, seeing that there are obviously some things which can be better managed in the former. We are far from having exhausted the possibilities of the influence of scientific discovery upon economic life, and through it upon social and political life. Both the relations of Nations and States to one another and the relations of the groups or communities within each State to each other may be affected in ways as yet scarcely dreamt of. Neither can we foresee the modes in which the scientific way of looking at all questions may come ultimately to tinge and modify men's habits of thought even in social and political matters. No institution was at one time more generally prevalent over the world, or seemed more deeply rooted, than Slavery; and slavery, which has now vanished from civilized communities, will soon have vanished from all countries. There is indeed hardly any institution for which permanance can be predicted except—and some will not admit even this exception—the Family.

Imagine a world in which all the hitherto unappropriated territories had been allotted to one or other of the few strongest States. Imagine tariffs abolished and the principle of equality of trade-facilities among States established. Imagine a system of international arbitration created under which the risks of war were so greatly reduced that the prospects of war did not occupy men's minds and give a military and aggressive tinge to their patriotism. The present relations of centripetal and centrifugal forces would under such conditions be greatly altered, as respects both the wide theatre of the world and the internal conditions of each particular State.

Imagine also a great advance in the desire to use governmental agencies for the benefit of the citizens, and a general conviction that such agencies could best be used by comparatively small communities rather than by the State as a whole. A new centrifugal force, centrifugal at least in respect of each State, would thereby have been called into action. No one will venture to foretell any of these things. But none of them is impossible; and it is plain that they might produce a set of conditions, and a play of forces, unlike the present, and unlike any period in the past. We must not therefore assume that the large States and the present structure and organization of States will be permanent.

Of the more remote future, History can venture to say little more than this—that it will never bring back the past. She recognizes that, as Heraclitus says, one cannot step twice into the same river. Even when she is able to declare that certain forces will assuredly be present, she cannot forecast their relative strength at any given moment, nor say what hitherto unobserved forces they may not, in their action upon one another, call into activity. All she can do for the lawyer, the statesman and the legislator, when they have to study and use the forces operative in their own time, is to indicate to them the nature and the character, the significant elements of strength and weakness, that belong to each and every force that has been heretofore conspicuous, so as to direct and guide them in observing and reflecting on the present. This is much less than has sometimes been claimed for history. Nevertheless it is a real service, for nothing is more difficult than to observe exactly, and the ripest fruit of historical study is that detachment of mind, created by the habit of scientific thinking, which prevents observation from being coloured by prejudice or passion.

V

PRIMITIVE ICELAND

ICELAND is known to most men as a land of volcanoes, geysers and glaciers. But it ought to be no less interesting to the student of history as the birthplace of a brilliant literature in poetry and prose, and as the home of a people who have maintained for many centuries a high level of intellectual cultivation. It is an almost unique instance of a community whose culture and creative power flourished independently of any favouring material conditions, and indeed under conditions in the highest degree unfavourable. Nor ought it to be less interesting to the student of politics and laws as having produced a Constitution unlike any other whereof records remain, and a body of law so elaborate and complex that it is hard to believe that it existed among men whose chief occupation was to kill one another.

With the exception of Madeira and the Azores, Iceland is the only part of what we call the Old World [1] which was never occupied by a prehistoric race, and in which, therefore, the racial origin of the population is historically known to us.

None of those rude tribes who dwell scattered over the north of Asia, Europe and America—Lapps, Samoyedes or Esquimaux—ever set foot in it. Adamnan, Abbot of Iona from A. D. 679 to 704, reports in his famous

---

[1] Though geographically Iceland belongs rather to North America than to Europe, geologically its affinities are with the Cape Verde Islands, the Canaries, Madeira, and possibly the Azores to the South, with Jan Mayen to the North, as it seems to owe its origin to a line of volcanic action stretching from the Cape Verde Islands to far beyond the Arctic Circle.

Life of St. Columba [1], a prophecy of the saint regarding
a holy man named Kormak, who, in Columba's days
(A. D. 521-597), made three long voyages from Ireland in
search of the ' Desert in the Ocean ' (*eremum in Oceano*),
a term so happily descriptive of Iceland that one is
tempted to believe it to be the region referred to.   A
little later the Venerable Beae (A. D. 673-735) speaks of
contemporaries of his own who, coming from the isle of
Thule, declared that in it the sun could be seen at mid-
night for a few days [2].   Still later the Irish monk Dicuil
(writing about A. D. 825) tells [3] of an isle lying far to the
North-West where monks known to him had spent the
summer some thirty years before.   And our earliest Icelandic authority, the famous *Landnámabók* (Book of the
Land-takings), mentions that when the first Norwegian
settlers arrived they found a few hermits of Irish race already established there, who soon vanished from the
presence of the stronger heathen, leaving behind books,
bells and staves (probably croziers).   The Norse settlers
called them Papas (*i.e.* priests), or Westmen, a term used
to describe the Scots of Ireland.   No doubt, then, the
earliest discoverers of the isle were these Celtic hermits,
who had crossed the wide and stormy sea in their light
coracles of wood and leather, consecrating themselves
to prayer and fasting in this inclement wilderness.   But
they contributed no element to the population of the
island, and can hardly be said to have a place in its
history, which begins with the great Norwegian
immigration.

The first Teuton to reach Iceland was a Norse Viking
named Naddoð, who was driven to the isle by a storm in

---

[1] *Vita S. Columbae*, cap. vi.

[2] Comment. on 2 Kings xx. 9.   The extreme northernmost point of Iceland just
touches the Arctic Circle.

[3] In his book *De Mensura Orbis Terrae*, cap. 7, he identifies the isle with Thule;
and the reports of the monks point rather to Iceland than to the Faeroe Isles, a
group which Dicuil mentions elsewhere, and which therefore he cannot mean by
his Thule.   The name Thule has of course been applied by different writers to
different lands.   When Tacitus says that it was seen in the distance by the fleet of
Agricola, he probably means either Shetland or the Fair Isle between the Shetlands and the Orkneys.

the latter half of the ninth century. He called it Snæ-land, or Snowland. A second visitor, a Swede named Gardar, sailed round it; a third (Flóki, a Norseman) landed, and gave it the name it still bears. But though the news of the discovery soon spread far and wide through the whole Northland, the isle might possibly have lain unoccupied but for the events that were passing in Norway. King Harald the Fairhaired was then in the full career of his conquests. The great battle of Hafrsfjord had established his power in Central and Southern Norway, and he was traversing the fjords with his fleet, compelling the petty chieftains who stood at the head of the numerous small independent communities that filled the country to acknowledge his supremacy, and imposing a tax upon the land-holding freemen.

The proud spirit of the warriors who for more than a century had been ravaging the coasts of all Western Europe could not brook subjection, and, being unable to offer a united opposition, the boldest and bravest among them resolved to find freedom in exile. Some sought the Orkneys, Shetlands and Faeroe isles, already settled by Northmen. Some joined the Norwegian set-tlers in Ireland, and drove the Celtic population out of some districts on its eastern coast. Others, again, fol-lowed Hrolf Ganger (Göngu Hrolfr) ('the Walker'), or Rollo as our books call him, a Viking who, having in-curred the wrath of Harald, sailed forth from his home on the fjords near Bergen to found in Northern Gaul a dynasty of Norsemen whence came the long line of Nor-man dukes and English kings, *Albanique patres atque altae moenia Romae.* And yet others, hearing the praises of the lately-discovered isle far off in the ocean, turned their prows to the west and landed on the solitary shores of Iceland. They embarked without any concert or com-mon plan; each chieftain, or head of a household, taking his own family, and perhaps a group of friends or de-pendents; and they settled in the new land where they pleased, sometimes throwing overboard as they neared

the shore the wooden columns, adorned with figures of
Thor and Oðin, of the high-seat in their old Norwegian
hall, and disembarking at the point to which these were
driven by the winds and currents. At first each took for
himself as much land as he desired, but those who came
later, when the better pastures had been already occupied, were obliged to buy land or to fight for it; and a
curious custom grew up by which the extent of territory
to which a settler was entitled was fixed. A man could
claim no more than what he could carry fire round in a
single day; a woman, than that round which she could
lead a two-year-old heifer. So rapid was the immigration, many colonists from Norwegian Ireland and the
Scottish isles, Orkneys, Shetlands and Hebrides (the
two former groups being then Scandinavian) joining
those who came direct from Norway, that in sixty years
the population had risen (so far as our data enable it to
be estimated) to about 50,000, a number which seems
not to have been exceeded down to the census of A.D.
1823. With those who came from Ireland and the Hebrides there came some small infusion of Celtic blood,
which we note in such names as Njál, Kjartan, and Kormak, given to men descended from the daughters of
Irish chieftains.

Planting themselves in this irregular way, and in a
country where the good land lay in scattered patches,
and where deserts, glaciers and morasses, as well as torrents, passable only with difficulty or even danger, cut
off one settlement from another, the first settlers did not
create, and indeed felt little need of, any political or social
organization. But after a time a sort of polity began to
shape itself, and the process of its growth is one of the
most interesting phenomena of mediaeval history. The
elements out of which it sprang were of course those two
which the settlers had brought with them from Norway,
and both of which were part of the common heritage of
the Teutonic race—the habit of joint worship at a temple,
and the habit of holding an assembly of all freemen to

discuss and dispatch matters of common interest, and more especially lawsuits [1]. This assembly resembled the Old English Folk Mot, and was called the Thing, a name which survives in our English word Hustings (Husting or House Thing), the platform from whence candidates spoke at parliamentary elections, which disappeared in A.D. 1872 when written nominations were prescribed by the statute which introduced vote by ballot. The Þing [2] was held at the temple, usually dedicated to Thor, the favourite deity of the Norsemen as Oðin was of the Swedes; since the place of worship was the natural centre of the neighbourhood, and the Þing was presided over by the local magnate or chief, who was usually also the owner or guardian of the local temple, there being among the Scandinavian peoples no special sacerdotal caste.

Now when a Norse chief settled himself in Iceland, one of his first acts was to erect a temple, often with the sacred pillars which he had brought from the ancestral temple in the old country. The temple soon became a place of resort, not only for his own immediate dependents, but also for those other settlers of the district who might not be rich enough to build and maintain a shrine of their own. Of this temple the chieftain and his descendants were the priests; and as the meetings of the local Þing were held in it, he was the natural person to preside over such meetings, both because he was usually (though not invariably) eminent by his wealth and power, and also because he offered the sacrifices and kept the sacred temple-ring on which judicial oaths were taken, as at Rome men swore at the Ara Maxima of Hercules. Thus the priest acquired, if he had not already enjoyed it, the position of a sort of local chieftain or magnate, not unlike those kings of heroic Greece whom we read of in

[1] Not but what the habit of holding such an assembly has existed among peoples of very diverse race in many parts of the world. It existed among the Greeks. It exists among the Kafirs of South Africa.

[2] I use the Icelandic and Anglo-Saxon letter Þ in this word to distinguish it from the common English word.

Homer, or those German tribe-princes whom Tacitus describes. Although his title was that of Goði [1] (originally Guði) or priest, a word derived from the name of the Deity, he lost in becoming the depositary of a certain measure of political power most of such religious character as his office had possessed. Nor did any sanctity attach to his person. In that age at least religion had come to sit rather lightly upon the Norsemen. Either from inner decay, or from the influence of the Christian peoples with whom they came in contact beyond the seas, the old faith was beginning to disintegrate. Worship was often cold or careless, and we read of men who regarded neither Þor nor Oðin, but trusted in their own might and main.

The Goði was therefore much more of a secular than of an ecclesiastical person, a chieftain rather than a priest in our sense of the word [2]. His powers as a chieftain were very indefinite, as indeed had been those of the local chieftains of Norway. He was only the first among a number of free and warlike land-owners, some of them equal or superior to him in lineage, with an official dignity which was little more than formal in the hands of a weak man, but might be turned to great account by a person of vigour and ability. As he presided in the Þing, so he was the appropriate person to see to the regularity of its judicial proceedings, to preserve order, and to provide for the carrying out of any measures of common concern on which it might determine. When any unforeseen danger or difficulty arose, he was looked to to advise or take the lead in action; the members of his Þing expected aid and protection from him, while he, like a thegn among the Teutons of contemporary England, expected support and deference from them. But he had no legal powers of coercion. Any one might op-

The term goði does not seem to have been used in Norway, but Ulfila, in his translation of the Bible into Gothic (in the fourth century A. D.), renders ἱερεύς by *gudja*. The ð is pronounced like th in 'then.'

[2] It is true that as the Sagas whence we draw our knowledge of the Goði were all written down at a time when heathenism had vanished, it is possible that they may not fully represent the original character of the office.

pose him in the Þing or out of it. Any Þing-man might withdraw at pleasure, join himself to some other Goði, and become a member of some other Þing¹. There was, it must be noted, no territorial circumscription corresponding to the Þing. Land had nothing to do with the position held by the Goði to the Þingmen, and herein, as well as in the absence of the relation of commendation and homage, we see a capital difference between this system and feudality. Nor was the post of Goði a place whence much emolument could be drawn. The Þingmen were indeed required to pay a sort of tax called the temple toll (*hoftollr*), but this did no more than meet the expenses to which the Goði was put in keeping up the temple, and feasting those who came to the sacrifices; it gave him no revenue which he could use to extend his authority. Accordingly, the Goðorð was regarded as implying power rather than property, and was not (after the introduction of Christianity) liable to the payment of tithe. A curious feature of the office was its alienability. Probably because it had arisen out of the ownership of the temple, it was regarded as a piece of private property which could be transferred by way of sale or gift, and could be vested in several persons jointly. And similarly a number of Goðorðs might by inheritance or purchase become vested in the same person.

Thus in the years immediately following the immigration there sprang up round the coasts of Iceland a great number of petty, unconnected and loosely aggregated groups of settlers. We must not venture to call them states, scarcely even communities, not principalities,

---

¹ The illustrious Konrad Maurer, to whose learned researches and sound judgement every one who writes about the constitutional antiquities of Iceland must feel infinitely indebted, thinks that the name of Goði was used in Norway before the emigration to Iceland, though probably the priest was there a less important person than he became in Iceland, where his custody of the temple put him to some extent in the position held in the Norwegian motherland by the hereditary chieftain, who was in Norway the natural president of the local Thing.

Those who desire to study the early history of Iceland may be referred to the writings of Dr. Maurer, and especially to his *Island bis zum Untergange des Freistaats* (Munich, 1874), and his *Beiträge zur Rechtsgeschichte des Germanischen Nordens* (Munich, 1852)

such as those which were beginning to spring up in Western Europe, not in a strict sense republics, yet nearer to republics than to principalities, organized, so far as they were organized at all, chiefly for the purposes of justice, and particularly for the exaction of fines for homicide, but with no settled plan of government, no written laws—if indeed writing was yet in use at all— no defined territory, and a comparatively weak cohesion among their own members, the Thingmen. The really effective tie was, in those ages, the tie of kindred; and the Þingmen of the same Goði were not kinsfolk, were not a clan or sept, like the Celtic communities of Scotland and Ireland. That tie was strong enough to involve a whole district in the blood-feud of a single man. For when any member of a family was killed, it was the duty of his nearest relatives to avenge his death, either by obtaining a full compensation in money, for which, if the offender refused to pay it, a lawsuit was brought in the Þing, or else by slaying the murderer or some member of his family. Thus a feud, like a *Vendetta* in Corsica or in Eastern Kentucky, might go on from generation to generation, each act of revenge drawing others in its train, and tending to draw more and more families into the feud, because when fights took place, the friends of each party often joined, and if some were killed, their relatives had a new blood-claim to prosecute.

Between the different communities that had thus sprung up there was no political tie whatever. There did not as yet exist any Icelandic nation, much less any common Icelandic State of which all the communities felt themselves members. Each was an independent body; and if a dispute arose between the members of two different Þings, there was no means of adjusting it except by voluntary submission to the award of some other Þing or else by open war. Seeing that slayings and plunderings and burnings were everyday occurrences in this fierce race, where Vikingry (*i.e.* piracy) was the most honoured pursuit, such cases were very frequent, espe-

cially as to take revenge for a kinsman's death was
deemed a sacred duty.

Even when the offender belonged to the same Þing
as the injured, it often happened that the influence of
his kindred, or the favour of the Goði of the place, or
some technical error in bringing the suit for compensation, prevented justice from being done. Accordingly
the need for some remedy, for some further political, or
rather judicial, organization of the island began to be
generally felt, for however fond men may be of killing
one another, the Norsemen were always also fond of
money, and would often prefer a blood-fine to the satisfaction of killing their enemy, could the blood-fine be
secured. Thus it came to pass that, about fifty years
after the first colonization, a chief named Úlfljót, venerable from his age and abilities, came forward to propose
a scheme. He urged the creation of one general Þing
for the whole country, where all matters of common interest might be discussed, and all suits which could not
be dispatched, or had not been fairly dealt with in the
local Þings, might be decided. Travelling round the
island, he brought over to his views the most influential
Goðis and other leading men; and at their request, sailed
to Norway to inquire into the laws prevailing there, and
to draw up regulations for this new general Þing; somewhat as envoys were, according to the Roman story,
sent from Rome to the Greek cities to bring back materials and suggestions for the legislation of the Decem-
virs. At the same time Úlfljót's foster-brother, Grím
Geitskór (' Goat's Shoe '), the fleetest man and nimblest
rock-climber in Iceland, was commissioned to traverse
the island in search of a place suitable for the meeting of
the proposed assembly. After long wanderings, Goat's
Shoe hit upon a spot to which the name of Þing Vellir [1],
' the plains of the Þing,' has ever since belonged, in

---

[1] Thing Vellir is the nominative plural, Thing Valla—the form in which the
word has become more familiar to Englishmen, and which remains in Thingwall
(near Liverpool), Tynwald (in the Isle of Man), and Dingwall (in Rosshire)—is the
genitive plural.

the south-west of the island, about eight hours' riding from where Reykjavík the present capital now stands, and within the district of the first temple that had been founded by Ingolf, the earliest Norwegian settler. This circumstance gave the place a sort of sacredness. There was plenty of water and pasture, and the lake which washed the plain of meeting abounded (as it does to this day) with trout and wild fowl. (It abounds also with most pernicious small black flies, whereon the trout grow fat, but which make fishing not always a pleasure.) Here, accordingly, Úlfljót having in the meantime returned from Norway with his materials for legislation, the first Alþing, or General Assembly of all Iceland, met in A.D. 930, and here it continued to meet, year after year, for a fortnight in the latter half of June, till the year 1800 [1], one of the oldest national assemblies in the civilized world, and one of the very few which did not, like the English Parliament and the Diet of the Romano-Germanic Empire, grow up imperceptibly and, so to speak, naturally, from small beginnings, but was formally and of set purpose established, by what would have been called, had paper existed, a paper constitution, that is to say by the deliberate agreement of independent groups of men, seeking to attain the common ends of order and justice.

There was thus created, before the middle of the tenth century, when Athelstan the Victorious [2] was reigning in England and defeating Scots and Northumbrians at Brunanburh by the help of the Icelandic warriors Thorolf and Egil, sons of Skallagrim [3], when the Saxon king Henry the Fowler was repelling the Magyar hosts and laying the foundations of the German Kingdom, and

---

[1] Since this lecture was delivered the Alþing which since 1843 had led a feeble life at Reykjavík as a sort of advisory council, has been re-established as a representative governing assembly under a new constitution granted to Iceland in 1874. It now meets every second year at Reykjavík.

[2] The Saga of Egil calls him Aðalsteinn hinn Sigrsæli (*lit.* 'blessed with victory'). It is curious that this title should have been preserved in Iceland and apparently have been forgotten in England.

[3] See *Egils Saga Skallagrimssonar*, chap. 54.

when the power of the last Carolingians was beginning
to pale in Gaul before the rising star of the Capetian line,
a sort of republic embracing the whole isle of Iceland, a
republic remarkable not only from its peculiar political
structure, but also, as will presently appear, from the
extremely limited range of its governmental activity.
About thirty years later its constitution was amended in
some important points, and forty years after that time,
about the year 1004, further alterations were made, the
details of which are too much disputed as well as too
intricate to be explained here. Its general outline, in its
completed shape, was the following. The total number
of regular Þings, and priest-chieftaincies or Goðorðs,
was fixed at thirty-nine, nine for each of the four Quarters into which the island was divided, except the North
Quarter, which, in order to allay certain local susceptibilities, was allowed twelve. Each of these thirty-nine
local Þings was presided over by its Goði. Then, for
certain purposes, three of these Þings were united to
form a larger Þing-district (Þingsokn), of which there
were therefore thirteen in all, viz. four for the North
Quarter, and three for each of the other Quarters.
There was also one still larger Þing for each Quarter,
called the Fjórðungsþing. It seems to have grown up
before the institution of the Alþing, and to have represented the first stage in the organization of a larger community out of the small local Þings. But it tended in
course of time to lose its importance.

Ordinary lawsuits and questions of local interest were
determined in these minor Þings, while graver suits, or
those in which the parties belonged to different Þings,
or where it was sought to reverse the decision of a local
Þing, as well as all proposals for alterations of the
general law, were brought before the Alþing, at its annual meeting in June. It seems to have been therefore
partly a court of first instance and partly a court of appeal. Now the Alþing was open, like other primary
Teutonic and Hellenic assemblies, to all freemen who

chose to attend ; but its powers were practically exercised by a limited number of persons, viz. the Goðis and certain members nominated by them.

For judicial purposes, the Alþing acted through four Courts, one for each Quarter. Each Quarter Court (fjorðungsdómr) consisted, according to one view, of thirty-six members, viz. the Goðis of the Quarter with twenty-four nominees, and, according to another view, of nine persons nominated by the Goðis of the Quarter. There was also a fifth Court (called the fimtardómr), instituted later than the others (A.D. 1004), on the suggestion of the famous jurist Njál, son of Thorgeir. This Court, which exercised jurisdiction in cases where one of the other Courts had failed, was composed in a somewhat different way, acted under a more stringent oath, and gave its decisions by a majority, whereas in other Courts unanimity was required. It seems to have been intended not only to avert armed strife by providing a better method for settling disputes, but also to organize the country as a whole and give it something approaching to a central authority. This result, however, was not attained, the social and physical obstacles proving insuperable.

In these judicial committees of the Alþing lawsuits were brought and argued with an elaborate formality and a minute adherence to technical rules far more strict than is now practised anywhere in Europe, a fact which will appear the more extraordinary when we remember that in those days both the law and all the appropriate forms of words which the parties were obliged to employ were not written, but preserved solely by the memory of individual men.

For legislative purposes the Alþing acted through another committee of 144 persons, only one-third (forty-eight) of whom, being the thirty-nine Goðis and nine nominees, had the right of voting. The nine nominees were persons chosen by the Goðis of the East, South, and West Quarters, three by each Quarter, in order to give each of these Quarters the same strength in the Committee as the North Quarter had with its twelve Goðis. Each of the forty-eight appointed two assessors who advised him, sitting one behind him and the other in front of him, so that he could readily seek their counsel, and thus the 144 were made up, the forty-eight being described as the Middle Bench. This Committee was called the Lögrétta (*lit.* ' Law Amending '), and by it all changes in the law were made, and all matters of common interest discussed. It was essentially an aristocratic body, as indeed the whole Constitution bore an aristocratic colour, though there was no such thing as a formal distinction of rank [1], much less any titled nobility. After the introduction of Christianity in A.D. 1000, the two bishops were added to the Lögrétta, while at the head of all, making up the number of members to 147, stood an elected officer, called the Speaker of the Law.

This last-named personage, the solitary official of the republic, is one of the most curious parts of the system. He was called the Lögsögumaðr, literally ' Law-sayman,' or, as we may render it, Speaker, or Declarer, of the Law, and was the depositary and organ of the unwritten common law of the country. It was his duty to recite aloud, in the hearing of the greater number of those present at the Þing, the whole law of Iceland, going through it in the three years during which he held office ; and to recite once in every year the formulas of actions, this being the part of the law which was of most practical importance. Besides this, he presided in the Lögrétta, giving a casting vote where the votes were equal ; and he was bound to answer every one who asked him what the provisions of the law actually were, although not required to advise applicants as to the course they ought to follow in a given case. When in any suit a question of what was the legal rule arose, reference was made to him, and his decision was accepted as final.

---

[1] Although the penalty for killing a man of high lineage was heavier than that for an ordinary freeman : and one perceives from the Sagas how carefully genealogies were preserved and what great respect was paid to long descent.

For these labours he received a yearly salary of two hundred ells of Vaðmál (the blue woolen cloth which then served as currency, and which continued to do so, for some purposes, down to our own time), besides one-half of the fines imposed at the Alþing. He was of course selected from the most accomplished lawyers of the time. His declarations of the law were conclusive, at least during his three years' term of office, in all causes and over all persons. Thus he exercised a kind of quasi-judicial or quasi-legislative power, and has been fancifully compared to the Roman Praetor, also an officer elected for a term, also by his edicts the declarer of the law he had to administer[1]. But the Law-Speaker was in reality neither judge nor magistrate, nor, indeed, a legislator, except in so far as the right to enounce and interpret borders on legislation. He delivered no judgements, he had no power of enforcing a decision or of punishing an offender. He did not even open the Alþing and take the responsibility for keeping order at it, for these functions belonged to the Goði of the district, called, because the Alþing met within his jurisdiction, the Allsherjargoði (priest of the whole host). The Lögsögumaðr was in fact nothing but the living voice of the law, enunciating those customary rules which had come down from the foretime, rules which all accepted, though they were not preserved in any written form, and though they must have been practically unknown to the great majority of the citizens.

The office, although more important in Iceland from the absence of a king or local prince, was one of which we find traces among other Scandinavian peoples, or at least among the Norsemen. It appears in Norway, in the Orkneys, and in the Hebrides (though there the name is Lögman, which in Iceland means merely one learned in the law).

Thingvellir, where the Alþing met from the year 930

---

[1] *Viva vox iuris civilis* was the description which the Romans used to give of their Praetor, as to whom see Essay XIV, p. 691.

down to a time within the memory of living men, is a spot not less remarkable physically than memorable for the stirring events of which it was the witness. It is a slightly undulating plain, some five miles long by three wide, washed on the south by a broad island-studded lake, and girdled in at its northern end by lofty mountains, their black volcanic rocks streaked here and there with snow-beds. The surface is all of lava, sometimes bare and rugged, sometimes covered with thin brushwood, dwarf birches and willows, sometimes smoothing itself out into sweeps of emerald pasture, but everywhere intersected by profound chasms, formed when the whole was a molten mass. East and west it is hemmed in by two lines of precipices, whose rugged sides seem to show that the plain between them has, at some remote period, perhaps when the lava-flood was cooling, sunk suddenly down, leaving these walls to be the edges of the plateau which stretches away backwards to the east and west. Under the western of these two walls, on the margin of the lake, just where it receives the stream which has flung itself in a sparkling cascade over the precipice, the place of meeting was fixed. The chieftains, who came from every corner of the island with a following of armed companions and dependents, because broils were frequent, and armed strife might interrupt the progress of a lawsuit, built their booths—erections of stone and turf roofed for the time with cloth or canvas—along the banks of the Öxará river, and turned out their horses to pasture by the lake. Places were appointed for the holding of the several courts, while the Lögrétta or legislative committee sat on a spot which nature seemed to have herself designed for the purpose. Two of the extraordinary chasms by which the plain is seamed, each some eighty feet deep, and filled for the lower fifty feet by bright green water, enclose a narrow strip of lava some two hundred yards long, cutting it off, except at one point where there is a narrow entrance which three men might hold, from the surrounding land. The surface is nearly level, covered by short grass now browsed by a few sheep; and there is nothing to tell that in this space, in the full sight of the assembled multitude, the heroes of ancient Iceland spoke and voted their laws, and gave their verdicts; while from an eminence in the midst of the enclosure, still called the Lögberg, or Hill of Laws, the Law-Speaker recited the law of the nation in the sight and hearing of the multitude that stood on the further side of the chasms[1]. Not only so: there is all round nothing whatever to show that the place has ever been different from what it is now. Between the Lögberg and the lake stand the little wooden church and its humble parsonage. No other house is near, nor any sign of human life. Only the islet is still pointed out in the river where the solemn duels which the laws of Iceland recognized were fought, and the deep green swirling pool into which women condemned for witchcraft were hurled from the brink of the precipice. In most of the spots to which the traveller is drawn, by memories of constitutional freedom or of political struggles, his imagination is aided by the remains of the buildings where assemblies met or monarchs sat enthroned. Here man has left nothing to speak of his presence, and it is hard to realize, when one looks on this silent and desolate scene, that it was once filled by so much strenuous life, and so often resounded to the clash of arms.

For the Alþing was not merely an assembly for the dispatch of business: it was the great annual gathering of the whole nation, a gathering all the more needed in a land where there are no towns, and most men live miles away from their nearest neighbours. To it chieftains rode with their wives and daughters and a band of armed retainers from the furthest corners of the country, taking, perhaps, as those must have done who came from the

---

[1] Since this was written, some eminent antiquaries, including my lamented friend Dr. Guðbrand Vigfússon, have argued that the true Lögberg is to be sought not in this spot which tradition indicates, but on the edge of the great lava rift called the Almannagjá to the west of the river. See *The Saga Steads of Iceland*, by W. G. Collingwood and Jón Stefánsson, 1899, pp. 14-17.

East fjords along the northern edge of the great central desert, a fortnight or more on the way. Shipmasters from Norway or Ireland brought their wares for sale. Artisans plied their trades. We are told that even jugglers' sheds and drinking-booths were set up, and games of all kinds carried on. It was a great opportunity not only for the renewing of friendships between those who lived in distant parts of the country, but for the arranging of adoptions and marriages; and the Sagas mention numerous instances in which proposals were made or betrothals entered into at a meeting of the Alþing, in most of which instances the will of the maiden seems to have prevailed over that of her parents. It was midsummer, when there is in those latitudes no night, but the glare of day subsides for a few hours into an exquisitely rich and tender twilight, clothing the sky with colours never seen in our duller air. And we can fancy how those who followed their fathers to the Alþing found compensation for all the loneliness and gloom of the long winter in this one fortnight of vivid mirth and excitement.

The meeting of the Alþing was not only the centre of the political life of the Republic. It was, so to speak, the Republic itself, for it was only then that the Republic became visible before men's eyes or acted as a collective whole. During the rest of the year lawsuits and everything else of public concern were left to the Quarter þings and local þings, and to the local Goðis. The few laws or resolutions of general concern which the Alþing passed—they were few, because its legislative activity was chiefly occupied in regulating its own judicial proceedings—were probably meant to be accepted and observed over the whole island, but the Alþing did not attempt to enforce them, and indeed had no machinery by which it could do so. Each Goði was, in a loose way, a sort of executive magistrate over his own þingmen; but he did not derive his authority from the Central or Federal Alþing, and he was not responsible to the Alþing for its exercise. The Republic, if we may so call it, had no

Executive whatever. Its sole official was the Law-Speaker (of whom more anon), but his function was only to declare the law, and was exercised only while the Alþing was sitting. At other times the constituent þings and Goðis were virtually quite independent, and might and often did carry on war with one another, subject to no penalty or liability for so doing, save in so far as an action for compensation might be brought against any one who had killed another. There was no police, no militia, no fleet, no army, nor any means, like those provided in the feudal kingdoms of contemporary Europe, of raising an army. The isle lay so far away from all other countries except Greenland, on which an Icelandic colony had been planted, that it happily did not need to have a foreign policy. There was neither public revenue nor public expenditure, neither exchequer nor budget. No taxes were levied by the Republic, as indeed no expenses were incurred on its behalf.

The Icelandic Republic was in fact a government developed only upon its judicial and (to a much smaller extent) upon its legislative side, omitting altogether the executive and international sides, which were in the Greek and Roman world, and have again in the modern world, become so important. For a community to exist with such an absence of administrative organization was obviously possible only in a region like Iceland, severed by a wide and stormy sea from the rest of the world, and with a very thin and scattered population; possible too only in a simple state of society where man's needs are few and every one fends for himself.

The system whose outlines I have sought to draw is full of interest and suggestion, as well to the student of legal theory as to the constitutional historian. Some modern theorists derive law from the State, and cannot think of law as existing without a State. A few among them have in England gone so far as to deny that Customary Law is law at all, and to define all Law as a Command issued by the State power. But here in Iceland we find Law, and indeed (as will appear presently) a complex and highly developed legal system, existing without the institutions which make a State; for a community such as has been described, though for convenience it may perhaps be called a Republic, is clearly not a State in the usual sense of the word. Of Iceland, indeed, one may say that so far from the State creating the Law, the Law created the State—that is to say, such State organization as existed came into being for the sake of deciding lawsuits. There it ended. When the decision had been given, the action of the Republic stopped. To carry it out was left to a successful plaintiff; and the only effect a decision had, so far as the Courts were concerned, was to expose the person resisting it to the penalties of outlawry—that is to say, any one might slay him, like Cain, without incurring in respect of his death any liability on the footing of which his relatives could sue the slayer. Law in fact existed without any public responsibility for enforcing it, the sanction, on which modern jurists so often dwell as being vital to the conception of law, being found partly in public opinion, partly in the greater insecurity which attached to the life of the person who disregarded a judgement. Yet law was by no means ineffective. Doubtless it was often defied, and sometimes successfully defied. That happened everywhere in the earlier Middle Ages, and happens to-day in semi-civilized peoples. But the facts that the Alþing maintained so active a judicial life, that the field of law was cultivated so assiduously, and the details of procedure worked out with so much pains and art, that lawsuits were contested so keenly and skilfully—all these facts seem to prove that law must have in the main had its course and prevailed, for it is hard to suppose that all this time and pains would have been during two centuries or more devoted to a pursuit which had no practical result. The contemporary kingdoms and principalities of the earlier Middle Ages lived by the vigour of the executive. There was in them very little of a State administration, and the law was in most or all of them older than the State—that is to say, it had existed in the form of customs recognized and obeyed before efficient means were provided for enforcing it. So far they resembled Iceland; and the same may be said of the city republics of Italy and Germany. But Iceland is unique as the example of a community which had a great deal of law and no central Executive, a great many Courts and no authority to carry out their judgements.

The process by which the law of Iceland grew, though less exceptional than was its political constitution, illustrates very happily the origin of Customary Law and the first beginnings of legislation. Law springs out of usage. The gathering of the neighbours develops into the Þing or local assembly of Norway and the Folk Mot of early England. It treats of all matters of common concern; and as it is the body before whom complaints of wrong are laid, it adopts by degrees regular set forms of words for the statements of a grievance, and for the replies to those statements. The usages become recognized customs, prescribing the cases in which redress may be claimed and the defences by which the claims may be repelled. The forms of words grow more elaborate and come to be considered so essential that a variation from them vitiates the claim. The body of rules thus formed becomes so large that only a few men, devoting themselves to the subject, are able to carry the whole in their memory. These men, proud of their knowledge, elaborate the rules, and particularly the set forms of words, still further, and in their enjoyment of technicalities attach more and more importance to formal accuracy. Thus Custom, which was loose and vague while held in solution in the minds of the mass, becomes crystallized into precision by the labour of the few whose special knowledge gives them a sort of pre-eminence, and even a measure of power. Then it is found that there are diversities of opinion among the experts in the law, or instances arise which show that some custom generally accepted is inconvenient. By this time Custom has acquired so much authority that the assembly, which has been also, and perhaps primarily, a law court, does not venture to transgress it, the men of legal learning being of course specially opposed to such a course. It therefore becomes necessary formally to change the Custom by a resolution of the body which is at once the Assembly and the Court. As this body consists of those who use, and whose progenitors have created, the custom, and as it continues to settle other matters of common concern affecting the district, it is the proper and only body to make the change. This, then, is legislation in its early stage. The law produced, which we may call Statute Law, is for many generations extremely small in proportion to the mass of law which rests upon Custom only. But the Statute Law is important because it is explicit, because it is sure to be remembered, because it deals with points comparatively large, since it would not be worth while to submit small ones to the assembly. Nevertheless legislation is among all peoples the smallest part of the work of primitive assemblies, be they Þings or Folk Mots or Agorai or Comitia. And the growth of the law of Iceland by custom, preserved and elaborated by a succession of law-sages, occasionally (though rarely) altered or added to by the vote of the Alþing, presents a lively picture of what must have been the similar process of the construction of early Roman law by the jurists (*prudentes*) and assembly (*comitia*).

Iceland, however, provided a means for the ascertainment and publicity of her law which Rome lacked. The Lögsögumaðr is an elegant (using the word in its strict Roman sense) complement to a system of Customary Law. His function was well designed to meet and cure the two chief defects in such a system, the uncertainty which existed as to what the rules accepted as law were and the difficulty which an individual desiring to take or defend legal proceedings found in discovering what the rule applicable to his case really was. The solemn reci-

tation of the whole law fixed it in the recollections of
those who busied themselves with such matters, and
gave everybody an opportunity of knowing what it covered. The right to interrogate the living depositary of
the law as to any special point whereanent the querist
desired to be informed was a great boon to private persons, who, since they might often have to suffer from
the extreme technicality of procedure, needed all the
more to be warned beforehand where the pitfalls lay.
In these respects the Icelandic system contrasts favourably with those of early Rome and early England. Till
the Twelve Tables were enacted the private citizen of
Rome had no means of ascertaining the law except by
asking some sage, who need not answer unless he
pleased, and whose view had no authority beyond that
which his personal reputation implied. Even after the
Twelve Tables had reduced much of the ancient Customary Law to shape, and made it accessible to the citizens at large, many of the forms of procedure, and the
rules as to the days on which legal proceedings could be
taken, were kept concealed by the patrician men of law
till divulged (at the end of the fourth century B.C.) by
Cn. Flavius. In England there was indeed no similar
effort to keep legal knowledge within the hands of a
few. But the customs were numerous, and many of
them were uncertain. There was no way of ascertaining them except by the judgement of a Court, a tedious
and expensive process, which after all decided only the
particular point that arose in the case that occasioned
the judgement. That means of determining a custom
to be valid and binding which the Icelanders had already
secured through their official in the last half of the tenth
century did not begin to be created by the action of the
English Courts till the end of the twelfth, and centuries
were needed to complete the process.

One of the things that most awakens our surprise in
the Icelandic Constitution is its extreme complexity. In
one sense simple and even rude, since it omits so much

we should have expected to find in a constitution, it is in another sense intricate, and puzzles us by the artificial character of the arrangements made for the composition of the various courts and of the legislative body, while the multiplicity of þings, and the distribution of powers among them, has given rise to many controversies among historians, some still unsettled. This phenomenon, however, finds a parallel in some of the constitutions of the Greek republics, not to speak of the elaborate systems of such cities as Florence and Venice in the fourteenth century. In Iceland the strong sense of independence which distinguished the Norsemen, and the jealousy the chiefs had of one another, made it necessary to devise means for securing equality and for preventing the influence of any group or district from attaining predominance. Herein the spirit of the Icelandic Constitution is singularly unlike that of the Roman. There, the intense realization of the unity of the city and the need for giving its government the maximum of concentration against neighbouring enemies caused vast powers to be entrusted first to the King and then to the Consuls or to a dictator. In Iceland, where no such need of defence existed, where there was no foreign enemy, and men lived scattered in tiny groups round the edges of a vast interior desert, no executive powers were given to anybody, and elaborate precautions were taken to secure the rights of the smaller communities which composed the Republic and of the priest-chieftains who represented them.

A like intricate character recurs in the system of legal procedure, but the cause is different and not peculiar to Iceland. The excessive technicality of Icelandic process, and the stress laid upon exact compliance with its rules, belong to that stage of the human mind in which form and matter have not yet been separated, and in which the respect for usage and tradition outweighs the sense of substantial justice. Simplicity in legal matters, instead of characterizing the state of nature, is the latest

legal achievement of a civilized age. In accounting for
the strictness of adherence to the letter, we must allow
something for the dread, natural enough in such an age,
that if deviations from the letter of the law were overlooked, if what we should call a power of amendment on
matters of form were entrusted to the Court, such discretion would be abused and confidence in the Courts
destroyed. But the reason is chiefly to be found, as in
the parallel case of those older forms of Roman procedure which continued terribly technical till the time of
Cicero, and as in the case of our own older law, to the
conservative spirit of the lawyers, attached to the forms
they had received and studied, and taking a professional
pride in working out their methods, a pride all the greater
the more technical those methods were, because the
more intricate the technicalities the higher the importance of the few who had mastered them. Substantial
justice is all the layman cares for. With the lawyer it
is otherwise. An eminent English judge used to remark
that of the questions argued before him, counsel showed
most interest in points of practice, costs came next,
while the merits of the case were last. The late Baron
Parke (Lord Wensleydale) was a type of the kind of
mind which flourished in Iceland in the eleventh century; and it was a type useful in its way, a type which
ought always to be represented in the legal profession,
for reverence for tradition and an acute interest in the
exactitude of form are hardly less necessary than a philosophic spirit and a zeal for progress.

How keen was the taste for legal subtleties and in-
tricacies is shown, not only by the existence of schools
of law in Iceland—young men gathering round sages
like Njál or Skapti Thoroddsson, just as the well-born
youth of Rome frequented the house of Tib. Corun-
canius or Q. Mucius Scaevola—but also by the evident
enjoyment which the authors of the Sagas show, and
which their public must evidently have taken, in the steps
in a lawsuit, or in the telling of some incident which

raises a nice point of procedure. In no other literature is fiction or history, by whichever name we describe the Sagas, so permeated by legal lore.

Our knowledge of the substance of early Icelandic law is derived partly from references or allusions in the Sagas, partly from some ancient law-books, the oldest of which belongs to the period of the Republic, and was compiled, probably about the middle of the twelfth century, out of materials some of them much older, and reaching back into the eleventh and even the tenth. Statutes had been passed during the course of the tenth century, and the Úlfljótslög of A.D. 930 is spoken of as a body of law prepared by Úlfljót after his journey to Norway and accepted by the Alþing, though it was probably a redaction of existing Norse customs, and does not seem to have been reduced to writing, as indeed it is improbable that any laws were written before the beginning of the twelfth century. The next effort at what has been called a codification of the law was made nearly two centuries after Úlfljót (about A.D. 1117), when a small commission was appointed which examined the customs, rejected some, approved or amended others, and created what is described as a sort of systematic collection. This is usually known as the Hafliðaskrá, from a prominent Goði and lawyer Hafliði Mársson, who was a member of the commission. This law is stated to have been accepted by the Alþing, and was no doubt preserved in writing, as the name Skrá (scroll) conveys.

The later book which used to be described as a Code survives in two MSS., differing a good deal from one another, and is commonly known as Grágás ('Grey-Goose')[1]. It is, however, really not a Code at all, and not even a single law-book, but a mass of matter of different dates and origins never reduced to any sort of

---

[1] The name Grágás (probably drawn from the binding in which a copy of it was preserved) seems to have originally belonged to a MS. of the Frostaþingslög, the law which prevailed round Throndhjem in Norway, and to have been applied by mistake in the seventeenth century to this Icelandic collection of customs, first published by the Arnamagnaean foundation in 1829.

unity. There are ordinances of the Alþing, decisions and declarations delivered by Law-Speakers, ecclesiastical regulations, formulas of legal procedure or legal transactions, memoranda of customs which seemed to those who recorded them to have obtained recognition and validity. It is full of instruction as a picture of primitive Teutonic institutions and life; and it throws a good deal of light both on the law of early England— English and Anglo-Norman—and upon some of the most curious features of early Roman law. Sometimes the references to the deliverances of a Law-Speaker as originating a rule make us think of the Roman Praetor, sometimes the concisely phrased records of what was settled by the Lögrétta remind us of our English reports of the judgements of the King's Courts in their early forms; while in one point the collection as a whole has a character which belongs to the earlier law-books as well of Rome as of England. Though the statutes of the Alþing are the most distinctly authoritative rules it contains, much whose authority would seem doubtful to a modern is set down in a way which clearly implies that it did possess authority. The line between absolutely binding law and all other law is not sharply drawn; indeed no such line exists. That which is recorded may be only a single instance of the observance of an alleged custom. It may be only the expression of the individual opinion of some learned lögmaðr (Lawman=jurist). Nevertheless it is a record which has come down from the past, and by which therefore the men of the present may seek to be guided.

In the law of Iceland, as it is presented in this ancient collection, we have, as in the Constitution of the island and the system of the Courts, a striking contrast between the rudeness of an extremely archaic society, in which private war is constantly going on, piracy is an honourable occupation, slavery exists, and there is no State administration and very little use of writing, and the refined intricacy of a system of law which makes

elaborate provision for the definition of legal rights and
their investigation and determination by legal process.
The time of day is fixed by guessing at the height of
the sun above the horizon. The wife is purchased. A
father may deliver his child into slavery, no doubt (as in
early Rome), a qualified slavery, for the payment of his
debts, and the insolvent debtor may be made a slave.
But, on the other hand, there are rules, not unlike those
of our modern Courts of Equity, regulating the guar-
dianship of the property of a minor, and permitting a
portion of it to be applied to the support of his indigent
father, brother or sister [1]. There are careful distinctions
as to who may sue for the penalty for homicide. If the
slain man is an Icelander, the action goes first to the son,
then to the nearest blood relation, then to the local Goði,
then to any member of the same Quarter, then to any
citizen (a sort of *actio popularis*). If the slain man was
not an Icelander, but one who used the ' Danish (or
northern) tongue,' *i.e.* if he was either a Norseman or
a Dane or a Swede, then any relative may sue; if a
stranger of any other nationality, only a father, son or
brother may sue. But for the protection of persons
coming in a ship, the comrade or partner [2] of the de-
ceased, whom failing, the skipper who has the largest
share in the ship, is a proper plaintiff.

It is curious to note that, although homicide and murder were common, the punishment of death is never
prescribed, even as in two or three of the Southern
States of America the death penalty is seldom inflicted,
while ' shootings at sight ' and lynchings abound. And
an interesting resemblance to early Roman law may be
found in the extreme severity of the law of slander and
libel. The truth of a defamatory statement is no defence.
To affix a nickname to a man is punishable by banish-

---

[1] This rule is ascribed to Guðmund Thorgeirsson, who was Law-Speaker from
1123 to 1135 A. D.

[2] Partner is félagi (English ' fellow'). Many further rules on this point are
contained in the passage, Grágás, chap. xxxvii (vol. ii. pp. 71-73 of the Arnamagnaean edition).

ment. No verses are to be made on a man, even in his praise, without his leave first obtained; and one who teaches or repeats the verses made by another incurs an equal penalty, the remedy extending even to verses made against the memory of the dead. A love poem addressed to a woman is actionable, the action being brought by her guardian if she is under twenty years of age [1].

Of the ramifications of the system of procedure into all sorts of Courts, besides the regular Þings, I have no space to speak; but one singular illustration of the faith which the Icelanders had in the efficacy of legal remedies deserves to be given, because in it these remedies reach beyond the present life. It comes from the Eyrbyggja Saga, one of the most striking of the old tales.

A chief named Thorodd, living at Fró á in Breiðifjörð, on the west side of Iceland, had just before Yule-tide been wrecked and drowned with his boat-companions in the fjord. The boat was washed ashore, but the bodies were not recovered. Thereupon his wife Thuríð and his eldest son Kjartan bade the neighbours to the funeral feast; but on the first night of the feast, as soon as the fire was lighted in the hall, Thorodd and his companions entered, dripping wet, and took their seats round it. The guests welcomed them: it was held that those would fare well with Rán (the goddess of the deep sea) who attended their own funeral banquet. The ghosts, however, refused to acknowledge any greetings, and remained seated in silence till the fire had burnt out, when they rose and left. Next night they returned at the same time and behaved in the same way, and did so, not only every night while the feast lasted, but even afterwards. The servants at last refused to enter the fire-hall, and no cooking could be done, for when a fire was lit in another room, Thorodd and his companions went there instead. At last Kjartan had a second fire lit in the hall, leaving the big one to the ghosts, so the cooking could now be

---

[1] See Grágás, chaps. civ-cviii, pp. 143-156 of vol. ii. in the Arnamagnaean edition.

done. But men died in the house, and Thuriŏ herself
fell ill, so Kjartan sought counsel of his uncle Snorri, an
eminent lawyer and the leading Goŏi of Western Iceland. By Snorri's advice Kjartan and seven others with
him went to the hall door and formally summoned Thorodd and his companions for trespassing within the
house and causing men's deaths. Then they named a
Door-Court (Dyradómr) and set forth the suits, following all the regular procedure as at a þing-Court. Verdicts were delivered, the cases summed up and judgement given; and when the judgement word was given on
each ghost, each rose and quitted the hall, and was never
seen thereafter.

Ghosts have given much trouble in many countries,
but it is only the Icelanders who have dealt with them
by an action of ejectment.

Although it is a remarkable evidence of the political
genius of the Norsemen that they should have been able
to work at all a legal system such as has been described,
it need hardly be said that it did not work smoothly.
The Icelanders were a people of warriors, little accustomed to restrain their passions, and holding revenge
for a sacred duty. The maintenance of order at the
Alþing was entrusted to the Goŏi of the spot, and it was
strictly forbidden to wear arms while the meeting lasted.
The closing of the Alþing was called Vápnatak (weapon-
taking, wapentake), because the arms that had been laid
aside were taken when men started to ride home from
the þing. But the arms were after all only left in the
booth, and more than once it happened that the party
which found itself unsuccessful in a lawsuit seized sword
and spear and fought out the issue in a bloody battle,
from which sprang again new blood-feuds and new lawsuits. It is not very often that the Sagas give us a
glimpse of the conduct of business at the Alþing; but
one such lawsuit, followed by a combat, which arose
when the suit broke down on a technical point, is described with wonderful force and spirit in the famous

Saga of Njál Thorgeirsson, a masterpiece of literature in the freshness and brilliance of its narrative.

We hear occasionally of the passing of particular laws at an Alþing. In A.D. 994, for instance, it was enacted that the suit for compensation for homicide which was brought, according to the general practice of the northern nations, by and for the benefit of the nearest relatives of the slain, a right which has survived in the law of Scotland under the name of Assythment, and has been partially introduced into the law of England by the Act 9 & 10 Vict. c. 93 (commonly called Lord Campbell's Act), should in future not be brought by a woman or by a child under sixteen years of age, but by the nearest male relative. This provision was suggested by a case that had occurred just before, when inadequate compensation had been recovered for the slaughter of a chieftain named Arnkel, owing to the mismanagement of the suit by his widow. Again, in A.D. 1006 we are told of the abolition of the judicial combat on the occasion of an indecisive duel between the poet and Viking Gunnlaug Ormstunga (Snake's tongue [1]) and another poet named Hrafn, the details of which are recorded in one of the most beautiful and touching of the early Sagas. Gunnlaug had been betrothed to Helga the Fair, one of the most famous heroines of Icelandic story, but having been detained in England by King Ethelred II, whose guest he had previously been in London [2] and whose praises he had been celebrating in verse, had failed to return at the appointed time, and found Helga, who had yielded to the importunities of her relatives, already married to Hrafn. According to the custom of the North, which then allowed any man to require another either to give up his wife and all his property or defend her and it by arms, Gunnlaug came to the Alþing and

---

[1] So called from his satirical powers.

[2] The Saga says (*Gunnlaugs Saga Ormstungu*, chap. vii) that in the days of Ethelred son of Edgar (Aðalráðr Játgeirsson) the same tongue was spoken in England and Denmark as in Norway, and that this continued in England till William the Bastard won England, after whom Welsh (Valsk = French) was spoken.

formally challenged Hrafn, and they fought, each with his second, a solemn duel on the island in the Öxará which was set apart for that purpose. A dispute arose after the first encounter, and the combatants were separated. Gunnlaug wished to resume the combat, but the law already referred to, prohibiting formal duels in future, was passed next day by the Lögrétta; and he unwillingly obeyed, for a breach of it would have exposed him to the penalties of outlawry. Helga, however, refused to live any longer with her husband Hrafn, and next year the two rivals sailed by agreement to Norway, just as, fifty years ago, persons fearing to fight a duel in England used to cross to Calais for the purpose. Years passed before they met in the wild country east of Throndhjem. There they fought out their quarrel. Gunnlaug smote off his enemy's foot, and then proposed to stop the combat. Hrafn however, supporting himself against a tree, wished to fight on, but as he was tortured by thirst, he besought his opponent to fetch him a draught of water from a brook hard by, promising not to deceive him. The chivalric Gunnlaug brought the water in his helmet, whereupon Hrafn, taking the water with his left hand, suddenly raised his sword and, with all his remaining strength, smote Gunnlaug on his bared head. ' Thou hast done ill and deceived me,' said Gunnlaug, ' seeing that I trusted you.' ' So is that,' answered Hrafn, ' but I grudged thee the love of Helga the Fair.' Then they fought on. Hrafn was slain, and in a few hours Gunnlaug died of his wounds [1]. The news was brought to Iceland, and after a time Helga, thinking ever of Gunnlaug, and often spreading out upon her knees a garment which Gunnlaug had given to her, pined away and died likewise.

Another striking scene at the Alþing has been pre-

[1] The Saga adds that very shortly after the combat, and long before the news of it could have reached Iceland, the ghosts both of Gunnlaug and of Hrafn appeared in dreams to their respective fathers in Iceland, and recited poems describing their deaths. Illugi the Black, Gunnlaug's father, remembered the poem he heard and repeated it aloud next day. The Saga gives both poems. This is one of the earliest Teutonic instances of a death-apparition.

served to us in the Saga which relates the introduction of Christianity. King Olaf Tryggvason, the most brilliant of all the Norwegian sovereigns, who, having been himself converted some ten years before, was hard at work converting the stubborn Norwegians by burning their houses and torturing themselves, had sent two missionaries to Iceland, one of whom, the priest Thangbrand, had been obliged to leave Norway on account of his violent life, and who signalized himself in Iceland by committing two murders in the course of his five months' stay, which was then summarily shortened. The unworthiness of the minister, however, does not seem to have injured the cause he championed. Several men of note embraced the new faith, which was of course well known to the Icelanders from their intercourse with Ireland and Britain, and had the promise of the future to recommend it. These men, and also some heathen chieftains who thought that acceptance was the best way of avoiding civil war, supported the envoys of Olaf, when, at the Alþing of the year 1000, they urged upon the assembly to decree the abolition of paganism. A story goes that, while the debate was at its height, a messenger arrived to tell that a volcano had broken out thirty miles to the south, and was pouring a flood of lava over the pastures. The heathen party accepted the news as an omen, and exclaimed, ' This is the wrath of the gods at these new rites ; see what you have to expect from their anger ! ' ' With whom, then,' said Snorri, a leading Goði who had not yet declared himself, ' with whom were the gods angry when this rock was molten on which we stand ? ' (pointing to the deep lava rifts that lay around the Lögberg). By the interposition of the Law-Speaker Thorgeir, that which he described as a compromise, but which was in reality a surrender by the heathen party, was at the same Alþing accepted. The people were to be baptized and declare themselves Christians, and the temples and images of the old gods were to be destroyed ; but those who liked to sacrifice at home might continue to do so; and two heathen customs, the exposure of new-born infants and the eating of horse-flesh, were to be permitted. Some difficulty arose over the reluctance of those who came from the North and East Quarters of the island to submit to immersion in cold water; but this difficulty was happily overcome by the use of the hot springs at Reykir for the rite.

The century and a half that followed the introduction of Christianity was the most brilliant period in the history of the island. It was not indeed a time of peace, for the old passions and the old superstitions were but little altered. Slayings and burnings of houses with their inmates went on pretty much as before. But there was now added to the stimulus which their free republican life and their piratical expeditions gave to the national spirit the influence of the learning and ideas which came in the train of the new faith. The use of writing soon spread, and the magnificent Sagas, which are among the noblest monuments of Northern genius, were nearly all of them produced in this age, though some were not committed to parchment before the end of the twelfth century.

For many years the Constitution of the Republic seems to have undergone no great alteration. The establishment of Christianity did indeed throw considerable power into the hands of the two bishops, and eventually produced a strife between the Church and the temporal magnates resembling that which distracted both the Romano-Germanic Empire and England. This scarcely affected the position of the Goði, whose authority had now lost so much as it originally possessed of a religious character. Snorri, whose appeal to geology is said to have decided the Alþing against paganism, was himself the priest of the most famous heathen sanctuary of the island. But in the beginning of the thirteenth century the delicately-framed fabric of the Republican Constitution began to break up. The tendency of a federation usually is to become less of a federation and more of a single united state. But in Iceland the federal bond, if one can use this name, was always weak, and when a powerful member became disobedient, there were no legal means of reducing him to submission. By degrees the number of priest-chieftainships diminished, the Goðorðs, which passed not only by inheritance but also by gift or sale, coming to be accumulated in the hands of a few great families, who thus acquired a predominant influence at the Alþing, were virtually masters of large districts of the country, and marched about like feudal lords attended by petty armies. Thus the old blood-feuds assumed more and more the aspect of civil wars. Piracy was now less practised, because the countries which had formerly been ravaged were better prepared for defence, so the energy that used to spend itself upon the coasts of Scotland and Ireland, of North Germany and Gaul, was now turned inward, and with fatal results.

I am not writing the history of Iceland, though indeed I wish I were doing so, for the theme is a fascinating one. But before closing these scattered observations, intended to stimulate rather than to satisfy curiosity, I will add three remarks suggested by the sketch that has been given.

The first remark is that Iceland presents one of the few instances in history of a breach in the continuity of institutional development. The settlers were all of Norse stock ; and Norway had in its petty communities a rudimentary system of institutions not unlike that described by Tacitus in his account of Germany, or that which the conquering Angles and Saxons brought to Britain. Each community was an independent Fylki (folk). In each Fylki there was a number of nobles, one of whom stood foremost as hereditary chieftain, and a body of warlike freemen, as well as a certain number of slaves. In each there was a popular assembly, the Þing, corresponding to our Saxon Folk Mot. Now owing to the way in which the settlers had planted themselves along the coasts of Iceland, and to the fact that they were less closely aggregated there than men had been in Norway, this organization did not reappear in the new land. There was indeed everywhere a þing, for the habit of meeting to deal with lawsuits and other matters of common interest was cherished as the very foundation of society. But an Icelandic community was not a Fylki. It was not an old natural growth, but rather a group of families whose tie was at first only that of local proximity and thereafter that also of worship at a common temple. The Goði, though he became the centre of this group, was not a chieftain with a hereditary claim to leadership, and was not necessarily of any higher lineage than some of his þingmen. Such eminent and high-born men as Njál for instance and Egil Skallagrimsson were not Goðis. The Goðorð was really a new institution, due to the special circumstances of Iceland, and apparently without precedent among the Teutonic races. Still more plainly was the organization of the Republic with its scheme of Courts and its Lögrétta a new creation, due to the wisdom and public spirit of the leading men of the nation, and not a purely natural growth.

Secondly, as the Icelandic Republic is a new form of political society, so the Alþing, in which the unity of the Republic found visible expression, is a unique body, which cannot be referred to any one of the familiar types of assembly. It is not a Primary Assembly, for though all freemen are present, only a limited number of persons are entitled to exercise either judicial or legislative functions. Neither is it a Representative Assembly, for no one was elected to sit in it as a delegate from others. The Goðis sat each by his own right, and the other members as nominees of the Goðis. Neither again is it a sort of King's Council, like the Curia Regis of mediaeval England, consisting of magnates and official advisers summoned by a monarch. If parallels to it are to be sought, they are to be sought rather in bodies such as the Roman Senate may have been in its earlier form, a

sort of council of the heads of organized communities;
yet the differences between the Roman *gentes* and the
Icelandic Þingmen, and the absence of an executive
magistrate like the Roman king, make the parallel anything but close. Still more remote is the resemblance
which the Alþing might be deemed to bear to the council of a league, such as was the Swiss Confederation before 1799, or such as the Diet of the Romano-Germanic
Empire in its later days.

The comparison of Iceland to a federation suggests
a third question. Why did not the Republic develop into
a united State, whether republican or monarchical, as did
most of the nations of mediaeval Europe?

Out of several reasons that might be assigned I will
mention three only, two of them political, the third
physical.

In Iceland there was no single great family with any
hereditary claim to stand above the others, while all
the leading families were animated by a high sense of
pride and a pervading sentiment of equality. This love
of equality remains among the sons of the old Norsemen both in Iceland and in Norway, and is indeed
stronger there than anywhere else in Europe.

Iceland had not, and could not have, any foreign wars.
There was therefore no external strife to consolidate
her people, no opportunity for any leader to win glory
against an enemy, or to create an army on which to base
his power. All the wars were civil wars, and tended to
disunion.

The third reason is to be found in the nature of the
country. The island, larger than Ireland, has practically
no land fit for tillage, and very little fit even for pasture.
Neither has it any internal trade. The interior is occupied by snow mountains and glaciers and lava-fields and
wastes of black volcanic sand or pebbles. Iceland is
really one huge desert with some habitable spots scattered along its coasts. It was the Desert that most of
all destroyed the chances of political unity under a re-

public by dividing the people into numerous small groups, far removed from one another, and in many places severed by rugged and barren wastes, or by torrents difficult to cross.

Nevertheless, although the Republic was evidently destined to perish, it is possible that had Iceland been left to herself the rivalry of the two or three great factions which divided it, and were usually in arms against one another, would have ended in the triumph of one of them, and in the establishment of a monarchy, or (less probably) of several independent rival principalities. But a new and more formidable figure now appeared on the scene. The successors of King Harald the Fair-haired had always held that the Icelanders, since their ancestors had come from Norway, ought to own their supremacy [1], and they argued that as monarchical government was divinely appointed, and prevailed everywhere in Continental Europe, no republic had a right to exist. King Hákon Hákonsson (Hákon IV), one of the greatest among the kings of Norway, now found in the distracted state of the island a better opportunity of carrying out the plans which his predecessors Olaf Tryggvason and Olaf the Saint had been obliged, by the watchfulness of the Alþing, to abandon. By bribes and by threats, by drawing the leading Icelanders to his Court, and sending his own emissaries through the island, he succeeded in gaining over the few chiefs who now practically controlled the Alþing, and at the meeting of midsummer, A.D. 1262 (one year before the battle of Largs, which saved Scotland from the invasion of this very Hákon), the Southern, Western and Northern Quarters accepted the King of Norway as their sovereign, while in 1264 (the year of the summoning of the first representative Parliament of England by Earl Simon de Montfort) the remaining districts which had

[1] This claim of a Crown to the allegiance of emigrants who had passed into new lands reminds one of that made by the British Government, down to 1852 and 1854, as respects the Dutch farmers who had gone forth into the wilderness of South Africa in 1836.

not yet recognized the Norwegian Crown, now held
by Magnus son of Hákon, made a like submission.
Thenceforward Iceland has followed the fortunes first
of Norway and then of Denmark. In 1814, when Norway was severed from the Danish and transferred to the
Swedish Crown, Iceland ought to have gone with Norway. But nobody at the Congress of Vienna knew or
cared about the matter [1] : and so Iceland remains attached to Denmark, for which she has little love.

With the free republic the literature which had given
it lustre withered up and disappeared. Only one work
of high merit, the religious poem called *The Lily*, was
produced in the centuries that succeeded down to the
Reformation, when the spirit of the people was again
stirred, and a succession of eminent writers began which
has never failed down to our own day. But in the darkest times, in the ignorance and gloom of the fifteenth
century, in the pestilences and famine caused by the terrible volcanic eruptions of the eighteenth, which are
said to have destroyed one-fifth of the population, the
Icelanders never ceased to cherish and enjoy their
ancient Sagas. No farmhouse wanted its tiny store of
manuscripts, which were and still are read aloud in the
long nights of winter, while the women spin and the
men make nets and harness. And it is beyond doubt
chiefly owing to the profusion and the literary splendour
of these works of a remote antiquity—works produced in
an age when England and Germany, Italy and France
had nothing better than dull monkish annalists or the
reciters of such a tedious ballad epic as the *Song of the
Nibelungs*—that the Icelandic language has preserved
its ancient strength and purity, and that the Icelandic
nation, a handful of people scattered round the edge of a
vast and dreary wilderness, has maintained itself, in face
of the overwhelming forces of nature, at so high a level
of culture, virtue and intelligence.

[1] The preliminaries to the Treaty of Kiel by which Norway was severed from
the Danish Crown to be attached to the Swedish refer to Iceland, the Faeroe
Isles, and Greenland as having 'never belonged to Norway.'

VI

THE UNITED STATES CONSTI-
TUTION AS SEEN IN THE PAST

THE PREDICTIONS OF HAMILTON AND TOCQUEVILLE

HE who desires to discover what have been the main
tendencies ruling and guiding the development of American institutions, will find it profitable to examine what
were the views held and predictions delivered, at different epochs in the growth of the Republic, by acute
and well-informed observers. There is a sort of dra-
matic interest in this method of inquiry, and it is calcu-
lated to temper our self-confidence in judging the phenomena of to-day. Besides, it helps us to realize, better
than we can do merely by following the course of events,
what aspect the political landscape wore from time to
time. When we read a narrative, we read into the events
our knowledge of all that actually flowed from them.
When we read what the contemporary observer expected from them as he saw them happening we reach
a truer comprehension of the time.

To collect and set forth a representative anthology of
political prophecies made at critical epochs in the history
of the United States, would be a laborious undertaking,
for one would have to search through a large number
of writings, some of them fugitive writings, in order to
present adequate materials for determining the theories
and beliefs prevalent at any given period. I attempt

nothing so ambitious. I desire merely to indicate, by a comparatively simple example, how such a method may be profitably followed, disclaiming any pretensions to dig deep into even the obvious and familiar materials which students of American history possess.

For this purpose, then, I will take two famous books —the one written at the very birth of the Union by those who watched its cradle, and recording incidentally, and therefore all the more faithfully, the impressions and anticipations of the friends and enemies of the infant Constitution; the other a careful study of its provisions and practical working by a singularly fair and penetrating European philosopher. I choose these books not only because both are specially representative and of rare literary merit, but because they are easily accessible to European as well as American readers, who may, by referring to their pages, supply the omissions which want of space will compel me to make, and may thereby obtain a more full and graphic transcript of contemporary opinion. One of these books is *The Federalist* [1]—a series of letters recommending the proposed Constitution for adoption to the people of New York, written in 1788 by Alexander Hamilton, afterwards Secretary of the Treasury, James Madison, afterwards President from 1809 to 1817, and John Jay, afterwards Chief Justice from 1789 to 1795. They were all signed *Publius*. The other, which falls not quite halfway between 1788 and our own time, is the *Democracy in America* of Alexis de Tocqueville.

I. THE UNITED STATES AT THE ADOPTION OF THE CONSTITUTION.

I begin by briefly summarizing the record which *The Federalist* preserves for us of the beliefs of the opponents and advocates of the Draft Constitution of 1787 regard-

[1] There are several good editions of *The Federalist*. The latest and one of the best known to me is that edited by Mr. Paul Leicester Ford (New York, 1898).

ing the forces then at work in American politics and
the probable future of the nation.

To understand those beliefs, however, we must bear
in mind what the people of the United States then were,
and for that purpose I will recall the reader's attention
to some of the more salient aspects of the Republic at
the epoch when its national life began.

In 1783 the last British soldier quitted New York, the
last stronghold that was held for King George. In 1787
the present Constitution of the United States was framed
by the Convention at Philadelphia, and in 1788 accepted
by the requisite number of States (nine). In 1789
George Washington entered on his Presidency, the first
Congress met and the machine began to work. It was
a memorable year for Europe as well as for America—
a year which, even after the lapse of more than a century, we are scarcely yet ripe for judging, so many sor-
rows as well as blessings, πολλὰ μὲν ἐσθλὰ μεμιγμένα, πολλὰ
δὲ λυγρά, were destined to come upon mankind from
those elections of the States-General which were proceeding in France while Washington was being installed
at Philadelphia.

All of the thirteen United States lay along the Atlantic
coast. Their area was 827,844 square miles, their population 3,929,214, little more than half the population of
New York State in 1900. Settlers had already begun to
cut the woods and build villages beyond the Alleghanies;
but when Kentucky was received as a State into the
Union in 1792, she had a population of only 80,000. The
population was wholly of English (or Anglo-Scottish)
stock, save that a few Dutch were left in New York, a
few persons of Swedish blood in Delaware, and some
isolated German settlements in Pennsylvania. But in
spite of this homogeneity the cohesion of the States was
weak. Communication was slow, difficult and costly.
The jealousies and suspicions which had almost proved
fatal to Washington's efforts during the War of Independence were still rife. There was some real conflict,

and a far greater imagined conflict, of interests between
the trading and the purely agricultural States, even more
than between the slave States and those in which slavery
had practically died out. Many competent observers
doubted whether the new Federal Union, accepted only
because the Confederation had proved a failure and the
attitude of foreign powers was threatening, could maintain itself in the face of the strong sentiment of local
independence animating the several colonies, each of
which, after throwing off the yoke of Britain, was little
inclined to brook any control but that of its own legislature. The new Constitution was an experiment, or
rather a bundle of experiments, whose working there
were few data for predicting. It was a compromise, and
its own authors feared for it the common fate of compromises—to satisfy neither party and to leave open rents
which time would widen. In particular, it seemed most
doubtful whether the two branches of the Legislature,
drawn from so wide an area and elected on different
plans, would work harmoniously, and whether general
obedience would be yielded to an executive President
who must necessarily belong to and seem to represent
one particular State and section of the country. Parties did not yet exist, for there was as yet hardly a nation; but within a decade they grew to maturity and
ferocity. One of them claimed to defend local self-government, the rights of the people, democratic equality;
the other, the principle of national unity and the authority of the Federal power. One sympathized with
France, the other was accused of leaning to an English
alliance. They were, or soon came to be, divided not
merely on burning questions of foreign policy and home
policy, but also—and this was an issue which mixed itself
up with everything else—as to the extent of the powers
to be allowed to the central Government and its relations to the States—questions which the curt though apparently clear language of the Constitution had by no
means exhausted.

Slavery was not yet a burning question—indeed it existed to some slight extent in the Middle as well as in the Southern States, but the opposition of North and South was already visible. The Puritanism of New England, its industries and its maritime commerce, gave it different sentiments as well as different interests from those which dominated the inhabitants of the South, a population wholly agricultural, among whom the influence of Jefferson was strong, and theories of extreme democracy had made progress.

There was great diversity of opinion and feeling on all political questions in the America of those days, and the utmost freedom in expressing it. Over against the extreme democrats stood an illustrious group whose leader was currently believed to be a monarchist at heart, and who never concealed his contempt for the ignorance and folly of the crowd. Among these men, and to a less extent among the Jeffersonians also, there existed no small culture and literary power, and though the masses were all orthodox Christians and, except in Maryland, orthodox Protestants, there was no lack of scepticism in the highest circles. One may speak of highest circles, for social equality, though rapidly advancing and gladly welcomed, was as yet rather a doctrine than a fact: and the respect for every kind of authority was great. There were neither large fortunes nor abject poverty: but the labouring class, then far less organized than it is now, deferred to the middle class, and the middle class to its intellectual chiefs. The clergy were powerful in New England: the great colonial families enjoyed high consideration in New York, in Pennsylvania, and above all in Virginia, whose landowners seemed to reproduce the later semi-feudal society of England. Although all the States were republics of a hue already democratic, every State constitution required a property qualification for the holding of office or a seat in the Legislature, and, in most States, a similar condition was imposed even on the exercise of the

20

suffrage. Literary men (other than journalists) were rare, the universities few and old-fashioned in their methods, science scarcely pursued, philosophy absorbed in theology and theology dryly dogmatic. But public life was adorned by many striking figures. Five men at least of that generation, Washington, Franklin, Hamilton, Jefferson and Marshall, belong to the history of the world; and a second rank which included John Adams, Madison, Jay, Patrick Henry, Gouverneur Morris, Roger Sherman, James Wilson, Albert Gallatin, and several other gifted figures less familiar to Europe, must be mentioned with respect.

Everybody professed the principles of the Declaration of Independence, and therefore held a republican form of government to be the only proper, or at any rate the only possible form for the central authority as well as for the States. But of the actual working of republican governments there was very little experience, and of the working of democracies, in our present sense of the word, there was really none at all beyond that of the several States since 1776, when they broke loose from the British Crown. Englishmen are more likely than other Europeans to forget that in 1788 there was in the Old World only one free and no democratic nation [1]. In Europe there now remain but two strong monarchies, those of Russia and Prussia, while the Western hemisphere, scarcely excepting Dutch and British Guiana and Canada, is entirely (at least in name) republican. But the world of 1788 was a world full of monarchs— despotic monarchs—a world which had to go back for its notions of popular government to the commonwealths of classical antiquity. Hence the speculations of those times about the dangers, and merits, and tendencies characteristic of free governments, were and must needs be vague and fantastic, because the materials for a sound induction were wanting. Wise men,

---

[1] The Swiss Confederation was hardly yet a nation, and few of the cantons were governed democratically.

when forced to speculate, recurred to the general principles of human nature. Ordinary men went off into the
air and talked at large, painting a sovereign people as
reckless, violent, capricious on the one hand, or virtu-
ous and pacific on the other, according to their own pre-
dilections, whether selfish or emotional, for authority
or for liberty. Though no one has yet written the natural history of the masses as rulers, the hundred years
since 1788 have given us materials for such a natural
history surpassing those which Hamilton possessed almost as much as the materials at the disposal of Darwin
exceeded those of Buffon. Hence in examining the
views of the *Federalist* writers [1] and their antagonists,
we must expect sometimes to find the diagnosis inexact
and the prognosis fanciful.

II. Predictions of the Opponents and Advocates of the Constitution.

Those who opposed the Draft Constitution in 1787,
a party both numerous and influential in nearly every
State, were the men specially democratic and also specially conservative. They disliked all strengthening of
government, and especially the erection of a central authority. They were satisfied with the system of sovereign and practically independent States. Hence they
predicted the following as the consequences to be expected from the creation of an effective Federal executive and legislature [2].

1. The destruction of the States as commonwealths.
The central government, it was said, would gradually
encroach upon their powers; would use the federal army

---

[1] Of these writers Hamilton must be deemed the leading spirit, not merely
because he wrote by far the larger number of letters, but because his mind was
more penetrating and commanding than either Madison's or Jay's. Madison rendered admirable service in the Philadelphia Convention of 1787, but afterwards
yielded to the influence of Jefferson, a character with less balance but more force
and more intellectual fertility.

[2] I take no account of those objections to the Constitution which may be
deemed to have been removed by the first eleven amendments.

to overcome their resistance; would supplant them in the respect of their citizens; would at last swallow them up. The phrase 'consolidation of the Union,' which had been used by the Convention of 1787 to recommend its draft, was laid hold of as a term of reproach. 'Consolidation,' the absorption of the States by or into one centralized government, became the popular cry, and carried away the unthinking.

2. The creation of a despot in the person of the President. His legal authority would be so large as not only to tempt him, but to enable him, to extend it further, at the expense of the liberties both of States and of people. 'Monarchy,' it was argued, 'thrown off after such efforts, will in substance return with this copy of King George III, whose command of the federal army, power over appointments, and opportunities for intriguing with foreign powers on the one hand and corrupting the legislature on the other [1], will render the new tyrant more dangerous than the old one. Or if he be more open to avarice than to ambition, he will be the tool of foreign sovereigns and the means whereby they will control or enslave America [2].

3. The Senate will become an oligarchy. Sitting for six years, and not directly elected by the people, it 'must gradually acquire a dangerous pre-eminence in

---

[1] See *The Federalist*, No. LIV.

[2] *The Federalist*, No. LXVI, p. 667. 'Calculating upon the aversion of the people to monarchy, the writers against the Constitution have endeavoured to enlist all their jealousies and apprehensions in opposition to the intended President of the United States, not merely as the embryo but as the full-grown progeny of that detested parent. They have to establish the pretended affinity, not scrupled to draw resources even from the regions of fiction. The authority of a magistrate in few instances greater, in some instances less, than those of a Governor of New York, have been magnified into more than royal prerogatives. He has been decorated with attributes superior in dignity and splendour to those of a King of Great Britain. He has been shown to us with the diadem sparkling on his brow and the imperial purple flowing in his train. He has been seated on a throne surrounded with minions and mistresses, giving audience to the envoys of foreign potentates in all the supercilious pomp of majesty. The images of Asiatic despotism and voluptuousness have scarcely been wanting to crown the exaggerated scene. We have been taught to tremble at the terrific visages of murdering janizaries, and to blush at the unveiled mysteries of a future seraglio.'

These were the days when Johnson and Gibbon ruled English style.

the government, and finally transform it into a tyrannical aristocracy [1].'

4. The House of Representatives will also, like every
other legislature, aim at supremacy. Elected only once
in two years, it will forget its duty to the people. It
will consist of 'the wealthy and well-born,' and will
try to secure the election of such persons only as its
members [2].

5. The larger States will use the greater weight in the
government which the Federal constitution gives them
to overbear the smaller States.

6. The existence of a strong central government is
not only likely, by multiplying the occasions of diplomatic intercourse with foreign powers, to give openings
for intrigues by them dangerous to American independence, but likely also to provoke foreign wars, in which
the republic will perish if defeated, or if victorious maintain herself only by vast expenditure, with the additional
evil of having created in an army a standing menace to
freedom.

That some of these anticipations were inconsistent
with others of them was no reason why even the same
persons should not resort to both in argument. Any
one who wishes to add to the number, for I have quoted
but a few, being those which turn upon the main outlines of the Philadelphia draft, may do so by referring
to the record, known at Elliott's Debates, of the discussions in the several State Conventions which deliberated
on the new Constitution. It is an eminently instructive
record.

I pass from the opponents of the Constitution to its
advocates. Hamilton and its friends sought in it a
remedy against what they deemed the characteristic
dangers of popular government. It is by dwelling on
these dangers that they recommend it. We can perceive, however, that, while lauding its remedial power,

---

[1] *The Federalist*, No. LXII.
[2] *The Federalist*, Nos. LVI and LIX.

they are aware how deep-seated such dangers are, and how likely to recur even after the adoption of the Constitution. The language which Hamilton held in private proves that he desired a more centralized government, which would have approached nearer to that British Constitution which he regarded as being, with all its defects (and partly owing to its corruptions!) the best model for free nations [1]. He feared anarchy, and thought that only a strong national government could avert it. And in a remarkable letter written in February, 1802, under the influence of disappointment with the course events were then taking, he describes, in his somewhat sweeping way, the Constitution he was 'still labouring to prop' as a 'frail and worthless fabric.'

We may therefore legitimately treat his list of evils to be provided against by the new Federal Government as indicating the permanently mischievous tendencies which he foresaw. Some of them, he is obliged to admit, cannot be wholly averted by any constitutional devices, but only by the watchful intelligence and educated virtue of the people.

The evils chiefly feared are the following:—

1. The spirit and power of faction, which is so clearly the natural and necessary offspring of tendencies always present in mankind, that wherever liberty exists it must be looked for [2].

Its causes are irremovable; all you can do is to control its effects, and the best prospect of overcoming them is afforded by the representative system and the wide area of the United States with the diversities among its population.

2. Sudden impulses, carrying the people away and inducing hasty and violent measures [3].

3. Instability in foreign policy, due to changes in the

---

[1] Though he, like other observers of that time, had not realized, and might not have relished, the supremacy, now become omnipotence, which the House of Commons had already won.

[2] *The Federalist*, No. X (written by Madison), and in other letters.

[3] *The Federalist*, No. LXII.

executive and in public sentiment, and rendering necessary the participation of a comparatively small council
or Senate in the management of this department.

4. Ill-considered legislation. 'Facility and excess of
law-making [1],' and 'inconstancy and mutability in the
laws [2],' form the 'greatest blemish in the character and
genius of our governments.'

5. The Legislature is usually the strongest power in
free governments. It will seek, as the example of the
English Parliament shows, to encroach upon the other
departments; and this is especially to be feared from
the House of Representatives as holding the power of
the purse [3].

6. The States, and especially the larger States, may
overbear the Federal Government. They have closer
and more constant relations with the citizen, because
they make and administer the ordinary laws he lives
under. His allegiance has hitherto belonged to them,
and may not be readily given to the central authority.
In a struggle, should a struggle come, State power is
likely to prevail against Federal power.

7. There is in republics a danger that the majority
may oppress the minority. Already conspicuous in some
of the State governments, as for instance in Rhode
Island, this danger may be diminished by the application of the federal system to the great area of the Union,
where 'society will be broken into so many parts, interests, and classes of citizens, that the rights of individuals or of the minority will be in little danger from
interested combinations of the majority [4].'

8. Another source of trouble is disclosed by the rash

---

[1] *The Federalist*, No. LXI.

[2] *The Federalist*, No. LXXII.

[3] 'The Legislative Department is everywhere (*i. e.* in all the States) extending
the sphere of its activity and drawing all power into its impetuous vortex. . . .
It is against the enterprising ambition of this department that the People ought to
indulge all their jealousy and exhaust all their precautions' (*The Federalist*, No.
XLVII). The people have now begun to resort to precautions; but it is not the
ambition of State legislatures that is feared, it is their subserviency to private
interests or the party machine.

[4] *The Federalist*, No. L.

and foolish experiments which some States have tried
in passing laws which threaten the validity of contracts
and the security of property. There are also signs of
weakness in the difficulty which State Governments have
found in raising revenue by direct taxation[1]. Citizens
whose poverty does not excuse their want of public
spirit refuse to pay; and the administration fears to
coerce them.

Not less instructive than the fears of *The Federalist*
writers are their hopes. Some of the perils which have
since been disclosed are not divined. Some institutions
which have conspicuously failed are relied on as full of
promise.

The method of choosing the President is recommended with a confidence the more remarkable because
it was the point on which the Convention had been most
divided and had been latest in reaching an agreement.

' If the manner of the appointment of the Chief Magistrate be not perfect, it is at least excellent. It unites
in an eminent degree all the advantages the union of
which was to be wished for. . . . The process of election affords a moral certainty that the office of President
will never fall to the lot of any one who is not in an
eminent degree endowed with the requisite qualifications. Talents for low intrigue, and the little arts of
popularity, may alone suffice to elevate a man to the
first honours in a single State, but it will require other
talents and a different kind of merit to establish him in
the confidence and esteem of the whole Union, or of so
considerable a portion of it as would be necessary to
make him a successful candidate for the distinguished
office of President of the United States. It will not be
too strong to say that there will be a constant probability
of seeing the station filled by characters pre-eminent for
ability and virtue[2].'

---

[1] *The Federalist*, No. XII.

[2] *The Federalist*, No. LXVII. In A.D. 1800, twelve years after Hamilton
wrote this passage, the contest for the Presidency lay between Jefferson and
Aaron Burr, and Hamilton was compelled by his sense of Burr's demerits to

It is assumed that America will continue an agricultural and (to a less extent) a commercial country, but that she will not develop manufactures; and also that the fortunes of her citizens will continue to be small [1]. No serious apprehensions regarding the influence of wealth in elections or in politics generally are expressed.

The contingency of a division of the States into two antagonistic groups is not contemplated. When the possibility of State combinations is touched on, it is chiefly with reference to the action of small and of large States respectively. In particular no hint is dropped as to the likelihood of the institution of slavery becoming a bond to unite the Southern States and a cause of quarrel between them and the Northern. Yet slavery had given trouble in the Philadelphia Convention, and an opposition of North and South grounded upon it soon emerged.

Although the mischiefs of faction are dwelt on, nothing indicates that its embodiment in highly developed party systems, whose organizations might overshadow the legal government, had occurred to any one's mind. Still less, of course, is there any anticipation of the influence to be exerted on politics by the distribution of offices. Not till long afterwards were they treated as ' spoils of war.'

urge his party to vote (when the choice came before the House of Representatives) for Jefferson, his own bitter enemy. What he thought of Burr, who, but for his intervention, would certainly have obtained the chief magistracy of the nation (and by whose hand he ultimately died), may be inferred from the fact that he preferred as President the man of whom he thus writes: ' I admit that his (Jefferson's) politics are tinctured with fanaticism; that he is too much in earnest in his democracy ; that he has been a mischievous enemy to the principal measures of our past administration ; that he is crafty and persevering in his objects ; that he is not scrupulous about the means of success, nor very mindful of truth ; and that he is a contemptible hypocrite. But, &c.' (Letter to James A. Bayard, Jan. 16, 1801.)

After this it is superfluous, as it would be invidious, to dwell on the deficiencies of some recent Presidents or Presidential candidates.

[1] 'The private fortunes of the President and Senators, as they must all be American citizens, cannot possibly be sources of danger' (*The Federalist*, No. LIV).

III. Criticism of the Predictions of 1788.

Let us now see which of these views and forecasts have been verified by the event.

Of those put forth by the opponents of the Constitution not one has proved true. The States are still strong, the President is not a despot, though for a time during the Civil War he came near being one, nor has he ever fallen under the influence of any European power. The House does not consist of the 'wealthy and well-born.' The larger States do not combine against nor press hardly on the smaller. No great country has had so few wars or indeed so few foreign complications of any kind[1]. The Senate is still often called 'an oligarchy,' but this means only that it consists of comparatively few persons, most of them wealthy, and that it has a strong corporate feeling in favour of the personal interests of each of its members. It is really as dependent on public opinion as the House, perhaps even more afraid of public opinion, and as directly the creature of party machinery, though less directly of popular election.

One is surprised to find that of the many arrows of accusation levelled at the Constitution, all should have flown wide of the mark.

The deeper insight and more exact thinking of Hamilton and Madison fastened upon most of the real and permanent weaknesses in popular government. Yet even they could not foresee the particular forms which those weaknesses would assume in the new nation. To examine in detail the eight points specified above would involve an examination of American history for a century. I shall therefore simply indicate in a word or two the extent to which, in each case, the alarms or predictions of *The Federalist* may be deemed well grounded.

---

[1] Three wars since 1789: that of 1812, that of 1845, and that of 1898. Every one of these might no doubt have been avoided with honour, and two of them savoured of aggression, but the same may be said of nearly all the wars of European States.

1. The spirit of faction has certainly, as Madison expected, proved less intense over the large area of the
Union than it did in the Greek republics of antiquity or
in the several States from 1776 to 1789. On the other
hand, the bonds of sympathy created by the Federal system have at times enabled one State to infect another
with its own vehemence. But for South Carolina, there
would have been no secession in 1861. Since 1880 the
' demon of faction ' has been less powerful in the parties
than at any previous date since the so-called ' Era of
Good Feeling ' in 1820.

2. Sudden popular impulses there have been. But
finding a ready and constitutional expression in elections, they do not induce a resort to arms, while the
elaborate system of checks on legislation seldom allows
them to result in the passing of dangerous measures by
Congress. In some States the risk of bad laws is serious,
but it is lessened by the provisions of the Federal Constitution as well as by the veto power of the State Governor and the restrictions of recent State Constitutions.

3. The early history of the Union furnishes illustrations of feebleness and inconstancy in foreign policy,
yet not greater than those which mark most monarchies.
Royal caprice, or the influence of successive favourites,
has proved more pernicious in absolute kingdoms or
principalities than popular fickleness in republics. That
the foreign policy of the United States was singularly
consistent down till 1898, when it suddenly took an entirely ' new departure,' was not due to the Senate. It
must be credited partly to the good sense of the people,
partly to the fact that the position and interests of the
nation prescribed certain broad and simple lines.

4. Whatever may be thought of its handling of private
bills, Congress was seldom prone to haste or reckless
expenditure in legislation on public matters, until it
passed the amazing Pensions Act of 1890. Nor has it
given the country too many laws. It has been on the
whole more blameable for what it neglects or postpones

than for what it enacts. The censure is more true of the
States, especially the newer Western States.

5. The House of Representatives has doubtless sought
to extend its sway at the expense of other departments. Whether it has succeeded is a question on which
competent observers in America itself differ; but the
fact of their differing proves that the encroachments
have not been considerable. Whenever the President is
weak or unpopular, Congress seems to be gaining on
the Executive Chief. When the latter is or seems
strong, he can keep the Legislature at bay.

6. In the struggle which never quite ceases, though
it is often scarcely noticed, between the States and the
Federal Government, the States have on the whole lost
ground. Nor are the larger States practically more
formidable than the small ones. The largest is small
compared with the immense Union. No State would
now venture to brave the Federal Judiciary as Georgia
did, and for a time did successfully (1832), in one of the
painful cases regarding the Cherokee Indians.

7. The so-called Tyranny of the Majority, a subject
too large to be fully examined here[1], has not hitherto
proved a serious evil in America. This, however, is due
rather to the character and habits of the people and their
institutions generally than to the mere extent and population of the Union, on which the *Federalist* writers relied.

8. There has been some unwise Congressional legislation, especially in currency matters, and, of course,
much more of unwise State legislation. But property
is secure, and the sense of civic duty seems, on the whole,
to be improving.

It will appear from this examination, and from the
fact (noted a few pages back) that some remarkable developments which political life has taken never crossed
the minds of the authors of *The Federalist*, that these
wisest men of their time did not foresee what strike us

[1] The subject is discussed in the author's *American Commonwealth*, chaps.
lxxxiv and lxxxv.

to-day as the specially characteristic virtues and faults of American democracy. Neither the spoils system nor the system of party nominations by wire-pullers crossed their minds. They did not foresee the inordinate multiplication of elections, nor the evils of confining eligibility for a seat in the legislature to a person resident in the electing district, nor the disposition to 'play down' to the masses by seductive proposals. That the power which money might come to exert lay quite out of their view is not to be wondered at, for no large fortunes then existed. No student of history will deem that these omissions detract from their greatness, for history teaches nothing more plainly than the vanity of predictions in the realm of what we call the moral and political sciences, in religion, in ethics, in sociology, in government and politics. Deep thinkers help us when they unfold those permanent truths of human nature which come everywhere into play. Historians help us when, by interpreting the past, they demonstrate what are the tendencies that have gone to create the present. Observers keen enough to interpret the underlying phenomena of their own time may help us by showing which of the tendencies now at work are likely to become ruling factors in the near future. But beyond the near future—that is to say, beyond the lifetime of the generation which already holds power—no true philosopher will venture. He may indulge his fancy in picturing the details of the remoter landscape; but he knows that it is a region fit for fancy, not for science. In the works of great thinkers there are to be found some happy guesses about times to come; but these are few indeed, compared with the prophecies whose worthlessness was so soon revealed that men forgot they had ever been made, or the dreams which, like those of Dante, idealized an impossible future from an irrevocable past.

As regards the views of Hamilton and Madison, who, be it remembered, do not present themselves as prophets, but as the censors of present evils which they are seeking to remedy, it may be added that the Constitution which they framed and carried checked some of these very evils (*c.g.* the unjust law-making and reckless currency experiments of the State Legislatures); and that it was obviously impossible till the Federal government had begun to work to say how the existing forces could adapt themselves to it. Hamilton remarks in one of his letters that he holds with Montesquieu that a nation's form of government ought to be fitted to it as a suit of clothes is fitted to its wearer [1]. He would doubtless have added that one cannot make sure of the fit until the suit has been tried on.

We must remember, moreover, that the causes which have affected the political growth of America are largely causes which were in 1788 altogether beyond human ken. The cotton gin, Napoleon's willingness to sell Louisiana, steam communications by water and land, Irish and German immigration, have swayed the course of that history; but even the first of these factors had not risen over the horizon in that year, and the last did not become potent till halfway through the nineteenth century [2].

What the sages of the Convention do show us are certain tendencies they discern in their contemporaries, viz. :—

Recklessness and unwisdom in the masses, producing bad laws.

Unwillingness to submit to or support a strong government.

Abuse by the majority of its legal power over the minority.

Indifference to national as compared with local and sectional interests, and consequent preference of State loyalty to national loyalty.

---

[1] 'I hold with Montesquieu that a government must be fitted to a nation as much as a coat to the individual ; and consequently that what may be good at Philadelphia may be bad at Paris and ridiculous at Petersburgh.' To Lafayette, Jan. 6, 1799.

[2] The first cargo of cotton was sent from America to Europe in 1791, and the cotton gin invented in 1793.

That each of these tendencies then existed, and might have been expected to work for evil, admits of no doubt. But if we ask American history what it has to say about their subsequent course, the answer will be that the second and third tendencies have declined, and do not at present menace the public welfare, while the first, though never absent and always liable to marked recrudescence, as the annals of the several States prove, has done comparatively little harm in the sphere of national government. As to the fourth, which Hamilton seems to have chiefly feared, it ultimately took the form, not of a general centrifugal force, impelling each State to fly off from the system, but of a scheme for the separation of the Southern or slave-holding States into a separate Confederacy, and in this form it received, in 1865, a crushing and apparently final defeat [1].

IV. TOCQUEVILLE AND HIS BOOK.

Fifty-one years after the recognition of the independence of the United States, sixty-seven years before the beginning of the twentieth century, Alexis de Tocqueville published his *Democracy in America*, one of the few treatises on the philosophy of politics which has risen to the rank of a classic. His book, therefore, stands rather further than halfway back between our own days and those first days of the Republic which we know from the writings of the Fathers, of Washington, Jefferson, Adams, Hamilton, Madison. It offers a means of measuring the changes that had passed on the country during the half-century from the birth of the Union to the visit of its most famous European critic, and again from the days of that critic to our own.

It is a classic, and because it is a classic, one may venture to canvas it freely without the fear of seeming

---

[1] When we come to Tocqueville, we shall find him touching but lightly on the two first of the above tendencies (partly, perhaps, because he attends too little to the State governments), but emphasizing the third and fearing from the fourth the dissolution of the Union.

to detract from the fame of its author. The more one reads Tocqueville, the more admiration does one feel for the acuteness of his observation, for the delicacy of his analysis, for the elegant precision of his reasonings, for the limpid purity of his style; above all, for his love of truth and the elevation of his character. He is not only urbane, but judicial; not only noble, but edifying. There is perhaps no book of the generation to which he belonged which contains more solid wisdom in a more attractive dress.

We have here, however, to regard the treatise, not as a model of art and a storehouse of ethical maxims, but as a picture and criticism of the government and people of the United States. And before using it as evidence of their condition seventy years ago, we must appraise the reliance to be placed upon it [1].

First let it be observed that not only are Tocqueville's descriptions of democracy as displayed in America no longer true in many points, but that in certain points they never were true. That is to say, some were true of America, but not of democracy in general, while others were true of democracy in general, but not true of America. It is worth while to attempt to indicate the causes of such errors as may be discovered in his picture, because they are errors which every one who approaches a similar task has to guard against. Tocqueville is not widely read in the United States, where the scientific, historical, and philosophical study of the institutions of the country, apart from the legal study of the Constitution, is of comparatively recent growth. He is less read than formerly in England and even in France. But his views of the American government and people have so passed into the texture of our thoughts that we cannot shake off his influence, and, in order to profit by it, are bound to submit his conclusions and predictions to a searching though always respectful examination.

[1] Some interesting remarks upon Tocqueville's tour in America and upon his views of American affairs may be found in President Gilman's Introduction to a recent edition (1898) of the English translation of Tocqueville's book.

The defects of the book are due to three causes. He had a strong and penetrating intellect, but it moved by preference in the *a priori* or deductive path, and his power of observation, quick and active as it was, did not lead but followed the march of his reasonings. It will be found, when his method is closely scrutinized, that the facts he cites are rather the illustrations than the sources of his conclusions. He had studied America carefully and thoroughly. But he wanted the necessary preparation for that study. His knowledge of England, while remarkable in a native of continental Europe, was not sufficient to show him how much in American institutions is really English, and explainable only from English sources.

He wrote about America, and meant to describe it fully and faithfully. But his heart was in France, and the thought of France, never absent from him, unconsciously coloured every picture he drew. It made him think things abnormal which are merely un-French; it made him attach undue importance to phenomena which seemed to explain French events or supply a warning against French dangers.

He reveals his method in the introduction to his book. He draws a fancy sketch of a democratic people, based on a few general principles, passes to the condition of France, and then proceeds to tell us that in America he went to seek the type of democracy—democracy pure and simple—in its normal shape.

' J'avoue que dans l'Amérique, j'ai vu plus que l'Amérique; j'y ai cherché une image de la démocratie elle-même, de ses penchants, de son caractère, de ses préjugés, de ses passions.'

Like Plato in the *Republic*, he begins by imagining that there exists somewhere a type or pattern of democracy, and as the American Republic comes nearest to this pattern, he selects it for examination. He is aware, of course, that there must be in every country and people many features special to the country which reappear

21

in its government, and repeatedly observes that this or
that is peculiar to America, and must not be taken as
necessarily or generally true of other democracies. But
in practice he underrates the purely local and special features of America, and often, forgetting his own scientific
cautions, treats it as a norm for democracy in general.
Nor does he, after finding his norm, proceed simply to
examine the facts and draw inferences from them. In
many chapters he begins by laying down one or two
large principles, he develops conclusions from them, and
then he points out that the phenomena of America conform to these conclusions. Instead of drawing the character of democracy from the aspects it presents in
America, he arrives at its character by a sort of intuitive
method, and uses those aspects only to point and enforce
propositions he has already reached. It is not democracy in America he describes, but his own theoretic
view of democracy illustrated from America. He is admirably honest, never concealing or consciously evading
a fact which he perceives to tell against his theories.
But being already prepossessed by certain abstract
principles, facts do not fall on his mind like seeds on
virgin soil. He is struck by those which accord with, he
is apt to ignore those which diverge from, his preconcep-
tions. Like all deductive reasoners, he is peculiarly exposed to the danger of pressing a principle too far, of
seeking to explain a phenomenon by one principle only
when it is perhaps the result of an accidental concurrence of several minor causes. The scholasticism we observe in him is due partly to this deductive habit, partly
to his want of familiarity with the actualities of politics.
An instance of it appears in his tendency to overestimate
the value of constitutional powers and devices, and to
forget how often they are modified, almost reversed, in
practice by the habits of those who use them. Though
no one has more judiciously warned us to look to the
actual working of institutions and the ideas of the men
who work them rather than to their letter, he has him-

self failed to observe that the American Constitution
tends to vary in working from its legal theory, and the
name Legislature has prevented him, like so many other
foreign observers, from seeing in the English Parliament an executive as well as a law-making body.

In saying that he did not know England, I fully admit
that his knowledge of that country and its free government was far beyond the knowledge of most cultivated
foreigners. He had studied its history and had gathered
from his reading the sentiments of its aristocracy and
of its literary men. But he did not know the ideas and
habits of the English middle class, with whom the Americans of his time might better have been compared, and
he was not familiar—as how could a stranger be?—
with the details of English politics and the working of
the English judicial system. Hence he has failed to
grasp the substantial identity of the American people
with the English. He perceives that there are many
and close resemblances, and traces much that is American to an English source. He has seen and described
with perfect justness and clearness the mental habits of
the English and American lawyer as contrasted with
those of the French lawyer. But he has not grasped, as
perhaps no one but an Englishman or an American can
grasp, the truth that the American people of 1830 was
a branch of the English people, modified in some directions by the circumstances of its colonial life and its
more popular government, but in essentials the same.
Hence much that was merely English appeared to
Tocqueville to be American or democratic. The functions of the judges, for instance, in expounding the Constitution (whether of the Federation or of a State) and
disregarding a statute which conflicts therewith, the responsibility of an official to the ordinary courts of the
land, the co-existence of laws of a higher and lower
degree of authority, seem to him to be novel and brilliant
inventions instead of mere instances of general doctrines
of English law, adapted to the circumstances of a colony

dependent on a home Government, or of a State partially
subordinated to a Federal Government. The absence
of what the French call ' Administration,' and the disposition to leave people to themselves, which strike him,
would not surprise an Englishman accustomed to the like
freedom. Much that he remarks in the mental habits of
the ordinary American, his latent conservatism for instance, his indifference to amusement as compared with
material comfort, his commercial eagerness and tendency to take a commercial view of all things, might
have been just as well remarked of the ordinary middle-
class Englishman, and had nothing to do with a democratic government. Other features, which he ascribes
to this last-named cause, such as habits of easy social
intercourse, the disposition to prize certain particular
virtues, the readiness to give mutual help, are equally
attributable to the conditions of life that existed among
settlers in a wild country where few persons were raised
by birth or wealth above their fellows, and every one had
need of the aid of others—conditions whose results remained in the temper of the people even when the community had passed into another phase, a phase in which
inequalities of wealth were already marked, and temptations had begun to appear which did not beset the Puritans of the seventeenth century.

It is no reproach to this great author that France
formed to him the background of every picture whose
foreground was the New World. He tells us frankly in
the Introduction that the phenomena of social equality,
as they existed in France, and the political consequences
to be expected from them, filled his mind when he examined the institutions of America; he hoped to find
there lessons by which France might profit: ' J'ai voulu
y trouver des enseignements dont nous puissions pro-
fiter.' But with this purpose before him, he could hardly
avoid laying too much stress on points which seemed
to have instruction for his own countrymen, and from
fancying those things to be abnormal, or at least spe-

cially noteworthy, which stood contrasted with the circumstances of France. Tocqueville is, among eminent French writers, one of the least prone to assume the ways and ideas of his own country to be the rule, and those of another country the exception; yet even in him the tendency lurks. There is more than a trace of it in his surprise at the American habit of using without abusing political associations, and at the disposition of Legislatures to try experiments in legislation, a disposition which struck him chiefly by its contrast with the immutability which the Code of the First Empire seemed to have stamped upon the private law of France.

His constant reference to France goes deeper than the method of the book. It determines his scope and aim. The *Democracy in America* is not so much a political study as a work of edification. It is a warning to France of the need to adjust her political institutions to her social condition, and above all to improve the tone of her politics, to create a moral and religious basis for her national life, to erect a new fabric of social doctrine, in the place of that which, already crumbling, the Revolution had overthrown. We must not, therefore, expect to find in him a complete description and criticism, such as a German would have given, of the government of America in all its details and aspects. To note this is not to complain of the book. What Tocqueville has produced is more artistic, and possibly more impressive than such a description would have been, as a landscape gives a juster notion of scenery than a map. His book is permanently valuable, because its reflections and exhortations are applicable not merely to the Frenchmen of sixty-five years ago, but to mankind generally, since they touch upon failings and dangers permanently inherent in political society. Let it only be remembered that, in spite of its scientific form, it is really a work of art quite as much as a work of science, and a work suffused with strong, though carefully repressed, emotion.

The best illustration I can give of these tendencies in

our author will be found in a comparison of the first part of the book, published in 1834, and now included in the first and second volumes of recent editions, with the second part published in 1840, and now forming the third volume. In the first part the author keeps near his facts. Even when he has set out on the *a priori* road he presently brings his theory into relation with American phenomena : they give substance to, and (so to speak) steady the theory, while the theory connects and illumines them. But in the second part (third volume) he soars far from the ground, and is often lost in the clouds of his own sombre meditation. When this part was written, the direct impressions of his transatlantic visit had begun to fade from his mind. With all his finesse and fertility, he had neither sufficient profundity of thought, nor a sufficient ample store of facts gathered from history at large, to enable him to give body and substance to his reflections on the obscure problems wherewith he attempts to deal [1]. Hence, this part of the book is not so much a study of American democracy as a series of ingenious and finespun abstract speculations on the features of equality and its results on modern society and thought, speculations which, though they have been singled out for admiration by some high judges, such as Ampère and Laboulaye, will appear to most readers overfanciful, overconfident in their effort to construct a general theory applicable to the infinitely diversified facts of human society, and occasionally monotonous in their repetition of distinctions without differences and generalities too vague, perhaps too hollow, for practical use.

How far do these defects of Tocqueville's work affect its value for our present purpose, that of discovering from it what was the condition, political, social, intellectual, of the United States in 1833, and what the forces

---

[1] Sainte-Beuve remarks of him, ' Il a commencé à penser avant d'avoir rien appris : ce qui fait qu'il a quelquefois pensé creux.' Thiers once said, in the Chamber, ' Quand je considère intuitivement, comme dirait M. de Tocqueville.'

that were then at work in determining the march of the nation and the development of its institutions?

It is but slightly that they impair its worth as a record of facts. Tocqueville is so careful and so unprejudiced an observer that I doubt if there be a single remark of his which can be dismissed as either erroneous or superficial. There is always some basis for every statement he makes. But the basis is occasionally too small for the superstructure of inference, speculation, and prediction which he rears upon it. To borrow an illustration from chemistry, his analysis is always right so far as it is qualitative, sometimes wrong where it attempts to be quantitative. The fact is there, but it is perhaps a smaller fact than he thinks, or a transient fact, or a fact whose importance is, or shortly will be, diminished by other facts which he has not adequately recognized.

When we pass from description to argument he is a less safe guide. By the light of subsequent experience we can perceive that he mistook transitory for permanent causes. Many of the phenomena which he ascribes to democracy were due only to the fact that large fortunes had not yet grown up in America, others to the absence, in most parts of the country, of that higher education and culture which comes with wealth, leisure, and the settlement of society. I have already observed that he sometimes supposes features of American politics to be novel and democratic which are really old and English; that he does not allow sufficiently for the imprint which colonial life had left on the habits and ideas of the people, an imprint which, though it tends to wear off with time, is yet also modified into something which, while you may call it democratic, remains different from the democracy of an old European country, and is not an index to the character of democracy in general.

It need hardly be said that the worth of a book like his is not to be measured by the number of flaws which can be discovered under the critic's microscope. Even a sovereign genius like Aristotle cannot be expected to

foresee which of the influences he discerns will retain
their potency: it is enough if his view is more piercing
and more comprehensive than that of his greatest contemporaries, if his record shows the high-water mark of
the learning and philosophy of the time. Had history falsified far more of Tocqueville's predictions than she has
done, his work would still remain eminently suggestive
and stimulating. And it is edificatory not merely because it contains precepts instinct with the loftiest morality. It is a model of that spirit of fairness and justice,
that love of pure truth which is conspicuously necessary,
and not less conspicuously difficult, in the discussion,
even the abstract discussion, of the problems of political
philosophy. Few books inspire a higher respect for
their writer.

V. Tocqueville's View of the United States.

Before we examine the picture of the social and political phenomena of America which Tocqueville has drawn,
let us see what were the chief changes that had passed
on the territory of the Union, on its material resources,
on the habits and ideas of the people, during the
forty-six years that elapsed from the publication of the
Federalist to that of the *Démocratie en Amérique*.

The territory of the United States had been extended
to include the whole valley of the Mississippi, while to
the north-west it stretched across the Rocky Mountains
as far as the Pacific. All beyond the Missouri was still
wilderness, much of it wholly unexplored, but to the
east of the Mississippi there were now twenty-four
States with an area of 2,059,043 square miles and a population of fourteen millions. The new Western States,
though rapidly increasing, were still so raw as to exercise comparatively little influence on the balance of national power, which vibrated between the free Northern
and the Southern Slave States. Slavery was not an
immediately menacing question, for the first wound it

made had been skinned over, so to speak, by the Missouri Compromise of 1820; but it was evidently pregnant with future trouble, for the number of slaves was rapidly increasing, and the slaveholders were already resolved to retain their political influence by the creation of new slave States. The great Federalist party had vanished, and the Republican-Democratic party, which had triumphed over it, had just been split into several bitterly hostile factions. Questions of foreign policy were no longer urgent, for Europe had ceased to menace America, who had now no neighbours on her own continent except the British Crown on the north and the Mexican Republic on the south and west. The protective tariff and the existence of the United States Bank were the questions most agitated, but the main dividing party lines were still those which connected themselves with the stricter or looser interpretation of the Federal Constitution—that is to say, they were questions as to the extent of Federal power on the one hand, as to the rights of the States on the other. New England was still Puritan and commercial, with a bias towards protective tariffs, the South still agricultural, and in favour of free trade. The rule of the masses had made its greatest strides in New York, the first, among the older States, which introduced the new methods of party organization and which thoroughly democratized her Constitution [1]. Everywhere property qualifications for office or the electoral franchise were being abolished, and even the judges formerly nominated by the State Governor or chosen by the State Legislature were beginning to be elected by manhood suffrage and for terms of years. In fact a great democratic wave was passing over the country, sweeping away the old landmarks, destroying the respect for authority, casting office and power more and more into the hands of the humbler classes, and causing the withdrawal from public life of men of education and refinement. State feeling was still

---

[1] The process of democratization was completed by the Constitution of 1846.

strong, especially in the South, and perhaps stronger
than national feeling, but the activity of commerce and
the westward movement of population were breaking
down the old local exclusiveness, and those who saw
steamboats plying on the Hudson and heard that locomo-
tive engines were beginning to be run in England, might
have foreseen that the creation of more easy, cheap, and
rapid communications would bind the sections of the
country together with a new and irresistible power. The
time was one of great commercial activity and great apparent prosperity; but large fortunes were still few,
while in the general pursuit of material objects science,
learning, and literature had fallen into the background.
Emerson was still a young Unitarian minister, known
only to the circle of his own friends. Channing was just
rising into note; Longfellow and Hawthorne, Prescott
and Ticknor had not begun to write. Washington Irving
was one of the few authors whose names had reached
Europe. How disagreeable the manners of ordinary
people (for one must of course except the cultivated
circles of Boston and Philadelphia) seemed to the European visitor may be gathered from the diaries of Richard
Cobden and Sir Charles Lyell, who travelled in America
a year or two after Tocqueville. There was a good deal
of ability among the ruling generation of statesmen—
the generation of 1787 was just dying out with Madison
—but only three names can be said to have survived in
the world's memory, the names of three party leaders
who were also great orators, Clay, Calhoun, and
Webster [1].

In those days America was a month from Europe and
comparatively little affected by Europe. Her people
walked in a vain conceit of their own greatness and
freedom, and scorned instruction from the effete monarchies of the Old World, which in turn repaid them

---

[1] To none of whom, oddly enough, does Tocqueville refer. He is singularly
sparing in his references to individuals, mentioning no one except President Jackson for blame and Livingston (author of the Louisiana Code and Secretary of
State, 1831-3) for praise.

with contemptuous indifference. Neither continent had realized how closely its fortunes were to be interwoven with those of the other by trade and the movements of population. No wheat, no cattle were sent across the Atlantic, nor had the flow of immigration from Ireland, much less from Central Europe, as yet begun.

The United States of 1834 had made enormous advances in material prosperity. Already a great nation, it could become a great power as soon as it cared to spend money on fleets and armies. The Federal government had stood the test of time and of not a few storms. Its component parts knew their respective functions, and worked with less friction than might have been expected. The sense of national unity, powerfully stimulated by the war of 1812, was still growing. But the level of public life had not risen. It was now rather below than above that of average private society. Even in the realm of morality there were strange contrasts. A puritan strictness in some departments of conduct and a universal recognition of the sanctions of religion co-existed in the North with some commercial laxity, while the semi-civilized South, not less religious and valuing itself on its high code of honour, was disgraced by the tolerance accorded to duels and acts of murderous violence, not to speak of the darker evils which slavery brought in its train. As respects the government of States and cities, democratic doctrines had triumphed all along the line. The masses of the people had now realized their power, and entered into the full fruition of it. They had unlimited confidence in their wisdom and virtue, and had not yet discovered the dangers incidental to the rule of numbers. The wise elders, or the philosophic minds who looked on with distrust, were either afraid to speak out, or deemed it hopeless to try to stem the flowing tide. They stood aside (as Plato says) under the wall out of the storm. The party organizations had just begun to spread their tough yet flexible network over the whole country; and the class of professional politicians, at once the creator and the creature of such organizations, was already formed. The offices had, three years before, been proclaimed to belong to the victors as spoils of war, but few saw to what consequences this doctrine was to lead. I will not say that it was a period of transition, for that is true of every period in America, so fast do events move even in the quietest times; but it was a period when that which had been democratic theory was passing swiftly into democratic practice, when the seeds sown long ago by Jefferson had ripened into a waving crop, when the forces which in every society react against extreme democracy were unusually weak, some not yet developed, some afraid to resist the stream.

VI. Tocqueville's Impressions and Prophecies.

Let us see what were the impressions which the America of 1832 made on the mind of Tocqueville. I do not pretend to summarize his account, which every student ought to read for himself, but shall be content with presenting the more salient points that ought to be noted in comparing 1832 with 1788 on the one hand, and 1900 on the other.

He is struck by the thoroughness with which the principle of the sovereignty of the people is carried out. Seventy years ago this principle was far from having obtained its present ascendency in Western Europe. In America, however, it was not merely recognized in theory, but consistently applied through every branch of local, State, and National government.

He is impressed by the greater importance to ordinary citizens of State government than of Federal government, and their warmer attachment to the former than to the latter. The Federal government seems comparatively weak, and in case of a conflict between the two powers, the loyalty of the people would be given rather to the State[1].

He finds the basis of all American government in the 'commune,' *i.e.* in local government, the ultimate unit of which is in New England the township, in the Southern and Middle States the county. It is here that the bulk of the work of administration is done, here that the citizens learn how to use and love freedom, here that the wonderful activity they display in public affairs finds its chief sphere and its constant stimulus.

The absence of what a European calls ' the administration ' is remarkable. Public work is divided up between a multitude of petty and unrelated local officials : there is no ' hierarchy,' no organized civil service with a subordination of ranks. The means employed to keep officials to their work and punish offences are two—frequent popular election and the power of invoking the ordinary courts of justice to obtain damages for negligence or unwarranted action. But along with the extreme 'administrative decentralization ' there exists a no less extreme ' governmental centralization,' that is to say, all the powers of government are collected into one hand, that of the people, the majority of the voters. This majority is omnipotent ; and thus authority is strong, capable of great efforts, capable also of tyranny. Hence the value of local self-government, which prevents the abuse of power by a central authority : hence the necessity for this administrative decentralization, which atones for its want of skill in details by the wholesome influence it exerts on the character of the people.

The judges enjoy along with the dignity of their European brethren the singular but most salutary power of ' declaring laws to be unconstitutional,' and thus they serve to restrain excesses of legislative as well as of executive authority.

The President appears to our author to be a com-

[1] His insistence on this point makes it all the more strange that he does not give any description of a State as a commonwealth, nor characterize the general features of its government.

paratively weak official. No person, no group, no party,
has much to hope from the success of a particular candidate at a Presidential election, because he has not
much to give away[!]. The elective system unduly
weakens executive authority, because a President who
approaches the end of his four years' term feels himself
feeble, and dares not take any bold step: while the coming in of a new President may cause a complete change
of policy. His re-eligibility further weakens and abases
him, for he must purchase re-election by intrigue and an
unworthy pandering to the desires of his party. It in-
tensifies the characteristic fault of democratic government, the predominance of a temporary majority.

The Federal Supreme Court is the noblest product of
the wisdom of those who framed the Federal Constitution. It keeps the whole machine in working order, protecting the Union against the States, and each part of
the Federal government against the aggressions of the
others. The strength of the Federation, naturally a
weak form of government, lies in the direct authority
which the Federal courts have over the individual citizen: while the action of these Courts, even against a
State, gives less offence than might be expected because
they do not directly attack its statutes, but merely, at the
instance of an individual plaintiff or defendant, secure to
him rights which those statutes may have incidentally
infringed.

The Federal Constitution is much superior to the
State Constitutions; the Federal Legislature, Executive
and Judiciary, are all of them more independent of the
popular majority, and freer in their action than the corresponding authorities in the several States. Similarly
the Federal government is better than those of the
States, wiser, more skilful, more consistent, more firm.

The day of great parties is past: there is now a feverish
agitation of small parties and a constant effort to create
parties, to grasp at some principle or watchword under
which men may group themselves, probably for selfish

ends. Self-interest is at the bottom of the parties, yet aristocratic or democratic sentiment attaches itself to each of them, that is to say, when a practical issue arises, the old antithesis of faith in the masses and distrust of the masses reappears in the view which men and parties take of it. The rich mix little in politics. Secretly disgusted at the predominance of the crowd, they treat their shoemaker as an equal when they meet him on the street, but in their luxurious homes lament the vulgarity of public life and predict a bad end for democracy.

Next to the people, the greatest power in the country is the press: yet it is less powerful than in France, because the number of journals is so prodigious, because they are so poorly written, because there is no centre like Paris. Advertisements and general news occupy far more of their space than does political argument, and in the midst of a din of opposing voices the ordinary citizen retains his dull fixity of opinion, the prejudices of his sect or party.

A European is surprised, not only at the number of voluntary associations aiming at public objects, but at the tolerance which the law accords to them. They are immensely active and powerful, and do not threaten public security as they would in France, because they admit themselves, by the very fact of their existence, to represent a minority of voters, and seek to prevail by force of argument and not of arms.

Universal suffrage, while it gives admirable stability to the government, does not, as people in Europe expect that it will, bring the best men to the top. On the contrary, the governors are inferior to the governed [1]. The best men do not seek either office or a seat in the House of Representatives, and the people, without positively hating the 'upper classes,' do not like them; and care-

---

[1] This is a common remark of visitors to America, but it arises from their mistaking the people they see in society for 'the governed' in general. They go carrying introductions to rich or educated people: if they mixed with the masses they would form a different notion of 'the governed,' as Tocqueville rather oddly calls the ordinary citizens.

fully keep them out of power. ' Il ne craint point les grands talents, mais il les goûte peu.'

The striking inferiority of the House to the Senate is due to the fact that the latter is a product of double election, and it is to double election that democracies must come if they will avoid the evils inseparable from placing political functions in the hands of every class of the people [1].

American magistrates are allowed a wider arbitrary discretion than is common in Europe, because they are more constantly watched by the sovereign people, and are more absolutely at their mercy [2].

Every office is, in America, a salaried office; nor can anything be more conformable to the spirit of a democracy. The minor offices are, relatively to Europe, well paid, the higher ones ill paid. Nobody wears any dress or displays any insignia of office [3].

Administration has both an unstable and an unscientific character. Few records are kept of the acts of departments: little information is accumulated: even original documents are neglected. Tocqueville was sometimes given such documents in answer to his queries, and told that he might keep them. The conduct of public business is a hand to mouth, rule of thumb sort of affair [4].

Not less instability reigns in the field of legislation. Laws are being constantly changed; nothing remains fixed or certain [5].

[1] It is surprising that Tocqueville should have supposed this to be the cause of the excellence he ascribes to the Senate, considering that the more obvious, as well as the true, explanation is to be found in the fact that the wider powers and longer term of the Senate made the ablest men seek entrance to it.

[2] The only instance given of this is in the discretion allowed to the officers of the New England townships, whose functions are, however, unimportant. The statement cannot have been generally true.

[3] This remained true till very recent years as regards public officials, save and except the Judges of the Supreme Court when sitting at Washington. But lately the Supreme Court Judges of some States have begun to wear gowns.

[4] This has ceased to be true in Federal administration, and in that of the more advanced States.

[5] Tocqueville does not say whether he intends this remark to apply to State legislation only or to Federal legislation also. He quotes dicta of Hamilton, Madison, and Jefferson to the same effect, but these testimonies, or most of them, refer to a

It is a mistake to suppose that democratic governments are specially economical. They are parsimonious in salaries, at least to the higher officials, but they spend freely on objects beneficial to the mass of the people, such as education, while the want of financial skill involves a good deal of waste. You must not expect economy where those who pay the bulk of the taxes are a mere fraction of those who direct their expenditure. If ever America finds herself among dangers, her taxation will be as heavy as that of European monarchies.

There is little bribery of voters, but many charges against the integrity of politicians. Now the corruption of the ' governors ' is worse than that of the ' governed,' for it lowers the tone of public morals by presenting the spectacle of prosperous turpitude.

The American democracy is self-indulgent and self-complacent, slow to recognize, still more slow to correct, its faults. But it has the unequalled good fortune of being able to commit reparable errors (*la faculté de faire des fautes réparables*). It can sin with impunity.

It is eminently ill-fitted to conduct foreign policy. Fortunately it has none.

The benefits which American society derives from its democratic government are summed up as follows :—

As the majority make the laws, their general tendency, in spite of many errors in detail, is to benefit the majority, because though the means may sometimes be ill chosen, the end is always the same. Hence the country prospers.

Every one is interested in the welfare of the country, because his own welfare is bound up with it. This patriotism may be only an enlarged egotism, but it is powerful nevertheless, for it is a permanent sentiment, independent of transient enthusiasms. Its character ap-

---

time anterior to the creation of the Federal Constitution. If it is true that State laws were being constantly changed in 1832, this can have been true only of administrative statutes, not of private law generally. One is tempted to believe that Tocqueville was unconsciously comparing America with France, where the Code has arrested legislation to an extent surprising to an English observer.

22

pears in the childish intolerance of criticism which the people display. They will not permit you to find fault with any one of their institutions or habits, not even if you praise all the rest [1].

There is a profound respect for every political right, and therefore for every magistrate, and for the authority of the law, which is the work of the people themselves. If there be exceptions to this respect, they are to be found among the rich, who fear that the law may be made or used to their detriment.

The infinite and incessant activity of public life, the responsibilities it casts on the citizen, the sense of his importance which it gives him, have stimulated his whole nature, and made him enterprising in all private affairs also. Hence, in great measure, the industrial prosperity of the country. Democracy effects more for the material progress of a nation than in the way of rendering it great in the arts, or in poetry, or in manners, or in elevation of character, or in the capacity for acting on other nations and leaving a great name in history.

We now come to the darker side of the picture. In democracies, the majority is omnipotent, and in America the evils hence flowing are aggravated by the shortness of the term for which a legislature is chosen, by the weakness of the Executive, by the incipient disposition to choose even the judges by popular vote, by the notion universally accepted that the majority must be right. The majority in a legislature being unchecked, laws are hastily made and altered, administration has no permanence, officials are allowed a dangerously wide range of arbitrary authority. There is no escape from the tyranny of the majority. It dominates even thought, forbidding, not indeed by law, but through social penalties no less effective than legal ones, the expression of any opinion displeasing to the ordinary citizen. In the-

---

[1] Every one knows how frequently European visitors used to comment upon this American trait. It is now much less noticeable than formerly. I can even say from experience that it has sensibly diminished since 1870.

ology, even in philosophy, one must beware of any divergence from orthodoxy. No one dare tell an unwelcome truth to the people, for it will receive nothing but incense. Such repression sufficiently explains the absence of great writers and of great characters in public life. It is not therefore of weakness that free government in America will ever perish, but through excess of strength, the majority driving the minority to despair and to arms.

There are, however, influences which temper the despotism of the majority. One is the existence of a strong system of local self-government, whereby nearly all administration is decentralized. Another is the power of the lawyers, a class everywhere disposed to maintain authority and to defend that which exists, and specially so disposed in England and America because the law which they study and practise is founded on precedents and despises abstract reason. A third exists in the jury, and particularly the jury in its action in civil causes, for it teaches the people not only the regular methods of law and justice, but respect for law and for the judges who administer it.

Next we come to an enumeration of the causes which maintain republican government. They are, over and above the constitutional safeguards already discussed, the following :—

The absence of neighbouring States, and the consequent absence of great wars, of financial crises [1], of invasions or conquests. How dangerous to republics is the passion for military glory is shown by the two elections of General Jackson to be President, a man of violent temper and limited capacity, recommended by nothing but the memory of his victory at New Orleans twenty years before [2].

---

[1] This observation seems strange indeed to any one who remembers the commercial history of the United States since the great crisis of 1838.

[2] Jackson's popularity began with his military exploit : but his hold on the people was due to other causes also. His election coincided with the rise of the great democratic wave already referred to.

The absence of a great capital.

The material prosperity of the country, due to its immense extent and natural resources, which open a boundless field in which the desire of gain and the love of independence may gratify themselves and render the vices of man almost as useful to society as his virtues. The passions which really agitate America are commercial, not political.

The influence of religion. American Protestantism is republican and democratic; American Catholicism no less so; for Catholicism itself tends to an equality of conditions, since it treats all men alike. The Catholic clergy are as hearty republicans as any others.

The indirect influence of religion on manners and morality. Nowhere is marriage so much respected and the relations of the sexes so well ordered. The universal acceptance of Christianity, an acceptance which imposes silence even on the few sceptics who may be supposed to exist there as everywhere, steadies and restrains men's minds. ' No one ventures to proclaim that everything is permissible in the interests of society. Impious maxim, which seems to have been invented in an age of liberty in order to give legitimacy to all tyrants to come.' The Americans themselves cannot imagine liberty without Christianity. And the chief cause why religion is so powerful among them is because it is entirely separated from the State [1].

The intelligence of the people, and their education, but especially their practical experience in working their local politics. However, though everybody has some education, letters and culture do not flourish. The Americans regard literature properly so called with disfavour: they are averse to general ideas. They have no great historian, not a single poet, legal commentators but no publicists, good artisans but very few inventors[!]

[1] I do not profess to summarize in these few lines all that Tocqueville says of the character and influence of Christianity in the United States, for he devotes many pages to it, and they are among the wisest and most permanently true that he has written.

Of all these causes, the most important are those which belong to the character and habits of the people. These are infinitely more important sources of well-being than the laws, as the laws are in turn more important than the physical conditions [1].

Whether democracy will succeed in other parts of the world is a question which a study of America does not enable the observer confidently to answer. Her institutions, however suitable to her position in a world of her own, could not be transferred bodily to Europe. But the peace and prosperity which the Union enjoys under its democratic government do raise a strong presumption in favour of democracy even in Europe. For the passions and vices which attack free government are the same in America as in Europe, and as the legislator has overcome many of them there, combating envy by the idea of rights, and the presumptuous ignorance of the crowd by the practice of local government, he may overcome them here in Europe likewise.

One may imagine institutions for a democracy other than those the Americans have adopted, and some of them better ones. Since it seems probable that the peoples of Europe will have to choose between democracy and despotism, they ought at least to try the former, and may be encouraged by the example of America.

A concluding chapter is devoted to speculations on the future of the three races which inhabit the territories of the United States. I need not transcribe what he says of the unhappy Indian tribes. Their fate was then already certain: the process which he saw passing in Alabama and Michigan afterwards repeated itself in California and Oregon.

The presence of the blacks is the greatest evil that threatens the United States. They increase, in the Gulf States, faster than do the whites. They cannot be kept

[1] Like most of his contemporaries, Tocqueville failed to appreciate the enormous influence of physical environment, which has, however, doubtless increased, so far as America is concerned, through the scientific discoveries made since the date of his journey.

for ever in slavery, since the tendencies of the modern world run strongly the other way. They cannot be absorbed into the white population, for the whites will not intermarry with them, not even in the North where they have been free for two generations. Once freed, they would be more dangerous than now, because they would not long submit to be debarred from political rights. A terrible struggle would ensue. Hence the Southern Americans, even those who regret slavery, are forced to maintain it, and have enacted a harsh code which keeps the slave as near as possible to a beast of burden, forbidding him to be taught and making it difficult for him to be manumitted. No one in America seems to see any solution. The North discusses the problem with noisy inquietude. The South maintains an ominous silence. Slavery is evidently economically mischievous, for the free States are far more prosperous: but the South holds to slavery as a necessity.

As to the Federal Union, it shows many signs of weakness. The States have most of the important powers of government in their hands; they have the attachment of the people; they act with vigour and promptitude, while the Federal authority hesitates and argues. In every struggle that has heretofore arisen the Federal Government has given way, and it possesses neither the material force to coerce a rebellious State nor a clear legal right to retain a member wishing to dissolve the Federal tie. But although the Union has no national patriotism to support it (for the professions of such patriotism one hears in America are but lip-deep), it is maintained by certain interests—those material interests which each part of the country has in remaining politically united with the rest. Against these one finds no strong interests making for material severance, but one does find diversities, not indeed of opinion—for opinions and ideas are wonderfully similar over the whole country—but of character, particularly between Northern and Southern men, which increase the chances of discord.

And in the rapid growth of the Union there lies a real source of danger. Its population doubles every twenty-two years. Before a century has passed its territory will be covered by more than a hundred millions of people and divided into forty States [1]. Now all partnerships are more difficult to keep together the more the number of partners increases [2]. Even admitting, therefore, that this hundred millions of people have similar interests and are benefited by remaining united, still the mere fact that they will then form forty nations, distinct and unequally powerful, will make the maintenance of the Federal Government only a happy accident. ' I cannot believe in the duration of a government whose task is to hold together forty different peoples spread over a surface equal to the half of Europe, to avoid rivalries, ambitions, and struggles among them, and to unite the action of their independent wills for the accomplishment of the same plans [3].'

The greatest danger, however, which the Union incurs as it grows is the transference of forces which goes on within its own body. The Northern States increase more rapidly than the Southern, those of the Mississippi Valley more rapidly still. Washington, which when founded was in the centre of the Union, is now at one end of it. The disproportionate growth of some States menaces the independence of others. Hence the South has become suspicious, jealous, irritable. It fancies itself oppressed because outstripped in the race of prosperity and no longer dominant. It threatens to retire from a partnership whose charges it bears, but whose profits it does not share [4].

Besides the danger that some States may withdraw

[1] There are now forty-five, with a population of nearly eighty millions.

[2] No proof is given of this proposition, which is by no means self-evident, and which has indeed all the air of a premiss laid down by a schoolman of the thirteenth century.

[3] He has, however, nowhere attempted to prove that the States deserve to be called ' nations ' or ' peoples.'

[4] The protective tariff was felt as a grievance by the South, being imposed in the interest of the Northern and Middle States. No doubt, the North got more pecuniary gain out of the Union than the South did.

from the Union (in which case there would probably be formed several federations, for it is highly unlikely that the original condition of State isolation would reappear), there is the danger that the central Federal authority may continue to decline till it has become no less feeble than was the old Confederation. Although Americans fear, or pretend to fear, the growth of centralization and the accumulation of powers in the hands of the Federal Government, there can be little doubt that the central authority has been growing steadily weaker, and is less and less able to face the resistance of a refractory State. The concessions of public territory made to the States, the hostility to the United States Bank, the (virtual) success of South Carolina in the Nullification struggle, are all proofs of this truth. General Jackson, now (1832) President, is at this moment strong, but only because he flatters the majority and lends himself to its passions. His personal power may increase, but that of the President declines. 'Unless I am strangely mistaken, the Federal Government of the United States tends to become daily weaker; it draws back from one kind of business after another, it more and more restricts the sphere of its action. Naturally feeble, it abandons even the appearance of force. On the other side, I think I perceive that in the United States the sentiment of independence becomes more and more lively in the States, and the love of provincial government more and more pronounced. People wish to keep the Union, but to keep it reduced to a shadow: they would like to have it strong for some purposes and weak for the rest—strong in war and almost non-existent in peace—forgetting that such alternations of strength and weakness are impossible.'

Nevertheless the time when the Federal power will be extinguished is still distant, for the continuance of the Union is desired, and when the weakness of the Government is seen to threaten the life of the Union, there may be a reaction in its favour.

Whatever may be the future of the Federation, that

of republicanism is well assured. It is deeply rooted not only in the laws, but in the habits, the ideas, the sentiments, even the religion of the people. It is indeed just possible that the extreme instability of legislation and administration may some day disgust the Americans with their present government, and in that case they will pass rapidly from republicanism to despotism, not stopping by the way in the stage of limited monarchy. An aristocracy, however, such as that of the old countries of Europe, can never grow up. Democratic equality will survive, whatever be the form which government may take.

This brief summary, which conveys no impression of the elegance and refinement of Tocqueville's reasonings, need not be pursued to include his remarks on the commercial and maritime greatness of the United States, nor his speculations on the future of the Anglo-American race. Still less shall I enter on the second part of the book, for (as has been observed already) it deals with the ideas of democracy and equality in a very abstract and sometimes unfruitful way, and it would need a separate critical study.

But before passing on to consider how far the United States now differs from the republic which the French philosopher described, we must pause to ask ourselves whether his description was complete.

It is a salutary warning to those who think it easy to get to the bottom of the political and social phenomena of a nation, to find that so keen and so industrious an observer as Tocqueville, who seized with unrivalled acuteness and described with consummate art many of the minor features of American politics, omitted to notice several which had already begun to show their heads in his day, and have since become of the first importance. Among these are—

The system of party organization. It was full grown in some States (New York for instance), and spreading quickly through the rest.

The influence of commercial growth and closer commercial relations in binding together different States of the Union and breaking down the power of State sentiment. He does in one passage refer to this influence, but is far from appreciating the enormous force it was destined to exercise, and must have exercised even without railways.

The results of the principle proclaimed definitely just before his visit, and already operative in some places, that public office was to be bestowed as a reward for political service, and held only so long as the party which bestowed it remained in power.

The assertion by President Monroe of the intention of the United States to regard as unfriendly (*i.e.* to do their best to resist) any extension of the 'European system' to the American Continent, and any further colonization thereof or intrusion by European powers thereon.

The rise of the Abolitionists (they had begun to organize themselves before 1830, and formed a National Anti-Slavery Society in 1833) and the intense hostility they aroused in the South.

The growth of the literary spirit, and the beginnings of literary production. The society which produced Washington Irving, Fenimore Cooper, Channing, Hawthorne, Emerson, Longfellow, Thoreau, Prescott, Ticknor, Margaret Fuller, Holmes, Lowell, Parkman—not to add some almost equally famous later names—deserved mention as a soil whence remarkable fruits might be expected which would affect the whole nation. Yet it is not once referred to, although one can perceive that Tocqueville had spent some time in Boston, for many of his views are evidently due to the conversations he held with the leading Whigs of that day there.

The influence of money on politics. It might surely have been foretold that in a country with such resources, and among a people whose restless commercial activity would be able to act on a vast scale, great piles of wealth would soon be accumulated, that this wealth would perceive objects which it might accomplish by legislative aid, would seek to influence governments, and would find ample opportunities for doing so. But of the dangers that must thence arise we do not hear a word.

VII. Examination of Tocqueville's Views.

Such was the aspect of the United States in 1832, such the predictions which an unusually penetrating and philosophic mind formed of its future. I will not attempt to inquire how far the details of the picture are accurate, because it would be unprofitable to contest statements without assigning one's own reasons, while to assign them would lead me into a historical disquisition. A shorter and simpler course will be to inquire in what respects things have changed since his time, for thus we shall be in a position to discern which of the tendencies he noted have proved permanent, what new tendencies have come into being, what are the main tendencies which are now controlling the destinies of the Republic.

I have noted at the end of last section the phenomena which, already existing in Tocqueville's day, he omitted to notice or to appraise to their due value. Let us see what time has brought forward since his day to alter the conditions of the problem as he saw it.

The great events that have befallen since 1834 are these :—

The annexation of Texas in 1845.

The war with Mexico in 1846, leading to the enlargement of the United States by the vast territories which are now California, Nevada, Utah, Idaho, Arizona, and New Mexico.

The making of railways over the whole country, culminating with the completion of four or five great Trans-Continental roads (the first in 1869).

The establishment of lines of swift ocean steamers between America and Europe.

The immigration from Ireland (immensely increased after the famine of 1846), and from Germany (beginning somewhat later), and from Scandinavia, Austria-Hungary, and Russia (later still).

The War of Secession, 1861-65; together with the extinction of Slavery.

The laying of submarine cables to Europe, and the extension of telegraphic communication over the whole Union.

The settlement of the Alabama claims, an event scarcely less important in American history than in English, because it greatly diminished the likelihood of a war between the two countries. In Tocqueville's time the hatred of Americans to England was rancorous.

The growth of great cities. In 1830, only two had a population exceeding 100,000. There are now (census of 1900) thirty-eight which exceed that population [1].

The growth of great fortunes, and of wealthy and powerful trading corporations; the extension of mining, especially silver and gold mining; the stupendous development of speculation, not to say gambling, in stocks and produce.

The growth of the universities and of many kindred literary and scientific institutions.

The war with Spain in 1898, and consequent annexation of Hawaii (which might probably not have been taken but for naval needs supposed to have been disclosed by the war), of Puerto Rico, and of the Philippine Isles.

These are events which have told directly or indirectly upon politics. I go on to enumerate the political changes themselves of the same sixty-seven years.

Democratization of State Constitutions, total abolition of property qualifications, choice of judges (in most States) by popular vote and for terms of years, restric-

---

[1] In 1790 there were only six cities with populations of at least 8,000. There are now 545. The percentage of urban to rural population (taking urban as that of a city of 8,000) was then 3.4 and is now 33.1.

tions on the power of State Legislatures, more frequent use of the popular vote or so-called Referendum [1].

Development of the Spoils System, consequent degradation of the increasingly large and important civil service, both Federal, State, and Municipal.

Perfection and hierarchical consolidation, on nominally representative but really oligarchic lines, of party organizations; consequent growth of Rings and Bosses, and demoralization of city government.

Enfranchisement of the negroes through amendments to the Constitution.

Intensification of National (as opposed to State) sentiment consequent on the War of Secession; passion for the national flag; rejection of the dogmas of State sovereignty and right of nullification.

Increased importance of currency and other financial problems: emergence of industrial questions as bases for party organization: efforts to found a Labour Party and a 'People's Party.'

To these I add, as powerfully affecting politics, the development not only of literary, scientific and historical studies, but in particular of a new school of publicists, who discuss constitutional and economic questions in a philosophic spirit; closer intellectual relations with Europe, and particularly with England and Germany; resort of American students to German Universities; increased interest of the best class of citizens in politics; improved literary quality of the newspapers and of periodicals (political and semi-political) generally; growth of a critical and sceptical spirit in matters of religion and philosophy; diminished political influence of the clergy.

We may now ask which of Tocqueville's observations have ceased to be true, which of his predictions falsified. I follow the order in which they were presented in the last section.

---

[1] Especially in the form of the amendment of particular provisions of State Constitutions.

Although the powers of the several States remain in point of law precisely what they were (except as regards the Constitutional amendments presently to be noticed) and the citizen depends as much now as then upon the State in all that relates to person and property, to the conduct of family and commercial relations, the National or Federal Government has become more important to him than it was then. He watches its proceedings more closely, and, of course, thanks to the telegraph, knows them sooner and more fully. His patriotism is far more national, and in case of a conflict between one or more States and the Federal power, the sympathies of the other States would probably be with the latter.

Local government has been maintained in its completeness, but it seems to excite less interest among the people. In the larger cities it has fallen into the hands of professional politicians, who have perverted it into a grasping and sordid oligarchy.

There is still, as compared with Continental Europe, little 'administration,' though more than in Tocqueville's time. But the influence of Federal legislation on the business of the country is far greater than it was, for the tariff and the currency, matters of increased consequence ever since the war, are in its hands.

The dignity of the judicial bench has in most States suffered seriously from the system of popular election for comparatively short terms. In those States where nomination by the Executive has been retained, and in the case of the Federal Judges (nominated by the President), the position is perhaps the highest permanent one open to a citizen.

The President's authority received a portentous enlargement during the War of Secession, and although it has now returned to its normal condition, the sense of its importance has survived. His election is contested with increasing excitement, for his immense patronage and the magnitude of the issues he may influence by his veto power give individuals and parties the strongest grounds for hope and fear. Experience has, on the whole, confirmed the view that the re-eligibility of an acting President (*i.e.* the power of electing him for an immediately succeeding term) might well be dispensed with.

The credit of the Supreme Court suffered somewhat from its pro-slavery decisions just before the war, and may possibly have suffered slightly since in respect of its treatment of the Legal Tender question. Nevertheless it remains respected and influential.

The State Constitutions, nearly all of which have been re-enacted or largely amended since 1834, remain inferior to the Federal Constitution, and the State legislatures are, of course (possibly with a very few exceptions in the New England States), still more inferior to Congress.

Two great parties reappeared immediately after Tocqueville wrote, and except for a brief interval before the Civil War when the Whig party had practically expired before its successor and representative the Republican party had come to maturity, they have continued to divide the country, making minor parties of slight consequence. Now and then an attempt is made to start a new party as a national organization, but it rarely becomes strong enough to maintain itself. The rich and educated renewed their interest in politics under the impulse of the Slavery and Secession struggle. After a subsequent interval of apathy they seem to be again returning to public life. The secret murmurs against democracy, whereof Tocqueville speaks, are confined to a handful of fashionable exquisites less self-complacent now than they were in the days when they learnt luxury and contempt for the people in the Paris of Louis Napoleon.

Although newspapers are better written than formerly and those of the great cities travel further over the country, the multitude of discordant voices still prevents the people from being enslaved by the press, which however shows an alarming capacity for exciting them. The habit of association by voluntary societies maintains itself.

The defects of the professional politicians, a term which now more precisely describes those whom Tocqueville calls by the inappropriate European name of ' the governors,' continue at least as marked as in his time.

So, too, the House of Representatives continues less influential than the Senate, but for other reasons than those which Tocqueville assigns, and to a less degree than he describes. The Senate has not, since 1880, maintained the character he gives it; and the fact that it is still chosen in the way which he commended shows that the merits he ascribed to it were not due to its mode of choice. Indeed in the judgement of most thoughtful men, popular election in the States would give a better Senate than election by the State Legislatures now does.

American magistrates never did in general enjoy the arbitrary power Tocqueville ascribes to them. They assuredly do not enjoy it now, but in municipalities there is a growing tendency to concentrate power, especially the appointing power, in the hands of one or a few officers in order that the people may have some one person on whom responsibility can be fixed. Such power is sometimes very wide, but it cannot be called arbitrary. A few minor offices are unsalaried; the salaries of the greater ones have been raised, particularly in the older States.

The methods of administration, especially of Federal administration, have been much improved, but are still behind those of the most advanced European countries, one or two departments excepted.

Government is far from economical. The war of the Rebellion was conducted in the most lavish way: the high protective tariff raises a vast revenue, and direct local taxation takes more from the citizen than in most European countries. An enormous sum is spent upon pensions to persons who purport to have served in the Northern armies during the Civil War [1].

Congress does not pass many public statutes, nor do they greatly alter ordinary law within the sphere open to federal legislation. Many legislative experiments are tried in the newer States, but the ordinary private law is in no such condition of mutability as Tocqueville describes. The law of England suffered more changes between 1868 and 1885 than either the common or statute law of the older States of the Union.

The respect for the rights of others, for the regular course of legal process, for the civil magistrate, remains strong; nor have the rich (although of late years more threatened) seriously begun to apprehend any attacks on them, otherwise than as stockholders in great railway and other corporations.

The tyranny of the majority is not a serious evil in the America of to-day, though people still sometimes profess alarm at it. It cannot act through a State legislature so much as it may have done in Tocqueville's days, for the wings of these bodies have been effectively clipped by the newer State constitutions. Faint are the traces which remain of that intolerance of heterodoxy in politics, religion or social views whereon he dilates [2]. Politicians on the stump still flatter the crowd, but many home truths are told to it nevertheless in other ways and places, and the man who ventures to tell them need no longer fear social proscription (at least in time of peace) in the Northern or Western States, perhaps not even in the Southern.

The Republic came scatheless out of a terrible civil war, and although the laurels of the general who concluded that war twice secured for him the Presidency, they did not make his influence dangerous to freedom.

[1] In 1892 the expenditure on this head was $155,000,000; in 1901 it was estimated at $142,000,000.

[2] Competent American observers in Tocqueville's own time thought he greatly exaggerated this danger. See a letter from Jared Sparks printed in Professor Herbert B. Adams' interesting monograph *Jared Sparks and Alexis de Tocqueville*, in Johns Hopkins University Studies, 1898.

There is indeed no great capital, but there are cities greater than most European capitals, and the Republic has not been imperilled by their growth. The influence of the clergy on public affairs has declined: whether or no that of religion has also been weakened it is more difficult to say. But all Americans are still agreed that religion gains by its entire detachment from the State.

The negro problem remains, but it has passed into a new and for the moment less threatening phase. Neither Tocqueville nor any one else then living could have foreseen that manumission would come as a war measure, and be followed by the grant of political rights. It is no impeachment of his judgement that he omitted to contemplate a state of things in which the blacks have been made politically the equals of the whites, while inferior in most other respects, and destined, apparently, to remain wholly separate from them. He was right in perceiving that fusion was not possible, and that liberation would not solve the problem, because it would not make the liberated fit for citizenship. Fit—that is to say, as fit as a considerable part of the white population —they will probably in the long run become, but even then the social problem will remain. His remark that the repulsion between the races in the South would probably be greater under freedom than under slavery has so far been strikingly verified by the result.

All the forces that made for the maintenance of the Federal Union are now stronger than they were then, while the chief force that opposed it, viz., the difference of character and habits between North and South, largely produced by the existence of slavery, tends to vanish. Nor does the growth of the Union make the retention of its parts in one body more difficult. On the contrary, the United States is a smaller country now when it stretches from the Bay of Fundy to the Gulf of California, with its seventy-six millions of people, than it was then with its thirteen millions, just as the civilized world was larger in the time of Herodotus than it is now,

for it took twice as many months to travel from Perse-
polis or the Caspian Sea to the Pillars of Hercules as
it does now to circumnavigate the globe, one was obliged
to use a greater number of languages, and the journey
was incomparably more dangerous. Before steamboats
plied on rivers, and trains ran on railways, three or four
weeks at least were consumed in reaching Missouri from
Maine. Now one goes in six days of easy travelling
right across the continent.

Nor has the increased number of States bred more
dissensions. The forty-five States of to-day are not as
Tocqueville assumes, and this is the error which vitiates
his reasonings, forty-five nations. The differences in
their size and wealth have become greater, but they work
more harmoniously together than ever heretofore, because neither the lines which divide parties nor the substantial issues which affect men's minds coincide with
State boundaries. The Western States are now, so far
as population goes, the dominant section of the Union,
and become daily more so. But their interests link
them more closely than ever to the North Atlantic
States, through which their products pass to Europe,
and the notion once entertained of moving the capital
from Washington to the Mississippi valley has been
quietly dropped.

VIII. CONCLUDING SUMMARY.

Before bidding farewell to our philosopher, let us
summarize his conclusions.

He sees in the United States by far the most successful and durable form of democratic government that has
yet appeared in the world.

Its merits are the unequalled measure of freedom,
freedom of action, but not of thought, which it secures
to the ordinary citizen, the material and social benefits
it confers on him, the stimulus it gives to all his practical faculties.

These benefits are likely to be permanent, for they rest upon the assured permanence of

Social equality;

Local self-government;

Republican institutions;

Widely diffused education.

It is true that these benefits would not have been attained so quickly nor in such ample measure but for the extraordinary natural advantages of the New World. Nevertheless, these natural advantages are but subsidiary causes. The character of the people, trained to freedom by experience and by religion, is the chief cause, their institutions the second, their material conditions only the third; for what have the Spaniards made of like conditions in Central and South America [1]?

Nevertheless, the horizon is not free from clouds.

What are these clouds?

Besides slavery and the existence of a vast negro population they are—

The conceit and ignorance of the masses, perpetually flattered by their leaders, and therefore slow to correct their faults.

The withdrawal from politics of the rich, and inferior tone of ' the governors,' *i.e.* the politicians.

The tyranny of the majority, which enslaves not only the legislatures, but individual thought and speech, checking literary progress, and preventing the emergence of great men.

The concentration of power in the legislatures (Federal and State), which weakens the Executive, and makes all laws unstable.

The probable dissolution of the Federal Union, either by the secession of recalcitrant States or by the slow decline of Federal authority.

There is therefore warning for France in the example

---

[1] The conditions of most parts of the tropical regions of South and Central America are in reality quite different from those of the American Union taken as a whole.

of America. But there is also encouragement—and the encouragement is greater than the warning.

Of the clouds which Tocqueville saw, one rose till it covered the whole sky, broke in a thunderstorm, and disappeared. Others have silently melted into the blue. Some still hang on the horizon, darkening parts of the landscape.

Let us cast one glance back at the course which events have actually taken as compared with that which Hamilton first, and Tocqueville afterwards, expected.

The Republic fared far otherwise than as Hamilton and his friends either hoped or feared. In this there is nothing to impeach their wisdom. They saw the dangers of their own time, and like wise and patriotic men provided the best remedies which existing conditions permitted. Some dangers they overcame so completely, particularly the financial misdoings of State legislatures, that these have now passed out of memory. They could not foresee what the power of money would become, because there was then little money in the country. They could not foresee the astonishing development of party machinery, because it is a perfectly new thing in the history of the world: and human imagination never does more, at any rate in the field of politics and sociology, than body forth things a little bigger than, or in some other wise a little varying from, what they have been before. It cannot create something out of nothing. Least of all could they divine what the results would be of the coexistence of the money power and the party machine. Nor did even Tocqueville, writing half a century later, when wealth had already appeared and the party machine was in places beginning to work, perceive what both had in store.

How would Tocqueville amend his criticisms were he surveying the phenomena of to-day?

He would add to his praise of the United States that its people re-established their government on firm foundations after a frightful civil war, that their army went back to its peaceful occupations, that they paid off their debt, that they have continued to secure a free field for an unparalleled industrial development and to maintain a hitherto unattained standard of comfort, that the level of knowledge and intellectual culture has risen enormously. He would admit that he had overrated the dangers to be feared from a tyrannical majority and had underrated the strength of the Union. But he would stand aghast, as indeed all the best citizens in the United States do now, at the mismanagement and corruption of city governments. He would perceive that the party organizations have now become the controlling force in the country, more important than the Legislature or the Executive. He would recognize the evils incident to the habit of regarding public office as a means of private advantage to its holder and the bestowal of it as a reward for party services. And he would, while gladly owning that the older forms of faction had ceased to be alarming, note a new development which the spirit of faction has taken in the tendency to look at and deal with both legislation and foreign affairs from the point of view of party advantage. Want of foresight or insight in those who direct the affairs of a mighty nation is at all times a misfortune: but when foresight and insight are set aside for the sake of some transitory party gain, the results may be even more serious.

This, however, is a tendency inherent in all schemes of government by party. It is familiar and formidable in European countries also.

VII

TWO SOUTH AFRICAN CONSTI-
TUTIONS[1]

I. THE CONDITIONS UNDER WHICH THESE CONSTI-
TUTIONS AROSE.

THE old Greek saying, 'Africa is always bringing something new [2],' finds an unexpected application in the fact that there exist in South Africa two Dutch republics possessing constitutions diverse in type from any of those which we find subsisting in other modern States. The system established by these two South African in-struments resembles neither the English, or so-called 'Cabinet,' system of government,—which has been more or less imitated by the other free countries of Europe, and has been reproduced in the self-governing British colonies,—nor the American, or so-called 'Presiden-tial,' system, as it exists in the United States and the several States of the American Union. And although it bears some resemblance to the constitution of the Swiss Confederation and to the constitutions of the cantons of Switzerland, this resemblance is not a close

[1] This Essay was composed early in 1896, and describes the Constitutions of the Orange Free State and South African Republic as they stood in December 1895, the month when the fatal invasion of the latter Republic by the police of the British S. Africa Company took place. I have left it, for obvious reasons, substantially un-changed, save that here and there I have corrected what seemed to be errors, have added one or two references to recent events, and have explained some constitu-tional points with more fullness. In its original form, the Essay appeared in the *Forum* in April 1896.

[2] Λέγεταί τις παροιμία ὅτι ἀεὶ φέρει Λιβύη τι καινόν. Arist. *Hist. Anim.* viii. 28.

one, and is evidently not due to conscious imitation, but to a certain similarity of phenomena suggesting similar devices. The constitutions of these two Dutch republics are the product, the pure and original product, of African conditions, having drawn comparatively little from the experience of older countries, or from the models their schemes of government afford. Moreover, these South African constitutions grew up upon a perfectly virgin soil. There was no pre-existing political organization, such as the old feudal polities supplied in some countries of Europe, out of which these Republics could develop themselves. There were no charters or guilds or companies, such as those which gave their earliest form to the governments of several of the older American States. Nor was there any home pattern to be copied, as the British colonies have, by the aid of statutes of the Imperial Parliament, copied the constitution of the United Kingdom.

This is one of the most interesting features of these Constitutions. They are not specifically Dutch. Neither are they English. Nothing is more uncommon in history than an institution starting *de novo*, instead of being naturally evolved out of some earlier form. The simple farmers who drafted the documents which I propose to describe, knew little about the systems either of Europe or of America. Few possessed any historical, still fewer any legal, knowledge. Many were uneducated men, though with plenty of rough sense and mother wit. They would have liked to get on without any government, and were resolved to have as little as possible. Circumstances, however, compelled them to form some sort of organization; and in setting to work to form one, with little except their recollections of the local arrangements of Cape Colony to guide or to assist them, they came as near as any set of men ever have come to the situation which philosophers have so often imagined, but which has so rarely in fact occurred—that of free and independent persons uniting in an absolutely new social compact for mutual help and defence, and thereby creating a government whose authority has had, and can have had, no origin save in the consent of the governed.

A few preliminary words are needed to explain the circumstances under which the constitutions of the Orange Free State and of the South African Republic (commonly called the Transvaal) were drawn up.

As early as 1820 a certain number of farmers, mostly of Dutch origin, living in the north-eastern part of Cape Colony, were in the habit of driving their flocks and herds into the wilderness north of the Orange River, where they found good fresh pasture during and after the summer rains. About 1828 a few of these farmers established themselves permanently there, still of course remaining subjects of the British Crown, which had acquired Cape Colony first by conquest and then by purchase in 1806 and 1814. In 1835-6, however, a much greater number of farmers migrated from the colony; some in larger, some in smaller bodies. They had various grievances against the British Government, some dating back as far as 1815: and they desired to live by themselves in their own way, untroubled by the Governors whom it sent to rule the country[1]. Between 1835 and 1838 a considerable number of these emigrants moved into the country beyond the Orange River, some remaining there, others pushing still further to the north-east into the hitherto unknown regions beyond the Vaal River, while a third body, perhaps the largest, moved down into what was then a thinly peopled Kafir land, and is now the British colony of Natal. This is not the place in which to relate the striking story of their battles with the Zulu king and of their struggle with the British Government for the possession of Natal. It is enough to say that this third body ultimately quitted Natal to join the other emigrants north of the moun-

[1] A concise account of these grievances and a sketch of the subsequent history of the emigrants may be found in Dr. Theal's *Story of South Africa* (published by Messrs. Putnam), and in my *Impressions of South Africa*, chaps. xi and xii. See also Dr. Theal's larger *History of the Boers in South Africa*.

tains; and that, after many conflicts between those emigrants and the native tribes, and some serious difficulties
with successive Governors of Cape Colony, the British
Government finally, by a Convention signed at Sand
River in 1852, recognized the independence of the settlers beyond the Vaal River, while, by a later Convention signed at Bloemfontein in 1854, it renounced the
sovereignty it had claimed over the country between the
Orange River and the Vaal River, leaving the inhabitants of both these territories free to settle their own
future form of government for themselves.

These two Conventions are the legal and formal
starting-points of the two republics in South Africa, and
from them the history of those republics, as self-governing states, recognized in the community of nations by
international law, takes its beginning. The emigrant
farmers had, however, already been driven by the force
of circumstances to establish some sort of government
among themselves. As early as 1836 an assembly of one
of the largest emigrant groups then dwelling in the
Orange River Territory, elected seven persons to constitute a body with legislative and judicial power. In
1838 the Natal emigrants established a Volksraad (council of the people) which consisted of twenty-four members, elected annually, who met every three months and
had the general direction of the affairs of the community, acting during the intervals between the meetings
by a small committee called the Commissie Raad. All
important measures were, however, submitted to a
general meeting called the Publiek, in which every
burgher was entitled to speak and vote. It was a primary assembly, like the Old English Folk Mot, or the
Landesgemeinde of the older Swiss Cantons. A somewhat similar system prevailed among the farmers settled
in the country beyond the Vaal River. They too had a
Volksraad, or sometimes—for they were from time to
time divided into separate and practically independent
republican communities—several Volksraads; and each

district or petty republic had a commandant-general. Their organization was really more military than civil, and the commandant-general with his Krygsraad (council of war), consisting of the commandants and field cornets within the district, formed the nearest approach to a regular executive. I have unfortunately been unable to obtain proper materials for the internal political history, if such a term can be used, of these communities before they proceeded to enact the constitutions to be presently described, and fear that such materials as do exist are very scanty. But, speaking broadly, it may be said that, in all the communities of the emigrant farmers, supreme power was deemed to be vested in an assembly of the whole male citizens, usually acting through a council of delegates, and that the permanent officials were generally a magistrate, called a landrost, in each village, a field cornet in each ward, and a commandant in each district. All these officials were chosen by the people [1]. In these primitive arrangements consisted the materials out of which a constitutional government had to be built up.

From this point the history of the Orange River Territory, which by the Convention of 1854 was recognized as the Orange Free State, and that of the Transvaal Territory begin to diverge. In describing the constitutions of the republics, I take first that of the Orange Free State, because it dates from 1854, while the existing constitution of the Transvaal is four years younger, having been adopted in 1858. The former is also by far the simpler and shorter document.

When the British Government in 1854 voluntarily divested itself of its rights over the Orange River Territory, greatly against the will of some of its subjects there, the inhabitants of that Territory were estimated at 15,000 Europeans, most of them of Dutch, the rest of

---

[1] I am indebted for most of these facts regarding the early organization of the emigrants to Dr. G. M. Theal's *History of the Boers in South Africa*, a book of considerable merit and interest, which, however, carries its narrative down only to 1854.

British origin. (The number of native Kafirs was much larger, but cannot now be estimated.) The great majority were farmers, pasturing their sheep and cattle on large farms, but five small villages already existed, one of which, Bloemfontein, has grown to be a town of 5,800 people, and is now the capital. The Volksraad, or assembly of delegates of the people, framed, and on April 10, 1854, enacted, a constitution for the new republic. This constitution was revised and amended in 1866, and again in 1879, but the main features of the original instrument remain. I proceed to deal with it as it now stands.

II. Constitution of the Orange Free State.

This Constitution, which is in the Dutch language, and is called *De Constitutie*, is a terse and straightforward document of sixty-two articles, most of which are only a few lines in length [1]. It begins by defining the qualifications for citizenship and the exercise of the suffrage (articles 1 to 4), and incidentally imposes the obligation of military service on all citizens between the ages of sixteen and sixty. Only whites can be citizens. Newcomers may obtain citizenship if they have resided one year in the state and have real property to the value of at least £150 sterling ($750), or if they have resided three successive years and have made a written promise of allegiance.

Articles 5 to 27 deal with the composition and functions of the Volksraad, or ruling assembly, which is declared to possess the supreme legislative authority. It consists of representatives (at present fifty-eight in number), one from each of the wards or Field Cornetcies, and one from the chief town or village of each of the (at present nineteen) districts. They are elected for four

---

[1] My thanks are due to the distinguished Chief Justice of the Free State (Mr. Melius de Villiers) for much information kindly furnished to me regarding this Constitution.

years, one-half retiring every two years. Twelve constitute a quorum. Every citizen is eligible who has not been convicted of crime by a jury or been declared a bankrupt or insolvent, who has attained the age of twenty-five years, and who possesses fixed (*i.e.* real) unmortgaged property of the value of £500 at least.

The Volksraad is to meet annually in May, and may be summoned to an extra session by its chairman, as also by the President (§ 34), or by the President and the Executive Council (§ 45).

The Volksraad has power to depose the President if insolvent or convicted of crime, and may also itself try him on a charge of treason, bribery, or other grave offence; but the whole Volksraad must be present or have been duly summoned, and a majority of three to one is required for conviction. The sentence shall in these cases extend only to deposition from office and disqualification for public service in future, a President so deposed being liable to further criminal proceedings before the regular courts.

The votes of members of the Volksraad shall be recorded on a demand by one-fifth of those present. The sittings are to be public, save where a special cause for a secret sitting exists.

The Volksraad shall make no law restricting the right of public meeting and petition.

It shall concern itself with the promotion of religion and education.

It shall promote and support the Dutch Reformed Church.

It may alter the constitution, but only by a majority of three-fifths of the votes in two consecutive annual sessions.

It has power to regulate the administration and finances, levy taxes, borrow money, and provide for the public defence.

Articles 28 to 41 deal with the choice and functions of the President of the state.

He is to be elected by the whole body of citizens, the Volksraad, however, recommending one or more persons to the citizens [1].

He is chosen for five years and is re-eligible.

He is the head of the executive, charged with the supervision and regulation of the administrative departments and public service generally, and is responsible to the Volksraad, his acts being subject to an appeal to that body. He is to report annually to the Volksraad, to assist its deliberations by his advice, but without the right of voting, and, if necessary, to propose bills. He makes appointments to public offices, and may fill vacancies that occur when the Volksraad is not sitting, but his appointments require its confirmation. (Such confirmation has been hardly ever, if ever, refused.) He may also suspend public functionaries, but dismissal appears to require the consent of the Volksraad.

Articles 42 to 46 deal with the Executive Council. It consists of five members, besides the State President, who is *ex-officio* chairman, with a deciding or overriding vote (*bestissende stem*). Of these five, one is the landrost (magistrate) of Bloemfontein, another the State Secretary, both these officials being appointed by the President and confirmed by the Volksraad; the remaining three are elected by the Volksraad. This Council advises the President, but does not control his action in matters which the Constitution entrusts to him, reports its proceedings annually to the Volksraad, and has the rights, in conjunction with the President, of pardoning offenders and of declaring martial law.

Regarding the judicial power only two provisions require mention. Article 48 declares this power to be exclusively exercisable by the courts of law established by law. Article 49 secures trial by jury in all criminal causes in the superior courts.

Local government and military organization, subjects

[1] In practice, the recommendation of the majority of the Volksraad is looked upon as likely to ensure the election of the person so recommended.

intimately connected in Dutch South Africa, occupy articles 50 to 56 inclusive.

A field cornet is elected by the citizens of each ward, a field commandant by those of each district, in both cases from among themselves [1]. In case of war, all the commandants and cornets taken together elect a Commandant-General, who thereupon receives his instructions from the President. Those who elected him may, with the consent of the President, dismiss him and choose another. Every field cornet and commandant must have landed property, the latter to the value of £200 at least.

Article 57 declares Roman Dutch law to be the common law of the state [2].

Articles 58 and 59 declare that the law shall be administered without respect of persons and that every resident shall be held bound to obey it, while articles 60, 61, and 62 guarantee the rights of property, of personal liberty, and of press freedom.

It will be convenient to defer general criticisms upon the frame of government established by this Constitution till we have examined that of the sister republic of the Transvaal, which agrees with it in many respects. But we may here briefly note, before passing further, a few remarkable features of the present instrument.

1. It is a Rigid constitution, *i.e.* one which cannot be changed in the same way and by the same authority as that whereby the ordinary law is changed, but which must be changed in some specially prescribed form—in this case, by a three-fourths majority of the Volksraad in two successive sessions [3].

2. The body of the people do not come in as a vot-

---

[1] In the earlier days of Rome the army elected its subordinate officers.

[2] Roman Dutch law is the common law all over South Africa, even in the almost purely English colony of Natal (though of course not in Portuguese or German territory). It has been largely affected, especially in the British colonies, by recent legislation.

[3] As to Rigid Constitutions, see Essay III.

ing power, save for the election of the President and Commandant-General. All other powers, even that of amending the constitution, belong to the Volksraad.

3. There is only one legislative chamber.

4. The President has no veto on the acts of the legislature.

5. The President has the right of sitting in and addressing the legislature.

6. The President's Council is not of his own choosing, but is given him by the legislature.

7. The heads of the executive departments sit neither in the Council nor in the legislature.

8. The legislature may apparently reverse any and every act of the President, save those (pardon of offences and declaration of martial law) specially given to him and the Executive Council.

American readers will have noted for themselves some few points in this Constitution which have been drawn from that of the United States. Others are said to have been suggested by the Constitution framed for the French Republic in 1848. Comparatively few controversies upon the construction of the Constitution have been debated with any warmth. One, which gave rise to a difference of opinion between the Volksraad and the Supreme Court of the state, arose upon the question whether the Volksraad has power to punish a citizen for contempt by committing him to prison for a long term, and to direct the State Attorney to prosecute him. The judges disapproved what they deemed an unconstitutional stretching of authority by the legislature. Using the opportunities of influencing public opinion which the delivery of charges to juries gave them, they ultimately so affected the mind of the people that the Volksraad tacitly retired from its position, leaving the question of right undetermined.

III. CONSTITUTION OF THE SOUTH AFRICAN REPUBLIC.

The South African Republic, or Transvaal State as it is popularly called, is ruled by a much longer, much less clear, and much less systematically arranged document than that established by its sister commonwealth [1]. A considerable part of the contents of this constitution is indeed unfit, as too minute, for a fundamental instrument of government; and, whatever the intention of its framers may have been, it has not in fact been treated as a fundamental instrument. Whether it is really such, in strict contemplation of law, is a question often discussed in professional circles in Pretoria and Johannesburg. I shall summarize the more important of its provisions—they occupy two hundred and thirty-two articles—and endeavour therewith to present an outline of the frame of government which they establish.

The Grondwet (Ground-law) or Constitution was drafted by a committee of an assembly of delegates and approved by the assembly itself in February, 1858. It is in Dutch, but has been translated into English more than once.

Article 6 declares the territory of the republic open to every stranger who submits himself to the laws—a provision noteworthy in view of recent events—and declares all persons within the territory equally entitled to the protection of person and property.

Article 8 states, *inter alia*, that the people 'permit the spread of the Gospel among the heathen, subject to prescribed provisions against the practice of fraud and deception'; a provision upon whose intention light is thrown by the suspicions felt by the Boers of the English missionaries.

Article 9 declares that 'the people will not tolerate

---

[1] I have to thank my friend Mr. J. G. Kotzé, late Chief Justice of the South African Republic, for information kindly supplied to me regarding certain points in this Constitution.

24

equality between coloured and white inhabitants either
in church or in state [1].'

Article 10 forbids slavery or dealing in slaves.

Article 19 grants the liberty of the press.

Articles 20 to 23 formerly declared that the people
would maintain the principles of the doctrine of the
Dutch Reformed Church, as fixed by the Synod of Dort
in 1618 and 1619, that the Dutch Reformed Church shall
be the Church of the State, that no persons shall be
elected to the Volksraad who are not members of that
Church, that no ecclesiastical authority shall be acknowledged save that of the consistories of that Church, and
that no Roman Catholic Churches, nor any Protestant
Churches save those which teach the doctrine of the
Heidelberg Catechism, shall be permitted within the republic. But these archaic provisions were in the revised
Grondwet of 1889 reduced to a declaration that only
members of a Protestant Church should be elected to
the Volksraad [2].

After these general provisions we come to the frame
of government. Legislation is committed to a Volksraad, ' the highest authority of the state.' It is to consist
of at least twelve members (the number is at present
twenty-four) who must be over thirty years of age and
possess landed property. Each district returns an equal
number of members. Residence within the district is
not required of a candidate. The members were formerly elected for two years, and one-half retired annually. Their term was afterwards extended to four years.
Every citizen who has reached the age of twenty-one
enjoys the suffrage [3] (persons of colour are of course

---

[1] The Boers are a genuinely religious people, and read their Bibles. But they
have shown little regard to 1 Corinthians xii. 13 ; Galatians iii. 28 ; and Colossians
iii. 11. The same may be said of the people of the Southern States of America ;
and is indeed also true of the less religious English both in South Africa and in the
West Indies.

[2] I am informed that even this restriction was abolished subsequently to 1895.

[3] The suffrage was by subsequent enactments restricted as respects immigrants
and the sons of immigrants ; and in 1895 a person coming into the country could not
obtain full electoral rights till after a period of twelve years. In July 1899, three

incapable of voting or of being elected). The unworkable provision of the old Grondwet that 'any matter discussed shall be decided by three-fourths of the votes' was subsequently repealed.

Three months are to be given to the people for intimating to the Volksraad their opinion on any proposed law, 'except laws which admit of no delay' (§ 12), but laws may be discussed whether published three months before their introduction or introduced during the session of the Volksraad (§ 43). The sittings are to open and close with prayer, and are to be public, unless the chairman or the President of the Executive Council deems secrecy necessary.

If the high court of justice declares the President, or any member of the Executive Council, or the Commandant-General, unfit to fill his office, the Volksraad shall remove from office the person so declared unfit and shall provide for filling the vacant office.

The administration, as well as the proposal, of laws was by the old Grondwet given to an Executive Council (§ 13). The revised instrument vests it in the State President. The President is elected for five years by the citizens voting all over the country. He must have attained the age of thirty and be a member of a Protestant (formerly of the Dutch Reformed) Church (§ 56). He is the highest officer of the state, and appoints all officials. All public servants, except those who administer justice, are subordinate to him and under his supervision. In case of his death, dismissal, or inability to act, his functions devolve on the oldest member of the Executive Council till a new appointment is made. The Volksraad shall dismiss him on conviction of any serious offence. He is to propose laws to the Volksraad—'whether emanating from himself or sent in to him by the people'— and support them in that body either personally or through a member of the Executive Council. He has,

months before the war which broke out in that year, the period was shortened to seven years owing to pressure by the British Government.

however, no right to vote in the Volksraad. He recom-
mends to the Volksraad persons for appointment to
public posts; and may suspend public servants, saving
his responsibility to the Volksraad. He submits an estimate of revenue and expenditure, reports on his own
action during the past year and on the condition of the
republic, visits annually all towns and villages where any
public office exists to give due opportunity to the inhabitants of stating their wishes.

The Executive Council consists of four official members besides the President, namely, the State Secretary,
the Commandant-General, the Superintendent of Native
Affairs, and the Keeper of Minutes (*Notulenhouder*), and
of two other members. All except the Commandant-
General are elected by the Volksraad; the Secretary for
four years, the two other members for three years. The
Commandant-General is elected by the burghers of the
whole republic for ten years. All, including the President, are entitled to sit, but not to vote, in the Volksraad.
The President and Council carry on correspondence
with foreign powers, and may commute or remit a penal
sentence. A sentence of death requires the unanimous
confirmation of the Council. The President may, with
the unanimous consent of the Council, proclaim war and
publish a war ordinance summoning all persons to serve
(§§ 23, 66, 84).

The provisions relating to the military organization
(§§ 93-114) are interesting chiefly as indicating the
highly militant character of the republic. Express provision is made not only for foreign war and for the
maintenance of order at home, but also for the cases of
native insurrection and of disaffection or civil war among
the whites. The officers are all elected by the burghers,
the Commandant-General by the whole body of burghers
for ten years, the commandants in each district for five
years, the field cornets and assistant field cornets in the
wards for three years.

The judiciary (§§ 115-135) consists of landrosts (magistrates who also discharge administrative duties), heemraden (local councillors or assessors), and jurors. The provisions regarding the exercise of judicial power are minute and curious in their way, but have no great interest for constitutional purposes. Two landrosts are proposed to the people of the judicial district by the Executive Council, and the people vote between these two. Minute provisions regarding the oaths to be taken by these officials and by jurymen, and regarding the penalties they may inflict, fill the remaining articles. A guarantee for the independence of the courts is to be found in the general statement in article 15 that 'the judicial power is vested in landrosts, heemraden, and jurors,' and in the declaration (§ 57) that the judicial officers are 'left altogether free and independent in the exercise of their judicial power.' A High Court and a Circuit Court, not provided for in the old Grondwet, appear in that of 1889, and are appointed for life. The High Court consists of a chief justice and four puisne judges.

The old Grondwet also contained some curious details relating to civil administration (which was primarily entrusted to the judicial officers, supported by the commandants and field cornets), and the revenue of the State, which was intended to be drawn chiefly from fees and licences, the people having little disposition to be directly taxed. The farm tax was not to exceed forty dollars, and the poll-tax, payable by persons without or with only one farm, was fixed at five dollars annually. Five dollars was the payment allowed to each member of the Volksraad for each day's attendance. Most of these provisions have disappeared from the instrument of 1889. The salary of the President of the Council, which had been fixed at 5,333 dollars, 2 schellings, and 4 stuivers, to be increased as the revenue increased, now amounts to £7,000 sterling ($35,000) per annum, besides allowances.

The most considerable change made since 1889 was

the establishment, in 1890, of a chamber called the Second Volksraad, which is elected on a more liberal basis
than the First Volksraad, persons who have resided
in the country for two years, have taken an oath of
allegiance and have complied with divers other requirements, being admissible as voters. This assembly, however, enjoys little real power, for its competency is confined to some specified matters, and to such others as
the First Volksraad may refer to it; and its acts may be
overruled by the First Raad, whereas the Second Raad
has no power of passing upon the resolutions or laws
enacted by the First Raad. The Second Volksraad is,
therefore, not a second chamber in the ordinary sense
of the term, such as the Senate in American States or
the House of Lords in England, but an appendage to the
old popular House. It was never intended to exercise
much power, and was, in fact, nothing more than a concession, more apparent than real, to the demands of
the Uitlanders, or recent immigrants excluded from
citizenship.

A few general observations may be made on this
Constitution before we proceed to examine its legal character and effect.

It was in its older form a crude, untechnical document, showing little trace on the part of those who
drafted it either of legal skill or of a knowledge of other
constitutions. The language was often vague, and many
of the provisions went into details ill-fitted for a fundamental law.

Although enacted by and for a pure democracy, it was
based on inequality—inequality of whites and blacks,
inequality of religious creeds. Not only was the Dutch
Reformed Church declared to be established and endowed by the State, but Roman Catholic churches were
forbidden to exist, and no Roman Catholic nor Jew nor
Protestant of any other than the Dutch Reformed
Church was eligible to the presidency, or to membership
of the legislature or executive council. In its improved

shape (1889) some of these faults have been corrected, and in particular the religious restrictions were reduced to a requirement that the President, the Secretary of State, the Landrosts and the members of the Volksraad should belong to a Protestant Church. The door, however, remained barred against persons of colour.

It contained and still contains little in the nature of a Bill of Rights, partly perhaps from an oversight on the part of its draftsmen, but partly also owing to the assumption—which the early history of the republic amply verified—that the government would be a weak one, unable to encroach upon the rights of private citizens.

The first legal question which arises upon an examination of this Constitution relates to its stability and permanence. Is it a Rigid or a Flexible Constitution? That is to say, can it, like the constitution of the Orange Free State and that of the United States, be altered only in some specially prescribed fashion? Or may it be altered by the ordinary legislature in the ordinary way, like any other part of the law?

In favour of the former alternative, that the constitution is a Rigid one, appeal has been made not only to the name Grondwet (Ground-law), but, which is of more consequence, to some of its language. The general declarations of the power of the people, the form in which they entrust power to the legislature, to the Executive Council, and to the judiciary respectively (as well as to the military authority), look as if meant to constitute a triad of authorities, similar to that created by the constitutions of American States, no one of which authorities may trespass on the province of the others. Some things seem intended to be secured against any alteration by the legislature, e. g., article 9 declares that 'the people will not allow of any equality between coloured and white inhabitants'; article 11 declares that 'the people reserve to themselves the exclusive right of protecting and defending the independence and inviolability of Church and State, according to the laws.'

On the other hand, it is argued that the constitution must be deemed to be a Flexible one, because it did not in its original form, and does not now, contain any provision whereby it may be altered, otherwise than by the regular legislature of the country acting according to its ordinary legislative methods. One cannot suppose that no change was intended ever to be made in the Grondwet. That supposition would be absurd in view of the very minute provisions on some trivial subjects which it contains. No distinction is drawn, by the terms of the instrument, between these minutiae and the provisions of a more general and apparently permanent nature. *Ergo*, all must be alterable, and alterable by the only legislative authority, that is to say, the Volksraad. This view, moreover, is the view which the legislature has in fact taken, and in which the people have certainly acquiesced. Some changes have been made—such as the admission to the electoral franchise of persons not belonging to the Dutch Reformed Church, the creation of a new supreme court, and the establishment of a Second Volksraad—which are not consistent with the Grondwet, but whose validity has not been contested.

The difficulty which arises from the fact that, whereas the framers of the Grondwet appear to have desired to make parts of their work fundamental and unchangeable, they have nevertheless drawn no distinction between those parts and the rest, and have provided no specific security against the heedless change of the weightiest parts, may be explained by noting that they were not skilled jurists or politicians, alive to the delicacy of the task they had undertaken. They expected that the Volksraad would continue to be of the same mind as they were then, and would respect what they considered fundamental; they relied on the general opinion of the nation. They had, moreover, provided a method whereby the nation should always have an opportunity of expressing its opinion upon legislation, namely, the provision (§ 12) that the people should have a period of three months within which to ' intimate to the Volksraad their views on any proposed law,' it being assumed that the Volksraad would obey any such intimation, although no means is provided for securing that it will do so.

This provision has given rise to a curious question. It excepts ' those laws which admit of no delay.' Now the Volksraad has in fact neglected the general provision, and, instead of allowing the three months' period, has frequently hastily passed enactments upon which the people have had no opportunity of expressing their opinion. Such enactments, which have in some instances purported to alter parts of the Grondwet itself, are called 'resolutions ' (*besluite*) as opposed to laws ; and when objection has been taken to this mode of legislation. these resolutions seem to have been usually justified on the ground of urgency, although in fact many of them, if important, could hardly be called urgent. They have been treated as equally binding with laws passed in accordance with the provisions of the Grondwet (for up to 1895 article 12 seems not to have been formally altered) ; and it is only recently that their validity has been seriously questioned in the courts. Those who support their validity argue that in passing such resolutions as laws, the Volksraad must be taken to have implicitly, but decisively, repealed the provision of article 12; or that, if this be not so, still the Volksraad is under article 12 the sole judge of urgency, and can legally treat things as urgent which are, in fact, not so; a view affirmed by the Chief Justice in a case (*State* v. *Hess*) which arose in 1895. They add that even apart from both these arguments the unbroken usage of the Volksraad during a number of years, tacitly approved by the people, must be deemed to have established the true construction of the Constitution, especially as according to Roman Dutch law, usage, whether affirmative or negative, can alter written enactments and could thus annul the directions of article 12. So it is written in the Digest of Justinian (I. 3. 32): ' Inveterata consuetudo pro lege custoditur . . . nam quid interest suffragio populus voluntatem suam declaret an rebus ipsis et factis? Quare rectissime etiam illud receptum est ut leges non solum suffragio legis latoris, sed etiam tacito consensu omnium per desuetudinem abrogentur.' To this, however, it is answered that the principle of obsolescence by contrary practice cannot fitly be applied where a statute is recent and express.

Until 1897, the High Court of the Transvaal had held that the resolutions as well as the laws passed by the Volksraad were fully valid, whether or no they had been submitted to the people for the period of three months, nor had the question of their being really urgent been raised. It had thus declared the Grondwet to be alterable by the Legislature, and so not a Rigid Constitution. In that year, however, in the case of *Brown* v. *Leyds*, the Court held, by a majority, that a law which had been passed without having been submitted to the people during the period prescribed by the Grondwet was unconstitutional and therefore void, thus appearing to assert (for the language of the judgement is not very clear) the view that the Grondwet was a Rigid Constitution, not alterable by the Legislature. This action was warmly resented by the Executive and Legislature: and the latter passed a resolution directing the President to require from every judge on pain of dismissal a declaration that he would in future recognize as valid every law passed by the Volksraad, and not again assert the so-called ' testing power' of inquiring whether a law conformed to the provisions of the Grondwet. The Chief Justice refused to make this declaration, and was accordingly dismissed, much to the regret of those who remembered his past services to the State.

On a review of the whole matter, apart from the political passion which has been brought into it, the true view would appear to be the following, though I state it with the diffidence becoming a stranger who is also imperfectly informed as to the constitutional history of the republic.

The Grondwet of the South African Republic, though possibly intended by its framers to be treated, in respect of its most important provisions, as a fundamental law not to be altered by the Volksraad in the exercise of its ordinary powers, is not really a Rigid constitution but a Flexible one. We have to look not so much at what the framers may have wished as at what the language employed actually conveys and imports; and the absence of any provision, such as that contained in the Constitution of the Orange Free State, for a special and peculiar method of change, is decisive upon this point. An American lawyer, accustomed to construe strictly documents which contain or modify powers, might be inclined to argue that the validity of laws (not dealing with matters which ' admit of no delay ') which had been passed as mere resolutions, ignoring article 12, may have been doubtful until the Volksraad modified that article by legislation. But the Transvaal High Court had held that the question of urgency was a question for the discretion of the Volksraad; and it must be added that persons accustomed to other legal systems do not necessarily proceed upon American principles. The Swiss, for instance, make their legislature the interpreter of the Constitution for the purpose of determining the extent of legislative power [1]. Allowing for this, and remembering that both the law courts and the whole people had until 1897 treated the Volksraad as an absolutely sovereign body, the action it took in asserting its sovereignty need excite no surprise. It was claiming nothing more than the powers actually enjoyed by the British Parliament. However, although the Volksraad was merely enforcing the rights which it reasonably (and I think correctly) conceived itself to possess, and could not have permitted the majority of the High Court to assert a power pre-

[1] See Essay III, p. 195.

viously unknown, a wiser course would have been to amend the Constitution in some way which would have given to the judiciary a more assured position than that which had been secured to them by a confessedly crude and imperfect instrument. It was through the confused language of the Grondwet that the whole difficulty arose, and while formally declaring that the Grondwet was not —as it certainly was not—a Rigid Constitution, the Volksraad ought to have endeavoured to render it more suited to the needs of a society which had grown to be different from that for which it had been originally enacted.

IV. OBSERVATIONS ON THE CHARACTER AND WORKING OF BOTH CONSTITUTIONS.

The principles of these Constitutions are highly democratic. They were intended so to be. Among the whites settled in these wide territories there prevailed a perfect social equality, a passionate love of independence, and a strong sense of personal dignity. They were as little influenced by political theories as it was possible for any civilized men in this century to be. Their wish for a government purely popular, and indeed for very little of any government at all, was due to their personal experience and to the conditions under which they found themselves in the wilderness; and one may doubt whether they would have established a regular government but for the dangers which threatened them from the warlike native tribes. Such sentiments as I have described would have disposed them, had they lived in a city, or in a small area like the cantons of Uri or Appenzell in Switzerland, to have kept legislation and the determination of all grave affairs in the hands of a general meeting of the citizens. But they lived scattered over a vast wilderness, with no means of communication save ox-wagons which travel only some twelve miles a day. In the Orange River Territory when it became a state there were probably less than three thousand citizens, though its area was nearly that of England. Hence primary assemblies were impossible, and power had to be entrusted to a representative body.

The predominance of the legislature is the most conspicuous feature of both these constitutions. The Transvaal Volksraad originally made all the appointments to the civil service, for the President had only the right of proposing, and even in the revised Grondwet of 1889 the Raad retains the right of approving or disapproving the President's appointments. In both republics the Volksraad appoints a majority of the Executive Council which surrounds the President, to advise, but also to watch and check him. It has complete control of revenue and expenditure. It may change the constitution, though, in the Orange Free State, only by a prescribed majority. The President has no veto on its acts; nor is it, as in most modern free countries, divided into two chambers likely to differ from and embarrass one another. Its vote, which may, if it pleases, be a single vote, given under no restrictions but those of its own making, is decisive.

The comparative feebleness of the other branches of government corresponds to the overwhelming strength of the legislature. The authority of the judiciary received from the first a somewhat vague recognition, and its independence was at one time, in the South African Republic, seriously threatened by the executive and legislature, and saved only by the exertions of the bench and bar, which aroused public opinion on its behalf. The later controversy between the Volksraad and the Chief Justice has been already discussed. In the Free State the Court's claim to be the proper and authoritative interpreter of the constitution, which would be clear upon English or American principles, was never formally admitted. And though the judges are in both republics appointed for life, their salaries are at the mercy of the legislature.

The executive head of the government has no doubt the advantage, as in an American State, of being directly chosen by the people, and not, as in France, by the legislature. But he has no veto on acts of the legislature, while his acts can be overruled by it, at least in the Orange Free State, for in the Transvaal this may be more doubtful. Its approval is required to any appointments he may suggest. He is hampered by an Executive Council which he has not himself selected, resembling in this respect an American State governor rather than the President of the Union. It may, in the Free State, try him and depose him if convicted. He has no military authority, such as that enjoyed by the British Crown and its ministers, or by the American President, for that belongs to the Commandant-General (though in the Orange Free State the Commandant 'receives instructions' from the President).

Against all these sources of weakness there are only two things to set. The President can speak in the Volksraad, and he is re-eligible any number of times.

The Executive Council, as already observed, seems intended to restrain the President, while purporting to aid and advise him. It may be compared to the Privy Council of mediaeval England, with the important difference that it is appointed, not by the executive, but partly by the legislature, partly by the people. As we shall see presently, it has proved to be an unimportant part of the machinery of government.

In all these points the two constitutions present a close likeness. They are also similar in the recognition which they originally gave, and have not wholly ceased to give, to a state church—an institution opposed to democratic ideas in America and in the British Colonies —as well as in their exclusion of persons of colour from every kind of political right. It would appear that upon this point there has never been any substantial difference of opinion in the two republics. Neither indeed is there much difference of opinion in the British parts of South Africa, for although the influence of English ideas has been so far felt that in Cape Colony persons of colour are permitted to vote, still the combination of a property qualification with an educational qualification greatly restricts their number. A republican form of government, therefore, does not necessarily appear to make for 'human rights' in the American sense of that term, any more than it did in the United States in 1788.

Speaking generally, these two Constitutions carry the principle of the omnipotence of the representative chamber to a maximum. This will be more clearly seen if we compare the system they create, first with the cabinet system of Britain and her self-governing colonies, and secondly with the presidential system of the United States.

The main differences between the South African scheme of government and the British may be briefly summarized.

The head of the executive is, in the South African republics, chosen directly by the people, whereas in Britain and her colonies the executive ministry is virtually chosen by the legislature [1], though nominally by the Crown or its local representative.

In these republics the executive cannot, as can ministers under the British system, be dismissed by a vote of the legislature, nor on the other hand has the executive the power of dissolving the legislature.

In these republics the nominal is also the real and acting executive head, whereas in the British system a responsible ministry is interposed between the nominal head and the legislature.

In all the above-mentioned points the South African system bears a close resemblance to the American.

---

[1] Using the expression which Bagehot has made familiar, though of course Parliament is far from determining the entire composition of a ministry, which may occasionally contain persons it would not have selected.

In these republics the President's Council need not consist of persons in agreement with his views of policy. It may even be hostile to him, as part of Warren Hastings's council at Calcutta was in permanent opposition to that governor. Nor does the Executive Council consist, like the (normal) British cabinet and United States Federal cabinet, of the heads of the great administrative departments, though several officials sit in it.

On the other hand, the South African system agrees with the British in permitting the head of the working executive to speak in the legislature, a permission which has proved to be of the highest importance, and which in America is given by usage neither to the Federal President [1] nor to a State governor.

The chief differences between the South African and the American system are the following:—

The President has, in the South African republics, far less independence than belongs in the United States to either a Federal President or to the Governor of a State. He has no veto on acts of the legislature, and less indirect power through the patronage at his disposal. Moreover, the one-chambered legislature is much stronger as against him than are the two-chambered legislatures of America, which may, and frequently do, differ in opinion, so that the President or Governor can play off one against the other. Further, as already observed, an American Federal President has a cabinet of advisers whom he has himself selected, and an American State governor has usually officials around him who, being elected by a party vote at the same election, are probably his political allies; whereas a South African President might possibly have an Executive Council of opponents forced on him by the Volksraad. And even in negotiations with foreign states, he cannot act apart from this Executive Council.

The distinctive note of both these South African Con-

---

[1] Although there is nothing in the federal constitution to prevent a President from addressing either House of Congress.

stitutions is the kind of relation they create between the Executive and the Legislature. These powers are not disjoined, as in the United States, because a South African President habitually addresses and may even lead the Volksraad. Neither are they united, as in Britain and her colonies, where the Executive is at the same time dependent on the legislature, and also the leader of the legislature, for the South African President is elected by the people for a fixed term, and cannot be displaced by the Volksraad. He combines the independence of an American President with the opportunities of influencing the legislature enjoyed by a British, or British colonial, Ministry. For nearly all practical purposes he is at the mercy of the legislature, because he has neither a veto, like the American President, nor a power of dissolution, like the British Ministry. The Volksraad could take all real power from him, should it be so minded. But he is strong by the possession of the two advantages just mentioned. He can persuade his Volksraad, which has not, by forming itself into organized parties, become inaccessible to persuasion. He can influence the opinion of his people, because he is their choice, and a single man in a high place fixes the attention and leads the minds of a people more than does an assembly.

It must, however, be remembered that the features— perhaps one may say the merits—which I have noted as shown in the working of the South African system, belong rather to small than to large communities. The Free State had in 1895 only some seventeen thousand voting citizens, the Transvaal not many more. Athens in the days of Themistocles had about thirty thousand. In large countries, with large Legislatures, whose size would engender political parties, things would work out differently. Furthermore, in a large State, the administrative departments would be numerous and their work heavy. The President could not discuss departmental affairs with the Raad, and could not easily be made personally responsible for all that his administrative officers

25

did. And the less knowledge he had of affairs and of persons, the less influence he exerted over the Raad, the more would his Executive Council tend to check him. Its members would probably intrigue with the leaders of parties in the Volksraad, and make themselves a more important factor in the government than they have been while overshadowed by his personality.

Any one who, knowing little or nothing about the social conditions and the history of these two republics, should try to predict the working of their governments from a perusal of their constitutions, would expect to find them producing a supremacy, perhaps a tyranny, of the representative assembly; for few checks upon its power are to be found within the four corners of either instrument. He would be prepared to see party government develop itself in a pronounced form. Power would be concentrated in the party majority and its leaders. The Executive would become the humble instrument of their will. The courts of law, especially in the Transvaal with its Flexible constitution, would be unable to stem the tide of legislative violence. The President might perhaps attempt to resist by producing a deadlock over appointments; and he would have a certain moral advantage in being the direct choice of the people. But the one-chambered Legislature would in all probability prevail against him.

Is this what has in fact happened? Far from it. Party government, in the English and American sense, has not made its appearance. The Legislature has not become the predominant power, subjecting all others to itself. It has, in general, followed the lead of the Executive. The Courts of law, though (in the Transvaal) at one moment menaced, have administered justice with fairness and independence. But in order to describe what has happened, I must, in a very few sentences, deal separately with the Orange Free State and the South African Republic, for though their constitutions are similar and the origin of their respective populations nearly identical[1], their history has been very different.

The Orange Free State had, for many years prior to 1899, a comparatively tranquil and uneventful career. One native war inflicted some injury upon it, but the result of that war was to give it a strip of valuable territory. It had joined the British colonies in a South African Customs Union, had placed its railroads under the management of the Cape Government, had maintained friendly relations with the two British self-governing colonies, had extended the franchise to immigrants on easy terms, and was at all times recognized as absolutely independent by the British Government. Internally its development, if not rapid, was both steady and healthful. There was no poverty among the people, and hardly any wealth. No exciting questions arose to divide the citizens, and no political parties grew up. The Legislature, although too large, has been a sensible, business-like body, which wasted no more time than debate necessarily implies. From 1863 to 1888 it was guided by the counsels of President Brand, whom the people elected for five successive terms, and whose power of sitting in it and addressing it proved of the utmost value, for his judgement and patriotism inspired perfect confidence. His successor Mr. Reitz, who was obliged by ill-health to retire from office in 1895, enjoyed equal respect and almost equal influence, when he chose to exert it, with the Volksraad, and things went smoothly under him, as they promised to do under President Steyn, who was elected in 1896, for the latter also was believed—so I heard when visiting the Free State in 1895—to possess the qualities which had endeared his predecessors to the community. The Executive Council has not proved to be a very valuable part of the scheme of government; and some judicious observers thought the constitution ought to be amended by strengthening

---

[1] The British element is larger among the citizens of the Orange Free State than it is in the burgher population of the Transvaal.

the position of the courts and introducing provisions for a popular vote on constitutional amendments, similar to those which exist in American States and in Switzerland. But, on the whole, the system of government worked smoothly, purely and efficiently; the Legislature was above suspicion, and the people were content with their institutions.

Very different had been the annals of the South African Republic. Soon after the Grondwet was adopted in 1858, a civil war broke out; and from that time onward factions and troubles of all kinds were seldom wanting. In 1877 the country, then threatened by native enemies, was annexed to the British dominions against the will of the people: in 1881 its autonomy was restored, subject to British suzerainty[1]. Its government, however, continued to be pressed by financial and other difficulties, till the discovery of rich gold-fields in 1884-6, while suddenly increasing the revenue, drew in a stream of immigrants which has steadily continued to flow, and therewith raised that new crop of political troubles of which all the world has heard[2]. The result has been that the Constitution has never had any period of comparative peace in which its working could be fairly tested. If it has not worked as smoothly as that of the Free State, this may be due not merely to inherent defects but to the strain which civil and foreign wars have placed upon it. The Legislature, however, has not played the leading part. President Burgers, who held

---

[1] A further convention was made in 1884, whose articles, omitting all reference to ' suzerainty ' conceded an independence qualified only in respect of the veto retained by Britain over treaties with foreign powers.

[2] When these immigrants from all parts of the world swarmed into the country, admission to the franchise was made more difficult, because the conservative section of the citizens naturally feared that the newcomers, many of whom did not intend to make the country their home, might, if they forthwith acquired voting power, soon secure a majority and overturn the existing system of the republic, including the official use of the Dutch language and the relations of Church and State. These non-burgher immigrants have been absurdly described as ' helots.' A closer parallel to them is to be found not in the semi-serfs of Sparta but in the class of resident aliens known at Athens as metics (μέτοικοι). But they were indeed far better off than that class, since they enjoyed full civic rights in all matters of private law, wanting only the right of sharing in the government.

office from 1872 till 1877, was, like President M. W. Pretorius before him, practically more powerful than the Volksraad; and since 1881 President Kruger, who has been thrice re-elected, has been the ruling force in the politics of the country. By his influence over the people, by his constant presence and speeches in the Volksraad, he threw its leaders entirely into the shade, and probably exerted more actual power than the chief magistrate of any other republic, though there was scarcely any other chief magistrate whose legal authority was confined within such narrow limits. So much may foreign troubles or economic and social facts, and so much do the qualities of individual men, affect and modify and prevail over the formal rules and constitutional machinery of government. The Legislature therefore has not had in the Transvaal that career of encroachment upon and triumph over the other authorities in the State which might have been predicted for it. Its turn might have come when external relations were tranquil and domestic controversies arose. When foreign affairs occupy men's minds and call for rapid decision as well as for continuity of policy, the Legislature is apt to be, in all countries, dwarfed by the Executive.

POSTSCRIPT.

Since the foregoing sketch of these remarkable experiments in the construction of Frames of Government was written (in 1896), both the Dutch republics have become involved in a deplorable war with England, which has lasted for many months, and still continues at the time of this writing. It has brought misery and desolation upon South Africa, and not least upon that singularly happy, prosperous, peaceful and well-governed community, the Orange Free State. While the flames are still raging, no one can conjecture in what form these two constitutions will emerge from the furnace, or whether indeed they will survive at all. In the midst of so terrible a catastrophe, a catastrophe unredeemed by any prospect of benefit to any of the combatants, and one whose results must be fateful in many ways for the future of South Africa, and possibly also of Britain, the destruction or transformation of constitutions seems but a small matter. But had these two republics been suffered to continue the normal course of their constitutional development, that development would have been full of interest. It might even have conveyed valuable instruction or suggested useful examples to other small commonwealths, for in the scheme of these Constitutions, and especially in that of the Free State, there are some merits not to be found either in the American or in the British system. These simple Free State farmers were wiser in their simplicity than some of the philosophers who have at divers times planned frames of government for nascent communities. But though Wisdom is justified of all her children, she cannot secure that her children shall survive the shock of arms.

VIII

THE CONSTITUTION OF THE COMMONWEALTH OF AUSTRALIA

I. INTRODUCTORY.

AUSTRALIA is the first instance in history of a whole continent whose inhabitants are all (if we exclude the vanishing aborigines) of one race and all owe one allegiance. Thus it has supplied the only instance in which a political constitution has been, or could have been, framed for a whole continent. It is moreover one of the very few cases in history in which a number of communities politically unconnected (save by their common allegiance to a distant Crown) who had felt themselves to be practically a nation have suddenly transformed themselves into a National State, formally recognizing their unity and expressing it in the national institutions which they proceeded to create. There could hardly be a more striking illustration of the speed with which events have been moving during the last and the present age than the fact that Australia, or New Holland as it was then called, was, except as to part of its coasts, marked as a *Terra Incognita* upon our maps so late as the beginning of the eighteenth century, that the first British settlement was not planted in it at Sydney (not far from Captain Cook's Botany Bay) till 1788, that responsible government was not conferred upon the oldest

colony, New South Wales, until 1855, nor upon West
Australia till 1890.

Besides the interest with which every one must see
the birth of a new nation, occupying a vast and rich
territory, the student of political science finds further
matter for inquiry and reflection in the enactment of an
elaborate constitution for the Commonwealth of Australia. Every creation of a new scheme of government
is a precious addition to the political resources of mankind. It represents a survey and scrutiny of the constitutional experience of the past. It embodies an experiment full of instruction for the future. The statesmen
of the Convention which framed this latest addition to
the world's stock of Instruments of Government had
passed in review all previous experiments, had found
in them examples to follow and other examples to shun,
had drawn from them the best essence of the teachings
they were fitted to impart. When the Convention prepared its highly finished scheme of polity, it delivered
its judgement upon the work of all who had gone before,
while contributing to the materials which will be available for all who come hereafter to the work of building
up a State.

Nearly all the precedents which the Australian Convention had at its disposal belong to very recent times,
in fact to the last century and a half. Though federal
governments are ancient—the oldest apparently is that
formed by the cities of Lycia in the fourth century B.C.
—the ancient federations scarcely got beyond the form
of leagues of small republics for the purpose of common
military defence. Such leagues never quite grew into
Federal States, properly so called, *i.e.* States in which
the central government exercises direct power over the
citizens of the component communities. The same remark applies to the confederacies of the Middle Ages,
such as that of the Hanse Towns and that of the old
Swiss Cantons, as well as to the United Provinces of
the Netherlands. The first true Federal State founded

on a complete and scientific basis was the United States, which dates from 1788, when its present Constitution was substituted for the Articles of Confederation of 1776. Next came the Constitution of the Swiss Confederation, enacted in 1848, and replacing a much looser form of union which had previously joined the Cantons of Switzerland. Its present amended form dates from 1874. The third was the Constitution of Canada, established by the British North America Act of 1867. Still later came the Constitution of the North German Confederation (1866) enlarged into that of the new Germanic Empire (1871), a remarkable Federal State with a monarch for its head, and including as its members both large kingdoms, such as Bavaria and Würtemberg, and the city republics of Lübeck, Bremen, and Hamburg [1]. But this last-named Federation, instructive as it is, deals with conditions too dissimilar from those of Australia to furnish many precedents in point. It was the Constitutions of the United States and of Canada which the Australians studied most carefully, and whence they drew as well inspiration as many useful suggestions. And the student who examines the Australian scheme will find it interesting to note many points that recall, by way either of likeness or of contrast, the systems of the United States, of Switzerland, and of Canada. It is only with these three that I propose to compare the Australian Constitution in the pages that follow. As I am writing not for lawyers but for students of history and of constitutions, who desire to understand the nature of this new Government sufficiently to follow with intelligence the course of political life under it, I shall pass lightly over its more technical and more purely legal aspects, and dwell rather upon those general features which will give to the future Australian polity its character and spirit.

---

[1] One might add the Constitution of the Austro-Hungarian Monarchy, which is a sort of double federation. But it is too peculiar to serve as an example to other peoples proposing to federalize.

II. The Movement for Federation.

Like the settlements of Britain in North America, the Australian settlements were organized as Colonies at different dates, and several of them independently of the others [1]. So, again like those of North America, each remained legally unconnected with the others, except through the allegiance they all owed to the British Crown, which sent out Governors to administer them. These officers were at first practically despotic; but when self-government was conferred upon a Colony, they became the nominal heads of an executive which in fact consisted of ministers responsible to the elective legislature of that Colony.

Little as there was in the way of official connexion between the scattered settlements, their inhabitants always deemed themselves Australians, giving their sentimental attachment rather to the country as a whole than to their respective colonies. They were all English; they all lived under similar conditions: their local life had not lasted long enough to form local traditions with which sentiment could entwine itself. The very names of some of the colonies did not favour individualization, for who would call himself a Newsouthwalesian? And the idea that the colonies ought to be united into one political body emerged very early. As far back as 1849 a Committee in England had recommended that there should be a Governor-General for all Australia, with power to convene a General Assembly to legislate on matters of common colonial interest, and a bill introduced into Parliament in that year contained clauses for establishing such a legislature. These provisions were dropped, for the time was not ripe, yet the idea continued to occupy the minds of Australian statesmen from that

[1] New South Wales in 1788, Tasmania in 1825, Western Australia in 1829, South Australia in 1836, Victoria in 1851, Queensland in 1859. Victoria and Queensland had however been originally settled (1836 and 1826), and for some time administered, from New South Wales, while Tasmania had been made a penal settlement as early as 1804.

year onwards; and it received a certain impulse from the creation of the Canadian Confederation in 1867. What it wanted was motive power, that is to say, a sense of actual evils or dangers to be averted, of actual benefits to be secured, by the union of the Colonies into one National State. Democratic communities, occupied by their own party controversies, are little disposed to deal with questions which are not urgent, and which hold out no definite promise either of benefit to the masses or of political gain to the leaders. However, in 1883 events occurred which evoked a new Pan-Australian feeling, and indicated objects fit to be secured by a united Australian government. The late Lord Derby, then Secretary of State for the Colonies, was the most cautious and unsentimental of mankind. He belonged to the old school of English statesmen who deprecated—and in some cases wisely deprecated—further additions to the territories and responsibilities of Britain. Disregarding the representations of the Governments of several among the Colonies, he neglected to occupy the northern part of the great neighbouring island of New Guinea which Australian opinion desired to see British, and permitted it, to their great vexation, to be taken by Germany. About the same time the escape of convicts into Australia from the French penal settlement in New Caledonia had caused annoyance, and movements were soon afterwards made by France which seemed to indicate an intention to appropriate the New Hebrides group of islands. These occurrences roused the Australians to desire an authority which might deliver their common wishes to the Home Government and take any other steps necessary for guarding their common interests. Accordingly a conference of delegates from all the Colonies, including New Zealand and Fiji, met in 1884, and prepared a scheme which was transmitted to England, and was there forthwith enacted by the Imperial Parliament under the name of The Federal Council of Australasia Act, 1885. This scheme was, how-

ever, (as I observed when it was under discussion in the
House of Commons) a very scanty, fragmentary and imperfect sketch of a Federal Constitution. It had no
executive power and no command of money. No colony
need join unless it pleased, and each might withdraw
when it pleased. Thus it befell that the plan excited
little popular interest, and gave such faint promise of
energetic action that only four colonies, Victoria,
Queensland, Tasmania, and South Australia, entered
into it; and of these South Australia presently with-
drew. Meanwhile the need for some general military
organization for all the Colonies began to be felt; and
further objects attainable by union floated before men's
minds. With the increase of trade and industry, the
vexation of tariff barriers between the colonies grew
daily less tolerable. Subjects emerged on which uniformity of legislation was felt to be needful. The irrigation question, one of great importance for so arid a
country, brings New South Wales, where some of the
large rivers have their source, into close relation with
Victoria and South Australia, and requires to be treated
on common lines. These and other grounds led to an
Inter-Colonial Conference of Ministers at Melbourne in
1890, and then to the summoning of a Convention of
Delegates from the Parliaments of all the Colonies, including Tasmania. This latter body, which included
many leading men, met at Sydney in 1891, debated the
matter with great ability, and produced a Draft Bill,
which became the basis of all subsequent discussions.
The movement, hitherto confined to a group of political
leaders, now began to be taken up by the people, and became, especially when the financial troubles of 1893 had
begun to pass away, the principal subject in men's minds.
That crisis had shown all the Colonies how closely their
interests were bound together, and had made them desire to remove every hindrance to an industrial and
financial recovery. A Conference of Prime Ministers
at Hobart in 1895 led to the passing by the several Co-

lonial Parliaments of enabling Acts under which delegates were chosen, this time (following recent American
precedents) by popular vote, to a new Convention which
met at Adelaide (in South Australia) in 1897. It produced a second draft constitution, based on that of 1891,
and laid it before the legislatures of the Colonies for
criticism. About seventy-five amendments were proposed, and were considered by the Convention at its
further sittings, which closed in March, 1898. The draft
Constitution was then submitted to a popular vote, a
new expedient in the British dominions, but one amply
justified by the need for associating the people with the
work. New South Wales alone failed to adopt it by the
prescribed majority, because a large section of her inhabitants thought that her interests had not been duly
regarded, but after a few amendments had been inserted at a conference of the Colonial Prime Ministers,
her people ratified it upon a second vote. On this vote
enormous majorities were secured in Victoria, South
Australia and Tasmania, smaller ones in New South
Wales and Queensland. The Constitution was then sent
to England and passed into law by the Parliament of
the United Kingdom under the title of The Commonwealth of Australia Constitution Act (63 & 64 Vict.
cap. 12). Action by the Imperial Parliament was not
only a convenient way of overriding all the colonial constitutions by one comprehensive Act, but was legally
necessary, inasmuch as some provisions of the Constitution transcended the powers of all the colonial legislatures taken together. Since it had from the first been
understood that the wish of the mother country was not
to impose her own views but simply to carry out the
wishes of the Colonies, only one slight alteration, an
alteration rather of form than substance, was made in
the draft as transmitted from Australia, the ill-considered notion of introducing a larger change having
been eventually dropped by the British Ministry.

I have mentioned these details in order to emphasize

the time, care and pains bestowed by the Australians—
for the work was entirely their own—upon this latest
effort of constructive statesmanship. The Constitution
of the United States was framed by a Convention which
sat at Philadelphia, with closed doors, for nearly five
months, and was accepted by Conventions in all the
thirteen States without change, though ten amendments
were immediately thereafter passed by general consent,
their adoption having been the price paid for the ratification of the main instrument by some doubtful States.

The Constitution of Canada took a little more than
two years to settle. The Resolutions on which it was
based were first of all drafted by a conference of delegates at Quebec. These were approved after full debate
by the legislatures of the Provinces, and were, after
some modifications, embodied in a Bill prepared by a
small conference of Canadian statesmen who met in
London. The Bill was then passed by the Imperial Parliament, never having been submitted to any popular
vote. But this Australian instrument is the fruit of debates in two Conventions, of a minute examination by
legislatures, of a subsequent revision by the second Convention, of further modifications in a few details by a
conference of Prime Ministers, and has after all this
preparation been sealed by the approval of the peoples
of the Colonies concerned. The process of incubation
lasted for nearly nine years, being all the while conducted
in the full blaze of newspaper reporting and under the
constant oversight of public opinion.

III. The Causes which brought about Federation.

The reasons and grounds assigned by the advocates
of Federation were more numerous than those urged in
the United States in 1787-9, or in Canada in 1864-6;
but none of them were so imperative, for the Australian
Colonies were far less seriously menaced by actually
insistent evils, due to the want of a common national

Government, than was the welfare either of the American States in 1787, or of Switzerland in 1848, or of Canada in 1867. In North America, it was the growing and indeed hopeless weakness and poverty of the existing Confederation, coupled with the barriers to commercial intercourse, the confusion and depreciation of currency, and the financial demoralization of some of the States, all of which had just emerged from an exhausting war, that drew the wisest minds of the nation to Philadelphia, induced them to persist in efforts to devise a better union, and enabled them to force its acceptance upon a people largely reluctant. In Switzerland it was the War of Secession (the so-called Sonderbund war) of 1847 that compelled the victorious party to substitute a new and truly federal constitution for the league which had proved too weak. In Canada the relations of the French-speaking and English-speaking Provinces (Lower and Upper Canada) had become so awkward that constitutional government was being practically brought to a standstill, and nothing remained but that the leaders of the two parties should devise some new system. Australia was in no such straits. Her colonies might have continued to go on and prosper, as six unconnected self-governing communities. It is therefore all the more to the credit of her people that they forwent the pleasures of local independence which are so dear to vivacious democracies, perceiving that although necessity might not dictate a federal union, reason recommended it.

The grounds which were used in argument to urge the adoption of the Federal Constitution may be summed up as follows :—

The gain to trade and the general convenience to be expected from abolishing the tariffs established on the frontiers of each colony.

The need for a common system of military defence.

The advantages of a common legislation for the regulation of railways and the fixing of railway rates.

The advantages of a common control of the larger rivers for the purposes both of navigation and of irrigation.

The need for uniform legislation on a number of commercial and industrial topics.

The importance of finding an authority competent to provide for old-age pensions and for the settlement of labour disputes all over the country.

The need for uniform provisions against the entrance of coloured races (especially Chinese, Malays, and Indian coolies).

The gain to suitors from the establishment of a High Court to entertain appeals and avoid the expense and delay involved in carrying cases to the Privy Council in England.

The probability that money could be borrowed more easily on the credit of an Australian Federation than by each colony for itself.

The stimulus to be given to industry and trade by substituting one great community for six smaller ones.

The possibility of making better arrangements for the disposal of the unappropriated lands belonging to some of the colonies than could be made by those colonies for themselves.

There was in these arguments something to move every class in the community. To the commercial classes, the prospect of getting rid of custom-houses and of finding a large free market close at hand for all products was attractive; as was also that of sweeping away the vexation of railway rates planned in the interests of each colony rather than for the common benefit of trade. Large-minded men, thinkers as well as statesmen, hoped that a wider field would bring a loftier spirit into public life. The working-classes might expect, not only advantages in the way of brisker employment, but the establishment of that provision for old age and sickness which a Government covering the whole country and commanding ample resources could make more efficiently and on more uniform lines than even the richest colony could do. Some of these grounds for union measure the distance which the world has travelled since 1788. Railways are far older than was self-government in the oldest Australian colony, far younger than the youngest of the original thirteen American States. Even so late as 1867, when Canada was confederated, no one thought of suggesting that the State should provide old-age pensions.

The opponents of Australian Federation, although they came more and more to feel their cause hopeless, were an active party, including many influential men. Besides denying that the benefits just enumerated would be attained, they dwelt upon the additional cost which a new Government, superadded to the existing ones, must entail. They fanned the jealousies which naturally exist between small and large communities, telling the former that they would be overborne in voting, and the latter that they would suffer in purse; and they wound up with the usual and often legitimate appeals to local sentiment.

The arguments drawn from considerations of expense and from local jealousies were met by a series of ingenious compromises and financial devices to which both the larger and smaller colonies were persuaded to agree, while the love of each community for its own political independence was overborne by the rising tide of national sentiment. An ambition which aspired to make Australia take its place in the world as a great nation, mistress of the Southern hemisphere, had been growing for some time with the growth of a new generation born in the new home, and was powerfully roused by the vision of a Federal Government which should resemble that of the United States and warn off intruders in the Western Pacific, as the American Republic had announced by the pen of President Monroe that she would do on the North-American Continent. The same nationally self-assertive spirit and desire for expansion which has recently spurred four great European Powers

26

into a rivalry for new colonial possessions, and which in 1899 made the United States forswear its old-established principles of policy, has been astir in the mind of the Australians. It had been stimulated by the example of a similar spirit in the mother country, and by the compliments which the English had now begun to lavish upon their colonies. It had gained strength with the growth to manhood of a generation born in Australia, and nurtured in Australian patriotism. Such a patriotism, finding no fit scope in devotion to the particular colonies, longed for a larger ideal. It supplied the motive force needed to create a national union. Without it, all the sober reasonings which counselled confederation might have failed to prevail. No equally strenuous or forward-reaching spirit moved the Canadians in 1867, nor are the traces of such a spirit conspicuous in the American debates of 1787-9. Some men were then solicitous for liberty, others for order and good government, but of imperial greatness in the present sense of the term little was said. Liberty and peace at home, not military strength and domination abroad, were the national ideals of those days.

The history of the Federation movement illustrates the truth that a great change is seldom effected in politics save by the coincidence of two moving forces—the prospect of material advantage and the power of sentiment. In every community there are many who can be moved only by one or other of these two forces, and nearly every man responds better to the first if he can be warmed by the second. In the American debates of 1788-9 feeling was mostly arrayed against the proposed federation, though reason was almost entirely for it. Reason prevailed, but prevailed with far more difficulty than the cause of Federalism, with less cogent economic grounds behind it, prevailed in Australia.

Like America in 1787, Australia was fortunate in having a group of able statesmen, most of whom were also lawyers, and so doubly qualified for the task of preparing a constitution. Their learning, their acuteness, and their mastery of constitutional principles can best be appreciated by any one who will peruse the interesting debates in the two Conventions. They used the experience of the mother country and of their predecessors in the work of federation-making, but they did so in no slavish spirit, choosing from the doctrines of England and from the rules of America, Switzerland, and Canada those which seemed best fitted to the special conditions of their own country. And like the founders of the American and Canadian Unions, they were not only guided by a clear practical sense, but were animated by a spirit of reasonable compromise, a spirit which promises well for the conduct of government under the instrument which they have framed.

IV. The Conditions for a Federal Commonwealth.

Before examining the provisions of the Constitution which is bringing the hitherto independent colonies into one political body, it is well to consider for a moment the territory and the inhabitants that are to be thus united.

The total area of Australia is nearly 3,000,000 square miles, not much less than that of Europe. Of this a comparatively small part is peopled by white men, for the interior, as well as vast tracts stretching inland from the south-western and north-western coasts, is almost rainless, and supplies, even in its better districts, nothing more than a scanty growth of shrubs. Much of it is lower than the regions towards the coast, and parts are but little above sea-level. It has been hitherto deemed incapable of supporting human settlement, and unfit even for such ranching as is practised on arid tracts in western North America and in South Africa. Modern science has brought so many unexpected things to pass, that this conclusion may prove to have been too hasty. Still no growth of population in the interior can be looked for corresponding to that which marked the development of the United States west of the Alleghanies in the beginning of the nineteenth century.

Of the six Australian colonies, one, Tasmania, occupies an island of its own, fertile and beautiful, but rather smaller (26,000 square miles) than Scotland or South Carolina. It lies 150 miles from the coast of Victoria. Western Australia covers an enormous area (nearly 1,000,000 square miles, between three and four times the size of Texas), and South Australia, which stretches right across the Continent to the Gulf of Carpentaria, is almost as large (a little over 900,000 square miles). Queensland is smaller, with 668,000 square miles; New South Wales, on the other hand, has only 310,000 square miles (*i.e.* is rather larger than Sweden and Norway and about the size of California, Oregon and Washington put together); Victoria only 87,000 (*i.e.* is as large as Great Britain and a little larger than Idaho). The country (including Tasmania) stretches from north to south over 32° of latitude (11° S. to 43° S.), a wider range than that of the United States (lat. 49° N. to 26° N.). There are thus even greater contrasts of climate than in the last-named country, for though the Tasmanian winters are less cold than those of Montana, the tropical heats of North Queensland and the shores of the Gulf of Carpentaria exceed any temperature reached in Louisiana and Texas. Fortunately, Northern Australia is, for its latitude, comparatively free from malarial fevers. But it is too hot for the out-door labour of white men. In these marked physical differences between the extremities of the Continent there lie sources whence may spring divergences not only of material interests but ultimately even of character, divergences comparable to those which made the Gulf States of the American Union find themselves drawn apart from the States of the North Atlantic and Great Lakes.

It must also be noted that the great central wilderness

cuts off not only the tropical north and north-west, but also the more temperate parts of the west from the thickly peopled regions of the south-west. Western Australia communicates with her Eastern sisters only by a long sea voyage [1]. She is almost in the position held by California when, before the making of the first transcontinental railway, people went from New York to San Francisco via Panama. Nor is there much prospect that settlements will arise here and there in the intervening desert.

The population of the Continent, which has now reached nearly 4,000,000, is very unequally distributed. The three colonies of widest area, Western Australia, South Australia, and Queensland, have none of them 500,000 inhabitants. Tasmania has about 170,000. Two others, New South Wales and Victoria, have each more than 1,000,000 [2]. This disparity ranges them for political purposes into two groups, the large ones with 2,500,000 people in two colonies, and the small ones with 1,500,000 in four colonies.

Against these two sets of differences, physical and social, which might be expected to induce an opposition of economic and political interests, there is to be placed the fact that the Australian colonies are singularly homogeneous in population. British North America is peopled by a French as well as by an English race, British South Africa by a Dutch race as well as an English. But Australia is purely British. Even the Irish and the Scotch, though both races are specially prone to emigrate, seem less conspicuous than they are in Canada [3]. Australia is to-day almost as purely English as Massachusetts, Connecticut, and Virginia were in 1776,

---

[1] It is four days' voyage from Adelaide, the capital of S. Australia, to Perth, the capital of W. Australia.

[2] Two-fifths of the population of Victoria live in Melbourne, one-fourth of the population of New South Wales in Sydney.

[3] In 1891, out of that part of the total population of Australia which had been born in the United Kingdom, about one-fourth had been born in Ireland and one-sixth in Scotland. Of the whole population of Australia, 95 per cent. are of British stock.

and probably more English than were the thirteen original States taken as a whole. In this fact the colonies found not only an inducement to a closer union, but a security against the occurrence of one of the dangers which most frequently threatens the internal concord of a federation. Race antagonisms have troubled not only Canada and South Africa but the United Kingdom itself, and they now constitute the gravest of the perils that surround the Austro-Hungarian monarchy.

Among the other favouring conditions may be enumerated the use of one language only (whereas in Canada and in South Africa two are spoken), the existence of one system of law, the experience of the same form of political institutions, a form modelled on that which the venerable traditions of the mother country have endeared to Englishmen in all parts of the world. It has also been a piece of good fortune that religion has not interposed any grounds for jealousy or division. The population of Australia is divided among various Christian denominations very much as the population of England is, and the chief difference between the old and the new country lies in the greater friendliness to one another of various communions which exists in the new country, a happy result due partly to the absence of any State Establishment of religion, and partly to that sense of social equality which is strong enough to condemn any attempt on the part of one religious body to claim social superiority over the others.

Finally, there is the unique position which Australia occupies. She has a perfect natural frontier, because she is surrounded by the sea, an island continent, so far removed from all other civilized nations that she is not likely to be either threatened by their attacks or entangled in their alliances. The United States had, when its career began, British possessions on the north, French and Spanish on the south. But the tropical islands which Holland, Germany and France claim as theirs to the north and east of the Australian coasts are cut off by a wide stretch of ocean [1]. They are not now, and are not likely at any time we can foresee, to contain a white population capable of disturbing the repose of Australia. Such a country seems made for one nation, though the fact that its settled regions lie scattered round a vast central wilderness suggests that it is better fitted for a federation than for a government of the unified type. But, on the other hand, this very remoteness might, in removing the force of external pressure, have weakened the sense of need for a federal union had there not existed that homogeneity of race and that aspiring national sentiment to which I have adverted.

Compare these conditions with those of the three other Federations. The thirteen colonies which have grown into the present forty-five States of the American Union lay, continuous with one another, along the coast of the Atlantic. England held Canada to the north of them, France held the Mississippi Valley to the west of them, and, still further to the west, Spain held the coasts of the Pacific. They had at that time no natural boundaries on land; and the forces that drew them together were local contiguity, race unity, and above all, the sense that they must combine to protect themselves against powerful neighbours as well as against the evils which had become so painfully evident in the governments of the several States. Nature prescribed union, though few dreamt that Nature meant that union to cover the whole central belt of a Continent. In the case of Canada, Nature spoke with a more doubtful voice. She might rather have appeared to suggest that this long and narrow strip of habitable but only partially inhabited land, stretching from the Gulf of St. Lawrence to Puget Sound, should either all of it unite with its mighty neighbour to the south, or should form three or four separate groups, separated by intervening wildernesses. Political feelings however, compounded of attachment to Britain and a proud resolve not to be merged in a rival

[1] The nearest point of Dutch New Guinea is about 150 miles from Australia.

power which had done nothing to conciliate them, led the Canadians to form a confederation of their own, which Nature has blessed in this point at least, that its territories are so similar in climate and in conditions for industrial growth that few economic antagonisms seem likely to arise among them.   Switzerland, however, is the most remarkable case of a Federation formed by historical causes in the very teeth, as it might seem, of ethnological obstacles.   Three races, speaking three languages, have been so squeezed together by formidable neighbours as to have grown into one.   The help of Nature has however been given in providing them with mountain fastnesses from which the armies of those neighbours could be resisted; and the physical character of the country has joined with the traditions of a splendid warlike heroism in creating a patriotism perhaps more intense than any other in the modern world.

V. The Constitution as a Federal Instrument.

In examining any Federal Constitution, it is convenient to consider the system it creates first as a Federation, *i.e.* a contrivance for holding minor communities together in a greater one; and then as a Frame of Government, composed of organs for discharging the various functions of administration.   Although the former of these influences the latter, because the federal character of a State prescribes to some extent the character of that State's governmental machinery, it conduces to clearness to deal with these two aspects separately.   Accordingly I begin with the federal aspect of the Constitution.

Federations are of two kinds.   In some, the supreme power of the Central Government acts upon the communities which make it up only as communities.   In others this power acts directly, not only upon the component communities, but also upon the individual citizens as being citizens of the Nation no less than of the several communities. The former kind of Federation may be described as really a mere League of States; the latter kind is a National as well as a Federal State.

The Australian Federation is of this latter type. So are the United States, the Swiss Confederation, and the Canadian Federation. It was however to the former type that both the United States before 1788 and Switzerland before 1848 belonged. So Germany was a mere League of States before 1866, but has been a National as well as Federal State since 1866 and 1871.

The essential feature of this latter type, with which alone we are here henceforth concerned, consists in the existence above every individual citizen of two authorities, that of the State, or Canton (as in Switzerland) or Province (as in Canada), to which he belongs, and that of the Nation, which includes all the States, and operates with equal force upon all their citizens alike. Thus each citizen has an allegiance which is double, being due both to his own particular State and to the Nation. He lives under two sets of laws, the laws of his State and the laws of the Nation. He obeys two sets of officials, those of his State and those of the Nation, and pays two sets of taxes, besides whatever local taxes or rates his city or county may impose.

Accordingly the character of each and every Federation depends upon the distribution of powers between the Nation and the several States, since some powers must be allotted to the larger, some to the smaller entity. With regard to certain powers there can be no doubt. The navy, for instance, the post-office, the control of all foreign relations, must obviously be assigned to the National Government, together with the levying of customs duties at the frontiers and the raising of revenue for the purposes above mentioned. On the other hand, matters of an evidently local nature, such as police, prisons and asylums, the system of municipal or county administration, with the power of taxing for these purposes, will be allotted to the State Governments. But between these two sets there lies a large field of legislation and administration which may, according to the circumstances of each particular country and the wishes of the people who enact their constitution, be granted either to the Nation or to the States. The law of marriage and divorce, for instance [1], criminal law [1], bankruptcy, the traffic in intoxicating liquors [2], the regulation of railways [2], the provision of schools or universities [3], are all matters which have both a national and a local significance, and may be entrusted either to the National legislature or to the State legislatures according as one or other aspect of them predominates in the mind of the people.

VI. Distribution of Powers between Nation and States.

Now the fundamental question in the distribution of powers between the Nation and the States is this—To which authority does the unallotted residue of powers belong? It has been found that no distribution, however careful, can exhaust beforehand all the powers that a legislature or an executive may possibly have to exercise, and it therefore becomes essential to provide, whenever a power not specifically mentioned needs to be exercised, whether it should be deemed to be rightfully exerciseable by the National or by the State authority. In other words, which of these authorities is to be deemed general legatee of any undistributed residue?

This question has been answered differently by different Federations. The United States and Switzerland leave to the States (to which they had belonged pre-

---

[1] In the U. S. A. a State, in Canada a Federal matter.

[2] In Switzerland a Federal matter, in the U. S. A. partly a Federal, partly a State matter.

[3] In the U. S. A. and Germany a State matter, in Switzerland and Canada partly a Federal matter.

viously) the undistributed powers. Canada (whose Provinces were in a different position) bestows them upon the National (Dominion) Government[1]. The question is the more important, because it creates in all sorts of doubtful matters a presumption in favour of the National Government or the State Governments, as the case may be. And it is specially important at the moment of creating a new Federation, because one of the difficulties always then experienced is to induce the States to resign powers they have hitherto enjoyed. Hence it reassures and comforts them to have the residue of powers not specifically distributed left still in their hands.

The Australians have followed the example of the United States and Switzerland rather than that of Canada; and they have done so for the sake of appeasing the local sentiment of the several colonies, and especially of the smaller colonies, who naturally feared that, as they would have less weight than their larger neighbours in the national legislature, they would be in more danger of being subjected to laws which their local opinion did not approve. Section 107 provides that—

'Every power of the Parliament of a Colony which has become or becomes a State shall, unless it is by this Constitution exclusively vested in the Parliament of the Commonwealth or withdrawn from the Parliament of the State, continue as at the establishment of the Commonwealth, or as at the admission or establishment of the State[2], as the case may be.'

Comparatively few powers of legislation are 'exclusively vested' in the Commonwealth Parliament; so that upon subjects other than these the State Parliaments retain for the present their previous power to legislate.

---

[1] See U. S. A. Constitution, Amendment X : Constitution of Swiss Confederation, Art. 3 : British North American Act (1867), sect. 91.

[2] These words are used to cover the case of the creation and admission of future States.

The name 'State,' which the Australians have substituted for 'Colonies,' is significant. It imports a slightly greater independence and has a more imposing sound than the Canadian term 'Province.'

But as it is also provided that all Acts of the Commonwealth Parliament, within the range of the powers granted, shall override laws of any State Parliament, such laws as the latter may pass upon subjects open to both legislatures are left at the mercy of the Commonwealth Parliament, which may, as and when it finds time or occasion, pass Acts extinguishing, or modifying the effect of, those enacted by the States.

Now the range of powers granted to the National or Commonwealth Parliament is very wide, wider than that of Congress or of the Swiss National Assembly, or even of the Dominion Parliament in Canada. I need not enumerate the powers granted, forty-two in number, for they will be found in sects. 52 and 53 of the Australian Constitution. Among them are the following, which are not specifically given to, and nearly all of which are not even claimed by, the United States Congress :—Powers to take over State railways, and to construct and extend railways (with the consent of the State in which the railway lies), to control telegraphs and telephones and also trading and financial corporations, to take over State debts [1], to legislate on marriage and divorce, on bills of exchange and promissory notes, on invalid and old-age pensions, on arbitration and conciliation in trade disputes (where these extend beyond one State), on bounties on the production or export of goods, on the service and execution throughout the Commonwealth of the civil and criminal process and judgements of the State Courts. If these powers come to be all put in force they may leave for State action a narrower and less interesting field than it enjoys in the United States, where nevertheless the State legislatures are bodies of no great account, seldom enlisting the services of men of first-rate capacity.

---

[1] Canada directs the Dominion to take over the Provincial debts existing at the time of the Union. In the U. S. A. the war debts of the States were taken over by the first Congress of the Union.

VII. Constitutional Position of the Australian States.

The Australian Constitution, like that of the United States, assumes the States to be already organized communities, and contains nothing regarding their constitutions. The case of Canada was different, because there the previous government of the Upper and Lower Provinces, which had been one, had to be cut in two, and arrangements made for duly constituting the two halves. But in the case of Australia, the pre-existing constitutions of the Colonies, granted by the Imperial Government at various times, go on unchanged, subject only to the supersession of some of their functions by the Commonwealth, and to one or two specifically mentioned restrictions. That these restrictions are comparatively few may be partly ascribed to that aversion which the English everywhere show to this kind of safeguard against the misuse of legislature power. The omnipotence of the British Parliament seems to have fostered the notion that all Parliaments ought to be free to do wrong as well as to do right. The only things from which a State is disabled are the keeping of a naval or military force (except with the consent of the Commonwealth Parliament), coining money, and making anything but gold and silver coin legal tender [1]. A State is not, as are the American States, forbidden to grant titles of nobility, or to pass any *ex post facto* law or law 'impairing the obligation of contracts.' That no such prohibitions exist in Canada may be ascribed to the fact that in Canada the National or Dominion Government has the right of vetoing laws passed by provincial legislatures, so that improper legislation can be in this way checked. The power is not often exercised in Canada, but when exercised has sometimes led to friction. This plan, however, is neither so respectful to the Pro-

---

[1] See sections 114 and 115 of Constitution, and compare Art. I. sect. 10 of Constitution of U. S. A.

vinces nor so conformable to general principles as is
the American plan, which leaves the States subject only
to the restrictions imposed by the Constitution, restrictions which *ipso iure* annul a law attempting to transgress
them.   And the Australians have wisely followed the
American rather than the Canadian precedent.   The
Australians have, to be sure, in reserve a power to
which nothing similar exists in America, viz. the right
of the British Crown at home to veto legislation. Rarely
as this right is put in force, it might conceivably be used
at the instance of the National Government to avert an
undesirable conflict between State statutes and National
statutes.   Note further that each Australian State is
left as free to amend its own constitution as it was
before, subject of course to the veto of the British
Crown, but to no interference by the Commonwealth,
whereas in Canada acts of the Provincial legislatures
amending their constitutions are subject to the veto
of the Dominion Government as representing the
Crown.

The omission of any provision similar to the famous
and much litigated clause which debars an American
State legislature from passing any law impairing the
obligation of contracts is especially noteworthy.   That
clause, introduced by the Philadelphia Convention in
order to check the tendency of some reckless States to
get rid of their debts, produced in course of time unexpectedly far-reaching results, from some of which
American legislatures and courts have made ingenious
attempts to escape.   It has indeed been thought that
several subsequent decisions of the Supreme Court are
not easily reconcileable with the famous judgement in
the Dartmouth College Case (A.D. 1818), in which the
full effect of this clause was for the first time displayed.
That effect has been to fetter legislation in ways which
are found so inconvenient in practice that they are
acquiesced in only because many State legislatures are
in the United States objects of popular distrust.   No

corresponding distrust seems to be felt in the British colonies, and therefore the Australians have not deemed any such prohibition needful, following the example of the British House of Commons, which in 1893 rejected a similar clause when moved as an amendment to the Irish Home Rule Bill of that year.

In another point the Australian States have been treated with respect. In each of them the nominal executive head has hitherto been a Governor appointed by the British Crown. This was the case in Canada prior to 1867: but when the Canadian Federation was formed, the appointment of the Governors of the several provinces was entrusted to the Governor-General of the Dominion, that is to say, to the Dominion Cabinet by whose advice the Governor-General, being a sort of constitutional monarch, is guided. In practice, therefore, these governorships have become rewards bestowed upon leading party politicians. The Australians wisely (as most Englishmen will think) avoided this plan. Neither did they adopt the American method of letting the people of each State elect the Governor, a method unsuited to government on the Cabinet system, because, as the State Governor is under that system only a nominal head of the Executive (the Cabinet being the real Executive), there was no good reason for setting the people to choose him, and good reasons against doing so, inasmuch as popular elections are invariably fought on party lines. Accordingly the Australians have preferred to let him continue to be appointed by the Home Government, and to allow him to communicate directly with the Colonial Office in London. His Ministers are indeed described in the Constitution (sect. 44) as being ‘the Queen’s Ministers.’

VIII. DIFFERENCES FROM THE UNITED STATES
AND CANADIAN FEDERATIONS.

Four other remarkable divergences, from both the
American and the Canadian Federal systems, remain
to be mentioned.

One relates to the judiciary. In the United States
there is a complete system of Federal Courts ramify-
ing all over the Union and exercising exclusive jurisdiction in all cases arising under Federal statutes, as
well as in a number of other matters specified in Art.
III. sect. 2 of the Constitution. But the State Courts
remain quite independent in all State matters, and determine the interpretation of the State Constitutions
and of all State statutes, nor does any appeal lie from
them to the Federal Courts. In Canada this was not
thought necessary, so there the same set of Courts
deals with questions arising under Federal statutes and
with those arising under Provincial Statutes, and the
Supreme Court of Canada receives appeals from all other
Courts. This is less conformable to theory than the
United States plan, but does not seem to have worked
ill. The danger that Courts sitting in the Provinces
would, under the influence of local feeling, pervert Federal law was not serious in Canada (though a similar
danger was feared in the United States in 1787), and
indeed all the Canadian judges are appointed by the Dominion Government, a further illustration of the preponderance which the Nation has over the Provinces.
The Australians have taken a middle course. They have
established a Federal Supreme Court, to be called ' The
High Court of Australia,' and have taken power for their
Parliament to create other Federal Courts. So far, they
follow the United States precedent. But they have
given power to the Commonwealth Parliament to invest
State Courts with federal jurisdiction, thereby allowing
those Courts to be, as in Canada, both State and Federal.
And they have also allowed an appeal from all State

Courts to the Federal High Court. By this plan the States are more directly connected with and subordinate to the National Government than they are in the United States. The Australian scheme has one great incidental advantage. In the United States the law of different States may and does differ, not only in respect of the difference between the statutes of one and the statutes of another, but also in respect of questions of common law untouched by statutes. The Supreme Court of Massachusetts may, for instance, take a different view of what constitutes fraud at common law from that taken by the Supreme Court of Pennsylvania, and there is no Court of Appeal above both these Courts to bring their views into accord. This has not happened to any great extent in Australia, because the British Privy Council has entertained appeals from all its Courts, and it will happen still less in future, because the Federal High Court will be close at hand to settle questions on which the Courts of different States may have been in disaccord.

A second point shows how much less powerful the sentiment of State sovereignty has been in Australia than it was in the United States. By an amendment (XI) to the American Constitution made in 1798 it is expressly declared that no State can be sued by a private plaintiff. But Australia expressly grants jurisdiction in such cases to its Federal High Court (sect. 75).

A third point is the curious and novel power given to a State of referring matters to the Commonwealth Parliament, and to that Parliament of thereupon legislating on such matters (sect. 51 (xxxvii)). Under this provision (which is not to be found in the Canadian Constitution [1]) there is no department of State law wherewith the National legislature may not be rendered competent to deal. It may be usefully employed to secure uniformity of legislation over all Australia on a number

---

[1] But see section 94 of the Canadian Constitution.

of subjects not within the specifically allotted field of the Commonwealth Parliament.

Finally, the Commonwealth Parliament may grant financial assistance to any State, and may take over the whole or a part of its debts as existing at the establishment of the Commonwealth [1]. Provisions such as these imply, or will involve if put in practice, a relation between the National Government and the States closer than that which exists in America.

To complete this account of the relation of the Nation to the States, let it be noted that a State may surrender any part of its territory to the Commonwealth, and that the Commonwealth is bound to protect each State against invasion or, on the application of the Executive of the State, against domestic violence [2]. This latter provision is drawn from the United States constitution [3], though in America it is from the State legislature, if then in session, that the application for protection ought to come. Australia is right in her variation, because in her States the Legislature acts through the Executive. Neither provision occurs in the Constitution of Canada, which assigns military and naval defence exclusively to the Dominion Government, and makes itself responsible for the maintenance of order everywhere. In Switzerland the management of the army, in which all citizens are bound to serve, is divided between Cantons and Confederation, the supreme control remaining with the latter (Artt. 18-22). The Confederation is bound to protect a Canton against invasion and disorders, and may even itself intervene if the Executive of the Canton cannot ask it on its own motion (Artt. 16 and 17). Australia, as we have seen, allows the States to maintain a force with the consent of the Commonwealth; and this is permitted by the American Constitution also.

[1] Sect. 105.   [2] Sect. 119.   [3] Art. II. sect. 3, and Art. IV. sect. 4.

IX. The Constitution as a Frame of National Government.

We may now pass on to consider the National Government, the construction whereof occupies by far the greater part of the Constitution, which, while it left the States pretty much as they were, had here to build up a new system from the ground.

The first point to be examined relates to the limitations imposed on the National Government as against the citizens generally, since I have already dealt with the limitations on its powers as against the States. Here a remarkable divergence from the American Constitution is disclosed. When that instrument was enacted, the keenest suspicion and jealousy was felt of the action of the Government to be established under it. It was feared that Congress might become an illiberal oligarchy and the President a new George the Third. Accordingly great pains were taken to debar Congress from doing anything which could infringe the primordial human rights of the citizen. Some restrictions are contained in the original Constitution: others fill the first nine amendments which were passed two or three years later, as a part of the arrangements by which the acceptance of the Constitution was secured. And down till our own time every State Constitution in America has continued to contain a similar ' Bill of Rights ' for the protection of the citizens against abuse of legislative power. The English, however, have completely forgotten these old suspicions, which, when they did exist, attached to the Crown and not to the Legislature. So when Englishmen in Canada or Australia enact new Constitutions, they take no heed of such matters, and make their legislature as like the omnipotent Parliament of Britain as they can. The Canadian Constitution leaves the Dominion Parliament unfettered save by the direction (sect. 54) that money shall not be appropriated to any purpose that has not been recommended to the House of Commons by the Executive, a direction embodying English practice, and now adopted by Australia also. And the Australian Constitution contains but one provision which recalls the old-fashioned Bill of Rights, viz. that which forbids the Commonwealth to ' make any law for establishing any religion or for imposing any religious observance or for prohibiting the free exercise of any religion.' The Swiss Constitution, influenced by French and American models, is in this respect more archaic, for it imposes a series of disabilities on its Legislature in the interest of individual freedom (sectt. 39, 49, 54-59). This diversity of attitude between the English on the one hand and both the Americans and the Swiss on the other is a curious instance of the way in which usage and tradition mould a nation's mind. Parliament was for so long a time the protector of Englishmen against an arbitrary Executive that they did not form the habit of taking precautions against the abuse of the powers of the Legislature; and their struggles for a fuller freedom took the form of making Parliament a more truly popular and representative body, not that of restricting its authority.

The point just examined is one which arises in all Rigid Constitutions, whether Federal or Unitary. But the next point is one with which only Federations are concerned; and it is one in which all the great Federations agreee. All have adopted the same method of providing both for the predominance of the majority of the people considered as one Nation, and for the maintenance of the rights of the States considered as distinct communities. The Americans invented this method: the Swiss, the Canadians, the Germans, and now the Australians, have imitated them. This method is to divide the Legislature into two Houses, using one to represent the whole people on the basis of numbers, and using the other to represent the several States on the basis (except in Germany) of their equality as autonomous communities. It was this device that made Federation possible in the United States, for the smaller States would not have foregone their independence in reliance upon any weaker guarantee.

X. The Legislature.

The Australian scheme provides (sectt. 7-23) for an Upper House or Senate of thirty-six members, six from each State, and a House of Representatives (sectt. 24-40) of seventy-five members, elected on a basis of population, so that forty-nine members will come from the two large States, New South Wales and Victoria, and twenty-six from the four small States. No Original State is ever to have less than five.

The equal representation of the six Original States is always to be maintained, but the number of Senators may be increased, and when new States come to be formed, the Parliament may allot to them such number of Senators as it thinks fit. Senators sit for six years, and do not all retire at the same time. These features are taken from the Constitution of the United States, which, as already observed, has been a model for subsequent Federal Upper Houses. But there are remarkable variations in the Australian scheme.

1. In the United States each newly-created State receives as a matter of right its two Senators. In Australia the Commonwealth may allot such number as it thinks fit.

2. In the United States one-third of the Senate retires every two years. In Australia one-half retires every three years.

3. In the United States the President of the Senate is the Vice-President of the United States, chosen by the people [1]. In Australia, the Senate is to choose its own President.

---

[1] *I.e.* practically by the people, though formally by a body of electors elected for that purpose.

4. In the United States the quorum is one more than a half of the total number; in Australia one-third of the total number.

5. In the United States the Legislatures of the several States elect the Senators. In Australia the Senators are elected by the people of the State.

This last point is one of great interest. Tocqueville, writing in 1832, attributed (erroneously, as the sequel has shown) the excellence of the American Senate to the method of election by the State Legislatures [1]. Since his days the American Senate has declined; and so far from this mode of election having tended to sustain its character, the general, though not unanimous, opinion of the wise in America deems the Senate to be injured by it, and desires a change to the method of election by direct popular vote. It was partly because the Australian Convention had become aware of this tendency of American opinion that they rejected the existing American plan; nor is it impossible that the Americans themselves may alter their system, which gives greater opportunities for intrigue and the use of money than popular election would be likely to afford. In Australia, the Senators are in the first instance to be elected by the people, each State voting as one electorate, but this may be altered (*e.g.* to a system of district elections) by the Parliament of the Commonwealth, or failing its action, by the Parliament of a State. It will be interesting to see what experiments are tried and how they work. District voting may give different results from a general State vote, and a party for the moment dominant may choose the plan that best suits it.

6. In the United States the Senate is an undying body, perpetually renewed by fresh elections, never losing more than one-third of its members at any one time. In Australia the Senate may be dissolved in case a deadlock should arise between it and the House of Representatives.

---

[1] See as to this, Essay VI, p. 336 and p. 352.

The Senate is the sheet-anchor of the four small States. Commanding a majority in it, they have consented to acquiesce in the great preponderance which their two larger neighbours possess in the House of Representatives. The numbers of the latter House are to be always as nearly as practicable double those of the Senate, a point whose importance will presently appear.

The House is to continue for three years (subject of course to dissolution), a term intermediate, though inclining in the democratic direction, between the two years of the American Congress and the seven (practically six) years of the British House of Commons. The Canadian term is five years. Until the Commonwealth Parliament otherwise provides, the electoral suffrage is to be (as in the United States) the suffrage prescribed by State law for the election of members of the more numerous State House, and it is expressly provided, doubtless with a view to the fact that women's suffrage already exists in two colonies, that no law shall prevent a State voter from voting at Commonwealth elections. So far from securing, as does the United States Constitution, that no person shall be excluded on the ground of race from the suffrage [1], Australia has expressly provided that persons belonging to a particular race may be excluded, for she declares (sect. 25) that in such case the excluded race is not to be reckoned among the population of the State for the purposes of an allotment of representatives. Plural voting is forbidden. The quorum of members is a mean between the inconveniently large quorum (one-half) of the American, and the very small one (forty) of the British House. The seat of any Senator or member of the House becomes *ipso facto* vacant if he fails (without permission) to attend any session for two continuous months. No person having any pecuniary interest in any agreement with the public service (except as member of an incorporated company of at least twenty-five persons), or holding any office of

[1] See Amendment XV to the Constitution.

profit under the Crown, can sit in either House, unless he be a Minister either of the Commonwealth or of a State. The exception is noteworthy, not only because it is framed with a view to the establishment of Cabinet Government, but also because it implies that a man may, contrary to American and Canadian usage, be at the same time both an executive official of a State and also a member of the Federal Legislature. It would appear that women are eligible to membership of either House. Every Senator and Representative is to receive a salary, fixed for the present at £400 ($2,000) a year.

XI. The Executive.

The Executive is to consist of the Governor-General and the Ministers. To the great convenience of the Australian people, the head of the Executive does not need to be elected either by popular vote (as in the United States) or by the Chambers, as in France and Switzerland. He is nominated by the British Crown, and holds office so long as the Crown pleases, receiving a salary fixed, for the present, at £10,000 ($50,000) a year (exactly the salary of the American President). He has an Executive Council, modelled on the British Privy Council (though the name Privy Council is not used as it is in the Canadian Constitution), and from it he chooses a number of Ministers (fixed for the present at seven) who are to administer the several departments of the public service. They must be members of one or other House of Parliament—a remarkable provision, for though this is a British practice, that practice has never been embodied in any positive rule. As the Governor-General is only a constitutional figure-head, these Ministers will in fact constitute the ruling executive of the Commonwealth.

XII. The Judiciary.

The Judiciary is to consist in the first instance of a Federal High Court (containing a Chief Justice and at least two other judges) capable of exercising both original jurisdiction in certain sets of cases, and also appellate jurisdiction not only from single Federal Judges and inferior Federal Courts, but also from the Supreme Courts of the States. Power is taken both to establish lower Federal Courts and to invest State Courts with federal jurisdiction. But besides this Judiciary proper, there is created a second Court for dealing with cases relating to trade and commerce, under the name of the Inter-State Commission (sect. 101). This remarkable and very important institution has doubtless been suggested by the United States Inter-State Commerce Commission created by Congress some eighteen years ago in order to deal with railway and water traffic between the States. Its functions will be half-administrative, half-judicial, and in questions of pure law an appeal will lie from it to the High Court, while a guarantee for its independence is found in the clause which declares that its members shall not be removed during their seven years' term of office. All Federal Judges are to be appointed by the Governor-General, that is to say, by the Executive Ministry. All trials (on indictment) for any offence against the laws of the Commonwealth shall be by jury, and held in the State where the alleged offence was committed. The judicial establishments of the States remain unaffected, and the judges thereof will continue to be appointed by the State Executives.

In determining the functions of the High Court there arose an important question which seemed for a moment to threaten the whole scheme of Federation. The draft Constitution which the Convention had prepared and which the people had approved by their vote provided that questions arising on the interpretation of the Con-

stitution as to the respective limits of the powers of the
Commonwealth and of the States, or as to the respective limits of the constitutional powers of any two or
more States, should be adjudicated upon by the High
Court of the Commonwealth, and that no appeal should
lie from its decision to the Queen in Council (*i.e.* to the
Judicial Committee of the Privy Council in England,
which is the Supreme Court of Appeal from the British
Colonies and India), ' unless the public interest of some
part of Her Majesty's dominions, other than the Commonwealth or a State, are involved.' When the draft
reached England to be embodied in a Bill, the British
Government took exception to this provision as tending
to weaken the tie between the mother country and the
colonies. There were many in England who thought
that it was not in the interest of Australia herself that
she should lose, in questions which might involve political feeling and be complicated with party issues, the
benefit of having a determination of such questions by
an authority absolutely impartial and unconnected with
her domestic interests and passions. How much better
(they argued) would it have been for the United States
at some critical moments could they have had constitutional disputes adjudicated on by a tribunal above all
suspicion of sectional or party bias, since it would have
represented the pure essence of legal wisdom, an unim-
peachable devotion to legal truth!

To this the Australians replied that the experience
of the United States had shown that in constitutional
questions it was sometimes right and necessary to have
regard to the actual conditions and needs of the nation ;
that constitutional questions were in so far political that
where legal considerations were nearly balanced, the
view ought to be preferred which an enlightened regard
for the welfare of the nation suggested ; that a Court
sitting in England and knowing little of Australia would
be unable to appreciate all the bearings of a constitutional question, and might, in taking a purely technical

and possibly too literal a view of the Constitution, give to the Constitution a rigidity which would check its legitimate expansion and aggravate internal strife. Australia must—so they pursued—be mistress of her own destinies, and as it is she that had framed and procured the enactment of this Constitution, so by her ought the responsibility to be borne of working it on its judicial as well as its executive and legislative side. Not only was this better for Australia herself, but it would be more conducive to the maintenance of the connexion between the Commonwealth and the mother country.

After some wavering, the British Government, perceiving the risk of offending Australian sentiment, gave way. They dropped in Committee of the House of Commons the alteration which they had introduced into the Australian draft, substituting for it an amendment which, while slightly varying the original terms of the draft, practically conceded the point for which the Australian Delegates, sent to England to assist in passing the measure, had contended. The Act as passed provides that no appeal shall lie to the Crown in Council upon the constitutional questions above-mentioned unless the High Court itself shall, being satisfied that the question is one which ought to be determined by the Privy Council, certify to that effect. In all other such cases its judgement will be final.

Appeals to the Privy Council in questions other than constitutional will continue to lie from the Supreme Courts of the States (with the alternative of an appeal to the High Court) and from the High Court itself, when special leave is given by the Privy Council. The Commonwealth Parliament may limit the matters in which such leave may be asked, but the laws imposing such limitations are to be reserved for the pleasure of the Crown.

The scheme of judicature above outlined follows in the main the model contained in the American Constitution. It does not draw the line between State and Federal matters and courts so sharply, for appeals are to lie from State Courts in all matters alike, and State Courts may receive jurisdiction in Federal matters. On the other hand, it is more conformable to principle than either the Canadian plan, which provides no Federal Courts save the Supreme Court and gives the appointment of all judges alike to the Dominion Government, or the Swiss plan, which refers questions of conflict between the Nation and the Cantons, or as to the constitutionality of Federal laws, not to the Judiciary at all, but to the Federal Legislature. Broadly speaking, the Australian High Court will have to fill such a place and discharge such functions as have been filled and discharged in America by that exalted tribunal which Chief Justice John Marshall and other great legal luminaries have made illustrious. In working out the provisions of the Constitution by an expansive interpretation, cautious but large-minded, it may render to Australia services not unworthy to be compared with those which America has gratefully recognized.

XIII. Working of the Frame of Government. The Cabinet.

Now let us see how this Frame of Government, which I have briefly outlined in its salient features, is intended to work.

Its essence lies in a matter which is not indicated by any express provision, the dependence of the Executive upon the Legislature. Herein it differs fundamentally from the American and Swiss systems. It reproduces the English system of what is called Cabinet or Responsible Government; that is to say, a Government in which the Executive instead of being, as in America, an independent authority, directly created by the people and amenable to the people only, is created by and responsible to the Legislature. As and when the British colonies respectively obtained self-governing institutions, each of them adopted this scheme, since it was the one familiar to them at home: and to it they seem all determined to adhere.

Its distinctive features are these.

The nominal head of the Executive, in Britain the Crown, in Australia the Governor-General as representing the Crown, is permanent, and is not responsible to the Legislature, because he acts not on his own views, but upon the advice of his Ministers.

The Ministers are responsible to the Legislature which virtually chooses them, and they depend upon its confidence for their continuance in office.

The Ministers are however not wholly at the mercy of the Legislature, because they may dissolve it, that is to say, may appeal to the people, in the hope that the people will elect a new Legislature which will support them. This kind of government accordingly rests on a balance of three authorities, the Executive, the Legislature, and the People, the people being a sort of arbiter between Ministry and Parliament. As the Ministry can at any moment appeal to the people, the threat of appealing puts pressure upon the Parliament, and keeps a majority cohesive. In the existence of this power of sudden dissolution there lies a marked difference from the American scheme, which some one has called Astronomical, because the four years' term of office of the Executive and the two years' term of the Legislature are both fixed by the earth's course round the sun.

I have spoken of the Legislature as the authority to which the Ministry is responsible. But what is the Legislature? In England, although Parliament consists of two Houses, the Minister-making power resides solely in the House of Commons. Being elective, the House of Commons has behind it the moral weight of the people and the prestige of many victories. Being the holder of the purse, it has the legal machinery for giving effect to its will, since without supplies administration cannot be carried on. Accordingly, though the existence of two often discordant Houses may arrest or modify legislation in Britain, it does not affect the executive conduct of affairs, save on the rare occasions when immediate legislation is deemed indispensable by the Executive. The same remark applies to Canada. There also one finds two Houses, but the Senate, being a nominated and not a representative body, holds an entirely secondary place. The Ministry may disregard a vote of want of confidence passed by it, just as in England they disregard an adverse vote of the House of Lords. In Australia, however, things will be quite different. There the Senate has been constituted as a representative body, elected by the peoples of the States; and as the protector of the rights and interests of the States it holds functions of the highest importance. Its powers (save in one point to be presently mentioned) are the same as those of the House. In whom then does the power of making and unmaking ministries reside? Wherever one finds two assemblies, one finds them naturally tending to differ; and this will be particularly likely to occur where, as in Australia, they are constructed by different modes of election. Suppose a vote of no confidence in a particular Ministry is carried in one House and followed by a vote of confidence passed in the other? Is the Ministry to resign because one House will not support it? It retains the confidence of the other; and if it does resign, and a new Ministry comes in, the House which supported it may pass a vote of no confidence in those who have succeeded it.

The problem is one which cannot arise either under the English or under the American system. Not under the English, because the two Houses are not co-ordinate, the House of Commons being much the stronger. Not under the American, because, although the Houses are co-ordinate, neither House has the power of displacing the President or his Ministers. It is therefore a new problem, and one which directly results from the attempt to combine features of both schemes, the Cabinet system of England and the co-ordinate Senate, strong because it represents the States, which a Federal system prescribes.

XIV. PROVISIONS AGAINST DEADLOCKS.

This, however, is only one, though perhaps the most acute, of the difficulties that arise from the existence of two co-ordinate Houses. Their differences upon questions of legislation are always liable to produce deadlocks. These annoying phenomena occur in England, though there the House of Lords, except upon Irish questions, usually gives way (even without a dissolution of Parliament), because it is afraid of incensing the people and thereby bringing about its own destruction if it continues to resist the national will. In Irish questions the Upper House has been apt to assume that the people of England and Scotland are not sufficiently interested to resent very keenly its difference from the Commons. In the United States there is no remedy for such deadlocks. They have to be endured, at whatever cost. The resistance of the Senate to various plans suggested by the House for dealing with the slavery question may be reckoned among the causes which brought on the War of Secession. The Australian colonies themselves have had frequent experience of deadlocks in matters of legislation between the two Houses, for in every colony there have been two Houses, though in every colony it is the more popular House which has controlled the Executive.

The difficulties I have indicated were fully before the minds of the statesmen who sat in the two Conventions. An ingenious device has been contrived for dealing with them (sect. 57). When the House passes a law and the Senate disagrees, the House may pass it again after three months, and if the Senate still disagrees, the Governor-General may thereupon dissolve both House and Senate together, unless the Parliament is within six months of its natural end by effluxion of time. If after such dissolution the new House again passes the measure, and the Senate once more disagrees, the Governor may convene a joint sitting of both Houses. If the proposed law is then passed by an absolute majority of the whole Parliament so convened in joint sitting, it shall be taken to have been duly passed by both Houses.

This method involves the expenditure of a good deal of time and the worry of a double general election, one for the House and one for the Senate. But it may prove to be the best method of solving a problem which neither Britain nor the United States has yet attempted to solve, and which certainly needs solution. The reader who remembers that the numbers of the House have been fixed to be always double those of the Senate, will now see how necessary such a provision was in order to secure that in this final trial of strength between Senate and House the principle of State rights and the principle of population shall each have its due recognition. Should these two principles come into collision, should, for instance, all the members from the four small States be of one mind and all the members from the two large States of another mind, the principle of population will prevail, for in the two Houses sitting together, the large States will have sixty-one votes (twelve senators and forty-nine representatives), whereas the small States will have only fifty (twenty-four senators and twenty-six representatives). Such a conjuncture may however never arise.

XV. RELATIONS OF THE TWO HOUSES.

The question remains which of the two Houses will hold the place of the British House of Commons as determining the tenure of office by Ministries. Upon this question light may be cast by the provisions with regard to money bills. The Constitution enacts (sect. 53) that

all bills appropriating revenue or imposing taxation
must originate in the House, and that the Senate may
not amend taxing bills, or those ' appropriating money
for the ordinary annual services of the Government,'
though it may return such bills to the House suggesting
certain amendments in them. The Senate may however
reject such bills. As this scheme, which somewhat resembles that of the American Constitution [1], itself suggested by the practice of England, seems to throw upon
the House the primary function of providing money for
the public service, and thus the primary control of the
national exchequer, it would seem that Ministers, unable without money to carry on that service, must stand
or fall by a vote of the House and not by a vote of the
Senate. Yet the Senate, though it cannot take the first
steps for granting money, can withhold money; and if
it does so in order to get rid of a Ministry it dislikes,
nothing short of the deadlock provision above described
can be invoked. Nor can the expedient of mixing up a
number of different taxing provisions in one Bill, or
inserting other matter in appropriation Bills ('tacking'),
be resorted to, for these are expressly prohibited by the
Constitution (sectt. 54, 55). Possibly in practice the
Houses will frequently agree to let the accustomed services of the year be provided for without much controversy, and will reserve their serious conflicts for new
proposals regarding taxation or appropriation.

Australians evidently expect that the usage hitherto
prevailing in all the Colonies of letting the Ministry be
installed or ejected by the larger House will be followed. Nevertheless the relations of the Commonwealth
Houses are so novel and peculiar, that the experience
of the new Government in working them out will deserve
to be watched with the closest attention by all students
of politics. Englishmen in particular have good reason

---

[1] In the U. S. A., however, the Senate may and does amend both revenue-rais-
ing and appropriation bills, and indeed frequently prevails against the House in
the quarrels which arise over these matters.

28

for doing so, because England, when she has substituted a representative Second Chamber for her present theoretically indefensible House of Lords, will have to devise some means for avoiding or solving deadlocks between such a Chamber and the House of Commons.

Some high Australian authorities have appeared to doubt whether two co-ordinate Houses can be made to work along with Cabinet Government. They observe that although there may be sometimes a willingness to make compromises for the sake of the public service, there is also in all governments, and certainly not least in those of the United States and the British Colonies, a tendency to press every legal right to its furthest limit, even if the machine should be stopped thereby. Were such stoppages to become frequent, Australia might, they think, be driven to amend her Constitution by so far disjoining the Executive from the Legislature as to give it something of the permanence it enjoys in America and Switzerland [1].

The relations of the Senate to the House may largely depend on factors still undetermined. One of these is the growth of population. Should the small Colonies grow rapidly, their representation in the House would before long be fairly proportionate to that which they enjoy in the Senate, so that the balance of parties might, so far as the size of States is concerned, tend to be nearly the same in both Houses. Another is the character of the controversies which will arise. These may not be such as to set the small States against the large ones, and the three party organizations, which are already strong, though they possess no such Machine System as America enjoys, may find their support pretty equally in all or most of the States, so that the balance of parties

---

[1] It was suggested in the Convention by Mr. Playford (then Prime Minister of South Australia) that the two Houses sitting together might appoint the Executive Ministry, but this plan deviated too far from British Colonial practice to find acceptance. A similar suggestion was made by Sir John Cockburn in the Sydney Convention in 1891. See his speech in an interesting volume published by him entitled *Australian Federation* (p. 139).

may in practice be found to differ but little in the Senate from what it is in the House. Thus these particular wheels or shafts of the constitutional machine, which are deemed less able than others to bear a severe strain, may not for a long while to come have any severe strain thrown upon them.

Another thing which may affect the relations of the two Houses is the comparative attractions which each will have for high political capacity. In the United States the Senate became, within thirty years from the establishment of the Constitution, an assembly much stronger, through the eminence of its members, than was the House of Representatives. As its term of membership was longer (six years against two years), and as it had certain quasi-executive functions in connexion with foreign relations and appointments, men of ability preferred it to the House, and the House constantly saw its best talent drawn off to its rival. The Senate has to-day no such intellectual ascendency as it had then, but capable men still migrate to it when they can from the House of Representatives. If the House establishes in Australia, as it will apparently do, its sole right to make and unmake Ministries, it will be the more tempting field for ambition: yet something will depend upon the amount of genius and character which the Senate attracts, for the presence of these in abundant measure will give it weight with the nation.

It has been suggested in Australia that the Senate with its thirty-six members is too small. The Senate of the United States however began with twenty-six; and it has been a great advantage to that body that its original numbers were small, for traditions more dignified than those of the tumultuous House were formed, and a somewhat stronger sense of personal responsibility was developed just because the individual was not lost in a crowd.

XVI. MISCELLANEOUS PROVISIONS.

Questions of trade and finance fill a chapter of the Constitution (sectt. 81-105); and it was indeed these questions, next to the issue between the large and the small States, that gave most trouble to those who framed the instrument. It is provided that the collection and control of all duties of customs and excise shall pass to the Commonwealth, but that not more than one-fourth thereof shall, for ten years at least, be retained by the Commonwealth, the other three-fourths being paid over to the several States, or applied to payment of the interest on their respective debts, should these debts be assumed by the Commonwealth. This arrangement was deemed needful to supply the States with funds for defraying their administrative expenses and the interest on their debts, seeing that the chief part of their revenue arose from customs and excise, the five which prepared the Constitution, except New South Wales, having adopted a protective policy. Bounties may be given either by the Commonwealth, or by the States with its consent. There are provisions regarding the collection of the customs, the control of railways and settlement of railway rates, the use of rivers for irrigation and water storage, and the State debts, but as these are largely temporary, and have little special interest for the student of constitutions, important as they are to Australian industries, I mention them only to show how elaborately the scheme of union has been worked out, and on how many perplexing topics, settled provisionally by the Constitution, the Commonwealth Parliament will have to legislate.

The question of the spot where the capital should be placed gave rise, as had happened in the United States and in Canada, to some controversy. It was adjusted by providing that the seat of Federal government should be in the colony of New South Wales, but at least 100 miles from Sydney. Here an area is to be set apart of not less than 100 square miles, which shall be under the jurisdiction of the Commonwealth, as the District of Columbia is under the authority of the National Government in the United States : and here a stately city will doubtless in time spring up.

Power is taken to admit new States, whether formed out of existing States or not, upon any terms and conditions (*e.g.* as to number of Senators) which the Parliament may fix, but if the new State is formed out of an old one, only with the latter's consent. The Parliament has also full power to accept and provide for the administration of any territory transferred to it by the Crown, so that no constitutional questions can arise resembling that which has occupied American lawyers since the annexation of Puerto Rico.

XVII. Amendment of the Constitution.

Last of all we come to the mode of amending the Constitution, a mode easier to apply than that prescribed for the United States, but showing the influence to some extent of the American though more largely of the Swiss model in its reference to the popular vote.

Every law proposing to alter the Constitution must be passed by an absolute majority of each House, and thereupon (after two but before six months) be submitted to the voters of every State. If in a majority of States a majority of the electors voting approve the proposal, and if these State majorities constitute a majority of all the electors voting over the whole Commonwealth, the amendment is passed, and is then to be presented to the Crown for assent. Should the two Houses differ, one passing the proposed law and the other rejecting it (or passing it with an amendment which the first-mentioned House rejects), the House which approves the proposal may again pass it, and if the dissenting House again dissents, the amendment may be submitted to the people as if both Houses had passed it. The decision of the people is final. To meet the fact that the suffrage is not in all the States confined to men, it is further provided that, in any State wherein all adults are entitled to vote, only one half of the vote shall be counted [1].

Thus the requirements for the passing of an Amendment are :—

1. Absolute majority in each House of Parliament, or else absolute majority in one House given twice, the second time after three months' interval, *plus* submission on both occasions to the other House.

2. Approval of the people in a majority of States (*i.e.* at present in four States at least).

3. Approval of a majority of the people voting over the whole Commonwealth.

The American Federal Constitution requires a two-thirds' majority in each House of Congress and a three-fourths' majority of States, or else the proposal of a Convention by two-thirds of the States and a three-fourths' majority of States approving what the Convention has settled, conditions extremely difficult to secure. The Swiss system permits the Constitution to be amended by the same process as is applied to the passing of laws, *plus* a popular vote which results in a majority of Cantons and in a majority of the people voting over the whole Confederation.

XVIII. Relations of the Australian Commonwealth to the Crown.

It has not seemed necessary to set forth the relations of the Commonwealth to the British Crown, because these relations are substantially those which have heretofore existed between the Crown and each of the self-

---

[1] But 'no alteration diminishing the proportionate representation of any State in either House of the Parliament, or the minimum number of representatives of a State in the House of Representatives, or increasing, diminishing or otherwise altering the limits of the State, shall become law unless the majority of the electors voting in that State approve the proposed law' (sect. 128).

governing colonies now united in the Federal Commonwealth. The chief difference is that the Commonwealth Parliament receives certain powers (as to extra-territorial fisheries and relations with the islands of the Pacific) which were previously exerciseable only by the (now extinct) Federal Council of Australasia (mentioned above), that it has a general power to legislate on ' external affairs ' (a somewhat vague term, sect. 51, xxix), and that it may ' exercise within the Commonwealth, at the request or with the concurrence of the Parliaments of all the States directly concerned, any power which can now be exercised only by the Parliament of the United Kingdom or by the Federal Council of Australasia ' (sect. 51, xxxviii). Apart from these provisions, which may give rise to some delicate questions, the principles and practice which have guided the action of the Home Government and of the Colonial Governors will apparently be preserved. Though the Imperial Parliament has an unquestioned right to legislate for every part of the British dominions so as to override all local legislation, it does not now exercise this power except for a few purposes of utility common to all, or many, British possessions, such as for the regulation of merchant-shipping or copyright, and when it does so, it secures the assent of the self-governing Colonies. So again, though the Crown has the legal right to withhold consent from Colonial Statutes, this right is rarely exerted, and then only in respect of some general imperial interest which it is supposed that the statute in question may prejudicially affect, *i.e.* the Crown's right is not exerted in the interest of any class of persons in the Colony or in pursuance of any particular view entertained either by the Governor there or by the Ministry at home. The new Australian Constitution provides (sectt. 58-60) that when a measure passed by the Parliament is presented to the Governor-General, he may either assent to it in the Queen's name (but subject to a power to the Queen to disallow the same within one year) or he may withhold assent; or he may reserve it for the Queen's pleasure, in which last case it shall not take effect unless he announces within two years that the Queen has assented to it. This right of veto, though it looks on paper larger than that which belongs to the President of the United States, seeing that the President's veto can be overridden by a two-thirds' majority in each House of Congress, is in reality far more limited, and will constitute no check (except where imperial interests may be affected) upon the practically sovereign power of the Commonwealth Parliament.

XIX. COMPARISON WITH THE CONSTITUTIONS OF THE UNITED STATES AND CANADA.

Before I make some general reflections on the character of this Australian Constitution, it is worth while to note summarily the principal points in which it differs from the two other Federal Constitutions which it most resembles.

The provisions which it has borrowed from the American Constitution have been already adverted to. It differs from that Constitution in the following (among other) respects:—

1. It is a longer instrument, going into much fuller detail on many topics.

2. It leaves less power to the States and gives more power to the Commonwealth; and it enables the Commonwealth Parliament to legislate for a State upon the State's request, a thing which lies quite outside the functions of Congress.

3. It does not establish a complete system of Federal Courts covering the whole area of the Commonwealth, but allows State Courts to be invested with Federal jurisdiction.

4. It makes the Federal High Court a Court of appeal from State Courts, whereas in the United States each State Supreme Court is final in its proper sphere.

5. It contains hardly any restrictions, in the nature of a ' Bill of Rights,' upon the power of the Federal Legislature over the individual citizen.

6. Instead of disjoining Legislature and Executive, it unites them closely by the system of Responsible or Cabinet Government, and so far from excluding every official from Congress, it makes a seat in Parliament a condition of Ministerial office.

7. It vests the choice of the Head of the Executive, not in the people, but in an external authority, the British Crown. To be sure, this Head is nominal and not responsible either to the people or to the legislature.

8. It vests the election of Senators in the people, not in State Legislatures, gives the Senate no power of amending but only of suggesting amendments in money bills, makes the Senate dissoluble in case of a deadlock between it and the House, and contemplates the possibility that new States may have a smaller representation in the Senate than original States.

9. It gives to the Executive no such veto on legislation as the President has in the United States. I have already explained that the veto of the Governor-General and the Crown is a different thing, and rarely employed.

10. It makes the amendment of the Constitution a much less tedious and difficult process.

Thus it may be said that, as compared with the American Constitution, it vests more power in the National Government as against the State Governments, and that, as between the various departments of the National Government itself, it concentrates power more fully in the hands of the Legislature and imposes fewer restrictions upon its action.

The Constitution of Canada seems at first sight nearer to that of Australia than does the American. It has a Monarch, represented by a Governor-General, for the head of its Executive. It contemplates a number of States small when compared with the forty-five of the

American Union. It has adopted the British system of Cabinet or responsible Government.

But the differences are really so considerable as to place Australia's scheme as far from that of her colonial sister as from the American. Among them are the following:—

1. The Canadian Constitution prescribes the Constitutions of the several Provinces, though it permits the Provincial legislatures to alter them (subject to a Federal veto). The Australian assumes its State Constitutions as existing, and makes no change in them, except so far as the Federation controls or supersedes them. Hence the antecedent power of changing them remains, so far as they are not affected by the Federal Constitution.

2. Australia leaves to the States all residuary powers (*i.e.* powers not expressly granted). Canada withholds them from the Provinces and vests them in the Dominion.

3. Australia leaves the State Governors to be appointed, as now, by the Home Government, apart from Federal interference. Canada gives the appointment of them to the Federal Ministry. And whereas in Canada a Provincial Governor cannot communicate directly with home but only with the Governor-General, in Australia the State Governor and his Ministers are in direct touch with the British Government in London.

4. Australia gives to the Federal Government no right whatever to interfere with State Statutes. Canada invests the Dominion Government with a veto on Provincial legislation by placing the Governor-General as regards such legislation in the place which the Queen holds as regards Dominion legislation.

5. Australia distinguishes Federal from State jurisdiction, taking power to establish Federal Courts other than her High Court, and to invest State Courts with Federal jurisdiction. Canada has no special Federal Courts other than the Supreme Court of the Dominion.

6. Australia makes her Senate an elective assembly. In Canada the Senate is nominated by the Dominion Government, and is therefore a weak body, quite unfit to try conclusions with the House which has the people behind it.

7. Australia provides a method whereby the Commonwealth may amend its Constitution. Canada has no such method, and thereby leaves amendment to the Imperial Parliament of the United Kingdom.

This comparison shows that the Australian scheme of Federal Government stands intermediate between that of the United States and that of Canada. In the United States, the Federal Government has less power as against the States than in Australia. In Canada, the Federal Government has more power, or at least a wider range of action. In other words, the Australian system approaches nearer, in point of form, to a Unitary Government than does the United States, but not so near as does Canada. I am speaking merely of form, that is, of the institutions as they stand on paper, for it does not necessarily follow that the spirit in which institutions are worked will precisely correspond to their form. The old Romano-Germanic Empire, for instance (1638-1806), was less unitary in practice than would have been collected from its form; the new German Empire (since 1871) is more unitary in spirit and working than its form would necessarily convey.

XX. General Observations on the Constitution.

Technically regarded, the Constitution is an excellent piece of work. Its arrangement is logical. Its language is for the most part clear and precise. The occasional, and perhaps regrettable, vagueness of some expressions appears due, not to any carelessness of the draftsmen, but to the nature of the subject-matter. The cumbrousness of the provisions regarding customs, duties, and the control of railways is the almost inevitable result of an effort to meet the claims and appease the apprehensions of neighbouring communities with interests that have been deemed opposed. Although it is much longer, as well as less terse, than the Constitution of the United States, going into fuller detail, and with more of the flavour of an English statute about it, it nevertheless, like that Constitution, leaves much to be subsequently filled up by the action of the legislature. A very large field of legislation remains common to the States and the Commonwealth Parliament; and though statutes passed by the latter will of course override or supersede those which may have been passed by the former, it may be many years before the higher Parliament finds leisure to cultivate all the ground which lies open before it. A further range of activity for that Parliament may disclose itself if the State legislatures should exert the power they possess of asking the Commonwealth to take over part of their work. And apart from both these lines of legislative action, the Parliament will find a very large number of matters which the Constitution has expressly directed it to settle by statutes. Till such statutes have been enacted, many points material to the working of the system will remain undetermined.

In two points the experience of the United States has been, consciously or unconsciously, turned to account. The complaint has often been made in America that the Constitution contains no recognition of the Supreme Being. The Australians have introduced such a recognition in the preamble of the Imperial Act establishing the Constitution, which runs as follows: ' Whereas the people of New South Wales, Victoria, South Australia, Queensland, and Tasmania, humbly relying on the blessing of Almighty God, have agreed to unite in one indissoluble Federal Commonwealth under the Crown of the United Kingdom,' &c. And they have also solemnly enounced in the same preamble that indissolubility of their union which the Americans did not enounce in 1788, and the absence of which from the instrument gave rise to endless argumentation on the part of those who maintained the right of a State to retire from the Federation.

The perfection of any Federal system may be tested by the degree of thoroughness with which the Federal principle is worked out in its application, not only to the legislative, but also to the executive and judicial branches of government. In this respect the Australian scheme is less perfect than the American; for the Commonwealth has received power to legislate, no doubt at the request of the State, on purely State matters, to return to the States part of the revenue it collects, and to assume the pecuniary liabilities of the States. There is also, as already noted, no such effort as in America to secure that questions of State law shall be determined solely by State Courts, for such cases may be appealed from State Courts to the Federal High Court. Thus the Nation looms large over the whole instrument, overshadowing the States. There are indeed many provisions for safeguarding the interests of the States, yet these are not so much recognitions of States' rights as stipulations made to secure material advantages, industrial or commercial or financial. An explanation of this remarkable feature of the scheme may be found in the phenomena of Australian as compared with those of American history. The thirteen States which united in 1788-9 had each of them a long history. The two oldest dated back to the beginning of the seventeenth century. The youngest had nearly sixty years of political life behind it. All were animated by a strong sentiment of local independence, and by a passion for liberty which had become associated with local independence. Their notions of a Unitary Government were formed from England, whose monarch they had latterly learned to hate as their oppressor. Hence their love for their States was largely sentimental. Their minds were filled, not by the mere sense of what they gained from their States as business men, but by the loyalty they bore to their States as protectors of their civic rights and embodiments of their historical traditions.

Very different were the feelings of the Australians. The oldest colony dated back scarcely more than a hundred years, and had enjoyed responsible government for less than fifty. Proud as each colony was of its progress, there had not been time for those political traditions to be formed in which the love of local independence roots itself. Neither were there between the several colonies such differences of origin or of usages and ways of life as separated the New Englanders from the men of Virginia and the Carolinas, for the Australians had emigrated so recently from Britain that no local types had yet been formed. Still less was there that aversion to a Unitary system of government which the strife with England had evoked among the Americans. The only political model which the Australians knew at first hand was the government of Britain by its Parliament, a government which had ceased in 1832 to be oligarchic, and had since 1867 begun to be democratic. Accordingly, among the Australians, State feeling had a thoroughly practical and business character. It took in each man the form of a resolve to secure the agricultural and trading interests of his own part of the country. It was in fact the wish to make a good bargain for his community and himself. Sentiment there was and is. But the sentiment gathered round the Commonwealth of the future rather than the Colony of the past. The same kind of feeling which attached the sons of the Cavaliers to Virginia and the Puritans of Massachusetts to the old ' Bay State ' made the Australians desire to found a great nation which should be the mistress of the Southern seas. Hence the absence of any jealousy of the central power beyond that which is suggested by the fear that local industrial or commercial interests might be unfairly dealt with.

This attitude of Australian feeling will therefore (if the view here presented be correct) work towards the development of those centralizing tendencies in the Constitution for which its terms give ample scope. In all forms of polity the influences which draw the members of a composite political community together and those which thrust them asunder are partly material, partly sentimental[1]. How the influences of material interest will work in Australia I will not attempt to predict. Some of them may prove centrifugal; others, such as those of trade, are clearly centripetal. The Constitution frankly recognizes that economic conditions prescribe a federal rather than a unitary government. But it is a significant fact that the influences of sentiment were arrayed on the side of the Nation rather than on that of the States. One can read this between the lines of the Constitution; and it explains why the Frame of Government is less consistently Federal than is that of the United States.

XXI. Modern and Democratic Character of the Australian Constitution.

The Australian instrument is the true child of its era, the latest birth of Time. Compared with it, the American Constitution seems old-fashioned, and parts of the Swiss Constitution positively archaic. Cabinet Government, whose fully developed form is scarcely a century old, is taken for its basis. Ideas and enterprises, problems and proposals, so new that they are only just beginning to be seriously discussed, figure in it. As slavery, an institution almost coeval with the human race, but essentially barbarous, survived to be mentioned (under a transparent euphemism) in the Constitution of the United States, so a new industrial question—viz. the struggle between white labour and free coloured labour—makes its appearance in this Australian document. Here too are the new products and new methods of science, telegraphs and telephones and the keeping of meteorological observations; here is the extension of

[1] See Essay IV.

the suffrage to women; here are the new troubles which spring from contests between employers and workmen; here the new proposals for throwing on the State the function of providing for its members in sickness and old age; here an express recognition of the right of a State to control the traffic in intoxicating liquors. And above all these one perceives through the whole instrument that dominant factor of our age, the ever-present and all-pervading influence of economic forces, of industrial production, of commerce, of finance. The increased and increasing importance of these influences in the life of the modern world, stimulated as they have been by the amazing progress of scientific discovery, finds a fuller expression in this Constitution than in any other yet framed.

As in these points this Constitution is at least abreast of European and American theory, and ahead of European or American practice, so also it represents the high-water mark of popular government. It is penetrated by the spirit of democracy. The actual everyday working of government in the Australian Colonies is more democratic than in Britain, because Britain has retained certain oligarchical habits, political as well as social. It is more democratic than in the United States, because there both the States and the Union are fettered by many constitutional restrictions, and because wealth has there (as indeed in Britain also) been able to exert a control none the less potent because half-concealed. But the Constitution of this Federal Commonwealth is more democratic than are the Constitutions of the several Australian colonies, in some of which property qualifications and nominated second chambers have survived till now. It prescribes no qualification for a Senator or Representative beyond his having attained the age of twenty-one and being himself qualified to become an elector. He need not even be a resident in the State where he seeks election. The Senate as well as the House is elective; both are chosen directly by the people, and on the basis of the suffrage which each State prescribes for the election of its more popular House. The duration of the House is only three years. The direct popular vote, an institution specially characteristic of advanced democracy, which has been developed independently in the United States and in Switzerland (where it has taken the double form of a Referendum to the people and an Initiative proceeding from the people), is here applied to the enactment of amendments to the Constitution, and, in the form of a general election of both Houses simultaneously, to the settlement of deadlocks between the Houses. There is no veto on the acts of the Legislature, for that vested in the Governor-General and in the Crown is not intended to be used except in the rare cases where imperial interests may be touched. In fact all those checks and balances in the English and American Constitutions by which the censors of democracy used to set such store, have here dwindled down to one only, viz. the existence of two Chambers. These two will be elected on the same franchise and composed of similar men, but the tendency to dissension so natural to rival bodies may sometimes interpose delays and ought certainly to make the criticism of proposals more searching. If the principle of popular sovereignty is expressed with equal clearness in the Constitutions of America and Switzerland, it assumes in this Australian Constitution a more direct and effective form, because many of the restrictions which the two former constitutions (and especially that of America) impose on the legislature in the supposed interests of the people are absent from the Australian instrument. In Australia the people, through their legislature with its short term, are not only supreme, but can, by the legislature's control of the Executive, give effect to their wishes with incomparable promptitude. For this purpose, the expression 'people' practically means the leader who for the time being commands the popular majority. Holding in his hand both the Executive

29

power of the Cabinet and the legislative power of Parliament, he has opportunities of effecting more than any one man can effect under the constitutions either of America or of Switzerland.

The solitary restraint which Australia provides is the co-ordinate authority of the Senate, a hostile majority in which may check or at least delay his legislative projects. Yet if his party in the country be well organized and his programme alluring to the masses he may control the Senate as well as the House, for it does not follow that because the smaller States have prudently placed their interests under the protection of the Senate, they will on the great issues of politics be usually found opposed to their larger neighbours [1].

This highly democratic character of their Constitution has been fully appreciated by Australian statesmen. The effusiveness with which they dwell upon it is probably more sincere than even that which is displayed by politicians in England, America, or France, when they chant the praises of the multitude. Australians are as sanguine in their temper now as Americans were in the days before the clouds of Slavery and Secession had begun to darken their sky.

XXII. Political Party in Australia.

Although the Constitution says no word about political parties, the fact that it contemplates a party system is written over it in bold characters. The sages of the Philadelphia Convention of 1787 neither intended nor expected that the scheme they devised would fall into the hands of parties. Indeed they had a touching faith, dispelled as soon as Washington retired from the scene, that the electors who were to be chosen to elect the President would select the best man in the nation irre-

---

[1] In the first election of members of the two Houses, which took place while these pages were passing through the press, every State was divided upon the issue of Free Trade *versus* Protection, though the Protectionist (or high-tariff) party secured more seats, in proportion, in the House than it did in the Senate.

spective of his political ties. The Swiss, strange as it
may seem to men of English or Anglo-American race,
have succeeded in keeping their Executive, elected
though it is by the Chambers, out of party politics altogether, nor do parties dominate the legislature and colour the public life of the nation as in America and England. But Government of the English ' Cabinet type '
is essentially party Government, that is to say, it has
been so hitherto both in England and wherever else it
has been tried, and no one has yet shown how it can be
made to work otherwise.

In America the great parties are younger than the
Constitution, which may be said to have created them.
In England they are older than Cabinet Government
proper, being practically contemporaneous in their rise
with that very rudimentary form of the Cabinet which
began to emerge in the time of King Charles II. In
Australia every colony has had such active and skilfully-
organized parties that no one doubts but what the Federal Legislature will find its first Ministry forthwith provided with a competent Opposition. It is generally
believed that the tariff will furnish the first, and for some
time the main, ground of party division, for the new
Government must begin by providing itself with an adequate revenue; the chief part of that revenue must be
raised by indirect taxation, and the issue of Free Trade
versus Protection has for years past been a burning one
in the largest Colonies.

I have observed that the Australian scheme contemplates a party system to work it. But what sort of a
party system? Obviously one in which there are two
parties only, each cohesive, each prepared to replace its
antagonist in the Executive. Such was the party system
of England till the present generation. Such has been
the party system of the United States. Exceptions indeed there have been, such as the Know-Nothing party
in 1852, the Greenback party in 1876, the Populist party
which arose in 1889, and is not quite extinct now (Febru-

ary 1901). In the United States the power of the two
great organizations is so vast, and the cost of creating
a new party so deterrent, that a third organization seldom appears, and if it appears, presently disappears.
But in France there have been and are several parliamentary groups, which frequently change their attitude
towards one another, sometimes combining to support
a Ministry, sometimes falling asunder and leaving it to
perish, because one group alone was not sufficient to
sustain it. Hence the lives of Cabinets have been short,
and would have been still shorter but for the fact that
an imminent peril to republican government itself has
sometimes compelled the various republican groups to
hold together. In Britain the same difficulty became
acute from 1880 onwards, as the Irish Nationalists consolidated themselves in a distinct Third Party; and it
may at any moment create serious embarrassment. It
exists in Germany also, and in the Reichsrath of the
Austrian half of the Austro-Hungarian Monarchy.
Now in several of the Australian Colonial Parliaments
a Labour party has recently arisen, which, keeping itself
independent of the two older parties, can throw its
weight on one or the other side and endanger the stability of Cabinets. Should this phenomenon reappear
in the Parliament of the Commonwealth, it will complicate still further a position which the co-ordinate
powers of Senate and House make complicated enough
already [1].

XXIII. POLITICAL ISSUES LIKELY TO ARISE IN AUSTRALIA.

The mention of parties suggests another question, the
last I shall attempt to discuss, viz. the lines on which
the political life of Australia is likely to move under her
new Constitution. It is a topic on which little will be

---

[1] Since these lines were written, the phenomenon has reappeared, for at the first elections, held in the spring of 1901, of the Senate and House, the Labour party obtained more than one-fifth of the seats in each House.

said by any one who remembers how seldom great constitutional changes have been followed by the results prophesied at the time. The Reform Bill of 1832 in Britain, the Civil War in the United States, the union of Italy under the dynasty of Savoy, not to speak of the French Revolutions of 1789 and 1848, all brought forth fruits very different from those predicted by some of the most judicious and unbiassed contemporary observers. Even the extension of the suffrage and redistribution of seats effected in Britain in 1884-5 were followed by a shifting of the balance of party strength exactly the opposite of that which the shrewdest party politicians had expected. But without attempting forecasts, one may try to indicate certain conditions likely to affect the development of Australian national and political life under the new form which this Constitution gives it.

First let us ask what are the controversies likely to occupy the nation and to supply a basis for national parties?

Taking one country with another, it will be found that the questions on which men have grouped themselves into parties may be classed under five heads, viz.:—

1. Questions of Race, such as those which have contributed to distract Ireland, which to-day trouble the Austrian Monarchy and (as respects the Poles) the Prussian Monarchy, which exist, though at present not acute, in Canada, and which are painfully acute in South Africa.

2. Questions of religion, now generally less formidable than they once were, yet embittering disputes regarding education in many modern countries.

3. Questions relating to foreign policy, whether as to the general lines on which it should be conducted, or as to the attitude to be held towards particular States at any given moment.

4. Questions regarding the distribution of political power within the nation itself.

5. Questions of an economic or economico-social

kind, *e.g.* regarding the disposal of land in public hands or its tenure in private hands, regarding the conditions of labour, regarding taxation and finance, the policy of Protection or Free Trade, the policy of progressive imposts, the propriety of assisting particular industries or particular classes out of public funds, whether national or local. Some of these may seem to be rather social than economic, but it will be found upon scrutiny that it is their economic aspect, *i.e.* their tendency to take money from or give money to some class in the community, that makes them bases for party combination. A purely social question seldom assumes great political significance.

(1, 2) Applying this classification to Australia we shall find that the first two sets of questions are absent. All the people are of practically the same race. None are animated by any religious passion, although controversies have sometimes arisen over theological teaching in State schools.

(3) Questions of foreign policy do not, strictly speaking, come within the scope of the Commonwealth Parliament, because they belong to the mother country. Nevertheless, it cannot be doubted that the Parliament will from time to time interest itself in them, especially as regards the isles of the Pacific and of the Eastern Archipelago, and will give forcible expression to its views should any crisis arrive. One can well imagine that the question of the attitude which the Commonwealth should assume, or urge the mother country to assume, towards Germany or France, or Holland, or even towards China or Japan or the United States, when any of these Powers may be taking action in the Western Pacific, might give rise to political contention.

(4) As respects the distribution of political power and the structure of the Federal Government, Australia is so democratic already that it cannot go much further. It will doubtless, however, be proposed to extend to women in all the States that right of voting at Common-

wealth elections which they already enjoy in South Australia and Western Australia, under the local law, or to apply more widely the institution of the direct popular vote; or to amend the Constitution in some point which will raise an issue between the more radical and the more conservative sections of opinion. That questions of constitutional amendment have played so small a part in American politics may be attributed to the extreme difficulty of securing the majorities required for altering the Constitution. In Australia the process will be far easier. The history of the United States during the first seventy years of the Constitution suggests that the question of the respective rights of the Federation and of the States may furnish a prominent and persistent issue. This is quite possible, for in Federations there is a tendency for many controversies of various kinds to connect themselves with, or to raise afresh, controversies regarding the true construction of the Federal instrument as respects the powers which it assigns to the Nation and to the component communities.

(5) It is however questions of the economic order that are likely to occupy, more than any others, the minds and energies of Australian statesmen. The tariff is a practically inexhaustible topic, because apart from the general issue between a Protective and Free Trade policy, the particular imports to be taxed and the particular duties to be imposed will furnish matter for debates that can hardly have finality, seeing that circumstances change, and that the financial needs of the Government will increase. It need hardly be said that in a new country like Australia direct taxation is difficult to collect and highly unpopular, so that larger recourse will be had to customs and excise than orthodox economists could justify in Europe. The financial relations between the Commonwealth and the States will be another fertile source of controversy. So may the regulation of the railways, which the Commonwealth seems likely to take over. So will the arrangements for secur-

ing the respective rights of different States as regards both irrigation and the navigation of the rivers, practically the only rivers of the Continent, which intersect the three south-eastern colonies. Among the labour questions likely to arise, one problem, much before the minds of Australians, may be found to cause difficulties in its details if not in its general principle; viz. the exclusion of immigrants of coloured race, Chinese, Japanese, Malays, and Indian coolies. The white labourers of the temperate colonies have been strongly opposed to the admission of such strangers, but the planters of the tropical north, who have used the labour of Pacific islanders on their sugar estates, take a different view of the case.

Some may think that the obvious line of party division will be found to be that which ranges the four smaller and the two larger States into opposite camps. If this should happen, which may well be doubted, it will be owing to a coincidence of economic interests, and not to the mere fact that the strength of one set of States lies in the House, that of the other in the Senate. The two largest States, New South Wales and Victoria, have hitherto been conspicuously divergent in their financial policy. In America, though the small States fought hard against the large ones in the Convention of 1787, the distinction has never since that date possessed any permanent political significance.

If parties form themselves on any geographical lines, the line will more probably be one between the tropical and the temperate regions. These tropical regions are at present much less populous and wealthy than is the temperate south-east corner of the Continent. They will doubtless increase both in wealth and in population, but as the strong sun forbids out-door labour to white men, the population enjoying political rights cannot, for generations to come, be a large one.

XXIV. POSSIBLE ENTRANCE OF NEW STATES.

The existing situation may be so materially affected by the entrance of new States that one naturally asks what are the prospects that new States will be admitted. As the whole Continent is already divided among the five existing States, new ones can come into being only by carving up the three larger of these. There has already been talk of dividing Queensland into two or perhaps three States. Others might be formed out of the now sparsely peopled regions of the north and northwest, when they have become more thickly inhabited. How fast the process of colonization will advance in these regions will depend upon what engineering science may be found able to do for the more arid tracts in the way of storing rain-water and raising it from deep wells, while something will depend on the disposition of the Federal Government to spend money for that purpose. Nor is another element to be overlooked. Vast as is the mineral wealth already known to exist in the explored parts of Australia, it may be equalled by that which exists in regions which have received no thorough geological examination. Should mines begin to be worked in the arid tracts, an additional motive would be given for the provision of water supplies there, for the existence of a population furnishing markets would stimulate men to develop the capacities of the soil for ranching and even for tillage. These possibilities show how many factors hitherto undetermined may go to moulding the political future of the country. The increase of population in regions now thinly peopled would either make the four smaller States, or some of them, the equals of the larger, or would, more probably, lead to the creation of new States, some of them with a character different from that of the two which now command a decisive majority in the House of Representatives. As the settlement of the Mississippi Valley changed American politics, so a filling up of large parts of the interior and north of Australia, unlikely as this now appears, might affect her constitutional growth in ways at which we can now only guess.

At present not only these tropical regions, but also the settled parts of Western Australia are separated by vast uninhabited spaces from the populous south-east corner of the continent. Hence just as in Canada an Intercolonial Railway to connect Nova Scotia and New Brunswick with Quebec and Ontario was provided for in the Constitution of 1867, and just as the construction of the great transcontinental Canadian Pacific line enabled Manitoba and British Columbia to become effective members of the Federation, so a line of railway from east to west across Australia, as well as the completion of the line, already partly constructed, from the south to the north, are among the political needs of the Commonwealth, and might do much to weld its people into an even more united nation.

One community remains to be mentioned whose geographical position towards Australia recalls the saying of Grattan that while the Ocean forbade Ireland to be politically severed from Britain, the Sea forbade an incorporating union. It has been hoped that New Zealand would enter the Federation, and she has herself seriously considered whether she ought to do so. With a healthy climate, a soil generally well watered, and an area not much less than that of the British Isles, New Zealand has evidently a great future before her. The population, now between 700,000 and 800,000, has tripled within the last thirty years; and the level of personal comfort and well-being is as high as anywhere in the world. Her accession would give further strength to the Federal Commonwealth. But New Zealand, as one of her statesmen observed, has twelve hundred reasons against union with Australia, for she is separated from the nearest part of Australia by twelve hundred miles of stormy sea, a distance more than half of that which divides Ireland from Newfoundland. She may therefore think that some sort of permanent league with Australia, for the purposes of combined naval defence and joint action in external questions of common concern, would conform better to her outlying position than would participation in a Legislature which must be mainly occupied with the affairs of Australia. Of the subjects assigned by the Constitution to the Commonwealth Parliament, there are several in which, because purely Australian, New Zealand would have no interest, some also with regard to which she could legislate better for herself than the Commonwealth could legislate for her, inasmuch as her economic and social conditions are not the same as those of Australia. An illustration is furnished by the difference between the native races in the two countries. The Australian aborigines, one of the most backward branches of the human family, are obviously unfit for the exercise of any political functions. They are not permitted to vote in any colony, and the Constitution provides that in determining the number of representatives to be allotted to a State they shall not be reckoned among its population. But the Maoris of New Zealand are an intelligent folk, to whom New Zealand has given the suffrage, and who are now on excellent terms with their white neighbours. It would no doubt be possible for the Commonwealth Parliament to legislate differently for them and for the ' black fellows ' of Australia ; but their dissimilar character shows the difference of the problems which arise in the two countries. New Zealand has however an interest in obtaining free access to the Australian markets, and her final decision as to entering the Federation may be influenced by the commercial policy which the larger country pursues [1].

In this changeful world, no form of government ever remains the same during a long series of years, and no Federation, however strictly the rights of its members

[1] While these pages were passing through the press, a Commission appointed in New Zealand to consider the question has reported strongly against her entrance into the Australian Federation.

may be secured by a Rigid Constitution, can continue to maintain exactly the same balance of powers between the Nation and the States. I have already expressed the opinion that the tendency is in Australia likely to be rather towards consolidation than towards a relaxation of the Federal bond, because not only national sentiment but economic influences also will work in that direction. Much however may depend on a factor still unpredictable, the relations between Australia, together with the British Empire generally, and the other Powers which are interested in the Western Pacific. Nothing does so much to draw together a people already homogeneous as the emergence of issues which threaten, or result in, a struggle against foreign States. The sentiment of internal unity is accentuated. Public attention is diverted from domestic controversies. Powers are willingly yielded to the Executive which would in days of peace be refused. The consequences may be good or evil—they have sometimes been in the long run evil—but either way they alter the character of the government. They may even give a new direction to its policy, as the United States has recently, and quite unexpectedly, discovered.

XXV. Future Relations of the Australian Commonwealth to Britain.

Australia however is not a State standing alone in the world, but a member of the British Empire, so we cannot close an examination of her Constitution without asking whether the union of her Colonies will affect her relations to the mother country.

When the first Convention to frame a Federal Constitution assembled in 1891, most Englishmen supposed that a Federated Australia would soon aspire to complete independence. Australian statesmen saw deeper, and predicted that the formation from the several Colonies of an Australian Nation would tend not to loosen, but rather to draw closer the ties that unite the people to Great Britain. So far as can be judged from the course of Australian opinion during the past ten years, this has been the result. There were at first some who advocated Federation as a means to independence. But they soon desisted, overborne by a different current. The same National feeling through which Federalism triumphed seems to have deepened the sense of unity with other members of the British race. And possibly that suspicion which colonies are apt to feel of a sort of patronage on the part of the mother country, and which sometimes disposes them to be self-assertive, may have vanished as they came to realize that the old country was proud of them and wished to treat them not only as a daughter but as an equal. Neither do they, democrats as they are, harbour distrust of a monarchy, or deem their freedom in any way hampered by it. The love for republicanism in the abstract, though far stronger in Continental Europe than in England, was everywhere a force in the first half of the nineteenth century. It has faded away in the second half throughout the British world, because the solid substance of freedom has been secured, because the old mischiefs of monarchical government have reappeared in republics, because men's minds have begun to be occupied with economic and social rather than with purely political questions. The fact that the British Crown is titular head of the Australian Commonwealth will not render the working of the Constitution less truly popular, any more than has befallen in Canada, a somewhat less democratic country. So far as the internal politics of Australia are concerned, she will take her own course, scarcely affected by her connexion with England. But the fact that she is, and seems likely to remain, a part of the British Empire, sharing in the enterprises and conflicts and responsibilities of that vast body, is a fact of the highest moment for her future and for the future of the world. Still more momentous might her relation to the Empire become should any scheme be devised for giving the self-governing Colonies of Britain a share in the financial liability for common defence, together with a voice in the determination of a common foreign policy. The difficulties of constructing any constitutional machinery for this purpose are obvious, yet perhaps not insurmountable. Should any such arrangement be ever reached, it will probably be reached through some crisis in the history of the Empire itself.

Sixty years ago it was generally believed that as soon as each British self-governing colony had become conscious of its strength, it would naturally desire, and could not be refused, its independence. But the last sixty years have brought with them many favouring conditions; and among these, one of which no one then thought, the long reign of a sovereign whose personal character, by its purity, simplicity and kindliness, won such reverence and affection, not only for herself, but also for the ancient institutions at the head of which she stood, that the prolongation of her life may be reckoned among the causes which have kept these far-off lands a part of the British realm and have given its actual form to the **Commonwealth of Australia.**